JONATHAN EDWARDS
and the
Covenant of Grace

The Jonathan Edwards Classic Studies Series

The Jonathan Edwards Center at Yale University is pleased to offer this volume, in grateful cooperation with Wipf & Stock Publishers, as part of its mission to encourage ongoing research into and readership of one of America's most original thinkers and one of its most significant historical and cultural figures. As much as the Edwards Center is devoted to presenting Edwards's own writings in a comprehensive and authoritative online format, we also see providing secondary resources as vital to supporting an ongoing understanding of Edwards's extensive and varied corpus, which can be accessed at http://edwards.yale.edu.
    Writings about Edwards's life, thought, and legacy continue to accumulate from authors representing a broad range of disciplines and agendas. Within the voluminous secondary literature, the Edwards Center recognizes the importance of insuring that certain key works—which sadly have gone out of print but yet remain in demand—are available for new generations coming to the study of Edwards and are recognized for their worth. These monographs represent some of the very best and most pioneering studies of Edwards, his times, and his influence, from scholars over the past half century and more. Indeed, these works not only greatly influenced the study of Edwards but American history in general. We hope these landmark studies, ranging from biography to intellectual and social history to philosophy and theology, continue to be sources of inquiry and inspiration for decades to come.

Harry S. Stout
Director
The Jonathan Edwards Center
Yale University

Jonathan Edwards Classic Studies Series

The Young Jonathan Edwards
William Sparkes Morris
With a new foreword by Kenneth Minkema

Jonathan Edwards, Pastor
Patricia Tracy
With a new preface by the author

Jonathan Edwards's Moral Thought and Its British Context
Norman Fiering
With a new foreword by Oliver Crisp

Beauty and Sensibility in the Thought of Jonathan Edwards
Roland A. Delattre
With a new foreword by Michael McClenahan

Religion and the American Mind
Alan Heimert
With a new foreword by Andrew Delbanco

Samuel Hopkins and the New Divinity Movement
Joseph A. Conforti
With a new foreword by Douglas Sweeney

Edwards on the Will: A Century of Anglican Theological Debate
Allen C. Guelzo
With a new preface/acknowledgements by the author

Jonathan Edwards: The First Critical Biography, 1889
Alexander V. G. Allen
With a new foreword by M. X. Lesser

Jonathan Edwards and the Covenant of Grace
Carl W. Bogue
With a new preface by the author

Future volumes are forthcoming. For current updates see http://edwards.yale.edu.

JONATHAN EDWARDS
and the Covenant of Grace

CARL W. BOGUE

WIPF & STOCK · Eugene, Oregon

Wipf and Stock Publishers
199 W 8th Ave, Suite 3
Eugene, OR 97401

Jonathan Edwards and the Covenant of Grace
By Bogue, Carl W.
Copyright©1975 by Bogue, Carl W.
ISBN 13: 978-1-60608-365-9
Publication date 12/2/2008
Previously published by Mack Publishing Company, 1975

ACADEMISCH PROEFSCHRIFT
ter verkrijging van de graad van Doctor in de Godgeleerdheid aan de Vrije Universiteit te Amsterdam, op gezag van de Rector Magnificus Mr. I. A. Diepenhorst, hoogleraar in de Faculteit der Rechtsgeleerdheid, in het openbaar te verdedigen op vrijdag 11 april 1975 te 13.30 uur in het hoofdgebouw der universiteit, De Boelelaan 1105 door

CARL W. BOGUE
geboren te Vincennes, Indiana, U.S.A.

1975 Mack Publishing Company

To
my Father and Mother

Preface to the 2009 Edition

The research for this book began almost a generation ago. At the time I had the sense that I was riding the wave of the renaissance of Edwardsian studies. The early volumes of the Yale University Press definitive edition of Edwards' writings had appeared. The interest was amazing and a stream of publications, academic and popular, was a delight to see. As a young student it was no small privilege to be granted access to the necessary manuscripts, many of them unpublished, wonderfully preserved in the Beinecke Rare Book and Manuscript Library at Yale University. What I never envisioned was that I was but riding the first of many "waves" in this resurgence of interest in Edwards and that the stream of publications would become a flood, relatively speaking, of available literature.

Since the publication of this book in 1975, the sheer volume of books, articles, and graduate dissertations about this Puritan giant living in Colonial America is staggering. In the Appendix of John H. Gerstner's three-volume work on Edwards, David F. Coffin, Jr. provides a list of all such writings he could find from 1979 to 1991. The list amounts to almost thirty pages and has around 450 publications. From 1991 to the present there would be no reason to expect that there were not at least that many additional publications.

Noting these things begs the question: Why, with so much material available, reprint a book over 30 years old? Through the years I have continued to receive inquiries as to whether it is still in print, how to get a copy, or whether I intend to reprint it. Happily, an easy answer is now at hand, thanks to the kindness of The Jonathan Edwards Center at Yale University.

At the time this work was published, there had been no comprehensive study of Edwards' doctrine of the covenant nor the distinctive relationship of this doctrine to the whole of Edwards' theology. Notwithstanding the huge volume of work on Edwards since, there still appears to be no such work. Also, however one might value the interpretive thesis of this work, it provides accessibility to the wealth of Edwards' comments on the covenant from sermons and miscellaneous writings that were unpublished.

The fact that Edwards himself never wrote a major treatise or book on the covenant does not argue the unimportance of the topic. I have attempted to show that covenant theology was a natural framework for Edwards' biblical thinking and in fact pervades the warp and woof of his systematic theological thinking. It certainly behooves a candid observer to bring the peculiar genius of Edwards to bear on contemporary discussions of federal theology in general and specific covenant issues in particular. Current debates about covenant theology have shifted from what they were a generation ago. Yet the modern scholar, hearing debate within Reformation theology today about new perspectives and visions in covenant theology, may profit from Edwards' stature as both a predestinarian and a covenant theologian.

One further question might well be raised as to whether a significant revision of this work would be preferable to a reprint. With the wealth of research and writing sparked in part by the ambitious publication project of Yale University Press, an expanded interaction with this literature might make the work more valuable. Apart from editorial and economic issues, however, such a project would be massive and well beyond the focus of this study. A mere annotated bibliography of the literature would be at least a graduate degree project.

Every generation has to some degree reflected a prevailing interpretation of Edwards which in one way or another is called into question by the next. Some make pilgrimages on a quest to return to the real Edwards, while others seek the real Edwards hidden beneath what seems apparent to the casual observer. Still others are willing to exalt what they admire in the man, with no sense of obligation to embrace the encumbrances of the Eighteenth Century trappings. And because of the obvious brilliance of the man, there will always

Preface to the 2009 Edition

be those who, intentionally or not, work to rehabilitate Edwards, making him fashionable with current trends in academia.

This work as it stands interacts with two prominent themes from a prior generation. I hope that the results of this interaction will still be of interest and in some ways helpful. However, everything that Edwards had to say about the covenant is of enduring interest. The research presented here, including the corpus of unpublished material preserved in manuscript form, I believe will be sufficient justification for the reappearance of this work.

Finally, I must add a few brief acknowledgments to those already in the original Preface. Since the original publication, a multitude, many unknown to me personally and some beyond the borders of the United States, have been a constant encouragement to me in their kind comments and reviews, their desire to obtain even a photocopy of the work, and their ongoing pressure and offers of help to see a reprinting for easy access. This was more than I could ever hope for growing out of a graduate dissertation.

I am especially indebted to Michael McClenahan, Fellow of The Jonathan Edwards Center at Yale University, who first contacted me about this possible avenue of getting *Jonathan Edwards and the Covenant of Grace* back into print and laid the foundation for moving ahead. I owe a special debt of gratitude to Kenneth P. Minkema, Executive Editor of *The Works of Jonathan Edwards* and Executive Director of The Jonathan Edwards Center at Yale University who took time from his busy schedule to counsel me in the final steps of this project.

A special tribute is reserved for my late wife, Rosalie, who not only typed the original first draft from my hand-written copy 35 years ago, but re-entered the entire work into the computer the year before her death, making possible the correction of various errors, correcting some imperfect grammar, and adding some minor revisions in the electronic version. Her ongoing suggestions and loving support were essential. My daughter, Katherine Chapman, was a major help in proofreading and providing improvements in the digital version. Finally, I thank God for my wife, Deborah, who

Preface to the 2009 Edition

has made certain I do not take retirement too seriously, encouraging me in several writing projects as well as ministerial opportunities.

Carl W. Bogue
November 2008
Scottsdale, Arizona

Contents

Preface vii

Part I
BACKGROUND

1. Contemporary Considerations 3
2. The Man and His Times 19
3. Is Theology Still Queen? 35
4. The Covenant of Grace in Theology 53
   The Covenant of Grace in Continental Reformed Theology .. 54
   The Covenant of Grace in Puritan Theology 67
5. History of Dogma Considerations 77
   Covenant, Calvinism, and Consistency 78
   Jonathan Edwards' Relation to His Background 86

Part II
THE COVENANT OF GRACE
IN A COVENANTAL FRAMEWORK

6. The Covenant of Redemption as Distinguished from the Covenant of Grace 95
   The Covenant of Redemption and Divine Sovereignty 96
   The Covenant of Redemption in Relation to the Covenant of Grace 103
7. The Covenant of Grace as Historical Manifestation of the Covenant of Redemption 115
8. Distinctive Aspects of Edwards' Doctrine of the Covenant of Grace 125
9. The Covenant of Grace in Relation to the Two Dispensations and the Covenant of Works 141
10. The Role of the Covenant Concept in Edwards' Theology 165

Part III
DOCTRINES RELATED TO THE COVENANT OF GRACE

11. Jonathan Edwards and Divine Sovereignty 177
12. The Self Binding of a Sovereign God in the Covenant of Grace 197
13. Grace and the Holy Spirit in the Covenant of Grace . 209
14. Justification by Faith in the Covenant of Grace ... 227
    The Nature of Covenant Faith 228
    Faith as Union with Christ 239
15. Faith as the Condition of the Covenant of Grace .. 253
16. Seeking Salvation in the Framework of Calvinist Covenant Theology 279

Part IV
CONCLUSION

17. Conclusion 301
    Bibliography 307

PREFACE

The renewal of interest in the life and thought of Jonathan Edwards in recent years may seem an historical curiosity to many. To one who has looked closely at Edwards it is not surprising. For though scholars from opposite personal convictions may reach different conclusions about him, few would dispute the fact that he was a truly remarkable intellect.

Among the enormous literature, past and present, dealing with Jonathan Edwards, I have yet to find any extensive treatment of his doctrine of the covenant of grace. Edwards' doctrine of the covenant of grace is frequently mentioned to illustrate either his Calvinism or his deviation from Calvinism. Still others will deny he taught the covenant of grace in order to affirm his Calvinism. There are excellent chapters dealing with the covenant in Conrad Cherry's *The Theology of Jonathan Edwards* and John H. Gerstner's *Steps to Salvation*. Such available sources enticed me to begin rather than conclude my research into this area.

Throughout this work three terms are frequently used, any one of which could serve as a basis for considerable historical discussion as to their precise meaning. They are Calvinism, Puritanism, and Arminianism. There is a general acceptance as to the broad meaning of these terms, and it is in that sense they are used. Calvinism is that theological system rediscovered at the time of the Reformation, articulated especially by John Calvin, and further systematized in succeeding centuries. Committed to doctrines such as the sovereignty of God, Scripture as the only rule of faith, enslavement of the human free-will after the fall of Adam, and justification by faith alone, Calvinism's distinctive doctrines of sin, gracious election, and assurance have come to be summarized in the so-called "five points of Calvinism." Puritanism, which can be defined in a limited technical way, is used in this work loosely and comprehensively for Episcopalians, Presbyterians, and Independents of Seventeenth and Eighteenth Century Britain and New England who held a Calvinistic creed and practiced personal piety. Arminianism, while encompassing far more as a system, reflects the popular Eighteenth Century use for designating deviations from the Calvinist doctrine of the enslaved will. Arminianism was thus a rejection of Calvinism's total inability, absolute predestination, and irresistible grace.

Published works of Edwards have appeared and reappeared throughout the last two centuries. Apart from the four volumes now available in the Yale edition of Edwards' works and certain individually published items, I have cited from the two volume London edition edited by Edward Hickman. While the Worcester and Dwight editions are more commonly cited, no one edition has unanimous acceptance, and I have preferred to use the two volume edition since it had the most material in the fewest volumes. Where the Yale edition is available, it is clearly to be preferred.

Much of Edwards' writing remains unpublished. The reader will note considerable reference to the unpublished manuscript material in this work. In most cases when a reference has appeared in published form, I cite that reference. Sermons, "Miscellanies," and "Interleaved Bible" citations identified as Yale MSS are part of the Yale Collection in the Beinecke Rare Book and Manuscript Library of Yale University. Sermons identified as Andover MSS are part of the Andover Collection of the Andover Newton Theological School.

In quoting from the unpublished material I have made only minor corrections necessary to put it in easily readable form. Changes include spelling out of abbreviations and arbitrary signs, bringing consistency to his use of capitals, and minimal alteration of punctuation to bring it more into conformity with current standards. I have attempted to leave the spelling unchanged. A question mark within a parentheses indicates that the preceding word is uncertainly deciphered. A bracket indicates the word or words are supplied by me in an effort to achieve the intended meaning.

I wish to acknowledge my gratitude to Yale University's Beinecke Rare Book and Manuscript Library for permission to examine the Edwards' manuscripts and to publish the relevant portions contained in this study. I am likewise grateful to Andover Newton Theological School for permission to cite relevant portions from sermons in their collection of Edwards' manuscripts.

During my visits to Yale University the staff of the Beinecke Rare Book and Manuscript Library extended to me every courtesy and assisted me greatly in examining the original Edwards' Manuscripts. Their kindness extended to microfilming for me many of their manuscripts, thus saving me countless trips to New Haven. I am indebted to Dr. Thomas Schafer of McCormick Theological Seminary, who personally assisted me in many ways on my first pilgrimage to Beinecke Library, not the least of which was permission to read his transcriptions of Edwards' "Miscellanies," which he is in the process of editing for publication in the Yale edition of Edwards' works. Only those who have examined Edwards' manuscripts and tried to decipher his handwriting can fully appreciate that assistance. I am likewise indebted to Dr. John H. Gerstner of Pittsburgh Theological Seminary for permitting me to check his transcriptions of important Romans sermons which he is preparing for publication in the Yale edition. And to the staff of the Barbour Library of Pittsburgh Theological Seminary I express my gratitude for their kind assistance in so many ways during my frequent visits, including access to the Anderson Room Rare Book Collections.

I am grateful for the training I received in excellent academic institutions. My personal debt to outstanding faculties is immeasurable. Three persons must receive special mention. Though he may be surprised to find his name here, Professor Roy Butler, then head of the Department of Philosophy at Muskingum College, greatly influenced my thinking. He stimulated, inspired, and guided my interest in philosophy and theology, opening up new horizons for which I will always be thankful. Of several outstanding teachers at Pittsburgh Theological Seminary I would single out Professor Dr. John H. Gerstner with special gratitude. It was he who first introduced me to the rewarding study of Edwards. That alone, though there is so much more, puts me in his debt. And what a privilege to add to this my gratitude to my *promoter*, Professor Dr. G. C. Berkouwer of the Free University of Amsterdam. His grasp of church doctrine, his ability to perceive the issues, and the humility and enthusiasm he brings to his theological work is an inspiration to his students. My appreciation extends to the other members of the theological faculty at the Free University from whom I had the privilege to learn.

Acknowledgment of personal help in the completion of this dissertation must begin and end with Dr. Berkouwer, who approved and guided the projected direction it would take, and who has offered critical evaluation after reading the manuscript. Professor Dr. J. van den Berg, also of the Free University of Amsterdam, provided many valuable criticisms and suggestions, causing me to think through far more carefully critical aspects of my research. On this side of the Atlantic I have received helpful comments and suggestions from Dr. Gerstner, whose specialized knowledge of Edwards brought added value to his contribution. The following also gave helpful assistance in reading and criticizing the manuscript: Rev. Joseph W. Atkins, Rev. Donald D. Crowe, Rev. James T. Dennison, Jr., Mr. Walter Wynn Kenyon, and Dr. Thomas Schafer. Mrs. Betty Hawley faithfully typed the final copy of the manuscript.

Many friends in the United States and The Netherlands

made the years of doctoral study a rewarding experience. The privilege to live in another country on another continent has been enhanced by our many Dutch friends, especially those in Dordrecht, where we lived and where our first child, Katherine, was born. Our faulty use of the Dutch language was no hindrance to their hospitality. To the Session and members of the Allenside United Presbyterian Church in Akron, Ohio, who adapted to the peculiar needs of a pastor researching and writing a dissertation, I owe a special debt of gratitude.

And how does one thank a wife for her part in such an undertaking? Rosalie has been a working wife, student's wife, minister's wife, and mother. She has typed and proof-read and served as a sounding board as my ideas developed. She has herself become a student of Edwards. Her love and support never failed.

I have reserved my parents for final acknowledgment. Not only their love and encouragement, but their many sacrifices, made possible my education. It is to them that I have dedicated this book. It is an inadequate tribute, but it at least symbolizes my love and my awareness of their influence on my life.

All of these blessings have come from my heavenly Father. The verse of Scripture which Edwards associates with his conversion gives a fitting conclusion to these remarks. "Now unto the King eternal, immortal, invisible, the only wise God, be honour and glory for ever and ever. Amen."

PART I

BACKGROUND

From my childhood up, my mind had been full of objections against the doctrine of God's sovereignty, in choosing whom he would to eternal life; and rejecting whom he pleased. . . . It used to appear like a horrible doctrine to me. . . . There has been a wonderful alteration in my mind, with respect to the doctrine of God's sovereignty, from that day to this. . . . I have often since had not only a conviction, but a *delightful* conviction. . . .

The first instance, that I remember, of that sort of inward, sweet delight in God and divine things, that I have lived much in since, was on reading these words, 1 Tim. i.17. *Now unto the King eternal, immortal, invisible, the only wise God, be honour and glory for ever and ever. Amen.* As I read the words, there came into my soul, and was as it were diffused through it, a sense of the glory of the Divine Being; a new sense, quite different from any thing I ever experienced before. . . .

From about that time I began to have a new kind of apprehensions and ideas of Christ, and the work of redemption, and the glorious way of salvation by him.[1]

---

1. This account in Edwards' own words of his conversion is found in a Memoir by Sereno Dwight. *The Works of Jonathan Edwards,* ed. Edward Hickman (2 vols.; London, 1879), hereafter cited as *Works,* I, liv-lv.

1
Contemporary Considerations

The renaissance of Edwardsean studies in this generation must appear an enigma to many. The unfortunate plight of Jonathan Edwards since his own day is that most people have an opinion about him, but apart from the serious student of Edwards few of them ever read his writings. The image of Edwards hangs suspended by the single thread of one sermon[1] over the pit of popular condemnation. If the theologian sympathetic with Edwards agonizes over that, the sympathetic philosopher is no less frustrated.[2] Edwards deserves better. Perry Miller, a secular historian whose name is synonymous with Puritan studies, has referred to Jonathan Edwards as "the greatest philosopher-theologian yet to grace the American scene."[3] The renewal of interest in this Puritan theologian cannot help but provide resounding confirmation of the truth of that statement.

Fortunately, some caricatures of many years are disappearing. There is no guarantee that new ones will not replace them, but the climate is greatly improved. Removing caricatures, however, is only a preparatory stage. Will the

---

1. The Enfield sermon on Deuteronomy 32:35, "Sinners in the Hands of an Angry God," because of its impact on the Great Awakening, its exemplification of "Puritan hell fire" preaching, and its literary form of creating images with words, has found its way into anthologies of American literature as a lone example of the "typical" Edwards.
2. *The Philosophy of Jonathan Edwards from His Private Notebooks*, ed. Harvey G. Townsend (Eugene, Oregon, 1955), p. x: "Edwards has often been praised for his relentless logic. But few have been able to say what his views of logic were."
3. In "General Editor's Note," *Freedom of the Will*, ed. Paul Ramsey, Vol. I of *Works of Jonathan Edwards*, ed. Perry Miller and John E. Smith (New Haven, 1962), p. viii.

flood of new literature provide a balanced view of the real Edwards? A danger in Puritan studies in general and Edwardsean scholarship in particular concerns a point of emphasis. The danger is that Edwards the theologian will be fit into the categories of other disciplines. It is true that there was considerable interest in Edwards the theologian during his lifetime and beyond. His published works, however, reflect limitations in this interest. Whether published during his lifetime or posthumously, they were selected more for their polemical relevance in that day rather than to provide a systematic presentation of his theology.

A survey of the vast literature about Edwards reflects an amazing preoccupation with seeing him as something other than a theologian. Ola Winslow in her prize-winning biography reflects this mentality. Jonathan Edwards has something to say, but someone other than Edwards is needed to find it. His mistake was that of "choosing to speak through an outworn, dogmatic system instead of letting the new truth find more appropriate form of its own."[4] The key to understanding Edwards comes "once his thought is taken out of the theological idiom."[5] Perry Miller, who more than any one else is responsible for renewed interest in Edwards, grounded his rehabilitation of Edwards on the thesis that there is a discrepancy between what Edwards said and wrote, and what he really thought.[6] This may make an eighteenth century Puritan palatable to "modern" thought, but suspicion is

---

4. Ola Elizabeth Winslow, *Jonathan Edwards, 1703-1758* (New York, 1941), p. 326.
5. Winslow, *Jonathan Edwards, 1703-1758*, p. 329.
6. Perry Miller, *Jonathan Edwards* (Cleveland, 1964). We are told, for example, that "Edwards' writing is an immense cryptogram.... The way he delivered his sermons is enough to confirm the suspicion that there was an occult secret in them: no display, no inflection, no consideration of the audience" (p. 51). "We are not sure whether we have to deal with a pathological secretiveness or an inherent inexpressibility in the thought itself." There is "an exasperating intimation of something hidden. There is a gift held back, some esoteric divination..." (p. 50). Not only is *Freedom of the Will* "an immense cipher" (p. 262), we are informed that "all Edwards writings" must be "read as a cipher" (p. 263). It is the "intellect behind the doctrines" that impresses Miller (p. 328).

aroused that the conclusion originates more from the esoteric powers of Professor Miller than from the documents.

Miller, of course, represents a sophisticated as well as extreme example of the varied attempts to understand Edwards. The preponderance of nontheological studies is not new. There are historical interpretations and psychological interpretations. There is the Edwards of Puritanical religiosity and Edwards the product of his cultural environment. Some find the key to Edwards in sociology; some say he makes sense only in light of the then current political aspirations of a young nation. Still others see the answer in the young Edwards, the youth thrilled at the discoveries of natural science and philosophy, the youth thwarted by a career as a pastor. The question almost asks itself, "What if Jonathan Edwards were first and foremost a Christian theologian willingly subjecting himself and his thoughts to the revelation of 'the King eternal, immortal, invisible, the only wise God'?"

Puritan covenant theology, and Edwards' relation to it, is part and parcel of these contemporary considerations. Interest in Puritanism resulted in renewed examination of Puritan covenant theology. But where is the emphasis? Jens Møller cites as a principal reason for the failure of current scholarship to adequately deal with the idea of the covenant "the fact that many of these scholars are primarily interested in sociology and less in theology."[7] The erudition of Perry Miller's work on seventeenth century New England is not questioned, but it is suggestive to note that his chapter on "The Covenant of Grace" is found in book IV with the general heading of "Sociology."[8] The theology of the covenant

---

7. Jens G. Møller, "The Beginnings of Puritan Covenant Theology," *Journal of Ecclesiastical History*, XIV (April, 1963), p. 46. "Another reason stems from the tendency to isolate the Puritans in England and New England from their English background as well as from their Continental forerunners and contemporaries. Interpretations which thus tend to neglect both theology and history necessarily lead to grave misunderstandings in the presentation of puritan covenant theology."

8. Perry Miller, *The New England Mind: The Seventeenth Century* (Cambridge, 1971), hereafter cited as *NEM: 17th Century*. The social and church

stands not in isolation from social and cultural concerns. But the primary concern is soteriological, and the theological questions must not be lost among related disciplines.

Had Perry Miller listened to his own comments earlier in the same volume, he might have been more hesitant to deal with the covenant of grace as "sociology."

> Recent writers on New England history have tended to minimize the importance of abstract theology and of the pulpit, to point out that whatever the theology, Puritan conduct can be explained without it. This conclusion has the advantages of appealing to an age that has no relish for theology....
>
> No doubt the importance of the creed can be overstressed; unless the sermons and the tracts are read with constant reference to social backgrounds and economic trends, there is every danger that the doctrine will be held responsible for traits which are simply those of the age...culture...or...new environment....
>
> ....
>
> Yet in their own eyes morality, however important, was secondary to the issues of salvation and regeneration. It may be that as a matter of historical fact many Puritan actions were largely determined by environment and economic interests, but Puritans themselves believed they followed from the condition of their souls.[9]

This recognition of the Puritan's self-testimony as to the priority of theology in their life may not be ignored. Furthermore, while psychological studies may rightly conclude that Puritans were "intoxicated with God," it may not be maintained to the exclusion of their reverence for reason.[10] When

---

covenants are also dealt with in this general heading, and not without justification.

9. Miller, *NEM: 17th Century*, pp. 47-49. The significance of this as a corrective is seen in the fact that Miller is a secular historian without sympathy or commitment for the theological doctrine in and of itself.

10. Miller, *NEM: 17th Century*, pp. 64-66. Miller goes on to say: "... The impression grows undeniably that though Puritanism was a piety, it was at the same time an intellectual system, highly elaborated and meticulously worked-out" (p. 67). "... Puritanism was, if not a rationalism, then decidedly a reasonableness" (p. 69). "The Catholic attack upon reason came in the form of 'fideism.' ... But from the Puritan point of view fideism was a wile of Babylon, a Papist trick to confuse the devout and mock the truth" (pp. 70-71). "... Protestant

Puritans themselves give priority to the issues of salvation and regeneration, and when they revere reason in opposition to fideism in whatever form, then the interpreter of a representative figure cannot claim academic integrity if he fails to let that figure speak for himself, on his own terms, with the preliminary assumption that he means what he says.

When Jonathan Edwards' position on the covenant of grace is under examination, he is the one to be heard from. One could hardly challenge his integrity, and much of his reputation rests on his logical acumen. In Chapter Three the priority which Edwards gives to theology will be indicated. The covenant of grace, dealing as it does with the soteriological relation of God and man in Christ, is a theological locus *par excellance.* Whatever Edwards has to say about it is certainly worth hearing. Any understanding of Edwards without it could only with qualification be called an understanding of Edwards at all.[11]

---

theologians strove with might and main to keep justification by faith from becoming a justification of illiteracy" (p. 73).

11. This plea to see a theological issue and its relation to a theologian in a theological way is not meant to be superficial. Joseph Haroutunian, *Piety versus Moralism; the Passing of the New England Theology* (New York, 1932), pp. xxii-xxiii, is critical of simplistic evaluations and criticisms which have frequently occurred. "The historians of the New England Theology have usually presented it as a minor chapter in the history of Christian theology. They have studied it from a strictly theological point of view, in the light of their own theological opinions, and have sought to criticize it by pointing out philosophical misconceptions and logical errors. The consequences of such treatments have been that the purport of the New England Theology has been misunderstood or overlooked, the causes of its passing have been misjudged, and its significance lost in doctrinal discussions and criticisms in terms of debatable philosophical issues." Whether one agrees with the conclusions of Professor Haroutunian regarding the passing of New England Theology or not, one can hardly dispute the fact that a grave injustice would be done to simply categorize New England Theology as Calvinistic or Puritan and then reject or criticize it from the basis of a non-Calvinistic or non-Puritan point of view. This does not argue against a proper investigation of Jonathan Edwards, for example, on a theological basis.

It should be noted also that Haroutunian's *Piety versus Moralism* predates much of the revival of interest in seeing the Puritan era in a more sympathetic light. Sympathetic does not mean agreement with, but at least, a lack of prejudice against, the topic under investigation.

In light of these considerations a discussion of Jonathan Edwards and the covenant of grace is actual and possible. The covenant of grace is a description of how the saints are related to God in faith. Nothing could be more fundamental to understanding a man's theology than understanding how he sees man in relation to God. Sovereignty and election, faith and obedience, grace and the Holy Spirit, all come into the discussion in their relation to Christ as mediator of the covenant. Center stage is the crucial issue of "unconditional election" and the "conditionality" of faith. The terrain is not unfamiliar, especially for theologians of the Reformation. To the extent that one has an ear to the Bible, the issues involved in the covenant of grace are contemporary.

The relevance of discussing Jonathan Edwards and the covenant of grace is also determined by factors from historical interpretation. Again we encounter the enormous prestige of Perry Miller. "Perry Miller's restoration of the Puritans is now so thoroughly accepted that it may be evaluated critically without seriously endangering the reputation of either the Puritans or of Miller himself."[12] And Miller's conclusion regarding Edwards and the covenant needs critical evaluation. In his interpretive *Jonathan Edwards* he sees an inconsistency between Calvinism and covenant theology, with Edwards adhering to the former while rejecting the latter. Focusing on the Boston lecture of 1731, "God Glorified in the Work of Redemption," Miller perceives an unmitigated Calvinism. He saw in the covenant idea, or "Federal Theology" as it was called, "a way for human enterprise in the midst of a system

---

See also Richard Schlatter, "The Puritan Strain," *Puritanism and the American Experience,* ed. Michael McGiffert (Reading, Massachusetts, 1969), p. 9: "To judge the Puritans by the yardstick of nineteenth-century liberalism is old-fashioned and unhistorical."

12. George M. Marsden, "Perry Miller's Rehabilitation of the Puritans: A Critique," *Church History,* XXXIX (March, 1970), p. 92. "Almost without a doubt Miller was the greatest American intellectual historian of our era; yet no historian is immune from the prejudices of his age.... It is possible... to discover in Miller's portrait of the Puritans aspects which reflect the values of twentieth-century America as much as those of seventeenth-century New England."

of determinism," and "Federal Theology is conspicuous in his sermon by its utter absence."[13] One readily sees the assumption of the very thing that must be proved, namely, that "unmitigated Calvinism" excludes the covenant of grace. Recent scholarship has retreated from Miller's conclusion suggesting his assumption was gratuitous and inconsistent with Edwards himself. The retreat has not resolved the issue, however, and a thorough examination of Edwards' position from his writings (including those never published) is needed.

Before leaving contemporary considerations the problem of biased interpretation needs to be elaborated. Hopefully the anti-Puritanism of the 1920's is disappearing. James Truslow Adams "was impatient with a Calvinism which proposed 'the utter surrender of one's own will to the divine will . . .' and which stripped 'God of every shred of what we consider moral character.' "[14] Vernon Parrington is of the same era with no less disdain for Edwards and Puritanism: "The theology of Calvin lay like a heavy weight upon the soul of New England."[15] While recent students of Puritanism find such hostile interpretation unsatisfactory, it does not preclude the danger of simply substituting one set of prejudices for another.

Samuel Eliot Morison, for example, is a founder of "modern" Puritan studies. A New Englander, his "objectivity" is argued on the basis that he "admired" the Puritans

---

13. Miller, *Jonathan Edwards*, p. 30. Miller's position, by virtue of its popular acceptance, will of necessity be dealt with at various points in our discussion.

14. Quoted in Schlatter, "The Puritan Strain," *Puritanism and the American Experience*, p. 8.

15. Vernon L. Parrington, "Jonathan Edwards Was an Anachronism," *Jonathan Edwards and the Enlightenment*, ed. John Opie (Lexington, Massachusetts, 1969), p. 92. "Unfortunate as those sermons were in darkening the frame of an acute thinker, . . . we cannot regret that Edwards devoted his logic to an assiduous stoking of the fires of hell. The theology of Calvin lay like a heavy weight upon the soul of New England, and there could be no surer way to bring it into disrepute, than to thrust into naked relief the brutal grotesqueries of those dogmas. . . . Once the horrors that lay in the background of Calvinism were disclosed to common view, the system was doomed."

without sharing their views. "The ways of the puritans are not my ways, and their faith is not my faith."[16] And Morison's most important associate, Perry Miller, not being a New Englander "had no local pride to justify," indeed, "as an outspoken atheist, he was just as detached from Puritan belief as Morison."[17] These men were apologetes for the Puritans, but hardly for reasons that would most satisfy the Puritans themselves. Jonathan Edwards may be a hero for Miller—but at what price?

It is axiomatic in contemporary historical research that one must ascertain the various historical conditions which form the context in which a given person worked and so arrive at some understanding of what he meant by what he said. Of course, seen in the total context, the result may well show that the person in question was in fact reacting against his traditions, or even molding new ones, rather than being molded by his environment.[18] The end goal is a noble one: What was said and what were the deepest intentions of the one who spoke. This valid historical method, however, is one of the easiest things to abuse. The form-content distinction can very subtly become a vehicle to import a new interpretation which an author finds suitable.

One must be very conscious of this danger in evaluating the almost revolutionary interpretation of Perry Miller. According to Miller, "the student of Edwards must seek to as-

---

16. Quoted in "Introduction," *The New England Puritans*, ed. Sydney V. James (New York, 1968), p. 5.

17. From the "Introduction," *The New England Puritans*, p. 6.

18. This is in fact what Miller finds in Edwards and what fascinates him, at least in the area of Edwards' originality. At the same time large portions of Edwards' thought remain with his tradition. Perry Miller, *Jonathan Edwards*, pp. 47-48, where we read: ". . . He was entirely satisfied to express himself, so far as content goes, in the received tenets of Calvinism." In order to see where his originality lies "one must seize upon occasional passages. . . . His originality was not substantive but primarily verbal . . . although his innovation in language portended an ultimate revolution in substance." Cf. Frederick J. E. Woodbridge, "Jonathan Edwards," *Philosophical Review*, XIII (July, 1904), p. 405: "He did not merely express the thought of his time. . . . He stemmed it and moulded it. . . . It was decidedly Arminian. He made it Calvinistic. . . . His time does not explain him."

certain not so much the peculiar doctrines in which he expressed his meaning as the meaning itself."[19] But to what extent can one reasonably assume such a duality of doctrine and meaning in Edwards? Was this man who could write so precisely, who was within a tradition without being a slave to it, really concealing a deeper secret with his doctrines, using them as a secret code for some mystical truth? Is there, in fact, justification for James H. Nichols' criticism "that the focus of interest has been less Edwards' own than Miller's"?[20]

Conrad Cherry has put his finger on the source of interpretive bias:

> ... Even when the stereotyped images are abandoned, interpreters of Edwards still feel uncomfortable with Edwards' Calvinism. To alleviate the pain of embarrassment, features of Edwards' thought are frequently searched out which "transcend" his Calvinism or which prefigure the post-Puritan era of American thought. Perhaps such a procedure would not be totally inappropriate if Edwards had not so obviously addressed himself to problems current in his eighteenth century or if he had not consciously chosen Puritan Calvinism as the framework for so much of his thought. One therefore suspects a ghost of the perspective yielding the older caricatures in a recent study of Edwards, which proceeds on the assumption that it is at the points where Edwards departs from main-line Puritan theology "that the present-day student has most to learn from America's most neglected theologian."[21]

Cherry also sees Miller in the same light. "Miller . . . leads one to conclude that Edwards is to be appreciated primarily at points other than where traditional Calvinist tenets receive extensive treatment."[22]

> For good or for ill, Edwards was a Calvinist theologian. . . . And though Edwards would have resisted having his thought reduced

---

19. In the "Foreword" of Perry Miller, *Jonathan Edwards*, n. p., where he further states: "It is this Edwards, the artist and the writer, that my volume seeks to expound."
20. James H. Nichols, Review of *Jonathan Edwards* by Perry Miller, *Church History*, XX (December, 1951), p. 79.
21. Conrad Cherry, *The Theology of Jonathan Edwards: A Reappraisal* (Garden City, New York, 1966), pp. 2-3. The reference is to Douglas J. Elwood, *The Philosophical Theology of Jonathan Edwards* (New York, 1960), pp. 10-11.
22. Cherry, *The Theology of Jonathan Edwards*, p. 3.

to that of his Puritan predecessors, he would have also insisted that if one learned from him *only* at the points where he departed from their thought, then one would not really learn from him at all....

To be sure, Edwards was no slave to his theological heritage....

... Edwards' intellectual interests were broad.... But the interest which occupied Edwards' chief attention were theological—interests which increasingly had their immediate occasions in the theological issues facing eighteenth-century New England. His philosophical and scientific interests were bent to a theological purpose. Edwards chose to broaden, impregnate and sometimes alter his Calvinist theology, rather than transcend it.[23]

Perry Miller's lack of emphasis on Scripture and doctrine suggests to George Marsden "that Miller realized that the Puritans could not be rehabilitated in the mid-twentieth century unless they were dissociated as far as possible from their exclusively Christian emphases."[24]

What emerges in this modern renaissance of Edwardsean scholarship reflects a rather clear pattern. The tendency of Edwards' interpreters is to be "uncomfortable" and "embarrassed" with his Calvinism. From that perspective one may simply reject as wrong large segments of Edwards' thought.[25] Or, one may choose to rehabilitate through demythologizing or changed emphases.[26]

---

23. Cherry, *The Theology of Jonathan Edwards*, p. 3-4.

24. Marsden, *Church History*, XXXIX, 95. "This suspicion receives further confirmation when we realize that Miller all but ignores the most crucial aspect of any Christian system—that of the person and work of Christ." Summarizing this aspect of his criticism Marsden writes: "By minimizing Scripture, systematic doctrine, and the role of Christ, Miller in effect seems to be engaging in a kind of demythologizing, or more properly 'de-Christianizing,' of Puritanism. This process is not by any means a fully developed thesis, but it is an undeniable subtle tendency" (p. 96).

25. Cf. for example, Edward H. Davidson, *Jonathan Edwards: The Narrative of a Puritan Mind* (Boston, 1966), p. 69. "... Edwards's idea of history is an odd fusion of stale Biblical analogies and pious trust that whatever was to be would eventually come to pass in just the way God intended it. Edwards seems to be aware of Biblical scholarship in his day.... Yet in almost every respect, from a modern point of view, Edwards's survey of history is worthless if not absurd.... And reading every text, whether it is Jacob's dream or the young man Solomon's rhapsody to his love, as if all were equally true puts Edwards far outside the way that history was to follow."

26. As has been indicated, Perry Miller is the preeminent example of this

The atmosphere of contemporary thinking exerts much influence in how one rightly understands Edwards. To what extent does Edwards satisfactorily explain Edwards, and to what extent must the modern visionary somehow penetrate through to the real Edwards? That answer is fundamental to the conclusions one discovers. Edwards, the meticulous scholar, was not prone to vague and unclear expression. He chose and defined his terms with great care. Is that the fundamental factor?[27]

Whether Jonathan Edwards speaks clearly enough to serve as his own interpreter will depend in part on how coherently the doctrine of the covenant of grace fits into his total teaching, or how consistently it is excluded. The covenant of grace concerns the relationship of God and man with respect to man's salvation. The clear testimony of Scripture indicates two dimensions to that relationship: man actively, voluntarily, turning or coming to God, and God turning or drawing man to Himself.[28] A writer who does biblical theology by choosing one or the other of these dimensions to the exclusion (implicit or explicit) of the other is superficial. A person who is under historical-theological examination, and who can legitimately be categorized as choosing a one-dimensional treatment of what is two-dimensional in Scripture, is a superficial thinker. The giants among Puritan theologians were not

---

approach. Cf. Miller in "General Editor's Note," *Freedom of the Will,* p. viii, having enthusiastically commended the reexamination of Edwards and past assumptions about him, says: "This is not to imply that today the precise doctrines that Edwards maintained, in the language in which he cast them, have been or should be extensively revived: indeed it is quite beside the purpose of this edition to promulgate them."

27. The shadow of Perry Miller is again present. According to Miller inconsistency just might be what sets Edwards above his contemporaries: "... We do not expect ... a unanimity of interpretation, or uncritical endorsement of Edwards' views.... If out of these several treatments various and sometimes contradictory interpretations emerge, we shall greet that result as a documented attestation to the range and complexity of Edwards' mind." In "General Editor's Note," *Freedom of the Will,* p. vii.

28. For an example of relevant texts stating these two aspects, and a statement of the issue involved, see Norman Pettit, *The Heart Prepared: Grace and Conversion in Puritan Spiritual Life* (New Haven, 1966), pp. 2-3, 8-9.

superficial thinkers. Certainly Jonathan Edwards was not. It simply will not do to interpret Edwards and the covenant in a way that implies Paul against the prophets, prophet against prophet, Peter against Paul, or even Paul against Paul. To interpret Edwards as polarized around faith *or* election, when Scripture holds them in correlation, is at best grossly unfair to Edwards' own intentions. It falsely assumes that for Edwards God electing and man responding are two "ways" rather than aspects of "one way." A statement by Edwards should reverberate throughout this study as a manifesto that he heard what Scripture said relevant to the covenant relationship. Concerning efficacious grace Edwards chooses neither God nor man to the exclusion of the other, nor part God and part man, but declares that *"God does all, and we do all."*[29]

We need finally to be alerted to the fact that clarification is needed on what is and is not relevant to a study about the covenant of grace. Edwards did not write a major chapter or separate publication on the covenant of grace. Our task is to ascertain whether he taught the doctrine and see how its presence or absence fits into his total thought. If the covenant of grace is there, it cannot be studied in quite the same way as the debates between Edwards and his opponents on the will, sin, revival practices and other polemical issues. We would expect to find it integrated into his writings on faith, election, grace, and similar theological loci. And while Edwards was not a slave to tradition, it would not be without justification to have an eye on the way the covenant of grace was handled by the theological predecessors whom Jonathan Edwards admired.

A study of the covenant of grace is further complicated by the fact, mentioned previously as a danger of emphasis, that the covenant of grace in many studies is seen merely as a part (not necessarily the most vital part) of the covenant

---

29. "Concerning Efficacious Grace," *Works,* II, 557 (Emphasis mine).

concept in Puritanism. The theological doctrine of the covenant of grace is threatened to be sacrificed to the broader covenant interests of church polity, sociology, or political science. This is precisely what occurs in volume after volume.

In the seventeenth century it became commonplace to discuss three covenants, "all three of them in theory quite distinct but in practice closely allied: the Covenant of Grace, the Church Covenant, and the Civil Covenant."[30] The covenant of grace was equated with the "invisible church," the elect who are united with Christ and known only to God. The Church covenant was the "visible church," the visible political union of saints. The civil covenant dealt with government and in reality was "merely physical enforcement and public advancement of whatever the churches desired." Perry Miller, in his second volume on *The New England Mind*, is careful to distinguish between the covenant of grace and the national covenant. Yet his real concern is "to show how the conception of a covenant was ... the master idea of the age."[31]

> The two covenants—personal and public—were 'branches' of the same, and yet distinct: saints dwelling alone may be in the Covenant of Grace without participating in a pledged society; a society may achieve this honor even though many (or most) of its citizens are not gracious.... This philosophy of the national covenant was not only a logical deduction from the Covenant of Grace, but also the theme of the Old Testament: Jacob wrestles in solitude with Jehovah, but Israel make their cohesion visible in an external organization—a church, a corporation, a nation, even a plantation.[32]

---

30. Herbert Wallace Schneider, *The Puritan Mind* (London, 1931), pp. 19-25.
31. Perry Miller, *The New England Mind: From Colony to Province* (Cambridge, 1967), hereafter cited as *NEM: Colony to Province*, p. 21.
32. Miller, *NEM: Colony to Province*, p. 21. "Theorists recognized at once that there are at least three respects in which a national covenant necessarily differs from the Covenant of Grace. A group exists only in this world: it does not migrate *in toto* to heaven.... It has to do with conduct here and now, with visible success or tangible failure. Secondly, since a society cannot be rewarded in heaven for its obedience ... and cannot be punished in hell ... it must perforce contract with the Almighty for external ends.... In the third place, a community

In historical interpretation the practical reality has dominated our understanding. That is, the various covenants were treated as aspects of one covenant, and practical considerations overshadowed theological issues.[33] The reality of this, however, in no way precludes an attempt to look at the covenant of grace as pre-eminently a theological doctrine. Indeed it appears not only justified, but required, that the covenant of grace (in this instance Edwards' view) be examined as much as possible in isolation from church and civil covenants.

Not only does Edwards' own interest require a theological approach, but there is historical justification as well. The phenomena of the Great Awakening was effectually eroding the practical unity of the three covenants. The individualism of the Awakening had "institutional effects." Gaustad writes:

> The emphasis upon a personal religious experience had then, as always, the effect of making converts less dependent on external authority—scriptural or ecclesiastical. Those to whom religion in the 1740's had suddenly become meaningful knew that the kingdom of God was within them; their private divine vocation, be it called new light, inner light, or sense of the heart, was their ultimate and occasionally their only appeal. To them only one covenant was of pressing significance: the covenant of grace. The church covenant was important, but secondary. Mediation was unnecessary, priesthood was universal. The civil covenant was obsolete, and society was shattered, but into members not classes.[34]

is not joined to God by so irrevocable a contract as will endure no matter how depraved it becomes. (A saint is at best imperfectly sanctified, but his sins have been atoned for; nothing he does . . . breaks that bond.) If a society . . . sinks so deep into corruption . . . the national covenant is ended" (pp. 21-22).

33. See Schneider, *The Puritan Mind*, pp. 24-25: "Thus it is evident that in practice, and to a large extent even in theory, the three covenants were really one. The Church Covenant gave form to the Covenant of Grace, and the Civil Covenant gave power to the Church Covenant. Society in New England was actually organized, as Baxter said it should be, into a Holy Commonwealth." Cf. Perry Miller, *NEM: Colony to Province*, pp. 72-73. Added to this situation is the historical interest in the "half-way covenant," which as a practical expedient had great importance for church history, but is relevant only incidentally as a covenant quite other than the theological covenant of grace.

34. Edwin S. Gaustad, *The Great Awakening in New England* (New York, 1957), p. 113.

Such an historical shift gives added weight to our method of examination. The opposite historical setting, however, would not fundamentally alter the principle which has been set forth. Only as we isolate the covenant of grace as a theological discussion point, can we approach the deepest intentions of Jonathan Edwards in relation to it.

2

The Man and His Times

The title is not meant to suggest a biographical sketch of one chapter. Many biographies of varying lengths (and quality) are available. Hopefully there will yet appear a definitive piece on the life and work of Edwards. No effort will be made here to provide even an outline of Edwards' life. Our concern is biographical only to the extent it assists our understanding of Edwards and the covenant of grace. His stature and abilities as well as the historical situation are relevant.

The genius of Edwards is underlined in a clever and perceptive way by Ola Winslow in her Pulitzer Prize winning biography: "It would be easier to derive Jonathan Edwards from his posterity than from his ancestors."[1] His intellectual ancestors, however, are illustrious in their own right.

A unique intellect he was. "Edwards is generally recognized to be the most eminent philosopher-theologian this country has produced, and some regard him as one of the greatest thinkers of all Christian history."[2] Georges Lyon, a French philosopher with little sympathy for Edwards the theologian, approvingly cites the concensus that Edwards is "the greatest metaphysician America has yet produced."[3]

---
1. Winslow, *Jonathan Edwards, 1703-1758*, p. 5.
2. Elwood, *The Philosophical Theology of Jonathan Edwards*, pp. 2-3.
3. Quoted in "Edwards and the New England Theology," B. B. Warfield, *Studies in Theology* (New York, 1932), p. 515. Lyon states further: "Who knows, they have asked themselves, to what heights this original genius might have risen, if, instead of being born in a half-savage country, far from the traditions of philosophy and science, he had appeared rather in our old world, and there received the direct impulse of the modern mind. Perhaps he would have taken a place between Leibniz and Kant among the founders of immortal systems, instead of the work he has left reducing itself to a sublime and barbarous theology, which astonishes our reason and outrages our heart, the object of at once our horror and admiration."

Nichols calls Edwards "the greatest intellect of the Awakening, and probably of colonial America generally."[4] John McNeill in his work on Calvinism declares that Edwards "must be regarded as the most eminent of American Calvinists."[5]

Not only the man but his works receive equal praise. Paul Ramsey, echoing Perry Miller's general comment, states that the one book, *Freedom of the Will*, "is sufficient to establish its author as the greatest philosopher-theologian yet to grace the American scene."[6] Ramsey further acknowledges the justification of Sereno Dwight's designation of four of Edwards' later works as "four of the ablest and most valuable works, which the Church of Christ has in its possession."[7] At the turn of the century John DeWitt expressed his belief that if Edwards had lived to complete his planned *History of Redemption*, "the world would have seen in it the fruit of a constructive genius not less great than that which appears in the *Summa* of St. Thomas or in the *Institutes* of Calvin."[8] An important observation regarding these later works is that they "involved no changes in his theology," but "they were the logical formulation of what he had long taught."[9] This observation is a sound one and should prevent any superficial impulse to set the "young Edwards" over against the "mature Edwards" in the question of the covenant of grace.

One of the remarkable aspects of Edwards' intellectual

---

4. James Hastings Nichols, *History of Christianity: 1650-1950* (New York, 1956), p. 75. "Edwards was startled at the response to his own preaching and could only explain it as God's ratification of the evangelical doctrines of grace and justification."

5. John T. McNeill, *The History and Character of Calvinism* (New York, 1954), p. 362.

6. "Editor's Introduction" in *Freedom of the Will*, p. 2.

7. "Editor's Introduction" in *Freedom of the Will*, p. 8. The four works are: *A Dissertation Concerning the End for Which God Created the World, A Dissertation Concerning the Nature of True Virtue, The Christian Doctrine of Original Sin Defended,* and *Freedom of the Will.*

8. John DeWitt, "Jonathan Edwards: A Study," *Princeton Theological Review*, II (January, 1904), p. 103.

9. Williston Walker, "Jonathan Edwards," *Jonathan Edwards: A Profile*, ed. David Levin (New York, 1969), p. 109.

life is the way mature writings are already present in embryo form in earlier work. The "Miscellanies," for example, are notes Edwards made for his private use, and they span his adult life. Frequently they find their way into both sermons and published works throughout his life. Not surprisingly, the sermons cited in this work reflect all periods of Edwards' preaching ministry. They do not show a difference in doctrine in different periods of his life. Consequently when seeking to ascertain Edwards' position on a doctrine such as the covenant of grace, one is able to look into his private notes and his sermons, as well as his scholarly writing for publication.

The man is preceded by the youth, and what a remarkable youth it was. The one overwhelming observation of all the biographies (and relevant specialized studies) is the precociousness of the boy. A cursory reading about Edwards reveals that he wrote his thousand-word essay, "Of Insects," at the age of twelve or thirteen. About that time also came forth a demonstration of the immateriality of the soul, as well as analyses of the rainbow and of colors demonstrating his having studied Newton's *Opticks* (or its essence via secondhand information). The incredibility of these achievements could serve as an argument against their genuineness[10] as long as there was any uncertainty regarding the manuscripts. Edwards entered Yale College in September 1716, aged thirteen. His formal academic training—the collegiate course, preparation for the ministry, and after a short pas-

---

10. B. B. Warfield cites the French philosopher Lyon in this regard in *Studies in Theology*, pp. 518-519, n. 7. "On this ground, indeed, Lyon, for example, refuses to believe in their genuineness. It is futile to adduce the parallel of a Pascal, he declares; such a comparison is much too modest; the young Edwards united in himself many Pascals, and, by a double miracle, combined with them gifts by virtue of which he far surpassed a Galileo and a Newton; what we are asked to believe is not merely that as a boy in his teens he worked out independently a system of metaphysics closely similar to that of Berkeley, but that he anticipated most of the scientific discoveries which constitute the glory of the succeeding century." Having cited evidence for their authenticity, Warfield concludes: "It is all, no doubt, very remarkable. But this only shows that Edwards was a very remarkable youth."

torate a return for his Master of Arts degree and the position of tutor—was equally impressive.

Concerning geographical background, two equally important observations need to be made. The Connecticut Valley was frontier America, far removed from the intellectual centers of Europe. Equally true, however, is the fact that Edwards to a large degree overcame that handicap by judicious use of the libraries at his disposal. If small, they were well chosen volumes and relatively current. Edwards also utilized personal and written contacts with whomever he could. The situation, if not ideal, was utilized by Edwards to the fullest degree, coupling his personal genius with extensive academic exposure.[11]

Apart from the externals of his training (though not divorced from them) Edwards had the gift of perception, the greatness of mind, to embrace the whole of Truth in its many facets. He was able to approach reality in a unified way; he was not forced to pit one aspect of reality over against another but saw instead the unity in the world he perceived.

> Jonathan Edwards was gifted with extraordinary vision and dialectical powers. His vision was at once a simple and immediate apprehension of a "divine and supernatural light" which flooded his world and his soul, and an extremely complex intuition in which Being, truth, virtue, beauty, and holiness fused into a splendor which ravished him all his days. . . . Mysticism and logic, delight and discourse, emotion and thought, were united one with another in Edwards' mind to produce writing which is poetry, philosophy, and theology, all at once. . . . God's love was to Edwards an intelligent love, at once benevolent and rational, without sentimentality and without frigidity. . . . The rare won-

---

11. For an extensive and informative study of the various influences on Edwards during his intellectual development see William Sparkes Morris, "The Young Jonathan Edwards: A Reconstruction" (Unpublished Ph.D. dissertation, University of Chicago, 1955). In this massive work of approximately 900 pages Morris treats, among other things, the books which Edwards owned or had access to, the curriculum of Yale, the viewpoints of his instructors, and his reaction to all these. Cf. also William S. Morris, "The Genius of Jonathan Edwards," *Reinterpretation in American Church History*, ed. Jerald C. Brauer (Chicago, 1968), pp. 29-65, which is an essay based on Morris' dissertation.

der of Edwards is the exhilarating union in him of many-sided sensibility with intellectual power.... His mind and heart, equally whole and vigorous, worked exuberant harmony one with the other. It is certainly a joy to know a man like him. One is reminded of Mozart.[12]

One readily detects in the history of doctrine the unfortunate results when such a unified view is missing.

The philosophical distinction between understanding and the will is a case in point, with the doctrine of faith serving as a particular application of his view. In a notebook on "Faith" Edwards lists as number one among "proper and important" inquiries concerning saving faith: "Whether justifying faith, in its proper essence, implies, besides the act of the judgment, also an act of the inclination and will?"[13] The question is not new to the history of theology, and the revival fires of the Great Awakening provided the issue for less sophisticated minds to take sides. Contrary to the intent of Calvinism and Puritanism to portray faith as a response of the whole man, there were those unable to keep the balance who emphasized either the will or the intellect as the principal faculty in true faith.[14] The primacy of the will, for example, grew out of an abuse of the emotional aspect of the revivals, while the primacy of the intellect had roots in an overreaction to the revival excesses.

Edwards saw faith as neither emotional or volitional response only nor mere rational assent. For Edwards faith was an act of the whole man:

> Upon the whole, the best, and clearest, and most perfect definition of justifying faith, and most according to the Scripture, that I can think of, is this, faith is the soul's entirely embracing the

---

12. Joseph Haroutunian in the "Preface" of Douglas Elwood, *The Philosophical Theology of Jonathan Edwards*, pp. vii-viii.
13. "Concerning Faith," *Works*, II, 588. Our intent here is not to have a discussion of faith but to see faith as an example of how Edwards had a unified view of reality.
14. Cf. William G. Wilcox, "New England Covenant Theology: Its English Precursors and Early American Exponents" (Unpublished Ph.D. dissertation, Duke University, 1959), pp. 156-160, and Cherry, *The Theology of Jonathan Edwards*, p. 12 ff.

revelation of Jesus Christ as our Saviour.... It is the whole soul according and assenting to the truth, and embracing of it. There is an entire yielding of the mind and heart to the revelation, and a closing with it, and adhering to it, with the belief, and with the inclination and affection.[15]

Not surprisingly, the work of the Holy Spirit influences, according to Edwards, both the mind and the will. In a sermon on spiritual illumination (Matt. 16:17) Edwards attributes to the Holy Spirit the gifts of a *"knowledge . . . which is above all others sweet and joyful"* and a *"light . . . such as effectually influences the inclination, and changes the nature of the soul"* (emphasis mine).[16]

Early in his life, in a list of subjects to be handled in a proposed "Treatise on the Mind," for which he had already compiled extensive notes, Edwards made his position clear:

> Concerning speculative understanding and sense of heart; whether any difference between the sense of the heart and the will or inclination; how the Scriptures are ignorant of the philosophic distinction of the understanding and the will; and how the sense of the heart is there called knowledge or understanding.[17]

---

15. "Concerning Faith," *Works*, II, 580. The relevance of this issue is reflected in the fact that it has surfaced in current theological discussions as a fundamental consideration in properly ascertaining the "Biblical view of man." For a good discussion of the theological importance of dealing with "the whole man" in an historical and contemporary context, see especially the chapter by that title in G. C. Berkouwer, *Man: The Image of God,* trans. Dirk W. Jellema (Grand Rapids, 1962), pp. 194-233.

16. "A Divine and Supernatural Light, Immediately Imparted to the Soul by the Spirit of God, Shown to be both a Scriptural and Rational Doctrine," *Works*, II, 17. Conrad Cherry indicates that Peter van Mastricht, a Dutch theologian highly valued by Edwards, "expressly called for an interpretation of grace in terms of both illumination and infusion. This meant for van Mastricht, as well as for most of Edwards' Reformed theological precursors, that the human agent is so constituted that grace must be two fold in its internal function: it must influence both the mind and the will. For 'if we should make the absurd supposition of the understanding's being most clearly enlightened, and yet the will not renewed,' said van Mastricht, 'the will would not follow the practical judgment, because in that case the understanding would not dictate agreeably to its propensity.' For faith to occur, the understanding must not only be illumined by a luminous principle; the will must also be bent by the infusion of a divine habit." *The Theology of Jonathan Edwards,* p. 34.

17. "The Mind," *The Philosophy of Jonathan Edwards,* p. 71. In the body of his notes on "The Mind" Edwards speaks of the will and its determination.

The Man and His Times

Perry Miller paints Edwards in bold relief against the backdrop of the revival conflict of rationalism and enthusiasm:

"The will . . . is not the greatest good apprehended, or that which is apprehended to be the greatest good; but the greatest apprehension of good. . . . The greatest mental existence of good—the greatest degree of the mind's sense of good—the greatest degree of apprehension, or perception, or idea of [one's] own good always determines the will. . . . It is utterly impossible but that it should be so that the inclination and choice of the mind should always be determined by good as mentally or ideally existing. It would be a contradiction to suppose otherwise, for we mean nothing else by good but that which agrees with the inclination and disposition of the mind. And surely that which agrees with it must agree with it. . . . For we mean nothing else by greatest good but that which agrees most with the inclination and disposition of the soul" (pp. 58-60). Edwards states with regard to "strong reason" that does not result in "just judgment": "It is not so much from a defect of the reasoning powers as from a fault of the disposition" (p. 66). Cf. number 2 in list of subjects to be dealt with in the "Treatise" which concerns "prejudices" and their bearing on the mind (p. 69).

One immediately recognizes here a philosophical-theological issue of momentous significance far beyond the scope of this work, yet the presupposition of which is fundamental to all aspects of Edwards' theology. In Perry Miller, *Jonathan Edwards*, to cite but one example, this unified approach of Edwards is frequently in view. For example: "Puritanism had always recognized a distinction between what is called 'speculative' religion and living religion. Any man could understand intellectually what a verse in the Bible or a doctrine of theology said, but not all could feel what it meant. . . . Puritanism of the seventeenth century had no explanation for the phenomenon except the caprice of God. . . . But Edwards entered upon his mission of reawakening New England armed with a scientific psychology wherewith to account, in the finest detail, for this riddle of experience. From Locke's demonstration that a thing cannot be the same to all perceptions, that it must exist for each perceiver as it is perceived, and from Locke's assertion that perception is an immediate, irresistible response of sensation to the impact of an object, Edwards concluded that as a man perceives, so is he—and that as he will perceive, so he is predestined to be. . . . 'He that is spiritually enlightened truly apprehends and sees it or has a sense of it.' To see is to have a sense; to have a sense is to have an inclination; and as a man inclines, he wills. . . . To perceive became to do. A man's act is not the result of a meshing of gears, but the expression—the 'image' he was later to say—of the whole man" (pp. 65-66). (If Miller, as he appears to do, gives the perception of man a logical or chronological priority to predestination, it is a gross misunderstanding of Edwards. If a cognitive priority from the standpoint of man is intended, as Miller's appreciation of Edwards' Calvinism would suggest he must mean, then one could wish for a clearer indication.) An appeal to the sermon, "A Divine and Spiritual Light," to show Edwards' "mysticism" misses the point according to Miller. The point he was striving to make, says Miller, is "that spiritual light is imparted not as a mystical infusion but as a rational conveyance through the senses" (p. 68).

Miller again brings up the point of will and understanding in his chapter on "Revivalism." Here he deals with Edwards' terms "natural" and "moral" orders. The "natural order" deals with natural "agreeableness"; the "moral" order is that

New England in the eighteenth century was a laboratory for America, and it divided itself in two, into "new lights" and "old lights." ... There was Davenport with all his passion; and there was Chauncy with all his rationalism. Out of his genius for definition, Edwards wrote a sentence that is applicable, in its recognition of ultimate significance, far beyond the borders of New England, far deeper into time than the eighteenth century: "Such distinguishing names of reproach, do as it were divide us into two armies, separated, and drawn up in battle array, ready to fight one with another; which greatly hinders the work of God."

---

fitness of relationship which depends upon the fashion in which an object 'affects' the perceiver.... It is the realm of values" (pp. 151-152). "...While atoms follow their courses, human experience is moral.... Perception has its logic.... But a man is affected by—that is, he loves or he hates—not things as they are in themselves, but things as he perceives them. We are 'capable of rationally determining for ourselves.'... But, because it is intelligent, it is aware of what it ought to be as well as of what is.... 'A man must answer with the disposition of the heart to do what is resolved to be done.' The difficulty of reconciling natural necessity with humanity's freedom to perceive in various ways disappears, or can be made to disappear, in the certainty that the newness and freshness of these things will affect the mind and work a free consent to reality" (pp. 152-153). "It is not a content, but a frame of conception; it is a consent, not to a syllogism or to a covenant, but to an experienced 'taste' or 'relish' which cannot be gainsaid. Regeneration is the convergence of the two orders upon a single perception, of the order of causes along with the order of morality, so that simultaneously there is given 'union to a proper object—and a relish of the object.' Redemption is a flash of experience, forever abiding, in which natural good and moral good merge in a sense of the real good" (p. 154).

Concerning the debate between Edwards and Chauncy dealing with "Religious Affections," Miller writes: "Chauncy persisted in arguing the whole case on the grounds of the scholastic psychology ... as though everybody in Christendom assumed that reason, imagination, and will were distinct 'faculties' and the affections a separate and autonomous power.... The irony is that the theological liberal, who in every trait stands for the rational Enlightenment, spoke in the language of outmoded science, and the defender of Calvinism put his case upon a modern, dynamic, analytical psychology in which the human organism was viewed, not as a system of gears, but as a living unit" (pp. 177-178).

John E. Smith, in the "Editor's Introduction," *Religious Affections,* ed. John E. Smith, Vol. II of *Works of Jonathan Edwards* (New Haven, 1959), p. 13, writes that what Edwards meant by the heart "has been obscured in the past because of a misapprehension according to which the heart is vaguely described as 'emotional' and set over against the 'head,' which is a symbol for reason and knowledge. *Edwards' analysis gives no warrant either for the identification or the opposition*.... The point almost invariably missed is that in Edwards' view the *inclination* (the faculty initially distinguished from the understanding) involves *both* the will and the mind."

These citations are not meant as definitive interpretations of Edwards' position, but rather to illustrate its importance and the way it functions in some of the issues in which Edwards was involved.

> ...The debate began as an argument concerning a work of God; it became, on both sides, contention about the nature of man....
> Neither side knew exactly what they were doing, or realized for decades what they had done, but Edwards knew at once. For that reason he centered his studies upon definitions of the human species, and pled with both camps not to cling to fragmentary, half-formed conceptions.... There must be light in the understanding, for heat without light is not heavenly; yet "where there is a kind of light without heat, a head stored with notions and speculations, with a cold and unaffected heart, there can be nothing divine in that light." These are not two opposites to be played off against each other: they can be made one in single perception: "if the great things of religion are rightly understood, they will affect the heart."[18]

The ability of Edwards to see the truth of both "sides" as "one in single perception" is indicative of his stature as a theologian and will manifest itself clearly in the divine-human polarity intrinsic to the covenant of grace.

Jonathan Edwards the preacher was no ranting revivalist. He spoke in a quiet voice and used few gestures. The logic of what he said and the work of the Holy Spirit were the relevant factors in his "success." In what is the best systematic treatment of the content of Edwards' preaching (*Steps to Salvation*), John Gerstner clearly demonstrates the vast wealth to be found in his homiletical labors. In a concluding chapter Gerstner provides some helpful insights about Edwards the preacher:

> Not only was he given to writing learned and profound treatises, but he preached solidly. He did not preach academically, certain-

---

18. Miller, *Jonathan Edwards*, pp. 178-179. Cf. Haroutunian in the "Preface" to Elwood, *The Philosophical Theology of Jonathan Edwards*, pp. viii-ix: "Those impressed by his spirituality have done no justice to his intelligence, and those impressed by his intelligence have been impervious to his 'sense of divine things.' But Edwards is his vision and his intellect. Without the one or the other he is not Edwards, and unless we see him as both we are bound to misunderstand him and deprive ourselves of his gifts.... Edwards not only insisted upon the immediacy of our knowledge of God but also argued it with the full use of his dialectical powers. With his vision he demolished deism and with his dialectics he demolished pantheism. He had his own way of combining Scripture and reason in our knowledge of God."

ly not pedantically. He made a distinction in method between the scholarly and the popular, but not in content. What he wrote in his treatises, he preached from his pulpit—and with basically the same arguments.

... He seemed to believe in the formula, "truth is unto godliness," and preached accordingly. He preached ... the whole truth, as he saw it. And he showed the people why he saw it so. His sermons explore the nature of God, the essence of virtue, the fine points of salvation, the controversial issues of theology....

... The preaching was always clear. I doubt if any ever thought of Edwards as going over their heads. Probably, they often wished he had.

Edwards was a preacher of the Word. In all his manuscripts I do not remember one that does not begin with a text and its exposition in context. All of his "doctrines" are drawn directly from the text. All of his "reasons" are implications of this and other texts, except for a rare flight of speculation of which he was fully conscious and about which he usually apologized.... He rested his final authority, however, on the authority of Scripture.

Furthermore, he preached every doctrine that he found in the Bible.... He preached about sovereignty and ... about responsibility; he preached about hell and about heaven; he preached about grace and about law; ... individual piety and ... social obligations; he preached about principles and about persons; he preached about terror and he preached about comfort.[19]

The popular image of Edwards as primarily a preacher of hell is without foundation.[20] It would be equally errant, however, to minimize it. Edwards preached on the reality of hell, and he meant what he preached.[21] As McNeill observes,

---

19. John H. Gerstner, *Steps to Salvation: The Evangelistic Message of Jonathan Edwards* (Philadelphia, 1960), pp. 189-190. The pastorate was no means to a greater vocational end for Edwards. And the significance of Edwards as a pastor can be appreciated to its fullest only when it is understood that he succeeded Solomon Stoddard (the "pope" of the Connecticut Valley) in the church of Northhampton (the most prestigious and influential church outside of Boston).

20. "Of the six hundred full-length manuscript sermons extant, about 25 percent are tentatively classified as evangelistic and only a few of these are of the threatening, imprecatory sort. A much larger percentage is typed as theological or as dealing with the Christian experience and with personal and social ethics. Of the seventy or so sermons already published, only about eight are denunciatory." Elwood, *The Philosophical Theology of Jonathan Edwards*, p. 163, n. 5.

21. Cf. Gerstner, *Steps to Salvation*, p. 24, where he observes: "What must have been especially terrifying to Edwards' audience listening to his merciless pictorial representations of the pit was the realization that they were not hearing

however, "even his lurid warnings were uttered in compassion, and his object in all preaching was to lead sinners to grace."[22] He warned sinners because he cared. Yet he is frequently judged unfairly at this point. Concerning his pleading with the unconverted, Gerstner perceptively observes: "This is not the spirit of sadism. Ironically, if Edwards, believing as he did, had been a sadist, he would never have said a word about perdition."[23]

Finally, what significance is the period of time in which Edwards lived to the understanding of Edwards? Much of the controversy in Edwardsean studies is related to the man and his times. Was he molded by his times, or did he mold them? Was he independent of his times, or did he react to them? Where among these questions can we find the man?

One commentary on the period for which there seems to be unanimity is that "decline" is an appropriate word to describe it. Edwards appears more a voice in the wilderness than the premier spokesman of an accepted way of life.

> In the year 1729, when Jonathan Edwards became full pastor of the church at Northampton, Mass., New England religion had already undergone a long process of decline. The theocratic ideal of the first settlers was disappearing, Calvinistic theology had become largely a matter of formality, and worldliness had been growing among the people. Calvinistic Christianity was being buried under a heavy coating of political and economic facts which had little relevance to its theology. It was not being effectively disputed, nor was it being openly discarded. It was simply

---

a sensationalistic ranter striving for an effect, but a prodigious and cool intellect driven by the purest moral earnestness seeking to approach some adequacy of representation for a transcendently awful fact."

22. McNeill, *The History and Character of Calvinism*, p. 362. Cf. Walker, *Jonathan Edwards: A Profile*, pp. 98-99. Walker finds Edwards' preaching of hell and the torments of the lost as objectionable but admits that it must be seen in perspective. "Repulsive as this presentation is, it is but fair to Edwards to remember that it seemed to him to be demanded no less by his philosophic principles than by his interpretation of the Bible. And it is merely justice to recall, also, that though the terrors of the law fill a large place in his pulpit utterances, no man of his age pictured more glowingly than Edwards the joys of the redeemed, the blessedness of union with Christ, or the felicities of the knowledge of God."

23. Gerstner, *Steps to Salvation*, p. 28.

being ignored as a matter of little consequence for practical living, by men who said one thing and did another. New England was becoming involved in the ways of the Old World, striving for commercial success, competing for profits, tasting power and assuming rights, ready to defend them legally or otherwise. The spirit of European nationalism, capitalism, and rationalism, with its apparatus of political and legal theory, was already growing strong. The theocentric piety of Calvinism seemed doomed.[24]

Frank Foster designates the close of the first century in New England, the point just prior to Edwards' emergence, as "the lowest point of religious decline reached in New England, whether it be considered from a practical or a doctrinal point of view."[25] In a highly condensed summary of Foster's work in *The New Schaff-Herzog Encyclopedia of Religious Knowledge,* he traces the theologically directed decline of the Calvinistic Puritanism that was imported from England. The movement was from the sovereignty of God to the emphasis on man's helplessness, to a decline of efforts to arouse sinners, to a paralysis within the churches, to an interest in externals and the arrival of the "Half-Way Covenant." The result was that "not only the Calvinistic theology, but even the religious life of New England was endangered.... New England was in a bad way.... Who would or could save it?"[26] His answer is implicit in the article by the space given to Edwards; in his book he is explicit: "The answer was providentially given in the birth and career of Jonathan

---

24. Haroutunian, *Piety versus Moralism,* pp. xx-xxi.
25. Frank Hugh Foster, *A Genetic History of the New England Theology* (Chicago, 1907), p. 43.
26. Foster, "New England Theology," *The New Schaff-Herzog Encyclopedia of Religious Knowledge,* ed. Samuel M. Jackson, VII (1953), p. 131. Cf. Peter Ymen De Jong, *The Covenant Idea in New England Theology, 1620-1847* (Grand Rapids, 1945), p. 123: "The Half-way Covenant as accepted by the Synod of 1662 did not bear the much-desired fruit.... Instead of a growing interest in the church and a deepening piety among the inhabitants of the land, New England experienced a time of grave laxness and gross indifference.... The most significant consequence was that during the next half century many of the churches openly acknowledged historical faith, or an intellectual acceptance of the Scriptural truths taught in the churches, as the only requisite to full membership. This decision was the result of the fearful religious decline suffered by the colonies during the period from the Synod of 1662 to the Great Awakening."

Edwards."[27] The issue becomes not whether, but how, he met the challenge, and with what implications for Calvinism!

There were important historical and sociological factors, but the primary issue was theological. Certainly Edwards thought so! The reaction against Calvinism, as we have seen, was well underway in Edwards' youth. ". . . By 1740, we find Jonathan Edwards leading, not a mighty Calvinistic army going forth conquering and to conquer, but an army desperately defending the citadel of New England Calvinism."[28] The theological terrain on which Edwards entered showed two equally unfortunate camps. On the one hand, there was a corrupted Calvinism whose doctrine of election tended towards fatalism rather than biblical predestination. Lack of responsibility and general indifference resulted. On the other hand, there was the Arminian assault in reaction to this sterile determinism.[29] Edwards with his unified perception of reality, Edwards the predestinarian preacher of "experimental" religion and human responsibility, saw the futility of both options. Therein he was the right man at the right time.

The theology of Jonathan Edwards, especially his view of the covenant of grace, developed in its historical context against the backdrop of the controversy between the so-called "consistent Calvinism" with its unconditional election and the increasingly expanding inroads of Arminianism. Other important issues were at stake. Yet in the broad historical sweep it was the Arminian controversy that was to alter the theological map of New England.

27. Foster, *A Genetic History of the New England Theology*, p. 47.
28. Frank A. Lawrence, "The Decline of Calvinism in New England Before Jonathan Edwards" (Unpublished Th.M. thesis, Pittsburgh-Xenia Theological Seminary, 1951), p. 2.
29. Cf. De Jong, *The Covenant Idea in New England Theology, 1620-1847*, p. 135, where he says: "Without a doubt this period was the lowest in degree of spirituality in the history of the first two centuries of New England Congregationalism. Both in theory and practice the gospel had lost its hold on the masses. THE TYPE OF PREACHING WAS EITHER A MORALISTIC ARMINIANISM OR AN EMASCULATED CALVINISM, WHICH IN ITS UNBALANCED STRESS ON ELECTION FORGOT THE COVENANT IDEA WHICH WOULD HAVE GIVEN ROOM TO HUMAN RESPONSIBILITY."

In his struggles with Arminianism, *Freedom of the Will* is a foundational work. The debate around the "will" would be determinative. It was a "no quarter" conflict. Paul Ramsey, in his introduction to *Freedom of the Will*, captures the importance this work had for Edwards: "Into the writing of it he poured all his intellectual acumen, coupled with a passionate conviction that the decay to be observed in religion and morals followed the decline in doctrine. . . ."[30] Edwards in his work *Original Sin* is still encountering Arminian notions. He refers the reader to *Freedom of the Will* but takes time to emphasize the cruciality of the question:

> There is no one thing more fundamental in their schemes of religion: on the determination of this one leading point depends the issue of almost all controversies we have with such divines. . . . I stand ready to confess to the forementioned modern divines, if they can maintain their peculiar notion of *freedom*, consisting in the *self-determining power of the will*, as necessary to *moral agency*, and can thoroughly establish it in opposition to the arguments lying against it, then they have an impregnable castle, to which they may repair, and remain invincible, in all the controversies they have with the reformed divines, concerning *original sin*, the *sovereignty* of grace, *election*, *redemption*, *conversion*, the *efficacious operation* of the Holy Spirit, the nature of saving *faith*, *perseverance* of the saints, and other principles of the like kind.[31]

The import of this for Edwards' position on the covenant of grace is fundamental. The whole point of the covenant concept, where maintained, is to define the relationship between God and man in the reality of salvation. With that we are at the very heart of the Arminian-Calvinist debate.

Jonathan Edwards—the man and his times! One can almost picture a solitary figure—a quixotic figure—resolutely taking on the seemingly irresistible, grinding wheels of his-

---

30. *Freedom of the Will*, pp. 1-2. In this work, Edwards "delivered the most thoroughgoing and absolutely destructive criticism that liberty of indifference, without necessity, has ever received" (p. 2). See also pp. 4-5 where Edwards is shown to believe doctrinal matters had wider implications for the general decline.
31. *Original Sin*, ed. Clyde A. Holbrook, Vol. III of *Works of Jonathan Edwards* (New Haven, 1970), pp. 375-376.

tory.³² What is utterly remarkable about the man is that he succeeded to a considerable extent. Haroutunian states: "Edwards revitalized religion for at least a part of New England."³³ Not without justification, B. B. Warfield summarizes Edwards' role and impact on the controversy in these words: "The movement against Calvinism which was overspreading the land was in a great measure checked, and the elimination of Calvinism as a determining factor in the thought of New England, which seemed to be eminent as he wrote, was postponed for more than a hundred years."³⁴

The flood still came! That Edwards postponed, rather than prevented, the flood of Arminianism and liberalism may lead some to conclude he failed. But is one's ability or the truth of his position always the determinative factor? Edwards, exerting himself to the fullest, committed the outcome to God's sovereign will. One is reminded of the text

---

32. To some, such activity was hardly praiseworthy. See, for example, Schneider, *The Puritan Mind*, p. 155: "As for Jonathan Edwards himself, he was a stumbling-block to his contemporaries, and a horrible example to his posterity. Whatever the value of his philosophy in its essential structure, the particular application he gave to it was even in his own day impractical, and today obviously absurd. Had his own love of God been less sentimental and pathological . . . his philosophy would have exercised more power. As it was, however, his philosophical insight was buried under the ruins of his religion. He failed to see the futility of insisting on the Puritan principles. He preached humility to the proud. He tried to awaken a sense of sin in those who were becoming constantly more self-reliant. He defended the glory of God to those who were beginning to revel in their own glory. He believed in submission at a time when his countrymen were raising the cry of independence. He could not stem the current. In 1758 he accepted the presidency of Princeton, and died. And with his death, his ideas lost their vitality."

33. Haroutunian, *Piety versus Moralism*, p. xxi. "For him religion was independent of the problems of social morality and civil government. He ignored the social principles in the Calvinistic idea of theocracy, and made Calvinistic piety a matter which concerned primarily the relation of the individual soul to God. Edwards put the theology of Calvinism upon the basis of an empirical piety, and defended its doctrines philosophically and rationally. He reinterpreted Calvinism as a religious philosophy of nature, and reasserted its doctrines in view of the facts of life as well as on scriptural foundations. Calvinistic theology was thus separated from its temporary social and political aspects, and restated as a religion of permanent human significance." This statement parallels the desire expressed in Chapter One to isolate the covenant of grace from the more general covenant concept.

34. Warfield, *Studies in Theology*, p. 532.

Edwards chose for the title page of *Freedom of the Will:* "Rom. ix. 16. It is not of him that willeth——." For him who has eyes to see, the renaissance of Edwardsean studies and new editions of his writings may be more than an historical curiosity.

3

Is Theology Still Queen?

The question "Is theology still queen?" is not a rhetorical one in certain quarters of modern Edwardsean scholarship. The opinion was previously cited[1] that Edwards erred in trying to express his ideas through the vocabulary of an "outworn, dogmatic system." Its demise notwithstanding, systematic theology was, according to Perry Miller, the "uncongenial thicket" chosen by Edwards. ". . . Theology was Edwards' medium, as blank verse was Milton's."[2] Miller refers to Edwards as "infinitely more than a theologian," but the relevant question of this chapter is whether Edwards would recognize anything (humanly speaking) as "more than" theology. The danger of this form-content distinction is that for one uncomfortable with the form (Calvinism), the "more than" can easily become "other than."

The question of the role of theology in Edwards' thinking is certainly not superfluous if for no other reason than his acknowledged stature as a philosopher. He has been linked with William James as representing the best in American philosophy.[3] Some would see him assuming a place between Leibniz and Kant had he stayed with philosophy and sci-

---

1. Cf. Miss Winslow's comments on p. 4.
2. In the "Forward" of Miller, *Jonathan Edwards*, n.p. ". . . Edwards was infinitely more than a theologian. He was one of America's five or six major artists, who happened to work with ideas instead of with poems or novels."
3. Cf. for example Chard Powers Smith, *Yankees and God* (New York, 1954), p. 247: ". . . He was America's first major modern mind. . . . If we were to select America's contribution to the gallery of the world's indispensable thinkers, we must mention James, and we must mention Edwards, and after that we must hesitate and weigh."

ence.⁴ Books, articles, and dissertations continue to be written, trying to probe the depths of Edwards the philosopher, notwithstanding the fact that the bulk of Edwards' efforts were put into theology. In fact, some commentators (Perry Miller, *et al.*) are so convinced that an intellect the likes of Edwards could not "waste" his talents on "outmoded" Calvinism, they search his theological writing for its hidden, yet real, meaning.

The relevance of philosophy to Edwards' thought cannot be ignored. He does not stand in isolation from The Enlightenment. His early notes show his intense interest in philosophy and natural science. Every biographer, superficial or penetrating, alludes to the "influence" of Locke (with less than unanimity on what that influence was), and few neglect to quote Edwards' glowing testimony of delight in Locke.⁵ Clearly he was sympathetic to an Age of Reason, though he disputed many of its fruits on the ground that they were unreasonable. "The apologist for emotion is no fundamentalist or anti-intellectual, and he could criticize the Enlightenment because he was enlightened."⁶ It is to the role of philosophy in Edwards' thought that we now turn, and that with an eye for our more fundamental question of its relevance to his theology.

The three most prominent names associated with Edwards in this context are Locke, Berkeley, and Newton. Their influence on Edwards has been and remains a source of much debate. We do not choose to enter that debate except to

---

4. Cf. quote of Lyon in note 3, p. 19.

5. Concerning Locke's *Essay on the Human Understanding,* Edwards says he was "enjoying a far higher pleasure in the perusal of its pages, than the most greedy miser finds, when gathering up handfuls of silver and gold, from some newly discovered treasure." "Memoirs," *Works,* I, ccxxiv.

6. Miller, *Jonathan Edwards,* p. 238. Prior to this Miller states: "To retreat into orthodoxy or the authority of a church, or to hold to faith apart from, in despite of, science and psychology, is to reject not rationalism but intelligence.... Edwards is a great modern in his refusal to confess that the eternal world is an utter mystery, by his summoning Christians to realize that 'to understand and know which, it chiefly was, that they had understanding given them'" (p. 237).

Is Theology Still Queen?

draw some reasonably sound conclusions as to how it relates to Edwardsean theology. For this we must of necessity rely on a sampling of conclusions made by those specializing in this aspect of Edwards.

In "An Essay on the Genius and Writing of Jonathan Edwards," Henry Rogers attributes Locke with the greatest influence: "At the age of fourteen, he perused or rather devoured Locke's Essay on the Understanding, a work which, more than any other, contributed to the formation of his intellectual character."[7] No one will assert that the role of Locke can simply be ignored. But what that role is continues to be debated.

The specter of Perry Miller appears again because of his contention that Edwards was so thoroughly persuaded by the empiricism of John Locke. He went to Northampton "to preach, to touch the people's hearts and not to store their heads, but his own head was full of Newton and Locke."[8] According to Miller, Edwards differs from Locke primarily in "redefining" and "going beyond" and "deepening," not in opposing.[9] Edwards "always exalted experience over reason" and "must be called . . . an empiricist."[10] Miller finds Edwards prepared for Locke by his concern for "divine things" coupled with "his inability to express what he felt."

> Then he read Locke, and the divine strategy was revealed to him. God's way, Locke made clear, is indirection, which is the only way, because speaking the unspeakable is impossible; God works through the concrete and the specific, and the mind (Edwards would add, the regenerate mind) must know enough "to stop when it is at the utmost extent of its tether."[11]

This word (Locke used capitals) "EXPERIENCE" was the

---

7. *Works*, I, x-xi.
8. Perry Miller, "The Rhetoric of Sensation," *Errand into the Wilderness* (New York, 1964), p. 175. This volume is a collection of Miller's essays with his more recent reflections preceding each.
9. Cf. for example, Miller, "The Rhetoric of Sensation," *Errand into the Wilderness*, pp. 175-182.
10. Miller, *Jonathan Edwards*, pp. 45-46. ". . . Edwards went to nature and experience, not in search of the possible, but of the given. . . ."
11. Miller, *Jonathan Edwards*, p. 53.

key to epistemology. "Men have to deal with things, but not with things as they lie in the divine mind or float in the ocean of being, but simply as they are registered on the human brain."[12] Edwards read Locke's work with ecstasy, continues Miller, and his thought "cohered firmly about the basic certainty that God does not impart ideas or obligations outside sense experience."[13]

Miller is certainly not representative. James Carse in a work on *Jonathan Edwards and the Visibility of God* concludes that Edwards abandoned Locke, and that not in favor of idealism, but a position "antithetical to idealism."[14] Whatever one concludes about Carse's judgment, he makes an observation about the character of Edwards that is not only true, but relevant to the issue of this chapter.

> In the writings of his adult years it was a . . . characteristic of his intellectual labor that he tirelessly hunted down every implication and consequence of an argument until he had proved it either true or absurd. There is no reason to think he was not doing that as a boy in these early pages. It would appear that he was undertaking a vigorous assault on the best philosophical arguments his age could provide him. He pursued each as far as it could take him, then, when he had perceived whither he had gone with it, he abandoned it.[15]

The significance of this is the confirmation it gives to the

---

12. Miller, *Jonathan Edwards*, p. 55.
13. Miller, *Jonathan Edwards*, p. 55. "To ask what the thing may be in itself is to ask what the sleeping rocks do dream of, since always, as soon as men take cognizance of anything, they deal with what they themselves have perceived" (pp. 64-65). The epistemological question with its technical implications was far less urgent for Edwards than has frequently been the case. ". . . Whether our ideas of objects correspond to the objects themselves—has no real urgency, as it never has to men in action or in suffering. Edwards could dismiss it, and would have saved the modern intellect an untold expenditure of time and paper had it heeded him, by the reflection arrived at in the 'Notes,' that since things exist to the mind as they are perceived, it is all one whether the so-called objects be mental or material" (p. 297).
14. James Carse, *Jonathan Edwards and the Visibility of God* (New York, 1967), p. 44. Cf. the whole chapter dealing with Locke, pp. 31-44.
15. Carse, *Jonathan Edwards and the Visibility of God*, p. 35.

integrity and originality of Edwards. Edwards felt no problem in using that which was good and true in a philosophy, but he also saw where he departed and chose to go down his own road.

What emerges as something of a consensus is that Locke indeed was a major factor in the philosophical development of Edwards, but not decisively. Leon Howard, who steeped himself in the textual problems of Edwards' "Notes on the Mind," is convinced that Edwards was critical in his acceptance of the Lockean treasure and was "more disposed to peck at Locke than to swallow him."[16] Paul Helm more recently reconsidered Locke and Edwards on philosophical grounds:

> There is no doubt that Locke's *Essay* was a major factor.... This undoubted influence is subject to important qualifications. Edwards was not an empiricist, and it is too much to say that his philosophy was Locke-inspired; he draws on arguments from "the new way of ideas" only when these serve his wider aims.[17]

Helm reiterates this need for qualification in the specific area of application. "... His account of religious experience cannot truly be characterized as Lockean or naturalistic without a great deal of further qualification."[18]

The influence of George Berkeley on Edwards is asserted almost as frequently as the influence of Locke. George Park Fisher declares emphatically what he perceives Edwards' position to be:

> Edwards was a Berkeleian.... Precepts of sense have no existence independently of mind; that, although they are not originated by us, but by a power without, that power is not a material substance or substratum, but the will of God acting in a uniform method.[19]

---

16. *"The Mind" of Jonathan Edwards: A Reconstructed Text,* ed. Leon Howard (Berkeley, 1963), pp. 121, 125.

17. Paul Helm, "John Locke and Jonathan Edwards: A Reconsideration," *Journal of the History of Philosophy,* VII (January, 1969), p. 51.

18. Helm, *Journal of the History of Philosophy,* VII, 60.

19. George P. Fisher, "The Philosophy of Jonathan Edwards," *Discussions in History and Theology* (New York, 1880), p. 229.

In their "Introduction" to a collection of selective writings of Edwards, Faust and Johnson indicate that it is unlikely that he abandoned his idealism and that it is "implicit in much of what he wrote."[20]

While few deny significant parallels to Berkeley, the consensus has grown that there is no evidence of Edwards ever reading Berkeley. This is not only a contemporary conclusion. At the turn of the century Fisher concluded that the parallel with Berkeley's idealism was a "coincidence" which "was owing to the powerful stimulus imparted ... by the writings of Locke," and this prompted him "to move on in a path of his own, quite beyond any conclusion reached in Locke's quickening essay."[21] More recently Townsend put forth a similar evaluation:

> Everything in the philosophy of Edwards resembling the thought of Bishop Berkeley can be accounted for without the supposition that he was acquainted with Berkeley's writing, by the simple hypothesis that he was led to his conclusions by reading and reflecting upon Locke as a passionate young Christian would reflect....
> ... There would have been less speculation on Edwards' debt to Berkeley if a more-adequate statement of his views had been generally available. For it is only in two or three isolated passages that the philosophy of Edwards resembles that of Berkeley.... The resemblance would more probably have suggested a common ancestry....[22]

Perry Miller says essentially the same thing and attributes the mistaken connection with Berkeley to an underestimating of Edwards.[23]

---

20. *Jonathan Edwards: Representative Selections, with Introduction, Bibliography, and Notes,* ed. Clarence H. Faust and Thomas H. Johnston (New York, 1962), p. xxviii. For a summary of the relation of Edwards to Locke and Berkeley, cf. p. xxiv ff.

21. *An Unpublished Essay of Edwards on the Trinity: With Remarks on Edwards and his Theology,* ed. George P. Fisher (New York, 1903), p. 18.

22. *The Philosophy of Jonathan Edwards,* p. vi.

23. Miller, *Jonathan Edwards,* p. 62. "Belief in the Berkeleyan influence springs from a reluctance to credit a mere boy with achieving such maturity—a strange inference for the century of Mozart—or else upon a superficial reading of the parallel. In Edwards, 'idealism' is an incidental argument...."

Is Theology Still Queen?

What we see is another instance of Edwards' relationship to his intellectual environment in which one may indeed speak of influence and/or parallel thought, but not without significant qualification. The philosophical truth, while not unimportant, has a kind of pragmatic qualification as it serves a higher aim. Regarding the idealism of Edwards, it is said that he perhaps "felt it unnecessary to complicate the various controversies in which he was engaged by insistence upon it," and "he had even in the beginning felt that it was of no practical importance."[24] Such an observation is based on Edwards' notes on "The Mind."

> Though we suppose that the existence of the whole material universe is absolutely dependent on idea, yet we may speak in the old way, and as properly and truly as ever. . . .
> . . . It is just all one, as to any benefit or advantage, any end that we can suppose was proposed by the Creator, as if the material universe were existent in the same manner as is vulgarly thought. For the corporeal world is to no advantage but to the spiritual; and it is exactly the same advantage this way as the other, for it is all one as to anything excited in the mind.[25]

"We may still talk as though bodies are where they appear to be whether or not anybody perceives them, because our problem as sentient beings is to find our way among them, truthfully and without sin."[26]

As suggested here, Berkeley is associated with the name of Edwards, though not necessarily because he was influenced by him. The third name mentioned in connection with Edwards' philosophy, and along with Locke could certainly be said to influence him, is Sir Isaac Newton. If he was not "delighted" in the same way he was with Locke, it was not because Newton had little impact on him. "Indeed, it is probable that he was acquainted with Newton before he dis-

---

24. *Jonathan Edwards: Representative Selections,* ed. Faust and Johnson, p. xxviii.
25. "The Mind," *The Philosophy of Jonathan Edwards,* pp. 39-40.
26. Miller, *Jonathan Edwards,* p. 63.

covered Locke."²⁷ We again find Edwards being influenced but subject to qualification.

> The records show that many saw in Newton's system of the world alarming atheistical and antireligious implications. Not so, Edwards. By temperament and early training he was already a rationalist. It seems to have been natural to his mind to suppose that the world is a completely rational system, plan, scheme, purpose. Whatever else he may have found in Newton, he must have found confirmation and strengthening of his natural inclination.
>
> Rationalism is not the whole of Edward's [sic] philosophy but it is the basis of it. The absolute reign of universal law was the presupposition of all his speculations and the object of his most ecstatic religious devotions.... The exaltation of God, His infinite majesty, wisdom, and power, are in dramatic contrast with man's littleness, ignorance, and folly.... After Edwards the main tendency of American philosophy exalted man rather than God.²⁸

Newton may have inspired mechanistic philosophies and deism, but for Edwards that was neither the only nor the right interpretation. Edwards was God-intoxicated. "... Immediate divine agency precludes the possibility of natural law as the deists conceived it," but "he was not rejecting science...."²⁹ Newton without God was nonsense. In his essay, "Of Being," Edwards stands in utter opposition to the deists: "... The constant exercise of the infinite power of God is necessary to preserve bodies in being," and from this "we learn that there is no such thing as mechanism... whereby bodies act each upon other purely and properly by themselves."³⁰

> As a student of Locke and Newton, Edwards saw at once that empiricists and naturalists were jumping to conclusions which neither Locke nor Newton would have drawn. He sensed a trend toward naturalistic religion.... He rejected both natural law and mechanical causation, reducing all causation to the "continued immediate efficiency" of God in creation.³¹

---

27. Townsend in *The Philosophy of Jonathan Edwards*, p. vii.
28. Townsend in *The Philosophy of Jonathan Edwards*, pp. viii-ix.
29. Elwood, *The Philosophical Theology of Jonathan Edwards*, p. 47.
30. "Of Being," *The Philosophy of Jonathan Edwards*, pp. 16, 19.
31. Elwood, *The Philosophical Theology of Jonathan Edwards*, p. 52.

Is Theology Still Queen? 43

In an age of enlightenment Edwards saw no need to escape to a storm-free haven of obscurantism or subjectivism to protect his faith and his God. Truth is truth. It is not sectarian or private. But neither was Edwards swept away by the currents of his time. He rejected deism, for example, not because it was un-Christian, but because it was untrue! He saw reality, with clearer perception than most men have ever been granted, *sub specie aeternitatis*. Such a vantage point was for Edwards divinely revealed, in contrast to the pantheisticly based view of Spinoza. The truth of philosophy was never more than or beyond the truth revealed by God. The Bible stood uniquely among the other books of Edwards' library. Of Holy Scripture Edwards writes:

> Nothing else pretends to set in view the whole series of God's works of providence from beginning to end, and to inform us how all things were from God at first, for what end they are, how they were ordered from the beginning, how they will proceed to the end of the world, what they will come to at last, and how then all things shall be to God.[32]

This statement, coming as it does near the end of "A History of the Work of Redemption," a work Edwards hoped to enlarge to what he planned as his greatest work, suggests the evaluation of the less sophisticated observer must also be the conclusion of a penetrating analysis. Jonathan Edwards was first and foremost a man of the Book. Theology is still queen.

In this framework we must see his relation to philosophy. "He welcomed Newton's physics and Locke's psychology, but there is no evidence that he was rejecting the Augustinian metaphysics which underlay original Puritanism."[33] Paul Ramsey, in his "Introduction" to *Freedom of the Will*, seeks to demonstrate

> how wrong it is to reduce JE's system to that of John Locke, while ignoring the traditional doctrine of infusion and not giving equal weight to his Augustinian doctrine of illumination. Insofar

---

32. "A History of the Work of Redemption," hereafter cited as "History," *Works*, I, 617.
33. Elwood, *The Philosophical Theology of Jonathan Edwards*, p. 6.

as Locke had great influence, it was not to make JE some sort of religious naturalist or sensational empiricist, but to provide him with a different philosophical manner of stating the truth contained in these earlier theological points of view.[34]

Edwards' reading of Locke did not confine him within narrow boundaries but "liberated him from this limited horizon and opened before him a new dimension of reality."[35] Paul Helm challenges the interpretation of Perry Miller as an exaggeration of Locke's influence on Edwards. "I want to argue," says Helm, "that Edwards used Lockean empiricism as a *model* for religious experience and nothing more."[36]

Not the fact of philosophical influence is at issue, but the emphasis. William Morris plays down the importance of Edwards reading Locke so young. "What matters," according to Morris, "is what he was able to assimilate from this Enlightenment thinker, and what stimulus he found in him for his own unusual powers."[37] While it should be noted that Edwards read Locke and Newton prior to his conversion, theological concerns still predominated, and the end result was not significantly altered. Alexander Allen, a nineteenth century biographer of Edwards, de-emphasizes the decisiveness of Locke and emphasizes the contrasting role of theology.

> The intellectual impulse came from the philosophy of Locke.... But even in his early adherence to the sensational philosophy he was still himself, independent, accepting or rejecting in accordance with an inward dictum which sprang from the depth of his being. LOCKE WAS AFTER ALL RATHER THE OCCASION THAN THE INSPIRING CAUSE OF HIS INTELLECTUAL ACTIVITY. HAD HE READ DESCARTES INSTEAD, HE MIGHT HAVE REACHED THE SAME CONCLUSION. Although Edwards came to his intellectual maturity before his religious experience had developed into what he called "conversion," yet his intellect was bound from the first with the idea of God. There is a peculiar charm in these early manuscripts written before his

---

34. *Freedom of the Will*, p. 43, n. 5.
35. Elwood, *The Philosophical Theology of Jonathan Edwards*, pp. 123-124.
36. Helm, *Journal of the History of Philosophy*, VII, 54.
37. Morris, "The Young Jonathan Edwards," pp. 180-181.

theology had received its final stamp. At times he seems as if almost losing himself in the realm of pure speculation. But the underlying motive in his Notes on the Mind or Natural Science is theological, not philosophical.[38]

The statement by Allen that "had he read Descartes instead, he might have reached the same conclusion" may be an overstatement. It is naive to think a person is totally unaffected by philosophical influences. Yet Allen's point is valid in pointing to the primacy of a theological framework.

William Morris probed perhaps as deeply as anybody the many elements that were formative in the younger years of Edwards. The following statement, with Locke's influence primarily in view, could nevertheless be instructive in Edwards' relation to any philosophical influences:

> *It cannot be too strongly stressed that before during and after his reading of John Locke, the main element in Jonathan Edwards' training, apart from the Bible and the scholastic analysis of the "Bible," was such scholastic disputation. Not only did he learn the theory of it in Burgersdicius and Heereboord, but also as this was a logic, essentially for exercise, and use, ever since the time of Ramus at least, and could be learned in no other way than through constant exercise and use, both the habits of thought and also many of the topics upon which he would use that thought were fixed for life in Edwards' mind.* The scholastics meant what they said when they contended that they were training men in *habitus*, and at no point does Edwards wholly succumb to the Lockean view that the whole content of the mind must be that which can be conscious to it at any one time.[39]

Later on in his dissertation Morris makes this helpful summary:

> But while Edwards acknowledges the great enthusiasm with which he read Locke, he does not say that he was converted to Locke, or that he owned him as master. According to Hopkins at no time did he own any man as master. An intellectual feast is

---

38. Alexander V. G. Allen, *Jonathan Edwards* (Boston, 1889), p. 5.

39. Morris, "The Young Jonathan Edwards," pp. 140-141. In note 1 on p. 107, Morris indicates the early reading of Locke as compared with reading Turretin much later. The point he wishes to stress then comes on p. 108 where he emphasizes that Edwards read Burgersdicius before reading either Locke or Turretin and brought this interpretive framework with him as he read.

not necessarily an intellectual enlightenment and certainly not a spiritual conversion. The age was one of transition; the methods were eclectic, the place of Locke in the esteem of the college and in the curriculum was yet to be definitively determined.[40]

The name of John Locke dominates this discussion as indeed it must. Morris' dissertation amply documents the fact that Locke was but one of many factors in Edwards' intellectual development. But Locke is used pre-eminently as evidence that Edwards succumbed to the wiles of philosophy. If, however, that is not the case (as the evidence would indicate), then the relation of Edwards to Locke would demonstrate all the more clearly that theology was the dominant factor in Edwards' life. Miller says of Edwards: "He is the last great American, perhaps the last European, for whom there could be no warfare between religion and science, or between ethics and nature."[41] To say Edwards was the last (unless the adjective "great" applies to none after Edwards) is at best naive. What he says about Edwards himself is a profound truth. The conclusion that Edwards "remained first of all a man of religion"[42] must never be separated from his conviction that what is true in theology can be shown to be philosophically true and reasonable as well.

At no point in Edwards' life is there a more relevant factor than his relationship to God. From his earliest youth, prior to conversion, the religious question was fundamental. "I made seeking my salvation the main business of my life."[43] His conversion is recorded in his own words,[44] and as a young man his life's resolutions were dominated by his commitment to the God of Scripture.[45] William Morris, who sought to track down all the relevant factors in Edwards' development, writes:

---

40. Morris, "The Young Jonathan Edwards," p. 241.
41. Miller, *Jonathan Edwards*, p. 72.
42. Warfield, *Studies in Theology*, p. 520.
43. "Memoirs," *Works*, I, liv.
44. "Memoirs," *Works*, I, liv-lvi.
45. "Memoirs," *Works*, I, lxii-lxv.

> ... The conversion of Edwards was regarded by Edwards himself as the central fact of his life. Not the reading of Locke, or the study of Newton, but the experience of conversion, the data which it gave him, and the new questions which it forced him to ask were the dominating factors in the whole of his subsequent life and thought.[46]

Two of the most significant interpretive keys for Edwards are delineated in the account of his conversion. At the heart of his conversion was "a sense of the glory of the Divine Being; a new sense, quite different from any thing I ever experienced before."[47] Equally important was his new attitude, a "delightful conviction" of "God's absolute sovereignty."[48]

Edwards entered college at age thirteen. His academic excellence exhibited itself in his formal training but was not an end in itself. Edwards' choice for utilizing his talent was as a minister of the Christian Gospel. Morris contends that Edwards' early training at Yale "has been most imperfectly understood" and affirms most emphatically that *Edwards had no intention that any new philosophy should bring in a new divinity.*"[49]

---

46. Morris, "The Young Jonathan Edwards," p. 33.

47. "Memoirs," *Works*, I, lv. Edwards cannot be understood apart from this dimension. Cf. for example the sermon on Matt. 16:17, "A Divine and Supernatural Light," *Works*, II, 12-17, and a "Miscellanies" entry published in "Jonathan Edwards on the Sense of the Heart," ed. Perry Miller, *Harvard Theological Review*, XLI (April, 1948), pp. 123-145. The "new sense" idea is seen all through Edwards and is relevant in understanding Edwards whether he is speaking "devotionally" or in full-blown apologetics.

48. "Memoirs," *Works*, I, lv. The doctrine of the absolute sovereignty of God is dealt with explicitly and implicitly by Edwards on many occasions. Edwards' first published work was a sermon on 1 Cor. 1:29, 30, 31, given at the Public Lecture in Boston, July 8, 1731, entitled "God Glorified in the Work of Redemption, by the Greatness of Man's Dependence upon him, in the Whole of it," *Works*, II, 3-7. While Perry Miller drew unwarranted conclusions from Edwards' emphasis on the divine sovereignty in this sermon, he is certainly correct in seeing it as basic to any right understanding of Edwards' thought. The circumstances were such that Edwards would want to say what he believed to have top priority, and he would want to say it well and without equivocation. See chapter one, Miller, *Jonathan Edwards*, pp. 3-34.

49. Morris, "The Young Jonathan Edwards," pp. 792, 810. It is true, he says, that Edwards read Locke and Newton, and that he had frequent contact with an ardent Lockean group. "But all of this must be appraised in the context of the *whole course of training* still required and pursued in the college" (p. 793). Morris sees the

Samuel Hopkins, a close friend of Edwards, saw him as "Calvinistic" in an unslavish way, with the Bible as the primary source of his principles.[50] The same conclusion is put forth by some more in disgust than praise:

> To grasp the temper of Voltaire's or Hume's histories, one must read the new philosophy and collections of state papers; to grasp the temper of Edwards' history, one must read the Church Fathers and the Scripture. However magnificent in conception, however bold in execution, Edwards' *History of the Work of Redemption* is a thoroughly traditional book, and the tradition is the tradition of Augustine.... For Edwards, the authority of the Bible is absolute.... In the modern sense, in the sense of Voltaire and Hume, almost none of Edwards' history is history—it is Calvinist doctrine....[51]

The fact that Peter Gay meant that pejoratively gives even added weight to our conclusion that this is indeed where Edwards stood.

---

influence of Locke on Edwards in the broader training he received at Yale (especially the standard textbooks of logic and metaphysics, the two most important of which were by Burgersdicius and Heereboord) and concludes that Edwards is indebted to them for giving him the academic tools "to mediate between the older logic and metaphysics of Scholastic Calvinism and Puritanism, and the newer logic and metaphysics of Locke" (pp. 794-795). Edwards would have learned from Heereboord "that there is no one and only logic as the way to truth. Eclecticism in logic was not only possible but might be desirable.... Philosophy was distinct from theology, and no harm need come to orthodox theology from any philosophy (e.g., the Cartesian) which one might adopt. Heereboord was a mediating theologian..." (p. 796). Another influence of Heereboord is that while "there is metaphysical truth," this "must serve theology as its handmaid" (p. 800). "There is no doubt whatsoever, that what was new in Locke was appreciated to the full by Edwards.... But there is no doubt also that the fundamental manner in which he approached and used Locke as a philosopher was determined, before he read Locke, by his reading of the Protestant Scholastics" (p. 807).

50. Samuel Hopkins, "The Life and Character of the Late Rev. Mr. Jonathan Edwards," *Jonathan Edwards: A Profile*, pp. 40-41. "He had an uncommon thirst for knowledge, in the pursuit of which, he spared no cost nor pains. He read all the books, especially books of divinity, that he could come at, from which he could hope to get any help in his pursuit of knowledge.... But he studied the Bible more than all other books, and more than most other divines do. His uncommon acquaintance with the Bible appears in his sermons, and in most of his publications.... He took his religious principles from the Bible, and not from any human system of body of divinity. Though his principles were *Calvinistic*, yet he called no man father. He thought and judged for himself, and was truly very much of an original."

51. Peter Gay, "The Obsolete Puritanism of Jonathan Edwards," *Jonathan Edwards and the Enlightenment*, pp. 102-103.

Paralleling this emphasis is the importance of Edwards' sermons. Especially during the twenty-three year pastorate at Northampton, "it was in his sermons that Edwards' studies bore their richest fruit."[52] Since "Edwards made no distinction between a scientific and a practical theology," says Allen, "his sermons are heavily freighted with the results of his speculative thought."[53] Exception must be taken, however, to Allen's statement that few of Edwards' sermons may be seen "as supplementing the general statement of his theology."[54] This may be truer for the published sermons, since they were frequently chosen on the basis of the same polemical and practical considerations which prompted some of Edwards' major works. Edwards' position on the covenant of grace was not a burning issue in the eyes of those who made selections for publication.[55] It has since become an issue, and it should not surprise us that there is a wealth of material to be mined from the vast number of extant manuscript sermons on this and other issues. It will not be of less value because it is a sermon.

With an eye to the "Contemporary Considerations" of Chapter 1, one suspects the resistance of many to see Edwards fundamentally as a "man of religion" (Calvinistic religion at that) is a result more of the interpreter's bias than of Edwards himself. To one unsympathetic with Calvinism, such a view of Edwards is at best "tragic." Townsend lessens the tragedy by providing an alternative:

> Had he lived in other circumstances or had he been in a secular profession, what were his private papers might have been his public ones. He was more churchman than philosopher, but his

---

52. Warfield, *Studies in Theology*, p. 523.
53. Allen, *Jonathan Edwards*, p. 103.
54. Allen, *Jonathan Edwards*, p. 103.
55. This is not to ignore the interpretation of Perry Miller which sees Edwards' vigorous Calvinism as self-evidently opposed to the covenant theology. However, such a conclusion is based primarily on implication and "silence" and remains the issue to be decided, not an assumption to be granted.

private papers show that under other stars he might have been more philosopher than churchman.[56]

The dilemma of one who is impressed with the genius of Edwards but abhors his doctrine is put in bold relief in an article by Clyde Holbrook:

> ... The common line which underscores these representative interpretations is one which either insists that his religious development hindered his development in other areas or regards his theology as an impossible vehicle for the presentation of his deepest and most valuable insights.[57]

The issue raised is

> whether theology as such is a worthy occupation for a first-rate mind and whether in fact the particular theology hammered out by Edwards was a valuable contribution in that area. The answer rendered by many of the critics to these questions would seem to be a muted negative to the first and an explicit and resounding negative to the second.[58]

The dilemma cannot be solved, however, by making Edwards something other than a biblical theologian. The Bible dominated his life, and any alternative conclusion will be based on the "fallacy of difference" which emphasizes the *special* rather than the *generic* when interpreting.[59]

In spite of those who refuse to accept Jonathan Edwards

---

56. *The Philosophy of Jonathan Edwards*, p. xix. Edwards would hardly credit his calling in life to which stars he was under!
57. Clyde A. Holbrook, "Jonathan Edwards and His Detractors," *Theology Today*, X (October, 1953), p. 391.
58. Holbrook, *Theology Today*, X, 392.
59. Vincent Thomas, "Edwards' Master Was the Bible, not Locke," *Jonathan Edwards and the Enlightenment*, p. 37. "The omission of any mention of the Bible from a catalogue of influences on Edwards can only be explained as the result of what Ralph Barton Perry has called the fallacy of difference. 'The tendency to conceive a sectarian doctrine in terms of its *special*, to the exclusion of its *generic*, characteristics is important enough to deserve a special name—"the fallacy of difference." ' It is true that one of the *specific* differences between Edwards and previous Puritans is the presence in his thought of elements that are derived from Newton and Locke. But when Edwards is looked at in the large, and the generic and specific characteristics of his thought are seen in their true proportions and weight, he remains, despite the influence of Newton and Locke, a medieval philosopher.... Edwards was a Puritan first, and a Newtonian or Lockean secondarily."

as first and foremost a theologian, the conclusion of Holbrook on this matter summarizes the only viable interpretation:

> The remarkable fact is that Edwards never seemed to take seriously at any time the possibility of becoming a scientist, a philosopher, or a man of letters. From first to last he was a theologian in the broadest sense....[60]

Many in this age would deem it unfortunate that any first-rate mind would operate under the "medieval" notion that theology is the queen of the sciences. If the form of the theology is Calvinism, such a critic may change his judgment from unfortunate to tragic. But that is where Jonathan Edwards stood. For those who stand where Edwards stood, with a common commitment to the Word—living and written—as the unique authority and ultimate source of truth, Edwards' work is far more than a museum piece. For those to whom Edwards represents fertile soil for an exercise in historical interpretation, their conclusions violate the canons of such interpretation if Edwards is not seen as being what he appears to be. By inclination, by training, by preaching and writing, Jonathan Edwards gave his whole life to the service of the Christ of Scripture.

---

60. Holbrook, *Theology Today*, X, 392.

4

The Covenant of Grace in Reformed Theology

Whether Jonathan Edwards deviated from his tradition may be debated. A deviation may not be assumed. The question of the "consistency" of his "Calvinism" may not jeopardize the historical reality that he is clearly within the Reformed and Calvinistic family. We may not conclude that because his tradition possessed the doctrine of the covenant of grace, he must necessarily possess the same doctrine. To ascertain the answer to such a question, however, a basic knowledge of the origins of such a doctrine would be very important.

Limitations dictate only a cursory survey. Certain basic elements should emerge, however, common to the various phases of development. Recent scholarship is turning up interesting parallel developments within the Calvinistic tradition and calling into question old theories as to the origin of covenant theology. Wilcox writes, for example:

> ... Covenant theology is no longer regarded as merely a theological offspring of John Calvin, a theory which was for many years accepted by most reputable scholars. Also, such a thesis as that propounded by George Park Fisher, who found the beginnings of covenant theology in the proclamations of the Dutch theologian Cocceius (d. 1669), is in disrepute.[1]

---

1. Wilcox, "New England Covenant Theology," pp. 2-3. Cf. also Gaustad, *The Great Awakening in New England,* pp. 7-8: "The covenant idea was not original either with German Reformed or English Puritan theologians. It has ample biblical basis (e.g., Isa. 42:6; Hos. 6:7; Heb. 9:15-17; Rom. 8:3; Lu. 22:20) and is prominent in the writings of Irenaeus. On the other hand, covenant theology, i.e., an entire theological system woven about the concept of the divine

In his dissertation, Wilcox outlines three sources of covenant theology: (1) the Rhineland Reformers (Zwingli, Bullinger, Bucer, Martyr, Ursinus, and Olevianus), (2) the theology of John Calvin (which he has well documented), and (3) English society that nurtured this system.[2] Perry Miller credits English Puritans with its origin (which they found in the Old Testament) and sees the doctrine having a triple life:

> ... In England it continued to be preached by various theologians; in Holland it became the doctrine of the Coccejan faction; and in New England it was from the beginning a fundamental tenet, the basis for much thinking which was ecclesiastical, political, and social as well as theological.[3]

Because of parallel developments and cross-fertilization of ideas it is less than ideal to compartmentalize historical considerations. For the sake of simplicity, however, we turn first to the Continental Reformers, and then their Puritan counterparts, to set forth the covenant doctrine inherited by Edwards.

The Covenant of Grace in Continental Reformed Theology

Covenant theology (frequently federal theology—Latin: *foedus*), and more specifically the covenant of grace, is a recognized type of Calvinistic or Reformed theology. There is considerable development in covenant theology from the 16th to 18th centuries. Of course, the covenant is not absent

---

covenants, is a phenomenon first appearing in the sixteenth century, becoming soon thereafter a recognized branch of Calvinistic or Reformed theology. This federal school (L. *foedus*, covenant) began in Germany in the sixteenth century, producing in the seventeenth century its best-known representative, John Koch (1603-1669). In the second half of the previous century, covenant theology appeared in English in the writings of John Preston (1587-1628) and William Ames (1576-1633) whose student Koch was. Popular authors of the following century, Baxter, Ussher, and Owen, adopted and dispersed this characteristic thought. From the English writers New England divines in the seventeenth century received their inspiration and pattern. When this federal school had invaded Puritanism in sufficient strength to be incorporated as an article in the Westminster Confession (chap. VII), its prominence in American theology—both Congregational and Presbyterian, and to a lesser extent also Baptist—was assured."

2. Wilcox, "New England Covenant Theology," pp. 3-39.
3. Miller, *NEM: 17th Century*, pp. 502-503.

in non-Reformed circles. The concept of covenant is too deeply implanted in Scripture to be ignored. "Covenant theology is, however, a distinguishing feature of the Reformed tradition because the idea of covenant came to be an organizing principle in terms of which the relations of God to men were construed."[4] Some[5] have distinguished between the "covenant idea" as "common Christian property" and "covenant theology" as distinctively Reformed. The covenant concept increasingly became a vehicle for expressing Reformed theology. De Jong suggests that the Reformation and the covenant were natural partners "in opposition to the mechanical theories of the Roman Catholic Church" in soteriology.[6]

In seventeenth century New England the covenant concept was applied to many areas of life. It was not always so:

It is with the Covenant of grace that the covenant theologians of the 16th century were concerned almost exclusively.... The Covenant of Grace... is constitutive of the history of redemption.

The Covenant of Grace from the earliest period of the Reformation was conceived of in terms of the administration of grace to men and belonging, therefore, to the sphere of historical revelation. It was regarded as having begun to be dispensed to men in the first promise given to Adam after the fall, but as taking concrete form in the promise to Abraham and progressively disclosed until it reached its fullest realization in the New Covenant.[7]

All the Reformers used the covenant of grace to express God's gracious dealings with His people, whether before or after the time of Christ.[8]

The covenant of grace played an important role for

---
4. John Murray, "Covenant Theology," *The Encyclopedia of Christianity*, ed. Philip E. Hughes, III (1972), p. 200.
5. Cf. for example W. Adams Brown, "Covenant Theology," *Encyclopedia of Religion and Ethics*, ed. James Hastings, IV (1911), pp. 216, 219.
6. De Jong, *The Covenant Idea in New England Theology, 1620-1847*, p. 17.
7. Murray, *The Encyclopedia of Christianity*, III, 204.
8. For a sampling of Reformed thinking cf. chapters 16 and 17 (pp. 371-447) of Heinrich Heppe, *Reformed Dogmatics*, ed. Ernst Bizer, trans. G. T. Thomson (London, 1950).

Zwingli (1484-1531) in favor of infant baptism and the salvation of children of believers.[9] Henry Bullinger (1504-1575) was apparently the first to write a treatise on the subject of the covenant. Appearing in 1534 under the title *De Testamento seu Foedere Dei Unico et Aeterno Brevis Expositio* Bullinger points the way covenant theology would proceed with his emphasis on the one covenant (of grace) which is eternal.[10] De Jong writes of Bullinger:

> He was the first to formulate clearly the ideas that all of religion consisted of the covenant relation in which man stood to God. The Biblical concept might not be reduced to a figure of speech borrowed from the realm of human relationships but expressed the essential nature of the bond between God and His people....[11]

He adds the general observation that "wherever the Reformed religion made its appearance, the idea of the covenant became prominent."[12]

Sooner or later one comes to Calvin with homage or hostility. In this case, does Calvin teach the covenant of grace, and if so, is he to be blamed or praised for it? It would indeed be a forced interpretation that would see Calvin as a covenant theologian in the sense that the covenant concept was an "organizing principle" in his theology. The covenant is not prominent in the *Institutes*, but the essentials are definitely present.

Calvin, like Zwingli, brings the covenant into relation with the sacraments. ". . . The Lord calls his promises 'cove-

---

9. De Jong, *The Covenant Idea in New England Theology, 1620–1847*, p. 23.

10. Cf. Murray, *The Encyclopedia of Christianity*, III, 204, and Brown, *Encyclopedia of Religion and Ethics*, IV, 220, where in note 3 he writes: "The design of Bullinger's treatise is to show that the gospel is older than Judaism, Muhammadanism, and Catholicism; indeed, that it goes back to 'Noah, Enoch, Seth, Abel, Adam, who without circumcision pleased God through faith.' He holds that there is no Christian virtue commended in the NT which was not equally exemplified in the words and deeds of Abraham."

11. De Jong, *The Covenant Idea in New England Theology, 1620–1847*, p. 24.

12. De Jong, *The Covenant Idea in New England Theology, 1620–1847*, p. 24.

nants' (Gen. 6:18; 9:9; 17:2) and his sacraments 'tokens' of the covenants...."[13] But more basic is Calvin's use of the covenant in demonstrating the unity of God's gracious dealings with men in both the Old and New Testaments. Chapter X of Book II of the *Institutes* deals with the similarity of both Testaments. "The covenant made with all the patriarchs is so much like ours in substance and reality that the two are actually one and the same."[14] Justification was always from grace alone, and Calvin declares that the "covenant of the gospel, the sole foundation of which is Christ," was made with the Jews in Old Testament times.[15] The "model" of Abraham is emphasized,[16] and in summary Calvin writes: "The Old Testament fathers (1) had Christ as pledge of this covenant, and (2) put in him all trust of future blessedness."[17]

The elements of later developments on the covenant of grace are not absent from Calvin. According to Calvin the reason why the spiritual alliance between God and us is comprehended under the word covenant is "because they be articles" on both God's side and man's side.[18] The "article" from man's side is uniquely the response of faith. Commenting on Genesis 17:9 Calvin says "a covenant is not otherwise confirmed, than as faith answers to it," and "as God binds himself to keep the promise given to us; so the consent of faith and obedience is demanded from us."[19] Since we have liberty to require God to fulfil his promises, says Calvin,

---

13. John Calvin, *Institutes of the Christian Religion*, ed. John T. McNeill, trans. Ford Lewis Battles, The Library of Christian Classics, XX-XXI (Philadelphia, 1960), hereafter cited as *Institutes*, I-II, (IV, xiv, 6), II, pp. 1280-1281. Cf. also (IV, xvi, 5, 6), II, 1327-1329, where the covenant of grace established with Abraham is the basis of infant baptism.
14. Calvin, *Institutes* (II, x, 2), I, 429.
15. Calvin, *Institutes* (II, x, 4), I, 431.
16. Calvin, *Institutes* (II, x, 11), I, 437-438.
17. Calvin, *Institutes* (II, x, 23), I, 448.
18. John Calvin, *The Sermons of Master John Calvin upon the fifth booke of Moses called Deuteronomie*, trans. Arthur Golding (London, 1583), hereafter cited as *Sermons on Deut.* (with text), (4:44-5:3), p. 177.
19. John Calvin, *Commentaries on the First Book of Moses Called Genesis*, Vol. I, trans. John King (Grand Rapids, 1963), pp. 451-452. Cf. also John Calvin,

"there must (say I) at leastwise be this mutual bonde betweixt us, that seeing God bindeth himself so unto us, we also must come and submit ourselves wholly unto him."[20] Calvin believes our lives must show "that hee hath not taken paynes with us in vaine," that we have not abused God's goodness, and that God "will have us to bee answerable againe on our side."[21] It is presumptuous, according to Calvin, to think the promises of God depend on man's doings. "... It is not for naught that Moses sayth, *The covenant of thy fathers*.... Every of us must apply it peculiarly to himselfe...."[22] God intends our assurance to come from relying on His promises. "... If we take not Gods promises as peculiar to our selves, it is unpossible for us to be grounded upon them...."[23]

The response of faith is thus a condition that binds God. "For hee is become our God uppon this condition, that we also should be his people."[24] Yet Calvin makes it absolutely clear that it was not man who made the covenant with God. "It is hee, that of his owne free goodnesse hath bound himselfe unto them. And for that cause is it sayd *that God sware to that covenant*...."[25] The covenant originates in the "infinite goodnesse" of God who is pleased "to binde himselfe interchaungeably unto us, whereas there is no cause why hee should bee bounde."[26] The emphasis is on the infinite distance between God and man as well as man's unworthiness.

Speaking of covenant, conditions, and boundness of God in no way contradicts the covenant of grace being a covenant of God's mercy. It is "foolish presumption" that "we should

---

Commentary on the Book of Psalms, Vol. III, trans. James Anderson (Grand Rapids, 1963), p. 254, where he speaks of "a mutual relation and correspondence between the covenant of God and our faith."
20. Calvin, *Sermons on Deut.* (26:16-19), p. 913.
21. Calvin, *Sermons on Deut.* (7:11-15), p. 324.
22. Calvin, *Sermons on Deut.* (4:23-26), p. 157.
23. Calvin, *Sermons on Deut.* (4:23-26), p. 158.
24. Calvin, *Sermons on Deut.* (26:16-19), p. 915.
25. Calvin, *Sermons on Deut.* (4:23-26), p. 158.
26. Calvin, *Sermons on Deut.* (4:44–5:3), pp. 179-180.

imagine that God respecteth our deservings, as we see that men are commonly given to think."[27] Calvin affirms that "all the promises which he maketh are conditionall," but then adds, "they have ill studied the holy scripture, when they cannot discerne betweene the promises as they are set down in the lawe, and the things God added to them to supply our default."[28]

> But (as I tolde you) the promises which import a condition depende herupon, that God hath received us for his people, and will have us to take him for our father. Now this thing is grounded on nothing else but upon his mercie.[29]

Calvin warns against beguiling ourselves in offering our own merits to God.

> ... On our part, all the covenants which are made in the lawe, are utterly vaine; and that all the promises which import any condition of well doing and of holy conversation, shoulde bee unavailable towards us, and never come to effect; unlesse wee resorted to this free promise, whosoever beleeveth that Jesus Christ dyed for our sinnes, and that God by his power hath raised him againe to make us righteous, beleeving the same in his heart and confessing it with his mouth; shal be saved.[30]

In an article "The Covenant of Grace in Calvin's Teaching" Anthony Hoekema stresses, as one must, Calvin's concern for *both* the responsibility of man *and* the sovereignty of God. He finds both of these truths merging in Calvin's doctrine of the covenant.[31] George Marsden rightly chides Perry Miller and his one-sided look at Calvin:

> Calvin's fullest exposition of the implications of the covenant of grace for understanding God's sovereignty and man's responsibility is found in his sermons on Deuteronomy, preached in 1555 and 1556. These sermons leave no doubt that Perry Miller was

---

27. Calvin, *Sermons on Deut.* (7:7-10), p. 317. Cf. *Sermons on Deut.* (7:11-15), p. 322: "But as soone as the ignorant sort doe heare of the woord condition, they beare themselves in hand that God maketh some payment, and that when he sheweth us any favour, he doth it in recompence of our deserts."
28. Calvin, *Sermons on Deut.* (7:11-15), p. 322.
29. Calvin, *Sermons on Deut.* (27:11-15), p. 923.
30. Calvin, *Sermons on Deut.* (27:24-26), p. 941.
31. Anthony A. Hoekema, "The Covenant of Grace in Calvin's Teaching," *Calvin Theological Journal*, II (November, 1967), pp. 134, 140 ff.

mistaken in supposing that the Puritans contrived the covenant concept in order to circumscribe the sovereignty of Calvin's God or to transform "the hitherto stern Deity" into a "condescending," "kindly and solicitous being."[32]

When Hoekema deals with the "human responsibility" side, he becomes misleading. Relating the covenant to particular election, he states that Calvin "does not identify membership in the covenant of grace with particular election."[33] Further, "Calvin clearly teaches that the adoption of people into the covenant of grace does not mean that each covenant member will invariably be saved."[34] The covenant members who are saved are "only those who 'participate in' the covenant, and ratify it by faith (thus stressing human responsibility)."[35] Particular election thus takes place within the "covenant." The problem is not with the conclusion that Calvin had a broader concept of covenant, perhaps suggestive of the later discussions about an "external" covenant as contrasted to the "internal" covenant. Calvin clearly knew of more than one kind of grace and was aware that the covenant God made with the nation of Israel, though a gracious covenant, did not guarantee the salvation of every Israelite. But to suggest that such is the only covenant Calvin taught, or that he meant that relationship to be equated to the covenant of grace, or that such a covenant was what he was setting forth in Book II, chapter X, of the *Institutes,* causes much confusion in understanding Calvin on the covenant of grace.

The crucial historical question is not whether Calvin had

---

32. Marsden, *Church History,* XXXIX, 102.
33. Hoekema, *Calvin Theological Journal,* II, 148.
34. Hoekema, *Calvin Theological Journal,* II, 150.
35. Hoekema, *Calvin Theological Journal,* II, 151. Covenant members who "remain true to God and continue to cling to Christ in faith" do so only because of "God's sovereign grace and is a sign of their particular election" (pp. 152-153). But this affirmation is rendered suspect by his statement that covenant membership (remember faith is not a concomitant to such membership according to Hoekema) "means that God will accept our imperfect works as if they were faultless" (p. 160). This sounds very much like the doctrine known as "evangelical obedience" which is utterly contrary to Calvinism. Whether that is Hoekema's intention, his language raises serious questions.

a fully developed covenant theology, but were the elements of the doctrine of the covenant of grace present. Norman Pettit claims general agreement that Calvin "was not a covenant theologian, in that covenant concepts were never the organizing principle of his theology."[36] Of course, this has no necessary bearing on whether Calvin taught the covenant of grace. The doctrine can be present without it being the organizing principle, as is suggested by Emerson in this statement:

> Indeed, Calvin was not a covenant theologian, but many of the implications of covenant theology—that man can know beforehand the terms of salvation, that man can prepare for salvation, that conversion is a process in which man's faculties are gradually transformed—all these are present in Calvin's teaching.[37]

Wayne Christy sees covenant theology in terms of supplement: "... It seems that the covenant theology had all that Calvin had and more.... It is a supplement to Calvinism...."[38]

As with Reformed theology in general, the doctrine of the covenant received an increasingly more systematic treatment.

> The covenant theologians who followed Calvin such as Jerome Zanchius, Zachary Ursinus, and Gaspar Olevianus adhere to a rather uniform pattern in expounding the doctrine of the Covenant of Grace. First of all ... they do not orient their exposition to a comparison and contrast with the Covenant of Works, as later theologians were wont to do....
> The covenant is that by which God reconciles us to Himself in Christ.... The emphasis falls to a large extent upon the gratuitous character.
> ....

---

36. Pettit, *The Heart Prepared*, pp. 39-40. This is said in the context of his study on the concept of "preparation" in Puritan theology. Calvin's doctrine of total depravity de-emphasized the concept of preparation, but Pettit acknowledges the fact that Calvin "did not deny preparation as such. Nor did he dismiss the biblical exhortations to preparation as 'useless' " (p. 40).
37. Everett H. Emerson, "Calvin and Covenant Theology," *Church History*, XXV (June, 1956), p. 141.
38. Wayne Herron Christy, "John Cotton: Covenant Theologian" (Unpublished Th.M. thesis, Pittsburgh-Xenia Theological Seminary, 1942), p. 69. Cf. further pp. 52-53, 69-70.

> The gratuitous and unconditional character of the covenant is not construed in any way as prejudicing the demand for faith. . . .
> In this early period there had not emerged the tension which developed in the 17th century on the question whether the covenant was to be conceived of as conditional or unconditional. It is apparent, however, that the question . . . had already been posed. . . .[39]

De Jong writes: "Thus in determining the boundary of the Covenant of Grace, Olevianus advocated the position that it was made by God with the elect in Christ."[40] The emphasis on election remains crucial throughout the history of the doctrine. Yet "from early times . . . the development of the covenant theology . . . has been deeply affected by the idea that a covenant is a compact or agreement between two parties."[41] Ursinus (1534-1583), in his *Commentary on the Heidelberg Catechism*, is representative when he defines covenant as

> a mutual promise and agreement, between God and men, in which God gives assurance to men that he will be merciful to them. . . . On the other side, men bind themselves to God in this covenant that they will exercise repentance and faith, or that they will receive with a true faith this great benefit which God offers, and render such obedience as will be acceptable to him.[42]

Perhaps no name is more frequently associated with covenant theology than Coccius (1603-1669). He utilized the covenant idea as the organizing principle of his system and on many points was in agreement with other Reformed theologians. Ironically, however, the prominence given him must be de-emphasized in terms of the Reformed tradition leading up to Edwards. The way Coccius distinguished the manner of forgiveness in the Old and New Testaments and his use of

---

39. Murray, *The Encyclopedia of Christianity*, III, 205-206. Cf. Brown, *Encyclopedia of Religion and Ethics*, IV, 220.

40. De Jong, *The Covenant Idea in New England Theology, 1620-1847*, p. 25.

41. John Murray, *The Covenant of Grace* (London, 1956), p. 5. Murray quotes from Bullinger as an early representative: " 'A διαϑήκη in the singular number signifies a pact and agreement and promise.' "

42. Zacharias Ursinus, *Commentary on the Heidelberg Catechism*, trans. G. W. Williard (Grand Rapids, 1956), p. 97.

distinct dispensations led him to conclusions resulting in accusations of heterodoxy. Whether justified or not, Cocceius is to some extent removed from the Reformed consensus on the covenant of grace.

Francis Turretin (1623-1687) and Peter van Mastricht (1630-1706) are not only important representatives of covenant theology, they are acknowledged favorably by Edwards. The line of transmission from the "federalism" of Turretin to the "Princeton theologians" is well known but is by no means limited to that. Not unthinkingly, nor without realizing the implications, would Edwards introduce a quote from Turretin with the phrase "the great Turretine."[43]

Turretin has a major section on the covenant of grace in his *Institutio Theologiae Elencticae*.[44] Having defined the various biblical terms which are used, Turretin defines the covenant of grace as

> a gratuitous pact entered into in Christ between God offended and man offending, in which God promises remission of sins and salvation to man gratuitously on account of Christ, man, however, relying upon the same grace promises faith and obedience.[45]

The gratuitous nature of the covenant is seen in that God is the author ("*Author* & efficiens principalis").[46] There are three contracting parties in the covenant: "*God* offended, *Man* offending and *Christ*, the Mediator, reconciling offending man to God offended and angry."[47] The things covenanted are "promised blessings" on God's part and prescribed duties on the part of man.[48]

---

43. *Religious Affections*, p. 289, n. 4.
44. Francis Turretin, *Institutio Theologiae Elencticae*, 3 volumes (Utrecht, 1734). All English quotations from Turretin are taken from a mimeographed reproduction of portions of a translation by George Musgrave Giger, Professor of Latin at Princeton University (1854-1865). This reproduction was made by the Pittsburgh Theological Seminary in 1965, and the original manuscript is located at Princeton Theological Seminary. Citations will be listed as *Institutio*, with the location in the Latin edition, followed by the page in the English translation.
45. Turretin, *Institutio* (*Loc.* XII, Q. II, v), II, 191 (Eng. p. 294).
46. Turretin, *Institutio* (*Loc.* XII, Q. II, vi), II, 191 (Eng. p. 294).
47. Turretin, *Institutio* (*Loc.* XII, Q. II, ix), II, 192 (Eng. p. 295).
48. Turretin, *Institutio* (*Loc.* XII, Q. II, xvii), II, 196 (Eng. p. 298).

Turretin goes on to deal with the "conditionality" of the covenant (how it is and is not conditional), the contrast of the covenants of works and of grace, the unity of the covenant in both dispensations, the extent of the covenant, and numerous other topics. What is significant is that Turretin, a predestinarian Calvinist whose consistency is perhaps his greatest fault in modern eyes, held a full doctrine of the covenant of grace without compromising his "Calvinism." If this is the case, it should suggest caution in drawing a premature conclusion that either Edwards was not a covenant theologian because he was a Calvinist, or that he was not a Calvinist because he was a covenant theologian.

Peter van Mastricht significantly influenced New England theology as well.[49] Edwards' praise for him includes a confirmation of his high regard for Turretin as well. In a letter to his friend Joseph Bellamy he wrote that van Mastricht's system of divinity was "better than Turretine or any other book in the world, excepting the Bible, in my opinion."[50] This is the testimony of one not prone to cite other authors frequently or favorably.

As did Turretin, van Mastricht devotes an entire section in *Theoretico-practica Theologia* to the doctrine of the covenant of grace, which is then followed by a chapter on Christ as the mediator of the covenant of grace.[51] His text for the chapter as a whole is the promise of Genesis 3:15. This first

---

49. Having indicated the importance of Ursinus as a standard author in 17th century New England, Perry Miller, *NEM: 17th Century*, p. 96, writes: "At the beginning of the eighteenth century Cotton Mather and the mentors of New England were enthusiastically recommending Petro van Mastricht's *Theoretico-Practica Theologia*. In its 1300 pages the whole of Christian theology and morality, theory and practice, is laid out with a minuteness and precision that bring a hundred years of methodizing to a stupendous fulfillment. Beyond this limit no mortal could go."
50. "Six Letters of Jonathan Edwards to Joseph Bellamy," ed. S. T. Williams, *New England Quarterly*, I (April, 1928), p. 230. Cf. also *Religious Affections*, p. 337, where Edwards writes: "as the great Mastricht expresses it."
51. Peter von Mastricht, *Theoretico-practica Theologia* (Utrecht, 1699). Liber V, "De Redemptione Christi," Caput I, "De Foedere Gratiae," pp. 389-409. Cf. Dutch translation, *Beschouwende en Praktikale Godgeleerdheit*, trans. Cornelius vander Kemp, 4 vols. (Rotterdam, 1749).

announcement of the covenant of grace, according to van Mastricht, contains most of the Gospel's main points: God is the cause of all our salvation and blessedness; man by his violation of the "natural covenant" is miserable; the mediator is promised who would redeem and remove man's enmity with God; the mediator would be a man (but also God) and defeat Satan; Satan would claim his own but through the Spirit's work rebirth, faith, repentance, and sanctification would come; the seed of the woman (the elect) are distinguished from Satan's seed; a church will be formed from the seed of the woman; and the gathering of them will be the means of making known the promise of restoration to the sinner.[52] Further expounding the elements of the covenant of grace, van Mastricht writes: "God is the author of the covenant of grace" thus indicating that it is of "pure grace."[53] "The covenanting parties are on the one side the Triune God and on the other side the *Christus mysticus*, i.e., Christ with His own."[54] The covenanting itself is then defined as "a mutual promise, where God promises redemption of the fallen sinner through a mediator, the mediator accepts the task of redemption, and His seed on their part accept the mediator and his redemption."[55] He concludes this summary by stating that "the form of the covenanting is a mutual agreement of the parties."[56]

In rounding out a brief look at Reformed theology on the covenant, the confessional statements must not be overlooked. The Westminster symbols explicitly set forth the covenant of grace.[57] That they are a notable exception in this regard necessitates two observations. Jonathan Edwards,

---

52. Mastricht, *Theoretico-practica Theologia* (*Lib.* V, *Cap.* I, iii), p. 392.
53. Mastricht, *Theoretico-practica Theologia* (*Lib.* V, *Cap.* I, iv), p. 393. This edition has paragraph iv misprinted as paragraph v. We are citing it as it should be printed.
54. Mastricht, *Theoretico-practica Theologia* (*Lib.* V, *Cap.* I, iv), p. 393.
55. Mastricht, *Theoretico-practica Theologia* (*Lib.* V, *Cap.* I, iv), p. 393.
56. Mastricht, *Theoretico-practica Theologia* (*Lib.* V, *Cap.* I, iv), p. 393.
57. "Confession of Faith," VII; XIV, ii; XXVIII, i; "Larger Catechism," 30-36, 166; and "Shorter Catechism," 20, 94.

whose view on the covenant of grace we seek to ascertain, showed no hesitation in his willingness to subscribe to the Westminster Confession of Faith.[58] Furthermore, the absence of explicit treatment of the covenant of grace in earlier confessions argues not for its absence in substance. John Murray expresses surprise at the absence of the term "covenant" precisely because "the confessions were framed in terms of the truths which covenant grace represents and that both the concept and the term occupied so important a place in the thinking" of those influential in their preparation.[59] De Jong attributes this absence to the newness of the covenant of grace as a developed doctrine and the fact that it was in the process of development during the credal formulations.[60] In essence, however, the covenant of grace is indeed present.

The issue was and is whether the very essence of Calvinism can be formulated in covenantal language. Nothing so illustrates the tension as the question of "conditionality" implicit in covenantal language. A statement of the question by John Murray will serve as a good conclusion to this section and a bridge to the Puritan treatment of the covenant of grace.

> The question which aroused the most ardent dispute in the 17th century, especially in the British Isles, was whether the covenant is to be conceived of as conditional or unconditional. Lest the nature of the dispute be misunderstood, there are certain considerations that must be kept in mind. (1) No theologian within the Reformed camp took the position that, in the saving provisions of which the Covenant of Grace is administration, the

---

58. In a letter to John Erskine in response to his question whether Edwards could subscribe to the Westminster Confession and Erskine's offer to assist Edwards find a congregation in Scotland, he wrote: "As to my subscribing to the substance of the Westminster Confession, there would be no difficulty...." "Memoirs," *Works*, I, clxiii.

59. Murray, *The Encyclopedia of Christianity*, III, 207.

60. De Jong, *The Covenant Idea in New England Theology, 1620-1847*, p. 32. He further suggests that the emphasis of the Reformed creeds on sovereignty and election, with less emphasis on human response to the Gospel call, may have been a factor in the creedal statements (pp. 47-48). Whether indeed there was "less emphasis" on human response is debatable. The boundaries of that response were indeed different from the non-Calvinists.

thought of condition is to be completely eliminated. Those who were most jealous for the unconditional character of the covenant as an administration of grace to men were insistent that for Christ as the Mediator of the covenant there were conditions which had to be fulfilled.... Christ's fulfilment of the conditions [is the] ... reason ... why the covenant, as it respects men, is without condition. (2) Those who maintained the conditional nature of the covenant were jealous at the same time to maintain that the fulfilment of the conditions on the part of men was wholly of God's grace. There was no thought of the covenant as contingent upon human autonomy.... (3) The dispute was to a large extent focused upon the relation which faith, repentance, obedience, and perseverance sustained to the covenant. None held that the covenant relation obtained or that its grace could be enjoyed apart from those responses on the part of the person in covenant fellowship with God.[61]

The Covenant of Grace in Puritan Theology

Across the Channel the covenant idea fell on fertile soil. There is debate on whether the seeds are imported or domestic. A common tendency is to conclude that Puritan theology in general, and Puritan covenant theology in particular, came from the Continent. This is applicable by extension to New as well as Old England. Perry Miller comments:

> Obviously, the major part of Puritan thought was taken bodily from sixteenth-century Protestantism. From the great reformers came the whole system of theology.... In fact, Puritan thinking was fundamentally so much a repetition of Luther and Calvin, and Puritans were so far from contributing any new ideas, that there is reason to doubt whether a distinctly Puritan thought exists. The theologians simply took up residence in a vast and already constructed mansion of theory.... In time they did effect some drastic alterations, but they did so inadvertently, and often without conscious realization.[62]

Miller is quick to acknowledge that "the Puritans would indignantly have denied" their ideas were derived from the Reformers. "Their convictions came from the Bible, and if men in the previous century had maintained the same opin-

---

61. Murray, *The Encyclopedia of Christianity*, III, 208-209. Cf. also Heppe, *Reformed Dogmatics*, pp. 378-386, where the conditional nature of the covenant is treated.
62. Miller, *NEM: 17th Century*, p. 92.

ions it was because they too had sat under the same schoolmaster."[63]

The development of covenant theology among the Puritans is seen by others as parallel to, rather than derived from, Continental theology.[64] De Jong indicates that independent development is generally accepted and concludes: "This would seem to prove that a type of Federal theology is a universal phenomenon wherever Reformed theology is seriously pursued."[65] George Marsden reverses the argument, suggesting that the parallel and independent development of the covenant doctrine points to a "recovery of biblical teaching" as its source:

> That this is the case is supported by the fact that the covenant doctrine began to appear in numerous places almost as soon as the Reformation had begun. Zwingli, Oecolampadius, Bullinger, Bucer, Tyndale, and several lesser figures developed early formulations of the concept. The connections among these as well as their connections with the Puritans are not entirely clear. But a major part of the explanation is most likely that they all read the same source.[66]

What is clear is the striking uniformity of Puritan covenant thinking. Trinterud points out that "scarcely a single important figure was not a covenant theologian" in the early

---

63. Miller, *NEM: 17th Century*, p. 93. George Marsden prefers the Puritans' own explanation: "... It seems that Miller has slyly substituted his plot for the actual development of the covenant doctrine. First of all, he minimizes the extent to which the concept of the covenant of grace was derived directly from Scripture.... It is of course possible that he is correct in suggesting that the covenant became popular in the sixteenth and seventeenth centuries because of its usefulness in explaining man's responsibilities to a sovereign God. The simpler explanation, and the one the Puritans themselves would have given, however, seems far more probable. The covenant doctrine was emphasized primarily because it was discovered to be a central biblical concept.... The development of the covenant doctrine was basically one more instance of the Protestant recovery of biblical teaching." *Church History*, XXXIX, 99-100.

64. Cf. William Wakefield McKee, "The Idea of Covenant in Early English Puritanism (1580-1643)" (Unpublished Ph.D. dissertation, Yale University, 1948), pp. 36-37, and Ernest F. Kevan, *The Grace of Law: A Study of Puritan Theology* (Grand Rapids, 1965), p. 40.

65. De Jong, *The Covenant Idea in New England Theology, 1620-1847*, p. 30.

66. Marsden, *Church History*, XXXIX, 100.

seventeenth century.[67] McKee, in his dissertation dealing with the covenant in early English Puritanism, writes:

> There was really no fundamental disagreement about the covenant. In a day of heated religious controversies there is surprisingly no evidence of any attack upon the covenant idea either from within Puritan ranks or from outside.[68]

Such silence speaks loudly for general approval of the covenant doctrine.

One of the early Scottish exponents of the covenant of grace is Robert Rollock (1555-1598). At the conclusion of the first section of this chapter the importance of the "conditionality" question is indicated. Murray concentrates on this in his treatment of Rollock:

> It is of particular interest to observe how Rollock answers the question of *condition* as it pertains to the Covenant of Grace. "The very name of the Covenant of Grace," he says, "might seem to require no condition, for it is called a free covenant, because God freely, and, as it might seem, without all condition, doth promise herein both righteousness and life.... But we are to understand that grace here, or the particle freely, doth not exclude all condition, but that only which is in the Covenant of Works, which is the condition of the strength of nature, and of works naturally just and good ... which can in no wise stand with God's free grace in Christ Jesus" (*Select Works*, Edinburgh, 1849, I, 39). This condition is none other than faith as that which comports with Christ and with God's free grace. And faith itself is also of grace and is the free gift of God.... Faith as the condition is brought into clearer focus and its relation to the covenant carefully defined so as in no way to prejudice free mercy and grace.[69]

It would be folly not to acknowledge the ever present danger of incipient Arminianism in speaking of covenant conditions. There is, however, the danger of interpretive error in finding incipiency where it is not, simply because one speaks of conditions.

---

67. Leonard J. Trinterud, "The Origins of Puritanism," *Church History*, XX (March, 1951), p. 50.
68. McKee, "The Idea of Covenant in Early English Puritanism (1580-1643)," p. 142.
69. Murray, *The Encyclopedia of Christianity*, III, 206-207.

Two of the best known English covenant theologians in the late sixteenth and early seventeenth century were William Perkins (1558-1602) and William Ames (1576-1633). In reference to Perkins, Jens Møller reminds us that systematic theology, especially in the sixteenth and seventeenth centuries with its continual restating of Reformation ideas, is "international." "This means that the theology, whether in Cambridge or Edinburgh, Leyden or Heidelberg, was basically the same, i.e. the theology of Calvin."[70]

> Perkins was a Calvinist.... The decree as concerning man is predestination. The election is performed through Christ but has also 'outward meanes'. These outward meanes are 'God's covenants, and the seale thereof'. Thus, when Perkins introduces the covenant (chap. xix), the background is God's free election and the sovereignty of God is safeguarded.... 'Gods covenant ... consists of ... Gods promise to man ... whereby he bindeth himself to man to be his God, if he performe the condition...'. ... We do not find any substantial deviation from Calvin in *Golden Chaine*.[71]

As a covenant theologian, Perkins did not infringe on God's sovereignty. Even the will to become regenerate Perkins attributes to regeneration having already begun.[72] "... Man in preparation must first have the 'seed' of grace, which is a 'true faith' though not a 'strong faith.' "[73]

While much of his labor and influence occurred during his years in the Netherlands, William Ames (1576-1633) was a Puritan whose intellectual roots were in England (especially in the person of William Perkins), rather than the Continent.[74] Ironically, his greatest influence was in New England,

---

70. Møller, *Journal of Ecclesiastical History*, XIV, p. 58.
71. Møller, *Journal of Ecclesiastical History*, XIV, pp. 59-60.
72. Pettit, *The Heart Prepared*, p. 62.
73. Pettit, *The Heart Prepared*, pp. 63-64.
74. Cf. McKee, "The Idea of Covenant in Early English Puritanism (1580-1643)," pp. 36-37, where he speaks of a cross fertilization between England and the Continent, yet with England covenant thought having its own history. "The fact that Ames' most influential and important work, the *Medulla Theologica*, was published in Leyden so soon after he left England would indicate that the idea of covenant expressed therein was well formulated in his mind before he left England rather than in any real sense being inspired abroad. It was William Perkins

The Covenant of Grace in Reformed Theology 71

where he himself planned to go. On both sides of the Atlantic he was a giant.

> For a century and a half William Ames's *Marrow of Theology* held sway as a clear, persuasive expression of Puritan belief and practice. In England, Holland, and New England nearly all those who aspired to the Puritan way read the book. No matter what their aspirations, undergraduates at Emmanuel College, Leyden, Harvard, and Yale had to read the *Marrow* in Latin as part of basic instruction in divinity.... The first Latin edition of 1623 appeared as *Medulla theologica* under an Amsterdam imprint. Twelve Latin printings followed, circulating widely in England, New England, and on the Continent. Jonathan Edwards (1703-1758) came into possession of a copy of the 1634 edition in New Haven; he twice signed it and added notes which bespeak his indebtedness.[75]

Eusden writes that "in early American theological and intellectual history, William Ames was without peer," and of more particular interest for our study, that Edwards "often began with the thought of the Franeker professor."[76] In his dissertation on "The Young Jonathan Edwards," Morris speaks of Edwards "mastering Ames."[77] As well as this direct influence on Edwards, it should also be noted that van Mastricht was strongly influenced by Ames and was in turn influential on Edwards.[78]

Ames, though not officially a delegate, participated as a "consultant" in the famous Synod of Dort. Eusden writes:

> What disturbed him about the Remonstrants was their failure to give the sovereignty and working power of God a primary place in theology; they had, in his mind, placed the Almighty at the beck and call of man. For this they surely deserved censure. But Ames,

---

to whom Ames more than once affirmed his indebtedness, so that Ames may more truly be regarded a disciple of Perkins rather than to have been molded decisively by continental influence."

75. In the "Introduction" of William Ames, *The Marrow of Theology*, ed. and trans. John E. Eusden (Boston, 1968), pp. 1-2. "The Edwards copy, autographed in 1721 when the owner was eighteen, is in the Beinecke Rare Book and Manuscript Library, Yale University." Jonathan Edwards was also in possession of other important works by Ames.
76. Ames, *The Marrow of Theology*, p. 11.
77. Morris, "The Young Jonathan Edwards," p. 83.
78. Ames, *The Marrow of Theology*, p. 65.

almost alone in the orthodox party, found that the Remonstrant insistence on man's response in the drama of salvation was a needed corrective for Reformed theology. In the *Marrow* he parallels one thrust of the original 1610 Remonstrance: "True Christian faith ... always leans upon divine testimony.... But this testimony cannot be received without a genuine turning of the will towards God. John 3:33, *He who receives his testimony has sealed that God is true."* ... Ames did not believe a sweeping, syllogistical declaration of the sufficiency of God settled the problem of salvation. There was much that man had to do.... It is not being suggested here that Ames was an Arminian-within-the-gates, or a quasi Remonstrant, but it is true that among orthodox theologians he was the most sensitive to the criticisms advanced by the opposition party.[79]

John Smith echoes this emphasis in writing that part of Ames' value for New England theology "lay in its explication of the covenant idea, especially its emphasis upon the voluntary character of the covenant type of agreement."[80] Thus, on the one hand, Ames reflected the Puritan emphasis that the covenant of grace was twofold: conditional and absolute. On the other hand, he was uncomfortable with the inherent dangers of defining the covenant in conditional terms and insisted that the condition, faith, was itself a part of the covenant promise and thus a gift of God.[81] Such explicit care as Ames took in giving proper attention to both aspects of the biblical understanding of the relation between God and

---

79. Ames, *The Marrow of Theology*, p. 7. One is not surprised to see a re-examination of the Arminian-Calvinist controversy, such as Dort, in an effort to see if some of the conflict might reside in misunderstanding because of a zeal for one truth element to the exclusion of another (as in sovereignty-responsibility issue and the conditionality of faith). G. C. Berkouwer is an example of a contemporary theologian whose writing is shaped in part by such unfortunate historical controversies (unfortunate only with regard to misunderstanding). In *Divine Election,* trans. Hugo Bekker (Grand Rapids, 1960), pp. 49-50, Berkouwer writes in connection with the historical perspective: "It is not difficult to realize that synergism usually originated as a defense against and reaction to fatalism and determinism. But the fact that a defense is necessary does not make synergism legitimate. Scripture fully honors man's activity; ... but never makes it part of a synergistic synthesis.... It is the nature of the relationship between God's grace and man's act that is at stake."

80. *Religious Affections,* p. 68.

81. Cf. John von Rohr, "Covenant and Assurance in Early English Puritanism," *Church History,* XXXIV (June, 1965), pp. 199-202.

man should preclude superficial either/or interpretations of Ames or his admirers on the question of relating divine sovereignty to human response. It should not surprise us if a similar situation prevailed in Edwards' thought.

We mention in passing one other author of the English Puritans. John Flavel (1630-1691) does not rank with Perkins or Ames, nor for that matter with other influential authors we could mention. What attracts our attention is the conclusion of William Morris that Flavel was high on Edwards' list of important works and his "favorite" author.[82]

> There is so much else of spiritual sustenance which Edwards must have drawn from Flavel that it is a pity that one can only mention key points, like these: That faith is or results in a mystical union with Christ in which we partake of his nature; that God acts efficaciously upon the will by drawing it to himself in a physical as well as a moral way; that God acts by his Holy Spirit implanting new principles and infused habits of grace in it by conversion; that in so doing he gives us a new quality of life and excellency and that however long and gradual the process of conversion may be, the actual moment of it is (as Edwards had himself described it) as instantaneous as the moment of the first creation.[83]

One can see in this summary elements common to the doctrine of the covenant of grace.

The doctrinal position of English Puritanism formed the intellectual bridge across the ocean to New England. De Jong states not only that they brought the idea of the covenant of grace with them from England, but that "this doctrinal emphasis was largely in accord with the line of development from Calvin through Amesius."[84] In his effort to determine the mind of New England, Perry Miller cites as a prime source English theologians and preachers "under whom New England studied":

---

82. Morris, "The Young Jonathan Edwards," pp. 832, 839. Cf. *Religious Affections*, pp. 60-62.
83. Morris, "The Young Jonathan Edwards," p. 357.
84. De Jong, *The Covenant Idea in New England Theology, 1620-1847*, p. 87.

Though these men never set foot in America, they exerted so deep and pervasive an influence upon the colonial intellect that their books must be treated to all intents and purposes as though they were productions of that intellect.... Three great teachers in particular were responsible for much of the New England creed: William Perkins, William Ames, and John Preston.[85]

The bridge to New England was also undergirded by the confessional fruit of the English and Scottish Puritans. The Westminster symbols were raised over New England, and no less a New Englander than Jonathan Edwards paid his allegiance when called upon to do so.

In New England, many who became leaders "were known to each other" before they left England and "were united ... by their common allegiance to a few great theologians."[86] In the "Foreward" to *The New England Mind* Miller writes:

My project is made more practicable by the fact that the first three generations in New England paid almost unbroken allegiance to a unified body of thought, and that individual differences among particular writers or theorists were merely minor variations within a general frame. I have taken the liberty of treating the whole literature as though it were the product of a single intelligence....[87]

In Chapter 2 we saw that Edwards arrived on the scene in a period of decline. This disintegration of a "unified body of thought," plus a desire to let Edwards speak for himself, dictates the brevity with which we treat New England Puritans themselves.

The most prominent representatives of New England covenant theology "were famous in their own right before they left Mother England." These were John Cotton, Thomas Hooker, and Peter Bulkeley.[88] "Of all the men of the first generation in America none wrote more profusely on the

---

85. Miller, *NEM: 17th Century*, pp. 432-433.
86. Miller, *NEM: 17th Century*, p. 432.
87. Miller, *NEM: 17th Century*, p. vii.
88. Wilcox, "New England Covenant Theology," pp. 43-45.

Covenant of Grace and its implications for the Christian life than John Cotton."[89]

> Most of Cotton's works were occasioned writings. In his day two "heresies" were on the rise, "Antinomianism" and "Arminianism." Antinomianism asked, "If salvation is by election and is settled once and for all, why need there be any scruples about conduct?" Arminianism emphasized man's conduct as a basic factor in achieving salvation. The covenant theology of New England arose in part as a reaction against both of these movements.[90]

His success is tempered by questions and controversy.[91]

Thomas Hooker, in *The Covenant of Grace Opened,* defines the covenant of grace as

> the speciall communication of God to a people that he will choose such, wherby he ingages himself to be their God and to make them to be his people. I adde that, to make them to be his people, because that is it, that bears up the Covenant and confirms it.[92]

"... With Peter Bulkeley, covenant theology came to its full flowering in early New England.... Bulkeley ... was a covenant theologian in the purest sense of the term."[93] There is in Bulkeley a clear emphasis on the mutuality of the covenant. "A Covenant properly binds both parties, and hath a condition annexed."[94] He speaks of the expressions used in Scripture which speak of "a Covenant *commanded*" and "a Cove-

---

89. De Jong, *The Covenant Idea in New England Theology, 1620–1847,* p. 81.
90. Christy, "John Cotton: Covenant Theologian," pp. 15-16.
91. Christy, "John Cotton: Covenant Theologian." pp. 73-74, speaks of Cotton "modifying" Calvin and sees an inconsistency between Cotton's Arminianizing tendency and his emphasis on election. Cf. also De Jong, *The Covenant Idea in New England Theology, 1620–1847,* pp. 92-93, re: dangers resulting from "emphasis" rather than "positive error." Regarding Cotton's problems with Anne Hutchinson and the Antinomian controversy, cf. further De Jong, pp. 95-96, and Pettit, *The Heart Prepared,* pp. 141-155.
92. Quoted in Christy, "John Cotton: Covenant Theologian," p. 55.
93. Pettit, *The Heart Prepared,* p. 114. It should be noted that Pettit's evaluation is based on his seeing in Bulkeley a view of "preparation" which suggests a degree of autonomy for man. If that were an accurate interpretation, it would mean Bulkeley represented a deviation, rather than a climax, of covenant theology.
94. Quoted in Christy, "John Cotton: Covenant Theologian," p. 56.

nant *promised,*" the "promise from God to us" and the "duty from us to God."⁹⁵

This survey covers many years and many authors from before Calvin through seventeenth century New England. We have purposely avoided developments regarding church and social covenants which increasingly became part of the picture. For while the Puritans saw such developments as part of the covenant framework, it is nevertheless possible to concentrate on the purely theological issue. To what extent there was a consistent development in this period⁹⁶ cannot be fully answered in the scope of this work, but some of the issues relevant to finding that answer will appear in the next chapter.

Edwards came out of this tradition. His position on the covenant of grace is not thereby determined. Neither may his intellectual ancestry be ignored. We turn now to a problem in historical interpretation, after which we want to listen carefully to Jonathan Edwards himself.

---

95. Quoted in Christy, "John Cotton: Covenant Theologian," p. 56.

96. Many see a deviation from Calvinism in the Puritan development of the covenant of grace. The issue is of burning importance in the next chapter, but an example of this viewpoint can be seen in Elwood, *The Philosophical Theology of Jonathan Edwards,* p. 106: "John Wollebius, Francis Turretin, and Petrus van Mastricht, for instance, whose Latin tomes underlay Puritan writings, were more Biblical in their conception of the covenant. But, as it was formulated by William Ames, William Perkins, and John Preston, this strange theology began to represent a progressive promise and command, and tended toward the common-law conception of a formal agreement of legal validity, requiring assent and obligation of both parties to the contract."

5

History of Dogma Considerations

No issue is so fundamental to the understanding of Edwards the theologian as the Calvinist-Arminian controversy.[1] The covenant of grace is integral to that controversy. In 1734 Edwards fired a broadside at the Arminians via a series of sermons on "Justification by Faith Alone,"[2] even though Perry Miller's study indicates at that time "none in New England was an avowed follower of Arminius."[3] According to Miller, Arminianism in New England need not come directly from Arminius; "it had imperceptibly pervaded the nation, although the victims . . . were not yet aware that they were infected."[4]

The relationship of Arminianism to the question of Edwards and the covenant of grace is put in bold relief by Miller's extensive and influential interpretation. While acknowledging the imported Arminian authors being read at that time, what he finds to be decisive is that "this imported Arminianism fell in with a home-grown variety."[5] The "Arminianizing 'tendency' " was directly related to the covenant, "and the concept of conditional faith thus degenerated into mere performance."[6] According to Thomas Schafer, covenant theology "placed great emphasis on the 'condi-

---

1. Cf. the latter part of Chapter 2 concerning the times in which Edwards lived and his part in those times. Edwards saw Arminianism as *the* issue and *the* enemy in the New England of his day.
2. "Justification by Faith Alone," *Works,* I, 622-654.
3. Miller, *Jonathan Edwards,* p. 107.
4. Miller, *Jonathan Edwards,* p. 108.
5. Miller, *Jonathan Edwards,* p. 112.
6. Miller, *Jonathan Edwards,* pp. 112-113. The relation of covenant thinking and Arminianism is treated by Miller in "The Marrow of Puritan Divinity," *Errand into the Wilderness,* pp. 48-98.

77

tional' nature of God's promises and implied that God, in bestowing the promised salvation, took account of some value in the fulfillment of the condition on man's part."[7]

While it is true that Schafer's comment was not in direct reference to Edwards, and while it is also very likely that various theologians using the covenant doctrine succumbed to degrees of Arminianism, it is not true that covenant theologians of stature placed any "value in the fulfillment of the condition on man's part," if "value" is to be understood in a meritorious sense. The whole emphasis of covenant theology, as surveyed in the last chapter, was in total opposition to any meritorious value on man's faith. And certainly Edwards had the same emphasis.

Whether Edwards is a covenant theologian is one question. Whether covenant theology is inconsistent with Calvinism is a preliminary consideration to which we now turn. What is clear, and what is part of the motivation for this study, is summarized well in a statement by George Marsden: "As for the thesis that the covenant of grace represented a revision of Calvinism, Miller has created a myth that has been so elegantly presented and widely repeated that it will be difficult to destroy."[8]

Covenant, Calvinism, and Consistency

When considering the covenant of grace and Calvinism in the first half of the eighteenth century two things need to be distinguished: what the situation is, and why it is that way. It is possible to rightly describe a period of history and wrongly conclude what causes produced it.

The noted historian Williston Walker believes he has found a "law of the development of a declining Calvinism" which is everywhere applicable and entails four stages.[9] Stage

---

7. Thomas A. Schafer, "Jonathan Edwards and Justification by Faith," *Church History*, XX (December, 1951), p. 55.
8. Marsden, *Church History*, XXXIX, 105.
9. Walker, "Jonathan Edwards," *Jonathan Edwards: A Profile*, pp. 95-96.

one is the emphasis on pure sovereignty and human inability. With a spiritual decline comes stage two asking what men can do, not to save themselves, but "to put themselves in a position where God is more likely to save them." The third stage moves from the emphasis on means to a belief that God will accept a "sincere but imperfect obedience as satisfactory." This was known by the name of Arminianism. The fourth stage is a degeneration to the point where Christianity is equated with "the practice of morality." Walker sees English Puritanism at the fourth stage and New England at the third stage when Edwards began his ministry. It is not the purpose of this study to challenge such an analysis. What does concern us is whether a covenant theologian is automatically assigned to a latter stage of this decline, or indeed, whether the covenant of grace is part and parcel of such a decline!

The actuality of such a question stems from the fact that the doctrine of the covenant of grace emphasizes strongly the human response in relation to God's grace, and it is precisely a type of human response that Walker and others identify with a declining Calvinism. It is the activism in covenantal theology that has caused suspicion about the authenticity of Puritan Calvinism. Thus to some, Edwards was less than Calvinistic because he held the doctrine, and others, because of his Calvinism, conclude that he was not in agreement with the Puritans in general who held to the covenant doctrine.

Dutch Calvinists, who tend to identify Edwards with Puritanism in general, are inclined to view the covenant of grace as taught in Puritan theology as the hole in the dike through which the Arminian flood poured. Jan Ridderbos, for example, who has much praise for Edwards in his fine systematic treatment of Edwards' theology, nevertheless states: "His theology cannot serve as a type of a pure Reformed system...."[10] Ymen Pieter De Jong, writing a few

---

10. Jan Ridderbos, *De Theologie van Jonathan Edwards* (The Hague, 1907), p. 316. Ridderbos puts Edwards over against the decline in Reformed theology in the eighteenth century (pp. 5-11), but Edwards is not without taint in his eyes.

years after Ridderbos' work, was perhaps even more explicit. Not only was Edwards unfaithful to historic Calvinism, according to De Jong, his revival theology was itself the cause of Edwardsean theology later passing into Arminianism.[11]

Historical interpretation not infrequently tends to see a conflict between covenant theology and predestination, and hence Calvinism. Gottlob Schrenk, in a work on the covenant in early Protestant theology, saw in the entry of the covenant concept as a "fundamental, dogmatical, principle" a precursor to a "new train of thought" modifying or weakening the "rigid predestination" motif.[12] He cites Veluanus as an example of Bullinger's successors for whom covenant theology goes "hand in hand with a rejection of double predestination, especially predestination to damnation."[13]

More recently, amid all the renewed interest in Puritan studies, such interpretation still prevails. Arminianism and covenant theology are cited in conjunction as responsible for modifying Calvinism.[14] Clyde Holbrook, in the "Editor's

---

11. Ymen Pieter De Jong, *De Leer der Verzoening in de Amerikaansche Theologie* (Grand Rapids, 1913), p. 17. "In these days of ferment and turmoil Jonathan Edwards, Sr., steps forward not only as a supporter of the revival, but also as a defender of Calvinism, when this is being attacked and fought by the Arminian school of Withby and Taylor. He himself, however, does not remain faithful to historical Calvinism." The cause of Edwardsean theology passing into Arminianism, according to De Jong, is Edwards' attempt to find a place for the revival practice in his theology. How strong this conviction was is illustrated by a remarkable proposition De Jong defended in conjunction with this published doctoral dissertation. In "proposition" three he states: "The distinction between natural and moral inability, however well intended, has nevertheless led to Pelagianism in Edwardsean theology" (n. p.). (Translations mine.)

12. Gottlob Schrenk, *Gottesreich und Bund in älteren Protestantismus vornehmlich bei Johannes Cocceius* (Darmstadt, 1967), p. 44: "Und die universalistische Tendenz, die durch die Bedanken Bullingers hindurchgeht, gibt gleich zu Beginn der Bundeslehre eine Vorahnung davon, dasz sich hier eine Theologie emporringt, die den starren Prädestinatianismus durch eine neue Gedankenreihe ergänzt."

13. Schrenk, *Gottesreich und Bund,* p. 52: "Diese Bundestheologie geht bei Veluanus hand in hand mit einer Ablehnung der doppelten Prädestination, bezonders derjenigen zur Verdammnis. Es wird die universalistische Gnadeneinladung hervorgehoben und gesagt: 'der gute Gott gönnt allen Berufenen die Seligkeit'."

14. Cf. for example Peter Toon, *Puritans and Calvinism* (Swengel, Pennsylvania, 1973), p. 85: "The seventeenth century witnessed various forces modifying

Introduction" to Edwards' *Original Sin*, concurs with the notion that the American soil was prepared beforehand for the imported seeds of Arminianism and Pelagianism:

> The mischief had begun innocently enough with the teachings of such Covenant or Federal theologians as William Perkins, William Ames, Richard Sibbes, and John Preston. . . . There was great comfort in the notion that God had willingly bound himself in covenant with the Puritan venture in the New World. Man was a sinner, of course, but the fall of Adam had not totally deprived him of the proper use of reason or certain seminal inclinations to virtue. Therefore he was capable of taking some faltering steps toward his own salvation by "closing" with the Covenant of Grace, which God mercifully extended to him. . . .
>
> The great God still loomed in the background. . . . But a definite direction that narrowly skirted some form of Arminianism was set in New England thought. Men could do something about their salvation, at least by way of preparation, since God . . . had opened the way to them. . . . Men could take a firmer grasp on their own destinies. . . .
>
> The sense of divine sovereignty was by no means dead. . . . But somehow, by the opening of the eighteenth century, the traditional doctrines had lost their vigor.[15]

C. C. Goen, in the "Editor's Introduction" of *The Great Awakening*, paints a similar picture:

> . . . For at least half a century the whole basis of church life in New England had been shifting imperceptibly to human effort and moral striving, so that quite unawares many orthodox ministers were encouraging a subtle form of salvation by works. Indeed, this is what "Arminianism" meant in mid-eighteenth-century New England: it had less to do with Jacobus Arminius (1560-1609), the Dutch theologian from whom it took its name, than with a mood of rising confidence in man's ability to gain some purchase on the divine favor by human endeavor.[16]

Though Goen says, "Miller probably went too far toward reducing the covenant of grace to man's contractual bargain with the Almighty,"[17] the current retreat is partial at best.

---

and extending Calvin's doctrines of grace. Of these, three of the most important were Arminianism, New Methodism, and Federal Theology."

15. *Original Sin*, pp. 4-7.
16. *The Great Awakening*, ed. C. C. Goen, Vol. IV of *Works of Jonathan Edwards* (New Haven, 1972), p. 10.
17. *The Great Awakening*, p. 11, n. 8.

It is an interesting development in dogma historical studies, that while Puritanism in general and Puritan theology in particular lay in disrepute especially in the United States, secular historians provided the impetus for the current renaissance of Puritan studies. From this source come two widely held conclusions we confront in some degree in most writers today. First, New England covenant theology is a departure from Calvinism. And secondly, Jonathan Edwards is an exception to this, being a "true" Calvinist in contrast to his contemporaries.

Samuel Eliot Morison is a formative representative. He writes: "Predestination... was not stressed by the New England puritans.... I feel qualified to deny that the New England puritans were predestinarian Calvinists."[18] Their reverence for Calvin was, according to Morison, a token allegiance; he was not their true "saint." Morison believes this is what he sees in their practice:

> The puritan sermons assume (when they do not directly teach) that by virtue of the Covenant of Grace, and through the efforts of the churches, salvation lay within reach of every person who made an effort; Christ helped those who helped themselves. Fatalism is completely wanting in the New England view of religion or of life.[19]

This evaluation makes Puritan religion appear simplistic if not crude. The problem may lie in Morison's apparent use of predestination and fatalism interchangeably. One can only wonder if he honestly believed the Puritans did not know the difference, or if he himself was unaware of the tremendous (may we say contradictory) difference between them. In any event Morison calls Edwards "the first New England Calvinist."[20] While we would maintain, and our historical survey would confirm, that covenant theology and predestination are not mutually exclusive, fatalism contradicts not only

---

18. Samuel Eliot Morison, *The Intellectual Life of Colonial New England* (New York, 1956), p. 11.
19. Morison, *The Intellectual Life of Colonial New England,* p. 11.
20. Morison, *The Intellectual Life of Colonial New England,* p. 159.

History of Dogma Considerations

covenant theology but Scripture as well. If Edwards is a Calvinist, and Calvinist equals fatalist, the conclusion would be inevitable if both these premises are true. And if Perry Miller has a similar mentality, one can easily see how Edwards' sermon on God's absolute sovereignty precluded Miller's openness to the possibility of Edwards accepting the doctrine of the covenant of grace.

The emphasis on sovereignty (Calvin) is thus seen to be qualified by New England Puritans. According to Morison:

> The God of John Calvin was both absolute and arbitrary. . . . But the God of New England, though absolute, was not arbitrary. So far as his dealings with men were concerned, he had voluntarily placed himself under a code: the Covenant of Grace. This, as interpreted by our theologians, meant that God's redeeming grace was bestowed on any person who sincerely and completely believed in God, and surrendered himself to God. Such a one, no matter how grievously he had sinned, could join the Covenant, and lay hold on Grace.[21]

The issue seems clear to Morison: covenant of grace or the sovereignty of Calvinism, but not both.

Miller continues this tradition. He is insistent that it is a misrepresentation of himself that New England parted from Calvinism. It was indeed a modification or revision, but still Calvinism.[22] "The covenant doctrine did not . . . intend to depart from essential Calvinism. . . . The final outcome . . . was a shamelessly pragmatic injunction."[23]

> For all ordinary purposes He has transformed Himself in the covenant into a God vastly different from the inscrutable Divinity of pure Calvinism. He has become a God chained—by His own consent, it is true, but nevertheless a God restricted and circumscribed—a God who can be counted upon, a God who can be lived with.[24]

---

21. Morison, *The Intellectual Life of Colonial New England*, p. 160.
22. Miller, "The Marrow of Puritan Divinity," *Errand into the Wilderness*, p. 49.
23. Miller, *NEM: 17th Century*, p. 395.
24. Miller, "The Marrow of Puritan Divinity," *Errand into the Wilderness*, p. 63.

The result was "that man can by fulfilling terms extort salvation from God."²⁵

Perry Miller's conclusion essentially is that Puritan theology moved to soften Calvinism (election), but they would not accept the option of Arminianism. The implication which appears throughout much of his writing is, however, that their logic should have led them there. Miller believes Edwards saw the option, choosing Calvin and rejecting the covenant of grace.

> It is also not surprising to find that when Jonathan Edwards came to feel that rationalism and ethics had stifled the doctrine of God's sovereignty and dethroned the doctrine of grace, *he threw over the whole covenant scheme,* repudiated the conception of transmission of sin by judicial imputation, *declared God unfettered by any agreement or obligation, made grace irresistible,* and annihilated the natural ability of man. *It was Jonathan Edwards* who went back to the doctrine from which the tradition had started; went back, not to what the first generation of New Englanders had held, but to Calvin, and *who became, therefore, the first consistent and authentic Calvinist in New England*²⁶ (Emphasis mine).

The pattern, as with Morison, appears to be: consistent Calvinism or covenant of grace, but not both.

If the sheer weight of numbers, the quantity of persons speaking in these terms, were the test for truth, then we could conclude our thesis at this point. The voices seem overwhelming which speak of "revision," "modification," and "softening" of Calvinism. A good summary of this view of covenant theology is in Ola Winslow's biography of Edwards, though she, like Miller, puts Edwards more on the Calvinist side of the covenant versus Calvinist mentality.

> ... Calvin's God had not crossed to the American continent at all, but by 1620 had already suffered comfortable modification at the hands of various Cambridge divines: John Preston, William

---

25. Miller, "The Marrow of Puritan Divinity," *Errand into the Wilderness,* p. 73.

26. Miller, "The Marrow of Puritan Divinity," *Errand into the Wilderness,* p. 98.

Perkins, Richard Sibbes, and notably William Ames, whose *Medulla Sacrae Theologiae* became the vade mecum of Harvard and Yale divinity students for another hundred years. During this same first century, New England Dissent through its own spokesmen, John Cotton, Thomas Hooker, John Davenport, and Peter Bulkeley, had modified Calvinistic doctrine still further in the direction of a reasonable rather than an arbitrary God, until by 1731 a theological system with a strongly legalistic bias had been developed. The "covenant of grace" amounted in effect to a contract, almost as binding on God as on man. Salvation was on terms. God bestowed it. Man did not deserve it, but he might know the terms, and if he chose to fulfill them, God was virtually in his power. ... Generally speaking, the arbitrariness of an inscrutable Deity had been brought within predictable bounds. Neither the sovereignty of God nor the depravity of man had been denied, but both had been decidedly bleached.[27]

As we will see later from Edwards himself (and that not contrary to the general doctrine of the covenant of grace), Miss Winslow's statement that the covenant of grace is "almost as binding on God as on man" shows a misunderstanding of the doctrine. For covenant theologians the very assurance of salvation was founded on God's being absolutely bound to the covenant, not through man's power, but because of who God is and the fact that He bound Himself. God's boundness to the covenant is equivalent to the statement that God's promises are absolutely and infallibly trustworthy.

The extent to which the covenant of grace is, or must be, seen as a deviation from Calvinism is undergoing revision currently. Certainly in light of the history of the doctrine such revision is needed. Not only did covenant theology develop hand in hand with Calvinism, but in New England it arose in part as a reaction against Arminian tendencies. If

---

27. Winslow, *Jonathan Edwards, 1703-1758*, pp. 154-155. Cf. Claude M. Newlin, *Philosophy and Religion in Colonial America* (New York, 1962), p. 4: "And since God also had made promises which he was bound to honor, the exercise of his sovereignty could not be quite as arbitrary as it might otherwise have seemed to be." George P. Fisher, *History of Christian Doctrine* (New York, 1896), p. 348, states that covenant theology "softened the rigor of Calvinistic teaching by setting up jural relations in the room of bare sovereignty."

there was a shift of emphasis, we may not prematurely conclude that the emphasis is either unbiblical or contrary to the previous emphasis. McKee writes:

> The covenant comes to overshadow predestination as the way God effects the salvation of men. To be sure the idea of God's predestination is always inferred, and the idea of covenant is clearly rooted in God's election, yet the tendency was to substitute the act of covenant for the decree of predestination as the explanation of man's salvation. . . . The covenant came to be the concept which revealed and explained all theology.[28]

The last sentence is perhaps too broad, but one is reminded of the healthy tension within Scripture regarding both election and human responsibility. Biblically speaking, to neglect either would be to err.[29]

When Jonathan Edwards himself is considered, when his loyalty to Scripture and his intellectual stature is taken into account, it would be unjust to begin with the assumption that Edwards chose either the divine sovereignty of God or the responsible activity of man in relation to God.

Jonathan Edwards' Relation to His Background

H. Richard Niebuhr, writing on the relation of the covenant to American democracy, reminds us of an important fact. While the covenant idea had many sources—Calvin, contract law, reaction to a mechanical Calvinistic determinism—"its chief source in the Scriptures was available to all men

---

28. McKee, "The Idea of Covenant in Early English Puritanism (1580-1643)," p. 145.
29. In an article by Gerald J. Goodwin, "The Myth of 'Arminian-Calvinism' in Eighteenth-Century New England," *New England Quarterly*, XLI (June, 1968), pp. 213-237, the interpretation of Miller, which sees Arminian theology in Calvinist dress via the covenant, is attacked as a myth. Goodwin says: "Arminian-Calvinism never existed," "eighteenth-century Puritan theologians understood the difference," and "they condemned Arminianism by name and by doctrine" (pp. 215-216). He further notes that when Arminians did appear "they did so as Arminians. . . . They got their theology by rejecting or radically altering New England's Calvinism, *not by elaborating the Covenant Theology* (emphasis mine). . . . Arminian-Calvinism existed only as a myth created by historians who fastened onto fragmentary evidence which bore out their expectations of theological change" (pp. 236-237).

History of Dogma Considerations

and not only available but pervasively present."[30] Jonathan Edwards, of course, came out of this environment. But the issue is much broader than the mere acknowledgment that the covenant idea is in Scripture, though that in itself is important background.

The major contention of this work will be that Jonathan Edwards, with all his intellect, creativity, originality, and historical environment, was clearly what we identify with the name "Calvinist." Equally true, and consistent with his Calvinism, Edwards taught the doctrine of the covenant of grace. On the issue of Calvinism and the covenant of grace he was a both/and theologian—and was so consistently. Much of current scholarship correctly asserts the pure Calvinism of Edwards but errs in claiming he abandoned the covenant of grace. Similarly, those concluding that Edwards is a covenant theologian are indeed correct, but many of them err in further concluding that he thereby deserted Calvinism.

That Edwards is a Calvinist is admitted by those for whom that is his glory as well as those for whom it is an enigma. An example of the latter is Peter Gay, who in reaction to those who would praise Edwards for his modernity, writes: "In the midst of the greatest revolution in the European mind since Christianity had overwhelmed paganism, Edwards serenely reaffirmed the faith of his fathers."[31] Disappointedly, if not pejoratively, Alfred Aldridge bemoans the oneness of Edwards with Calvinism as a lack of originality.

> Practically any one of his works could serve as a commentary on any other. But all that Edwards' extraordinary logical consistency really means is that he adhered rigidly to Calvinistic theology on which every part of his own system is based. If the doctrines of Calvinism fit together as a system, Edwards' philosophy can do no less.[32]

---

30. H. Richard Niebuhr, "The Idea of the Covenant and American Democracy," *Puritanism and the American Experience*, p. 220.
31. Peter Gay, "The Obsolete Puritanism of Jonathan Edwards," *Jonathan Edwards and the Enlightenment*, p. 101.
32. Alfred Owen Aldridge, *Jonathan Edwards* (New York, 1964), p. 165.

While Edwards called no man master, he was a consistent exponent of Calvinism. Nichols writes: "The most conspicuous single theological rationale of the Awakening was the 'consistent Calvinism' of Edwards and Hopkins."[33] Warfield had written earlier: "The system to which he gave his sincere adhesion . . . was simply Calvinism."[34] Warfield makes an observation with a great deal of merit regarding Dwight's statement that Edwards did not believe doctrines simply because Calvin believed them:

> This very disclaimer is, however, a proclamation of agreement with Calvin, though not as if he 'believed everything just as Calvin taught'; he is only solicitous that he should be understood to be not a blind follower of Calvin, but a convinced defender of Calvinism.[35]

As a bridge between the Calvinism of Edwards and his teaching of the covenant, we cite one example where both are manifest together. Edwards' sermons on justification exhibit Calvinism's[36] attack on Arminianism as clearly and purely as any author has. Goen, attributing the revival of the Westminster doctrines in the Connecticut Valley to Edwards, writes:

> Convinced that the doctrine of human ability which underlay the gradual shift to Arminian principles was a dangerous heresy, he preached in 1734 a series of five sermons on justification by faith alone. These messages were broadsides of pure and uncompromised Reformed doctrine that all men justly deserve instant and total damnation, that none has any claim upon God's mercy, that salvation is a gracious gift of God through Jesus Christ who dies to save sinners, that it is appropriated through faith which itself is a gift of God—all these points were hammered home with a relentless force that scarcely can be appreciated by the reader today.[37]

---

33. Nichols, *History of Christianity*, p. 193.
34. Warfield, *Studies in Theology*, p. 528.
35. Warfield, *Studies in Theology*, p. 531.
36. It should be understood that Calvinists such as Edwards do not see themselves as followers of Calvin as such but rather as agreeing with him as to the truth of Scripture.
37. C. C. Goen, *Revivalism and Separatism in New England, 1740–1800: Strict Congregationalists and Separate Baptists in the Great Awakening* (New Haven, 1962), p. 7.

At the end of these sermons Edwards treats the importance of the doctrine and writes: "It is in this doctrine that the most essential difference lies between the covenant of grace and the first covenant."[38] Edwards himself thus draws the parallel between the covenant of works and justification by works on the one hand, and the covenant of grace and justification by faith alone on the other.

> ... By the covenant of grace we are not thus justified by our own works, but only by faith in Jesus Christ. It is on this account chiefly that the new covenant deserves the name of a covenant of grace, as is evident by Rom. iv. 16. "Therefore it is of faith, that it might be by grace."[39]

Clearly Edwards was aware of no inconsistency between the Calvinistic understanding of justification by faith alone and the doctrine of the covenant of grace. Edwards has them essentially related. Yet Miller can write: "The scandal of Edwards' discourses on justification ... was his rejection of the covenant...."[40]

It is a gratuitous assumption which sees in the "naked sovereignty" and "unconditional election" of Calvinism an exclusion of the covenant of grace. Those who maintained the covenant doctrine were often the most insistent upon the absolute sovereignty of God. Edwards clearly belongs to this tradition. He stressed more vigorously than most the need for active response on man's part. But who more clearly than Edwards articulated the absolute sovereignty of God. In this light it should not be surprising that some will see Edwards as neither inconsistent, nor as choosing for one side or another, but as a "predestinarian evangelist" who "was himself a covenant theologian and saw in it no compromise whatever with Arminianism."[41]

It is certainly clear, and will become more so, that Edwards does in fact deal with the covenant of grace in explicit

---

38. "Justification by Faith Alone," *Works*, I, 652.
39. "Justification by Faith Alone," *Works*, I, 653.
40. Miller, *Jonathan Edwards*, pp. 115-116.
41. Gerstner, *Steps to Salvation*, p. 14.

terms. Those who say he abandoned the covenant doctrine surely know this and must therefore draw their conclusions on implicit grounds. We have suggested dangers in historical interpretation that could result in such a situation. We deny that they may do so legitimately.

To defend the thesis that Edwards was a covenant theologian one must exercise caution. Edwards was an astute thinker and saw more clearly than most the dangers of the covenant terminology. In an entry in the unpublished "Miscellanies" which deals with the covenant, he warns of the confusion and difficulties arising from such "wrong" language for "right" thinking, especially to "call the receiving of life the 'condition' of receiving of life."[42] His eye is clearly on the central biblical truth that Christ fulfilled the condition of our righteousness and hence our justification.

Superficially, on the basis of this one reference, one might conclude that Edwards abandoned the doctrine of the covenant of grace. The problem that this would pose, however, is that Edwards, in both his preaching and writing, frequently teaches the covenant of grace. If you add to this the implicit presupposition of a covenantal framework in much of his theology, that problem is magnified.

One possible solution to such a problem is that Edwards was hopelessly inconsistent, that he contradicted himself throughout his intellectual life. Yet all we know about this man refutes such a conclusion. To even suggest that Edwards frequently did not really mean what he said belies any claim to understand him. Far more likely is that Edwards labored under the frustration, common to any perceptive theologian,

---

42. "Miscellanies," No. 2. The "Miscellanies" consist of eight volumes and an index volume. These are part of the Yale Collection, Folders XIII-XXI, located in the Beinecke Rare Book and Manuscript Library. A microfilm copy was kindly supplied by the Beinecke Library and is used with their kind permission. I have also had access to a transcription of the "Miscellanies" made by Dr. Thomas A. Schafer, and with his gracious consent I am utilizing his expertise contained therein for modernization of punctuation and spelling and for help in passages unclear in the original text.

which comes from translating divine and infinite truth into finite human language. Edwards saw the imperfection of human language in capturing this most profound relationship between the eternal God and finite man. Acknowledgment of the inherent difficulties in covenantal language does not constitute an abandonment of the doctrine of the covenant of grace. Indeed the use which Edwards makes of covenantal language suggests his preference for this human formulation rather than some alternative.

It is true that Edwards did not spell out a detailed and systematic exposition of the covenant of grace in the way Turretin or van Mastricht did in their systematic theological works, or in the way some of his Puritan predecessors did in treatises on the subject. Yet implicitly and explicitly it pervaded his work. While we have set Edwards within his tradition, we must also lift him out of it for our final conclusions. Whether other Puritans remained faithful to Scripture in honoring the absolute sovereignty of God and the human response as they expounded the covenant of grace must be determined on their own merit. Here we can only speak, with any degree of comprehensiveness, for Jonathan Edwards. It is possible, of course, that the conclusion concerning Edwards will be suggestive of other Puritans as well.

As we conclude Part I, it would be well to emphasize two important factors drawn from this background which will be critical to a proper understanding of Edwards and the covenant of grace. On the one hand, both his contemporaries and subsequent biographers agree that Edwards was one of those unique individuals who creatively breaks new ground and is not dependent upon spoon-fed answers. He had that rare ability to take what was given, think through all the implications creatively and with originality, and arrive at valid conclusions, all without the help most people need from commentators and tradition. While he was not impoverished as far as great authors were concerned, and though he sought out the great literature and was judicious in his selection, the fact that he lived in "culturally deprived," "frontier" America put this dimension of Edwards in bold relief.

On the other hand, Edwards did not choose a career in philosophy or natural science. He chose the discipline of "The Book." Furthermore, he placed himself clearly and without apology in the specifically defined tradition of orthodox Christianity. He felt no compulsion to throw off the shackles of his tradition; he was comfortable with the "faith of his fathers," his spiritual ancestors. And unless he declares otherwise on a specific point of doctrine, there should be a prejudice in favor of the assumption that Edwards agreed with, rather than departed from, his tradition.

In regard to these two factors, some reject the latter because of the former. To the unsympathetic, the latter is a "tragedy" in light of the former. But any attempt to pit these against one another, or to affirm one at the expense of the other, would fail to show the true Edwards.

To obtain a fair interpretation of Edwards, therefore, one can assume a significantly large degree of agreement with his theological ancestors: Calvin via Turretin, van Mastricht, Ames, and similar authors. Therein lies the validity of an historical interpretation. At the same time, however, the first of the two factors mentioned above means you can look at Jonathan Edwards in and of himself, let him speak, without being a slave to a forced historical interpretation. Thus as we consider the covenant of grace and Jonathan Edwards, we will consider most carefully his own words, but always with an eye on the tradition out of which he writes.

PART II

THE COVENANT OF GRACE IN A COVENANTAL FRAMEWORK

Another covenant that Christ has regard to in the execution of his mediatorial office, is that covenant of grace which God established with man. . . . God does, as it were, make his promises which he makes to his creatures, his rule to act by: i.e., all his actions are in an exact conformity to his promises, and he never departs in the least degree from them. . . . But God's promises are consequent on his purposes, and are no other than the expressions of them. And the covenant of grace is not essentially different from the covenant of redemption: it is but an expression of it: it is only that covenant of redemption partly revealed to mankind for their encouragement, faith, and comfort. And therefore the fact that Christ never departs from the covenant of redemption, infers that he will never depart from the covenant of grace; for all that was promised to men in the covenant of grace, was agreed on between the Father and the Son in the covenant of redemption.[1]

---

1. Sermon on Hebrews 13:8, *Works,* II, 950.

6

The Covenant of Redemption as Distinguished from the Covenant of Grace

Central to Edwards' doctrine is his conviction that the covenants of redemption and grace are essentially one, yet distinguished. In a manuscript sermon on Hebrews 9:15-16, Edwards writes that the covenant of grace as Christ's last will and testament "is a twofold covenant of God relating to the salvation of men by Christ that ought not to be confounded but carefully distinguished."[1] The one is a "covenant that God the Father makes with Christ... wherein believers are looked upon as in Christ"; the other is "the covenant that is between Christ and believers themselves."[2] In his sermon on Hebrews 13:8 Edwards refers to the one as "the covenant of redemption, or the eternal covenant," and the other he identifies as "the covenant of grace."[3]

Such a distinction by Edwards must be seen in perspective. He is clearly uncomfortable with the potential dangers of such a distinction, though in practice he treats it as a necessary distinction. In his first entry on the covenant in his "Miscellanies" notebook he attributes many of the difficulties surrounding the covenant of grace (especially wrong

---

1. Sermon on Hebrews 9:15-16, Yale MSS, p. 3. Cf. "Miscellanies," No. 825, Yale MSS: "There are two covenants that are made that are by no means to be confounded one with another."
2. Sermon on Hebrews 9:15-16, Yale MSS, pp. 3-4.
3. Sermon on Hebrews 13:8, *Works,* II, 950.

thinking concerning conditionality) to such a distinction.[4] While Edwards apparently sees in the historical manifestation of God's plan of salvation a necessity to distinguish the two covenants, he prefers the divine perspective in which there is really only one covenant. In the immediate context of the above reference where Edwards distinguishes between the covenants of redemption and grace, he writes:

> ... God's promises are consequent on his purposes, and are no other than the expressions of them. And the covenant of grace is not essentially different from the covenant of redemption: it is but an expression of it: it is only that covenant of redemption partly revealed to mankind for their encouragement, faith, and comfort.[5]

While neither the covenant of redemption nor the covenant of grace are dealt with in published form by Edwards, at least not in the systematic fashion of many of his predeces-

---

4. "Miscellanies," No. 2, Yale MSS. Expressing his uneasiness with calling faith the condition of the covenant, Edwards writes: "Talking thus, whether it be truly or falsely, is doubtless the foundation of Arminianism and neonomianism, and tends very much to make men value themselves for their own righteousness." This danger, which for Edwards was not of the essence of "covenant" but an abuse of the concept, was seen by many critics as part and parcel of covenant theology. Cf. Miller, *NEM: 17th Century*, p. 375.

5. Sermon on Hebrews 13:8, *Works*, II, 950. The relation between the two covenants and whether it is best viewed as one covenant or two is a question not unique with Edwards. To cite but one example, Louis Berkhof sees a certain systematic advantage in seeing the parties of the covenant thus: "God the Father, as representing the Trinity, and Christ, as representing the elect." This unified view finds expression in the *Westminster Larger Catechism* as well as among Boston, Kuyper, and others. The view which sees two covenants is preferred for its clarity, however. The two are "the covenant of redemption (*pactum salutis*) between the Father and the Son, and, as based on this, the covenant of grace between the triune God and the elect or the elect sinner." This view, says Berkhof, "is followed by the majority of Reformed theologians." The important thing to note is his statement that "there is no *essential* difference between these two representations." And if Scripture is better elucidated by making the twofold distinction, it "'does not follow that there are two separate and independent covenants.... The covenant of grace and redemption are two modes or phases of the one evangelical covenant of mercy.'" Louis Berkhof, *Reformed Dogmatics*, 2 vols. (Grand Rapids, 1932), I, 247-248. Perry Miller, *NEM: 17th Century*, pp. 405 ff., attributes the origin of the covenant of redemption to the federal theologian's need for reinforcing the covenant of grace. Such a view, while not without some merit, hardly does justice to the biblical roots of the doctrine. Cf. Murray, *The Encyclopedia of Christianity*, III, 212-215, for an historical sketch of the development of the covenant of redemption.

sors, the doctrines are very much alive throughout his work on both an explicit and implicit level.

The Covenant of Redemption and Divine Sovereignty

Covenant theology has gone hand in hand with predestinarian Calvinism and its heavy emphasis on the absolute sovereignty of God. Edwards is no exception. The heart of the covenant concerns divine promises, and for Edwards "God's promises are consequent on his purposes, and are no other than the expressions of them."[6] The burden of one of Edwards' major works, "A Dissertation Concerning the End for which God Created the World," is that everything God did in the creation of the world and everything He did within that creation, though they may appear distinct and manifold, serves one, unified goal, namely, the glory of God.[7] Edwards writes:

> The emanation or communication of the divine fulness ... is *received* and *returned*. Here is both an *emanation* and *remanation*. The refulgence shines upon and into the creature, and is reflected back to the luminary. The beams of glory come from God, are something of God, and are refunded back again to their original. So that the whole is *of* God, and *in* God, and *to* God; and he is the beginning, and the middle, and the end.[8]

A necessary perspective, therefore, in a right understanding of God's dealing with man is the perspective of eternity, of God's eternal nature, expressed in His purposes and revealed in His Word.

The eternal nature, both past and future, of God's sovereign work of salvation is described in a manuscript sermon on Hosea 13:9. "Thus God is the sole author of the salvation of those that are saved even from the very first beginning of it in the eternal covenant of redemption even to the end and

---

6. Sermon on Hebrews 13:8, *Works*, II, 950.
7. "A Dissertation Concerning the End for which God Created the World," *Works*, I, 95-121.
8. "A Dissertation Concerning the End for which God Created the World," *Works*, I, 120.

consummation of it in the eternal glory of the saints."[9] In a manuscript sermon on Proverbs 8:31 Edwards states that Christ not only "delighted in the thought of saving poor sinners before the world was made," he "was appointed to save sinners and undertook it before the world was made."[10]

Though faith as well as unbelief takes place in time, an act of responsible, active persons, and though it may "appear" inconsistent with God's electing from eternity, Edwards, in a sermon on Ephesians 3:10, sees it as rather displaying the wisdom of God.

> At the very time that God uttered the threatening, "In the day thou eatest thereof thou shalt surely die;" and at the time that Adam had first eaten the forbidden fruit; there was then an existing promise, that many thousands of Adam's race should obtain eternal life. This promise was made to Jesus Christ, before the world was. What a difficulty and inconsistence did there seem to be here? But it was no difficulty to the wisdom of God, that the promise and the threatening should be both fully accomplished to the glory of God's truth in each of them. Psal. lxxxv. 10. "Mercy and truth are met together, righteousness and peace have kissed each other."[11]

In a sermon on 1 Peter 2:9 Edwards relates this electing from eternity to a covenant between the Father and Son.

> In election, believers were from all eternity given to Jesus Christ. As believers were chosen from all eternity, so Christ was from eternity chosen and appointed to be their Redeemer, and he undertook the work of redeeming them. There was a covenant respecting it between the Father and Son. Christ, as we have already observed, loved them before the creation of the world; and then he had their names, as it were, written in a book, and therefore the book of life is called the Lamb's book.... Christ often calls the elect those whom God had given him.[12]

Divine election may not be considered as something other

---

9. Sermon on Hosea 13:9, Yale MSS, p. 11.
10. Sermon on Proverbs 8:31, Yale MSS, p. 1. He indicates Christ undertook the task with delight, knowing what would occur in the end, and that he was motivated in this by "love to God the Father" and "love to sinners" (pp. 3-5).
11. "The Wisdom of God, Displayed in the Way of Salvation," *Works*, II, 149.
12. Sermon on 1 Peter 2:9, *Works*, II, 938.

than the grace of God revealed in Jesus Christ, and that election stands indissolubly related to the covenant of redemption.

One should be put on guard against any notion of the covenant of grace that would reflect disparagingly upon the absolute sovereignty of God in salvation. In a series of sermons on John 16:8 (one manuscript notebook) Edwards at one point presses relentlessly on the theme that any possibility of salvation by our own righteousness would mean the covenant of redemption was unnecessary.

> And what a reflection do you cast upon them as the contrivers of this wonderfully [sic] way. The persons of the Trinity . . . consulted from all eternity about it, as being the main work of divine wisdom. The Father entered into a covenant of redemption with the Son before the foundation of the world; and if your way be true, it was all for nothing; it was only a frivolous notion. The Father, Son and Holy Ghost . . . busied themselves about it needlessly. You by your practice reflect upon them, as tho they made a great ado, and consulted to do some great and strange thing to no purpose, but only to surprize and amuse the world.[13]

He continues at length in this sermon to show how a self-righteous scheme of salvation disparages each person of the Trinity.

What precisely is the covenant of redemption? A rather precise statement is found in the sermon on Hebrews 13:8 where Edwards is teaching the unchangeableness of Christ as applicable for reproof and encouragement. Christ as Mediator is guided by the twofold covenant (redemption and grace), and the covenant of redemption he defines as

> the eternal covenant that was between the Father and the Son, wherein Christ undertook to stand as Mediator with fallen man, and was appointed thereto of the Father. In that covenant, all things concerning Christ's execution of his mediatorial office, were agreed between Christ and his Father, and established by them. And this covenant or eternal agreement, is the highest rule that Christ acts by in his office; and it is a rule that he never departs from. He never does any thing, more or less, than is contained in that eternal covenant. Christ does the work that God gave him to do in that covenant, and no other: he saves those,

---

13. Sermons on John 16:8, Yale MSS, pp. 60-61.

and those only, that the Father gave him in that covenant to save; and he brings them to such a degree of happiness as was therein agreed. To this rule Christ is unchangeable in his regard; it stands good with Christ in every article of it, yesterday, to-day, and for ever.[14]

"A History of the Work of Redemption" is a series of sermons which were outlines of a great work Edwards envisioned, dealing with the eternal drama of salvation and involving the Trinity and all of mankind. Here redemption is not confined to the limited sense of the "purchase of salvation," but in the larger sense as

> not only the purchase itself, but also all God's works that were properly preparatory to the purchase, and accomplishing the success of it. So that the whole dispensation, as it includes the preparation and purchase, the application and success of Christ's redemption, is here called the work of *redemption*.... And it includes not only what Christ the Mediator has done, but also what the Father, or the Holy Ghost, have done, as united or confederated in this design of redeeming sinful men; or ... all that is wrought in execution of the external covenant of redemption.[15]

While Edwards is concerned primarily with the historical outworking of redemption, he emphasizes that "some things were done before the world was created, yea from eternity":

> The persons of the Trinity were, as it were, confederated in a design, and a covenant of redemption. In this covenant the Father had appointed the Son, and the Son had undertaken the work; and all things to be accomplished in the work were stipulated and agreed.[16]

For Edwards then, the three persons of the Trinity are harmoniously at work in this great plan of redemption. It is true that most references Edwards makes to the covenant of redemption, as with other covenant theologians, refer to the covenant God the Father makes with the Son.[17] But the Holy Spirit is by no means ignored. The series of sermons on John

---
14. Sermon on Hebrews 13:8, *Works*, II, 950.
15. "History," *Works*, I, 534.
16. "History," *Works*, I, 534.
17. Cf. for example, Sermon on Hebrews 13:8, *Works*, II, 950; Sermon on 1 Peter 2:9, *Works*, II, 938; and Sermon on Isaiah 55:3, Yale MSS, p. 7.

16:8 has as its doctrine: "That the work of the Holy Ghost as Christ's messenger is to convince men of sin, of righteousness and of judgment."[18] He writes:

> When man was first created, there was a consultation among the persons of the Trinity. God said, let us make man, etc. So it is in the work of redemption. The Father provides, chooses, sends and accepts a Saviour. The Son is the Saviour, who satisfies justice and answers the law, and buys redemption for his people. The Holy Ghost immediately confers the benefits of all this and actually makes the elect partakers of the salvation Christ has wrought.[19]

Edwards continues to spend a good deal of time in this sermon spelling out the work of the Holy Spirit in the covenantal relationship.

One of the inferences of the covenant language, confirmed of necessity by who the parties of the covenant are, is that it is a covenant of free mutuality. The traditional understanding on this point, common in the theological textbooks, is reflected in a statement from Heidegger: " 'While in respect of authority and power to make a pact the covenant of grace was μονόπλευρον, this one was plainly δίπλευρον, mutual, not only because of mutual terms but also because of the equal power and will of Father and Son.' "[20]

Edwards is operating with similar assumptions and speaks not only of the Father *giving* the elect to the Son, but also of the Son willingly *receiving* them. In a sermon on Romans 8:29 he writes:

> And this eternal foreknowledge implies three things: 1. God the Father's choosing them and 2. His giving them to the Son to be his as he did in the covenant of redemption. Christ speaks of those that the Father had given him, [John 6:37]. 3. It implies the Son's accepting them and looking on them as his from eternity.[21]

In the manuscript sermon on Hosea 13:9, emphasizing that

---

18. Sermons on John 16:8, Yale MSS, p. 3.
19. Sermons on John 16:8, Yale MSS, p. 4.
20. Heppe, *Reformed Dogmatics*, p. 379.
21. Sermon on Romans 8:29, Yale MSS, pp. 9-10.

God gives the redeemer and the redeemer is God, Edwards writes: "... Tho we read that he was sent by the Father and that he received commandments of the Father, yet the Father did not command him to undertake it, but when he had of his own accord undertaken it in the covenant of redemption, he thereby became ... subject to God and was commanded by him."[22] In his work "Justification by Faith Alone" Edwards makes an important statement on the situation before and after the Trinitarian agreement in the covenant of redemption:

> ... Christ was not obliged, on his own account to undertake to obey. Christ, in his original circumstances was in no subjection to the Father, being altogether equal with him.... There was a transaction between the Father and the Son, that was antecedent to Christ's becoming man, and being made under the law.... In order to estimate the value and validity of what Christ did ... we must look back to that transaction ... and see what capacity and circumstances Christ acted in them, and we shall find that Christ was under no manner of obligation.... After this he was equally under obligation to both; for henceforward he stood as our surety or representative.... But if we look to that original transaction between the Father and Son ... we shall find Christ acting with regard to both, as one perfectly in his own right, and under no manner of previous obligation to hinder the validity of either.[23]

Everything pertaining to our salvation is traced by Edwards back to the sovereign pleasure of God. In that momentous sermon "God Glorified in Man's Dependence" Edwards says: "As it is God that *gives*, so it is God that *accepts* the Saviour."[24] The doctrine of a manuscript sermon on 1 Corinthians 11:3 states: "God the Father acts as the head of the Trinity in all things appertaining to the affair of man's redemption."[25] If we hear what Edwards is saying, however, such a doctrine is assuming the existence of the covenant of

---

22. Sermon on Hosea 13:9, Yale MSS, p. 3.
23. "Justification by Faith Alone," *Works*, I, 637-638. This discourse is an edited form of a series of sermons on Romans 4:5 which Edwards preached with great spiritual blessing.
24. Sermon on 1 Corinthians 1:29-31, *Works*, II, 3.
25. Sermon on 1 Corinthians 11:3, Yale MSS, p. 2.

redemption. Concerning the doctrine of this 1 Corinthians 11:3 sermon, Gerstner writes:

> But it is to be remembered that this was because it was agreed that the Father should so act, not that the Father possessed any natural right so to do. If he had, a covenant would not have been necessary.[26]

It perhaps should only be noted that the "necessity" of a covenant in no way implies a lack of perfect unity or harmony in the Godhead.

The Covenant of Redemption in Relation to the Covenant of Grace

The covenant of redemption, with qualifications, contains the covenant of grace within its boundaries. According to Edwards "the covenant of grace is not essentially different from the covenant of redemption: it is but an expression of it...."[27] In his notes Edwards wrote: "The covenant that God the Father makes with believers is indeed the very same with the covenant of redemption made with Christ before the foundation of the world or at least is entirely included in it."[28]

Regarding covenant in the broader sense, as the eternal covenant of redemption manifest in time, Edwards states: "The excellency of this covenant and the great desirableness of an interest in its blessings is set forth here by two things: 1. that it is an everlasting covenant, 2. that the mercies promised in it are sure."[29] The comfort of the covenant of grace is thus anchored in the covenant of redemption. In this same sermon on Isaiah 55:3 Edwards contrasts the covenant of redemption, or "everlasting covenant," with "the covenant that God made with Adam," and the excellency of the covenant of redemption is that it is "made with ... an eternal

---

26. Gerstner, *Steps to Salvation*, p. 176.
27. Sermon on Hebrews 13:8, *Works*, II, 950.
28. "Miscellanies," No. 1091, Yale MSS.
29. Sermon on Isaiah 55:3, Yale MSS, p. 2.

person . . . from eternity . . . to eternity."[30] Furthermore, "the surety that is intrusted with the fulfillment of this covenant is everlasting and unchangeable in his fidelity."[31] The certainty stems from the fact that God established the covenant involving "each of the persons of the Trinity," that it was engaged "by promise and oath," and involves among other things "seals" and "pledges" of fulfillment.[32]

The certainty of the covenant of redemption is relevant to the believer because the believer in one sense participates in that covenant. "There is a covenant that God the Father makes with Christ . . . wherein believers are looked upon as in Christ."[33] Christ and believers "are considered together as one mystical person," and this mystical person (Christ and believers) is the "one party in the covenant" to whom promises are made, and "God the Father" is "the other party."[34] Christ and His church are together one party in the covenant.

As far as sinners are concerned, the covenant of redemption is the eternal basis for the covenant of grace. For Christ, however, it was a covenant of works rather than a covenant of grace. Righteousness and justice are no less eternal attributes of God than His love and mercy. In one of the earlier "Miscellanies" Edwards makes it very clear that eternal life is merited, though not by man.

> . . . If we speak of the covenant God has made with man stating the condition of eternal life, God never made but one with man, to wit, the covenant of works; which never yet was abrogated. . . . The covenant of grace is not another covenant made with man . . . but a covenant made with Christ to fulfill it.[35]

The covenant of grace for sinners is but the covenant of works fulfilled by Christ as the covenant head, meriting eternal life for those united to His mystical body.

---

30. Sermon on Isaiah 55:3, Yale MSS, p. 7.
31. Sermon on Isaiah 55:3, Yale MSS, p. 8.
32. Sermon on Isaiah 55:3, Yale MSS, pp. 10-12.
33. Sermon on Hebrews 9:15-16, Yale MSS, p. 3.
34. Sermon on Hebrews 9:15-16, Yale MSS, p. 3.
35. "Miscellanies," No. 30, Yale MSS.

The concept of covenantal obligations by means of covenant heads is brought out in a manuscript sermon on Psalm 111:5. Edwards mentions two kinds of covenant engagements: "1. Those that he enters into with the covenant head . . . wherein promises are made to man indirectly in their representatives, or 2. those that he enters into with men. . . ."[36] Of the first sort Edwards cites two examples: "That which was made with the first Adam" and "that which was made with the second Adam" (the covenant of redemption).[37] According to Edwards "they are both covenants of works" and are both related to the "eternal rule of righteousness."[38]

In his "Miscellanies" notebook Edwards provides a good summary of the notion that the covenant of grace is not a "new" covenant in contrast to the covenant of works made with Adam:

> Towards the rectifying of what has been already said about the covenants [Nos. 2, 30]. The covenant of grace or redemption (which we have shewed to be the same) cannot be called a new covenant, or the second covenant, with respect to the covenant of works; for that is not grown old yet, but is an eternal immutable covenant, of which one jot nor tittle will never fail. There have never been two covenants, in strictness of speech, but only two ways constituted of performing of this covenant: the first constituting Adam the representative and federal head, and the second constituting Christ the federal head; the one a dead way, the other a living way and an everlasting one.[39]

The relation of believers to Christ as their covenant head is seen in an important "Miscellanies" entry on "Covenant of Redemption and Grace."

> There is a covenant that God makes with believers in Christ that is different from the covenant of union between Christ and his spouse. There are promises of God the Father made to believers and not only made to Christ for them before the world was. And yet it will not follow there is a distinct covenant of grace between

---

36. Sermon on Psalm 111:5, Yale MSS, p. 4.
37. Sermon on Psalm 111:5, Yale MSS, p. 4.
38. Sermon on Psalm 111:5, Yale MSS, pp. 4-5.
39. "Miscellanies," No. 35, Yale MSS.

God the Father and believers besides the eternal covenant of redemption that God made with his Son. The promises that God in the covenant of redemption made to his Son . . . were properly made to Christ's mystical [body] for they were made to Christ as a publick person. . . . The promises are in effect not only made to Christ but his members, for they were made to the whole mystical Christ and tho the whole of Christ's mystical [body] was not yet in being, only the head of the body as yet is in being, and the members only existing in God's decree, and as in process of time the members one after another come into being and then the same promises that were virtually made to 'em before are expressly revealed to 'em and directed to 'em. Yet this does not make the promises as revealed and directly made to the members a different covenant from the promises that were before made to the Head that existed before 'em and stood for 'em. . . .

If Adam our first surety had fulfilled the covenant made with him . . . then his posterity . . . would all have had a title to eternal life by virtue of the promises made to Adam their surety. . . .

If God the Father before the foundation of the world makes a covenant with his Son concerning him and his future spouse and gives promises to both considered as those that are to be one, and afterwards when his spouse is obtained and he is united to her he brings this covenant and these promises in his hand and delivers it to her as a covenant made with them jointly, this don't make it now to become another covenant any more than if Christ's spouse had actually been with Christ when the covenant was first made and both had appeared in actual union before the Father in that transaction.

. . . .

So that altho undoubtedly besides the marriage covenant between Christ and his church there is a covenant that God the Father makes with believers of which Jesus Christ is the Mediatour; yet this covenant is in no wise properly a distinct covenant from the covenant God makes with Christ himself as the believers' head and surety and that he made with him before the world was. God the Father makes no covenant and enters into no treaty with fallen man distinctly by themselves; he will transact with them in such a friendly way no other way than by and in Christ Jesus as members and as it were parts of him.[40]

It is particularly in the "Miscellanies" that Edwards relates the two covenants which "are by no means to be confounded," yet are essentially one covenant. In one instance where he is simply identifying the two covenants he calls one

---

40. "Miscellanies," No. 1091, Yale MSS.

the Covenant of Grace

"the covenant of God the Father with the Son and with all the elect in him" and the other a "marriage covenant between Christ and the soul, the covenant of union . . . whereby the soul becomes united to Christ."[41] These are indeed distinct relations: God the Father and Christ; Christ and believers.

May we then speak of a covenant of grace between God the Father and men? This by-passes the distinction just made, and Edwards says if that is what we understand by the covenant of grace, it "is no other than a revelation of part of the covenant of redemption to men, even that part of [it] that contains promises of blessings to men . . . as in Christ."[42] Here too he calls the covenant between Christ and believers a "marriage covenant," but "the covenant between God the Father and believers is in some respect the same with the covenant of redemption between the Father and the Son."[43] In another "Miscellanies" entry Edwards mentions the frequency in Scripture where God speaks of making a covenant with his people and compares it to "the covenant between husband and wife." According to Edwards this covenant is "the covenant between Christ and his people."[44]

Edwards is clearly as concerned to keep the twofold covenant distinguished as he is to insist upon its essential unity. In a major entry in the "Miscellanies" on the "Covenant of Grace" he writes a considerable amount about the similarities and differences of the two covenants. He begins by stating:

> It seems to me there arises considerable confusion from not rightly distinguishing between the covenant that God makes with Christ and with his church or believers in him, and the covenant between Christ and his church or between Christ and men. There is doubtless a difference between the covenant that God makes with Christ and his people, considered as one, and the covenant of Christ and his people between themselves. . . . These covenants

---

41. "Miscellanies," No. 825, Yale MSS.
42. "Miscellanies," No. 919, Yale MSS.
43. "Miscellanies," No. 919, Yale MSS.
44. "Miscellanies," No. 617, Yale MSS.

are often confounded and the promises of each called the promises of the covenant of grace without due distinction.[45]

While Edwards declares that the promises of both covenants are "conditional," he points out their conditions differ: the condition of the covenant of redemption is Christ's redemptive work, and the condition of the covenant of grace is that men "should close with" Christ and "adhere" to Him (i.e., faith).[46] Though the question of "conditionality" will be dealt with at length at a later point, we must remember here that in "Miscellany" No. 2 Edwards was critical of calling faith the condition of salvation.[47] It is difficult to maintain that faith is not a meritorious work, which was a paramount concern of Edwards, if it is called a condition. Whether from the pressure of accepted usage or the lack of a better alternative, Edwards' references to faith as a condition of the covenant of grace were not occasional slips but words chosen by design.

Both covenants are similar in that there are promises. They differ, however, in what the promises are.

> The sum of what is promised by the Father in the former of these covenants is Christ's reward for what he has done in the work of redemption . . . and the sum of what is promised in Christ's marriage covenant with his people is the enjoyment of himself and communion with him in the benefits he himself has obtain'd of the Father by what he has done and suffered.[48]

Edwards prefers the analogy of marriage to illustrate the covenant of grace between Christ and His bride, and the covenant of redemption then becomes analogous to "the covenant that a father makes between a son and his wife . . . considered as one."[49] Which of these dimensions we are operating in will have an important bearing on the conditions and promises.

---

45. "Miscellanies," No. 617, Yale MSS.
46. "Miscellanies," No. 617, Yale MSS.
47. "Miscellanies," No. 2, Yale MSS.
48. "Miscellanies," No. 617, Yale MSS.
49. "Miscellanies," No. 617, Yale MSS.

Hence it appears that many of the things promised in both these covenants are the same, but in some things different so that those things that are promises in one of these covenants are conditions in another. Thus regeneration and closing with Christ is one of the promises of the covenant of the Father with Christ but is the condition in the covenant of Christ with his people. So on the other hand the incarnation, death and sufferings of Christ are promises in Christ's covenant with his people, but they are the conditions of the covenant of the Father with his Son.[50]

On the one hand the covenants are closely related; on the other they are "entirely different and not at all to be confounded."

It is also noted that "both these covenants are revealed to us and we are concerned in both":

> We are concerned in the covenant between the Father and Son because in that covenant God transacted with him as a publick person or as our head and therefore transacts with believers as in Christ or as being parts of Christ. We are concern'd in the covenant between Christ and us as being one of the parties contracting. In the former we are concern'd as being of one of the parties contracting or belonging to it but in the latter we are concerned as being distinctly and by ourselves one of the parties contracting. . . .
> The promises of the former of these covenants being revealed to become the promises of the Father to believers, these are the promises that are given us in Christ, that is they are promises made to us by the Father as being in Christ, being parts of Christ and so having a right to the same blessings that are promised to Christ himself our head.[51]

The covenant of grace, between Christ and His Church, is thus distinct from the covenant of redemption. It is

> the covenant by which Christ's disciples become interest[ed] in that eternal life and kingdom which God the Father did by covenant make over to Christ as a publick person agreeable to those words of our Saviour to the disciples. Luke 22.29. And I appoint unto you a kingdom as my Father had appointed unto me. The words in the original are literally translated thus: *I by covenant dispose* [or make over] *unto you as my Father by covenant hath disposed unto me a kingdom.*[52]

---

50. "Miscellanies," No. 617, Yale MSS.
51. "Miscellanies," No. 1091, Yale MSS.
52. "Miscellanies," No. 1091, Yale MSS.

It is the conviction of Edwards that a clear understanding of the proper distinctions between these two covenants, as well as an awareness of wherein they are one, would go a long way in reconciling the differences between the divines who think the covenants are the same and those who think they are different.[53]

While it involves some speculation as to Edwards' intention, he apparently was alluding to an example of identifying the covenants in a reference to Thomas Boston. At the conclusion of a letter to Edwards Thomas Gillespie asked: "Are the works of the great Mr. Boston known in your country, *viz.* the Fourfold State of Man, View of the Covenant of Grace, and a Discourse on Afflictions, and Church Communion, &c."[54] In the letter Edwards sent to Gillespie in return he closes with an answer concerning Boston:

> As to Mr. Boston's *View of the Covenant of Grace,* I have had some opportunity to examine it, and I confess I do not understand the scheme of thought presented in that book. I have read his *Fourfold State of Man,* and liked it exceedingly well. I think, in that, he shows himself to be a truly great divine.[55]

On the surface that is a rather strange comment from Edwards about a work dealing with so common a doctrine by an author the stature of Boston. The answer may be in the relation of the two covenants.

Historically the covenant of grace was first formulated as a way of expressing God's dealings with men. A further development was seen in the emphasis on the Trinitarian *pactum salutis,* the covenant of redemption, and its relation to the covenant of grace. But Boston exhibits yet a new dimension which Edwards warned against, namely, confounding the two covenants. Boston writes: "The Covenant of Redemption and the Covenant of Grace are not two distinct covenants, but one and the same."[56]

---

53. "Miscellanies," No. 1091, Yale MSS.
54. "Memoirs," *Works,* I, cxxviii.   55. "Memoirs," *Works,* I, cxxxiii.
56. Thomas Boston, *A View of the Covenant of Grace* (Philadelphia, 1827), p. 32.

the Covenant of Grace

The issue becomes very confused then when Boston speaks of the condition of the covenant of grace. He writes:

> ... Receiving is not the thing, upon which the buyer's right and title to the commodity, or the hireling's right and title to the reward, is founded: therefore, though it may be called a *condition of connexion* in the respective covenants, yet it cannot, in any propriety of speech, be called the condition of them.[57]

Boston writes at some length to show that Christ is the condition of the covenant of grace. "... The *condition of the covenant of Grace*, properly so called is, Christ in the form of a bond-servant, as last Adam...."[58] Since Edwards defines the covenant of grace as that existing between Christ and believers, it is obvious that to call Christ the condition of the covenant so defined would make no sense. This is why Edwards insists on not confounding the two covenants, as Boston has done, even though he is equally concerned to show that the covenant of grace is but an expression in time of the eternal covenant of redemption. Whether an equating of the two covenants is the source of Edwards' remarks on Boston's view of the covenant of grace is not provided in Edwards' writing. He would surely find it puzzling to refer to Christ and His work as the condition of the covenant of grace. Though as we have seen, he would insist that the work of Christ is the condition of the covenant of redemption.

According to Edwards the covenant of redemption is the foundation, an eternally sure foundation, of the covenant of grace. Had there been no covenant of redemption, there would be no covenant of grace. The new covenant which God makes with men is an everlasting covenant, whose efficacy is anchored in the eternal covenant between the persons of the Trinity. Salvation is by faith alone; faith is the entry into the covenant of grace. But it is the covenant of redemption that provides the faith and its application by the Holy Spirit, as well as the surety for the performance of all the promises of God relating to salvation.

---

57. Boston, *A View of the Covenant of Grace*, p. 84.
58. Boston, *A View of the Covenant of Grace*, p. 84.

What we have seen thus far in Edwards' doctrine is not at odds with the doctrine of those authors he valued highly. William Ames, for example, writes:

> 3. The agreement between God and Christ was a kind of advance application of our redemption and deliverance of us to our surety and our surety to us. Upon that latter redemption, to be completed in us, it has the effect of a kind of an efficacious example; the former is a representation of the latter and the latter is brought into being by the former.
>
> 4. Thus our deliverance from sin and death was not only determined by the decree of God but also granted and communicated to Christ and to us in him before it was known by us. Rom. 5:10, 11, *We have been reconciled to God by the death of his Son . . . through whom we have now received a reconciliation.*[59]

Van Mastricht, in the exegetical section of his chapter on the covenant of grace, writes that the work of redemption was determined by God in the eternal decree, and that redemption was provided for and applied in time.[60]

The eternal counsel of God, carried out in time and formulated in terms of the covenant, has continued as standard fare in Reformed theology. Bavinck, to cite a twentieth century example, indicates three matters as the content of the counsel of God: "The first is election" (unconditional), the second is the counsel of redemption which contains "the achievement of that whole salvation which God wants to grant to His elect," and the third is "the working out and the application of the salvation wrought by Christ" (covenant of grace).[61]

Jonathan Edwards was concerned about time as well as eternity. Sinners needing salvation are in time. Edwards humbled himself before the sovereign God as reverently as any theologian, but he passionately believed that what occurs in time is rooted in eternity and serves the ultimate glory of

---

59. Ames, *The Marrow of Theology,* p. 149.
60. Mastricht, *Theoretico-practica Theologia* (*Lib.* V, *Cap.* I, ii), p. 390.
61. Herman Bavinck, *Our Reasonable Faith,* trans. Henry Zylstra (Grand Rapids, 1956), pp. 266-268. Cf. H. Bavinck, *Gereformeerde Dogmatick,* 4 vols. (Kampen, 1895-1901), III, p. 206.

God. The covenant of grace is the historical implementation of the eternal covenant of redemption. We have noted a caution from Edwards about covenantal language, especially the issue of conditionality. Critics have claimed he threw over the covenant to protect his doctrine of divine sovereignty, or that he weakened his doctrine of divine sovereignty because of his covenant doctrine. What Edwards himself taught regarding the covenant of grace is the prime consideration to which we now move.

7

The Covenant of Grace as Historical Manifestation of the Covenant of Redemption

The covenant of grace and the covenant of redemption are inseparably united in Edwards' thought. As this chapter title suggests, the covenant of grace is identified primarily as a manifestation of the eternal covenant of redemption. It is in a very real sense a part of that eternal covenant. Yet Edwards, as we have seen, is insistent upon there being a twofold covenant. In this he was echoing the Reformed teaching before him. Van Mastricht, to cite but one example, writes:

> Est autaem foedus gratiae duplex: *aternum* alterum, alterum *temporale*. Illud ab aeterno coiit inter Patrem & Filium, super restitutione peccatoris electi; hoc in tempore coit inter Deum & peccatorem electum.[1]

The type of distinctions implied are partly revealed in the different parties covenanting, as well as in the way the distinct persons of the Trinity are involved in the eternal covenant.

The hope for sinners is founded in the relationship between the two covenants. In a manuscript sermon on 2 Samuel 23:5 Edwards states: "The covenant of grace is

---

1. Mastricht, *Theoretico-practica Theologia* (*Lib.* V, *Cap.* I, vi), p. 393. This edition has paragraph vi misprinted as paragraph vii. We are citing it as it should be (vi) instead of as printed. Cf. Turretin, *Institutio* (*Loc.* XII, Q. II, xii) II, 193-194 (Eng. p. 206).

every way so ordered as is needful in order to its being made firm and sure."[2] The basis of this, according to Edwards, is "the covenant of redemption, which God made with Christ from all eternity." "Surely God will fulfill the engagements that he from all eternity entered into with his own Son."[3]

Without the covenant of redemption there would be no covenant of grace. Whether the covenant of grace is "firm and sure" is an irrelevant question if there is no covenant of redemption. It is equally true, however, that the covenant of redemption without the covenant of grace would be a charlatanic doctrine as far as man's hope of salvation is concerned. It would be a plan to accomplish redemption without a plan to apply that redemption. Consequently, the fact of the covenant of grace—call it by whatever name you will—is fundamental in the revelation of the Gospel of salvation.

The Westminster Confession, concerning God's gracious covenant with man, states: "There are not, therefore, two covenants of grace differing in substance, but one and the same under various dispensations."[4] In an article on covenant theology John Murray writes:

> The Covenant of Grace from the earliest period of the Reformation was conceived of in terms of the administration of grace to men and belonging, therefore, to the sphere of historical revelation. It was regarded as having begun to be dispensed to men in the first promise given to Adam after the fall, but as taking concrete form in the promise to Abraham and progressively disclosed until it reached its fullest realization in the New Covenant.[5]

As soon as the framework of historical revelation is suggested, "A History of the Work of Redemption" emerges as a work of major importance from the pen of Edwards.

When Aaron Burr, president of the College of New Jersey, died in 1757, Jonathan Edwards was chosen to be the successor. In a letter to the trustees expressing his doubts

---

2. Sermon on 2 Samuel 23:5, Yale MSS, p. 5.
3. Sermon on 2 Samuel 23:5, Yale MSS, p. 6.
4. "Confession of Faith," VII, vi.
5. Murray, *The Encyclopedia of Christianity*, III, 204.

the Covenant of Redemption

about accepting such a position he mentions some projects which had long occupied his attention and which he hoped to complete. One of these was the planned "History."

> But besides these, I have had on my mind and heart (which I long ago began, not with any view to publication) a great work, which I call a *History of the Work of Redemption,* a body of divinity in an entire new method, being thrown into the form of a history . . . beginning from eternity, and descending from thence to the great work and successive dispensations. . . .[6]

The draft for this work consisted of a series of sermons he gave in 1739 and which were published posthumously.

This work, "beginning from eternity" and surveying history, has considerable reference to the covenant of grace. Yet Edwards himself in this very work places salvation and the covenant of grace inseparably together. "For salvation is the sum of all those works of God by which the benefits that are by the covenant of grace are procured and bestowed."[7] So central is the covenant of grace to this work one could almost substitute the title of "A History of the Covenant of Grace."

According to Edwards, Christ began his mediatorial work as soon as man fell, and "the gospel was first revealed on earth, in these words, Gen. iii.15. 'And I will put enmity between thee and the woman. . . .' "[8] Edwards calls this "the first revelation of the covenant of grace." Though the first surety had failed, in these words "there was an intimation of another surety to be appointed for man"; "it was an obscure yet comprehensive revelation of the gospel."[9] Soon after God revealed the covenant of grace, the custom of sacrificing was divinely appointed "to be a standing type of the sacrifice of Christ till he should come," and "it is probable . . . that

---

6. "Memoirs," *Works,* I, ccxvi-ccxvii.
7. "History," *Works,* I, 533.
8. "History," *Works,* I, 536-537. One should be clear that for Edwards this is not a "reaction" solution to the problem of sin. The whole point of the covenant of redemption is that redemption begins "from eternity." As he says in his sermon on Hebrews 13:8, "God's promises are consequent on his purposes." *Works,* II, 950.
9. "History," *Works,* I, 537.

Adam and Eve were the first fruits of Christ's redemption."[10]

Edwards was firmly within his theological tradition in beginning with this Genesis text. Van Mastricht, for example, not only began with this text, but he used Genesis 3:15 as the foundational text for his entire chapter on "De Foedere Gratiae."[11] Although the form or the name is not yet present, van Mastricht sees in this text "all the material and essential parts of the covenant of grace."[12] There is condemnation and judgment against the tempter with deliverance for the tempted; there is not only enmity with Satan but the implication of friendship, restoration, repentance, and faith on the positive side.[13]

Edwards places the flood in the history of redemption as part of the fulfillment of the covenant of grace revealed to Adam. "This was ... a destruction of the seed of the serpent" as well as "God's wonderfully preserving that family of which the Redeemer was to proceed."[14] The "new grant" of the earth given to Noah and God's acceptance of Noah's sacrifice are "founded on the covenant of grace."[15] Had the first (covenant of works with Adam) not been broken, the

---

10. "History," *Works*, I, 537-538.
11. Mastricht, *Theoretico-practica Theologia* (*Lib.* V, *Cap.* I), pp. 389-409. This interpretation of Genesis 3:15 continued to be the common view among Reformed theologians since Edwards. Bavinck for example writes: "Principicel bevat Genesis 3 heel de historie der menschheid, alle wegen Gods tot redding van het verlorene en tot overwinning der zonde. Zakelijk is hier het gansche evangelie, heel het verbond der genade aanwezig. Al het volgende is ontwikkeling van wat thans als kiem reeds geplant is.... Toch wordt in Gen. 3 het woord verbond nog niet genoemd; eerst bij Noach, Abraham en Israel aan den Sinai is er sprake van." *Gereformeerde Dogmatiek*, III, 191. Cf. also Bavinck in *Our Reasonable Faith*, p. 271, where he writes: "In this mother-promise is contained nothing less than the ... institution of the covenant of grace.... There is nothing conditional and uncertain about this. God Himself comes to man, He Himself plants the enmity, He initiates the warfare, and He promises the victory. Man has no part in this except to listen to it and to accept it in childlike faith. Promise and faith are the content of the covenant of grace which is now set up for man...." Cf. Berkhof, *Reformed Dogmatics*, I, 283-285.
12. Mastricht, *Theoretico-practica Theologia* (*Lib.* V, *Cap.* I, ii), p. 389.
13. Mastricht, *Theoretico-practica Theologia* (*Lib.* V, *Cap.* I, ii), p. 390.
14. "History," *Works*, I, 541.
15. "History," *Works*, I, 541.

flood would not have been sent to destroy the world. To the "new grant" there is "a promise annexed, that now the earth should no more be destroyed, till the consummation of all things."

> The reason why such a promise . . . was added to this grant made to Noah, and not to that made to Adam, was because this was founded on the covenant of grace, of which Christ was the surety, and therefore could not be broken. . . . Though the wickedness of man has dreadfully raged, . . . yet God's patience holds out . . . according to his promise . . . and his grant established with Noah and his sons abides firm and good, being founded on the covenant of grace.
> . . . God renews with Noah and his sons the covenant of grace. . . . It was a covenant already in being, and that Noah would understand by that determination the covenant of grace.[16]

In a note on Genesis 9:12 ff. Edwards speaks of the rainbow as a fitting "token of the covenant." "This is on many accounts a token of God's covenant of grace, and his special promise of no more overthrowing the earth with a flood in particular."[17] The covenant of grace was not a new thing with Noah, but it was renewed with him.

The covenant of grace was revealed to our first parents and then to Noah, but with the call of Abraham the covenant of grace is revealed more fully and specifically. "It is now revealed to Abraham, not only that Christ should come; but that he should be his seed; and promised, that all the families of the earth should be blessed in him."[18] This promise was repeated four times to Abraham. The covenant with Abraham included temporal blessings, but the covenant of grace was central. In "A Humble Inquiry" Edwards writes:

> . . . The substance and marrow of that covenant which God made with Abraham and the other patriarchs, was the *covenant of grace*, which is continued in these days of the gospel, and extends to all his spiritual seed, of the Gentiles as well as Jews. . . . There were other subservient promises which were typical of its benefits. . . .[19]

---

16. "History," *Works*, I, 541-542.
17. "Notes on the Bible," *Works*, II, 697-698.
18. "History," *Works*, I, 543.   19. "A Humble Inquiry," *Works*, I, 462.

In a manuscript sermon on Galatians 3:13-14 Edwards equates the blessings we have through Christ with the promises to Abraham as a revelation of the covenant of grace. "The apostle speaks expressly of the covenant God made with Abraham as the covenant of grace in the words immediately following the text."[20]

Edwards stresses the clarity with which Christ and His redeeming work manifests itself in this renewal of the covenant of grace with Abraham.

> In this renewal of the covenant of grace with Abraham, several particulars concerning it were revealed more fully than before; not only that Christ was to be of Abraham's seed, but also, the calling of the Gentiles, that all nations should be brought into the church, all the families of the earth made blessed. And then the great condition of the covenant of grace, which is faith, was now more fully made known. Gen. xv. 5, 6. "And he said unto him, So shall thy seed be. And Abraham believed God and it was counted unto him for righteousness." Which is much noticed in the New Testament, as that for which Abraham was called the father of believers.
>
> And as there was now a further revelation of the covenant of grace, so there was a further confirmation of it by seals and pledges; particularly, circumcision, which was a seal of the covenant of grace. . . . It was *a seal of righteousness of faith.* . . .
>
> Another remarkable confirmation Abraham received of the covenant of grace, was when he returned from the slaughter of the kings; when Melchisedec the king of Salem, the priest of the most high God, that great type of Christ, met him and blessed him, and brought forth bread and wine. The bread and wine signified the same blessings of the covenant of grace, that the bread and wine does in the sacrament of the Lord's Supper. . . .
>
> Another confirmation of the covenant of grace, was the vision he had . . . of the smoking furnace, and the burning lamp, that passed between the parts of the sacrifice. . . . The sacrifice signified that of Christ. The smoking furnace . . . signified the sufferings of Christ. But the burning lamp . . . signifies the glory . . . procured by them.
>
> Another remarkable pledge that God gave Abraham of the

---

20. Sermon on Galatians 3:13-14, Andover MSS, p. 2. This sermon exists in manuscript at Andover Newton Theological Seminary and is quoted with their kind permission. Future reference to this or other sermons from this collection will be cited as Andover MSS.

the Covenant of Redemption 121

> fulfilment of the covenant of grace, was his giving of that child of whom Christ was to come, in his old age ... and his delivering Isaac, after he was laid upon the wood of the sacrifice to be slain.[21]

One cannot help but be impressed with the frequency and centrality with which Edwards uses the doctrine of the covenant of grace.

"God again renewed and confirmed the covenant of grace to Isaac and Jacob,"[22] to Isaac in Genesis 26:3-4 and to Jacob in Genesis 27:29. Negatively, "Esau, not included in this blessing, missed of being blessed as an heir of the benefits of the covenant of grace."[23] In this contrast between Jacob and Esau the relationship between election and the covenant of grace is apparent. The covenant was renewed and confirmed with Jacob on several occasions. "Thus the covenant of grace was now renewed much oftener than it had been before."[24] As the appearing of Christ draws nearer, the light of the Gospel shines brighter.

The next major stage of revelation was Moses and the Exodus. Edwards writes:

> The first thing that offers itself is the redemption of the church of God out of Egypt; the most remarkable of all in the Old Testament, the greatest pledge and forerunner of the future redemption by Christ, and much more insisted on in Scripture than any other of those redemptions.[25]

Edwards refers to 1 Corinthians 10:11 and declares that the deliverance out of Egypt was one of those events that "happened unto them for *types.*"[26] In a sermon on 1 Corinthians 10:11 Edwards states as his doctrine: "The things which came to pass to the Children of Israel in travelling from Egypt through the wilderness to Canaan are resemblances of what comes to pass to souls in their spiritual travel."[27]

---

21. "History," *Works,* I, 543-544.
22. "History," *Works,* I, 545.
23. "History," *Works,* I, 545.
24. "History," *Works,* I, 545.
25. "History," *Works,* I, 546.   26. "History," *Works,* I, 548.
27. Sermon on 1 Corinthians 10:11, Yale MSS, p. 3.

David receives a central place in Scripture as regards salvation history and thus is seen by Edwards as central to his thesis. "The next thing to be observed here, is God's solemnly renewing the covenant of grace with David, and promising that the Messiah should be of his seed."[28] Edwards sees this covenant as identical with the offer of Christ to sinners.

> That this covenant, now established with David by Nathan the prophet, was the covenant of grace, is evident by the plain testimony of Scripture, Isa. lv. 1-3. There we have Christ inviting sinners to come to the waters, &c. And in the 3d verse, he says, "Incline your ear, and come unto me; hear and your souls shall live; and I will make with you an everlasting covenant, even the sure mercies of David." Here Christ offers to poor sinners, if they will come to him, to give them an interest in the same everlasting covenant that he had made with David, conveying to them the same sure mercies. But what is that covenant, in which sinners obtain an interest when they come to Christ, but the covenant of grace.[29]

The theme of Edwards' "History" continues even during the dispersed state of the Jews in captivity. He sees this as preparing the way for Christ in that "it showed the necessity of abolishing the Jewish dispensation, and introducing a new dispensation of the covenant of grace" and "of abolishing the ceremonial law, and the old Jewish worship."[30]

The middle section of Edwards' "History" deals with the years of Christ's sojourn on earth from the incarnation to the resurrection. Throughout this period and on into the final segment of history until the end of the world the covenant of grace remains in effect. Edwards refers to the designation "latter days" as signifying "the last period of the great work of redemption; which is as it were the sum of God's works of providence; the last dispensation of the covenant of grace on earth."[31]

---

28. "History," *Works*, I, 554.
29. "History," *Works*, I, 555. Edwards calls this "the fifth solemn establishment of the covenant of grace with the church after the fall.... The first was with Adam; the second with Noah; the third with the patriarchs, Abraham, Isaac, and Jacob; the fourth was in the wilderness by Moses; and now the fifth is made to David."
30. "History," *Works*, I, 563.   31. "History," *Works*, I, 583.

the Covenant of Redemption 123

In the final chapter of his work entitled "Improvement of the Whole" Edwards draws several conclusions, one of which is the unchangeableness of God's covenant of grace.

> From what has been said, we may see the stability of God's *mercy* and *faithfulness* to his people; how he never forsakes his inheritance, and remembers his covenant to them through all generations. Now we may see what reason there was for the words of the text, "The moth shall eat them up like a garment, and the worm shall eat them like wool; but my righteousness shall endure for ever and ever, and my salvation from generation to generation."[32]

The text referred to here is Isaiah 51:8 which is the text for the whole work. In a manuscript sermon on 2 Samuel 23:5, Edwards calls the covenant of grace an "eternal covenant" with all things necessary to make it firm and sure. He cites such things as its relation to the covenant of redemption, its revelation after the fall with its various renewals (as in the "History"), confirmation by oaths, each person of the Trinity witnessing to it, confirmation by seals, aspects already fulfilled, the assurance of our surety being already acquitted and justified by the resurrection, and similar things all showing that "the covenant of grace is ordered in all things, and sure."[33]

One can only marvel at the bias of some interpreters to exempt Jonathan Edwards from the category of a covenant theologian. W. Adams Brown, for example, says of Edwards' "History" that while the covenant is occasionally mentioned, "the reference is only incidental, and the idea exercises no formative influence upon the structure of the work."[34]

---

32. "History," *Works*, I, 618. In a manuscript sermon on 2 Samuel 23:5, Yale MSS, pp. 5-17, Edwards calls the covenant of grace an "eternal covenant" with all things necessary to make it firm and sure. He cites such things as its relation to the covenant of redemption, its revelation after the fall with its various renewals (as in the "History"), confirmation by oaths, each person of the Trinity witnessing to it, confirmation by seals, aspects already fulfilled, the assurance of our surety being already acquitted and justified by the resurrection, and similar things all showing that "the covenant of grace is ordered in all things, and sure."
33. Sermon on 2 Samuel 23:5, Yale MSS, pp. 5-17.
34. Brown, *Encyclopedia of Religion and Ethics*, IV, 223. Cf. De Jong, *The Covenant Idea in New England Theology, 1620-1847*, p. 149, where he writes the

One would only need to read the first page of Edwards' "History" to realize that the covenant of grace is integral to his theme. In the introduction he declares the happiness of the church of God to consist of the following:

> ... In God's righteousness and salvation towards them. By God's righteousness here, is meant his faithfulness in fulfilling his covenant promises to his church, or his faithfulness towards his church and people, in bestowing the benefits of the covenant of grace upon them. Though these benefits are bestowed of free and sovereign grace, as being altogether undeserved; yet as God has been pleased, by the promises of the covenant of grace, to bind himself to bestow them, they are bestowed in the exercise of God's righteousness or justice. And therefore the apostle says, Heb. vi. 10. "God is not unrighteous, to forget your work and labour of love." And 1 John i.9. "If we confess our sins, he is faithful and just to forgive us our sins, and to cleanse us from all unrighteousness." So the word *righteousness* is very often used in Scripture for God's covenant faithfulness. . . . So we are often to understand righteousness and covenant mercy for the same thing. . . .
>
> The other word used is *salvation*. Of these two, God's righteousness and his salvation, the one is the cause of which the other is the effect. God's righteousness, or covenant mercy, is the root, of which his salvation is the fruit. Both of them relate to the covenant of grace. The one is God's covenant mercy and faithfulness, the other intends that work of God by which this covenant mercy is accomplished in the fruits of it. For salvation is the sum of all those works of God by which the benefits that are by the covenant of grace are procured and bestowed.[35]

This is an extremely important statement concerning Edwards' view on the covenant of grace. We can only repeat what we said earlier, namely, that the name of this work might with qualification be "A History of the Covenant of Grace."

---

following about Edwards' "History": "In it Edwards consistently used covenant terminology without making the idea truly determinative." De Jong finds this interesting as a demonstration that "the covenant idea was not yet forgotten," but he sees it there as a vestige, not as an essential aspect of his thought.

35. "History," *Works*, I, 533.

8

Distinctive Aspects of Edwards' Doctrine of the Covenant of Grace

Perhaps the most distinctive way Edwards characterizes the covenant of grace is with the analogy of a marriage covenant. Especially in the "Miscellanies," but by no means only there, we see the covenant of grace in terms of marriage. ". . . The covenant between Christ and believers 'tis the marriage covenant."[1] The marriage analogy serves a dual purpose inasmuch as it is the primary analogy of the doctrine of union with Christ. This is appropriate since union with Christ is a key doctrine for Edwards and, as will be seen later, is directly related to the covenant of grace. In a "Miscellanies" entry on distinguishing the two covenants Edwards writes: "There is another covenant that is the marriage covenant between Christ and the soul, the covenant of union or whereby the soul becomes united to Christ."[2]

This same distinction is made in sermons where Edwards deals with the twofold covenant. In a sermon on Hebrews 9:15-16 he refers to "another covenant" besides the one between God the Father and Christ, namely, "the covenant that is between Christ and believers themselves."[3] This he calls a "marriage covenant." In a Psalm 111:5 sermon Edwards states that the covenant between Christ and the individual "is

---

1. "Miscellanies," No. 919, Yale MSS.
2. "Miscellanies," No. 825, Yale MSS.
3. Sermon on Hebrews 9:15-16, Yale MSS, p. 4.

what is properly called the covenant of grace" and in Scripture "symbolized as a marriage covenant."[4]

This relationship is also mentioned in passing where Edwards is dealing with other themes. In a sermon on "The Church's Marriage to her Sons, and to her God" Edwards uses the marriage concept to describe the union between a "faithful pastor and a Christian people."[5] He emphasizes, however, that this "blessed union . . . is but a shadow";

> . . . Christ is the true husband of the church, to whom the souls of the saints are espoused indeed, and to whom they are united as his flesh and his bones, yea and one spirit; to whom they have given themselves in an everlasting covenant, and whom alone they cleave to, love, honour, obey, and trust in, as their spiritual husband. . . .[6]

In his treatise on "Qualifications for the Lord's Supper" Edwards states that in the Lord's Supper there is "a mutual solemn *profession* of the two parties transacting the covenant of grace, and visibly united in that covenant."[7] He then utilizes the marriage analogy in illustrating the covenant transaction.

> Our taking the bread and wine is as much a *professing* to accept of Christ, at least, as a woman's taking a *ring* of the bridegroom in her marriage is a profession and seal of her taking him for her husband. The sacramental elements in the Lord's supper represent Christ as a party in covenant, as truly as a *proxy*, represents a prince to a foreign lady in her marriage; and our taking those elements is as truly a professing to accept of Christ, as in the other case the lady's taking the proxy is her professing to accept the prince as her husband.[8]

It is this "marriage" between Christ and the elect sinner that bridges the gap between God offended and man offending. The prime covenant is between God the Father and Christ, but it is Christ as united with His church. Thus the eternal decree is manifested in time only when the members

---

4. Sermon on Psalm 111:5, Yale MSS, p. 7.
5. Sermon on Isaiah 62:4-5, *Works*, II, 17-26.
6. Sermon on Isaiah 62:4-5, *Works*, II, 20-21.
7. "An Humble Inquiry," *Works*, I, 458.
8. "An Humble Inquiry," *Works*, I, 459.

the Covenant of Grace

of that church become united with Christ. To be outside of the "marriage covenant," the covenant of grace, is to be outside the covenant of redemption.

> God the Father makes no covenant and enters into no treaty with fallen man distinctly by themselves. He will transact with them in such a friendly way no other way than by and in Christ Jesus as members and as it were parts of him. The friendliness and favour shall not be to them in their own name, but it shall all be to Christ and all acts of friendship and favour shall all be to him and all promises made to him and the fulfilment of promises also shall be to him and to believers only as being in him and under the covert of his name and as being beheld and reckond as parts of him.[9]

From man's perspective all the covenant promises are contingent upon his being in Christ, and to be in Christ is to be in the covenant of grace.

The covenant of redemption is fully an eternal covenant. The temporal aspect of the covenant of grace, however, necessitates its completion in time. In an important "Miscellanies" entry on the covenant of grace Edwards adds the following corollary:

> Coroll. 1. The revelation and offer of the gospel is not properly called a covenant till it is consented to. As when a man courts a woman offers himself to her, his offer is not called a covenant tho he be obliged by it on his part. Neither do I think that the gospel is called a covenant in Scripture but only when the engagements are mutual.[10]

In another entry we find a similar statement:

> This covenant before marriage is only an offer or invitation. Behold I stand at the door and knock &c— In marriage or in the soul's conversion it becomes a proper covenant. This is what is

---

9. "Miscelanies," No. 1091, Yale MSS. Cf. Sermon on Hebrews 9:15-16, Yale MSS, pp. 4-6, where Edwards uses the illustration of a king covenanting with his son and his son's wife together as one party with the promise contingent upon the son's fulfilling a certain condition. This, he states, is a different covenant from that between the son and his wife. A similar illustration is found in "Miscellanies," No. 617, Yale MSS, where the example is a father who "gives an estate to his son and his future wife," and the son in turn "in the marriage covenant gives himself and his estate to her that he takes" as his wife, "yet the covenants are entirely different."

10. "Miscellanies," No. 617, Yale MSS.

called the covenant of grace in distinction from the covenant of redemption.[11]

It is this aspect of "becoming" a covenant which in part distinguishes the covenant of grace from the covenant of redemption.

Having emphasized these temporal features, however, it would be well to again see Edwards tie the covenant of grace into the covenant of redemption. He does this in the language of the marriage analogy and in the context of the incompleteness of the covenant of grace when he writes the following in one of his important "Miscellanies" on the covenant:

> If God the Father before the foundation of the world makes a covenant with his Son concerning him and his future spouse and gives promises to both considered as those that are to be one, and afterwards when his spouse is obtained and he is united to her, he brings this covenant and these promises in his hand and delivers it to her as a covenant made with them jointly, this don't make it now to become another covenant any more than if Christ's spouse had actually been with Christ when the covenant was first made and both had appeared in actual union before the Father in that transaction.[12]

In this succinct statement Edwards covers several important points. The covenant with the Son concerns His "future spouse" who obtains the covenant promises only after she is united with Him. It is the same covenant, however, between God the Father and Christ with His bride, whether viewed from eternity before the bride has actually been united in the marriage covenant with Christ or after that union. When it is remembered that Edwards, as well as other covenant theologians, referred to believers united to Christ by faith as promises given to the Son in the eternal covenant of redemption, it becomes clear that the Son's "future spouse" will infallibly exist and that the promises made to her in Christ are from the divine perspective made as though the union were already actual.

As we have seen, there are different parties involved in

---

11. "Miscellanies," No. 825, Yale MSS.
12. "Miscellanies," No. 617, Yale MSS.

the two covenants. There are also different conditions and different promises, and Edwards is concerned that a confusion of these differences will result in confusion in the two covenants. The reverse is also likely where failure to distinguish between the covenants results in a confusion of the conditions and promises. The framework of the marriage analogy is utilized by Edwards in speaking of these differences.

Regarding the conditions of the covenants, we find a statement by Edwards that will be important to remember when we deal with the question of conditionality in a later chapter. "All the promises of each of these covenants are conditional," and, according to Edwards, "to suppose that there are any promises of the covenant of grace, or any covenant promises that are not conditional promises seems an absurdity and contradiction."[13] The conditions are clearly different, however.

> The condition of the covenant that God has made with Jesus Christ as a publick person is all that Christ has done and suffered to procure redemption. The condition of Christ's covenant with his people or of the marriage covenant between him and men is that they should close with him and adhere to him.[14]

The contrast is between "doing," with its suggestions of working, earning, or meriting, and "closing" with Christ, implying receiving, accepting or in biblical terms, faith. In a sermon on Hebrews 9:15-16, Edwards says the condition of the covenant of redemption "is all that Christ has done and suffered" for our redemption and "is wholly performed by Christ," but the condition of the covenant of grace "between Christ and his people . . . is to be performed by believers and is faith in Jesus Christ."[15]

The promises of the two covenants are also different and correspond to the different conditions.

---

13. "Miscellanies," No. 617, Yale MSS.
14. "Miscellanies," No. 617, Yale MSS.
15. Sermon on Hebrews 9:15-16, Yale MSS, p. 3.

> The sum of what is promised by the Father in the former of these covenants is Christ's reward for what he has done in the work of redemption and success therein. And the sum of what is promised in Christ's marriage covenant with his people is the enjoyment of himself and communion with him in the benefits he himself has obtain'd of the Father by what he has done and suffered.[16]

The significance of the marriage covenant is that the persons covenanting give themselves *and* all that they possess to each other.

This union between Christ and His bride, with each party sharing with the other all they possess, has tremendous soteriological implications. In his notes Edwards writes the following:

> ... Indeed we may say that the sum of all that Christ promises in his covenant with his people is that he will give himself to them. In marriage the persons covenanting, giving themselves to each other, do give what they have to each. The union which they mutually consent to infers ... communion. This promise of the covenant of Christ with his people implies eternal life of both soul and body. The happiness of eternal life ... consists in the enjoyment of Christ, and in ... communion with him or partaking with him in the happiness and glory of his reward who is rewarded with the eternal life and glory of both soul and body. It includes sanctification and perseverance, these are included in the enjoyment of Christ and communion with Christ. It includes justification. This also is a part of believers' communion with Christ for they in their justification are but partaker[s] of Christ's justification, they are pardond and justified in Christ's acquittance and justification as mediatour. The promises of the incarnation of Christ and of his obdience and sacrifice were included in the covenant between Christ and believers before these things were actually accomplished. These were included in Christ's promise of giving himself to believers. If he gives himself to believers as is promised in this marriage covenant, then he must represent them. If Christ gives himself to sinners, of course justice done to the sinners takes hold on him, and all the sinners' obligations lie upon Christ. These things necessarily follow from Christ's making himself one with them as he doth in his marriage covenant.[17]

---

16. "Miscellanies," No. 617, Yale MSS.
17. "Miscellanies," No. 617, Yale MSS. Luther was particularly fond of the marriage analogy to illustrate the way Christ suffers for our sins (which become His in the marriage) and we receive His righteousness.

The mutuality of this covenant has crucial implications for Christ as seen in the latter portion of this quote. If the righteousness of Christ with its merited blessings belong to believers by means of this covenant, it is also true that the believers' sin with its merited punishment belong to Christ. That is the way Christ took our sins upon Himself. The sinner's debt became Christ's debt in their marriage, and the cross was where Christ paid off the debt in full.

Another designation used by Jonathan Edwards in describing the covenant of grace, a designation not uncommon in Reformed theology, is that of a last will and testament. The doctrine of a sermon-lecture on Hebrews 9:15-16 states: "The covenant of grace is as it were Christ's last will and testament."[18] In one of the "Miscellanies" Edwards uses the teaching of Scripture on this point to show that the parties of the covenant of grace are Christ and the church. He writes:

> ... This covenant is called a testament in Scripture and compared to a will that is confirmed by the death of the testatour. Now the testatour that died was Christ and not God the Father. If the covenant of grace was his will and testament to his church, then Christ and the church are the parties contracting.[19]

The testament idea is a solid scriptural designation. Turretin, for example, felt compelled to argue not for its acceptance as a valid understanding of διαθήκη but rather that its common acceptance as testament not exclude the covenant idea. He indicates that the testamentary notion is the principal meaning intended by the Apostle in Hebrews 9:15 with its emphasis on the death and satisfaction of Christ, but he also insists that it not be understood exclusive of the covenant relationship "which demands faith and obedience on man's part."[20]

---

18. Sermon on Hebrews 9:15-16, Yale MSS, p. 2.
19. "Miscellanies," No. 1064, Yale MSS.
20. Turretin, *Institutio* (*Loc.* XII, Q. I, vi), II, 187 (Eng. p. 291). He also states in paragraph v, p. 187 (Eng. p. 291), "... Although the testamental relation is connoted, the federal relation cannot and ought not to be excluded, because there are properly no sureties of Testaments, but between adverse parties a

In a sermon on John 14:27, published as "The Peace which Christ Gives His True Followers," Edwards teaches that the promises of the covenant of grace are given to believers in Christ's last will and testament.

> Christ at his death made over the blessings of the new covenant to believers, as it were in a will or testament.
>
> The new covenant is represented by the apostle as Christ's last will and testament. Heb. ix. 15, 16. "And for this cause he is the Mediator of the New Testament, that by means of death, for the redemption of the transgressions that were under the first testament, they which are called might receive the promise of eternal inheritance. For where a testament is, there must also of necessity be the death of the testator." What men convey by their will or testament, is their own estate. So Christ in the new covenant conveys to believers his own inheritance, so far as they are capable of possessing and enjoying it. They have that eternal life given to them in their measure, which Christ himself possesses. . . . They inherit his kingdom. . . .
>
> Men in their wills or testaments most commonly give their estates to their children: so believers are in Scripture represented as Christ's children. Heb. ii. 13. . . .
>
> This covenant between Christ and his children is like a will or testament also in this respect, that it become effectual, and a way is made for putting it in execution, no other way than by his death; as the apostle observes it is with a will or testament among men. "For a testament is of force after men are dead." Heb. ix. 17. For though the covenant of grace indeed was of force before the death of Christ, yet it was of force no otherwise than by his death. . . .[21]

In the manuscript sermon on Hebrews 9:15-16, a text referred to in the above quote, Edwards goes into some detail on "how" the covenant between Christ and believers is like a last will and testament. To begin with, the "eternal inheritance" which Christ gives "is his own independently and absolutely," and He may thus freely dispose of it as he desires.[22] One cannot give in a will what he does not possess. Furthermore, "that which Christ disposes of in the covenant

---

Mediator is appointed to reconcile them, and so unite them with each other by a covenant." Cf. Berkhof, *Reformed Dogmatics*, I, 268-269.

21. Sermon on John 14:27, *Works*, II, 90.
22. Sermon on Hebrews 9:15-16, Yale MSS, pp. 7-8.

of grace is his whole estate"; Christ who possesses all things gives "all that he has to be enjoyed by them."[23] Such blessings are also unmerited by believers. Christ does not give the inheritance to those who "pay" for it. "He conveys . . . this inheritance to believers of his own free will."[24] A will or testament is not valid if one is compelled to make it rather than freely decide on such a disposition. The testamentary character of the covenant of grace is further illustrated by the fact that it is Christ's children who inherit the heavenly estate ("Men in their last wills do most commonly dispose of their estates to their children."), and the covenant or testament "becomes effectual . . . by Christ's death."[25]

Much as we saw Edwards appeal to the covenant of redemption to anchor the believer's assurance of salvation on a firm foundation, so in the application of this important Hebrews sermon he teaches that the certainty of the divine promises can be seen in the fact that the covenant is like a last will and testament.

> Hence we learn what a sure foundation the faith of those that believe on Christ is built upon, the foundation of their faith in the covenant of grace which is a covenant well ordered in all things and sure. . . . Christ has not only promised the eternal inheritance to believers but has confirmed it to them in his last will and testament. And the testator has died to make his will effectual. . . . The testament of the dead is . . . a sacred thing and justly so.[26]

As with the word $\delta\iota\alpha\vartheta\acute{\eta}\kappa\eta$, so in Edwards' theology we see the concept of testament and covenant closely allied.

As well as the specific designations of the covenant of grace as a marriage covenant and a testament, the general frame of reference for Edwards is the covenant of grace in relation to the covenant of redemption. A key sermon already referred to in this relationship is a published sermon on

---

23. Sermon on Hebrews 9:15-16, Yale MSS, p. 9.
24. Sermon on Hebrews 9:15-16, Yale MSS, p. 11.
25. Sermon on Hebrews 9:15-16, Yale MSS, pp. 12-15.
26. Sermon on Hebrews 9:15-16, Yale MSS, p. 19.

Hebrews 13:8. To show how Christ always "acts by the same rules in the execution of his mediatorial office," Edwards refers first to the eternal covenant of redemption and then says this with regard to the covenant of grace:

> Another covenant that Christ has regard to in the execution of his mediatorial office, is that covenant of grace which God established with man. Though indeed this be less properly the rule by which Christ acts as Mediator, than the covenant of redemption, yet it may be called a rule. God does, as it were, make his promises which he makes to his creatures, his rule to act by: i.e. all his actions are in an exact conformity to his promises, and he never departs in the least degree from them, as is the case with men with regard to what they make the rule of their actions. Yet it is not a rule to God in the same sense as a rule is to a created agent, which must be considered as something antecedent to the purposes of the agent, and that by which his purposes are regulated. But God's promises are consequent on his purposes.... Therefore the fact that Christ never departs from the covenant of redemption, infers that he will never depart from the covenant of grace; for all that was promised to men in the covenant of grace, was agreed on between the Father and the Son in the covenant of redemption. However, there is one thing wherein Christ's unchangeableness in his office appears: that he never departs from the promises that he hath made to man. There is the same covenant of grace in all ages of the world. The covenant is not essentially different now from what it was under the Old Testament, and even before the flood; and it always will remain the same. It is therefore called an everlasting covenant, Isa. lv. 3.[27]

When Edwards designates the covenant of grace as an "everlasting covenant," it is essential to remember the integral relationship of this covenant to the covenant of redemption. The eternal covenant of redemption is an eternal covenant in the fullest sense of the word. The covenant of grace is not less of an eternal covenant since it is integrally related to the covenant of redemption. But it is eternal in a derivative rather than an absolute sense. As Edwards stated in the above quote, Christ acts in exact conformity with His promises to man, and "all that was promised ... was agreed on ... in the covenant of redemption." Because the covenant

---

27. Sermon on Hebrews 13:8, *Works*, II, 950.

the Covenant of Grace

of grace is an historical manifestation of the eternal covenant of redemption and not an autonomous or self-standing covenant, it can rightly be called an eternal or everlasting covenant.

One of the factors that qualifies the covenant of grace as not eternal in an absolute sense is that man is a participant in that covenant. This was brought out early in this chapter where the covenant of grace was likened to a marriage covenant. In corollary number one of note No. 617 of the "Miscellanies" Edwards states that the "offer of the gospel is not properly called a covenant till it is consented to," even as an offer of marriage is only an offer and not the covenant of marriage itself.[28] Though the covenant of grace is an everlasting covenant, it is not in effect until the person actually believes in Jesus Christ. "The elect are chosen from eternity, to be sure, but they are not admitted to the covenant of grace until the moment they accept Jesus Christ as their redeemer."[29]

The fact that the sinner's acceptance of the covenant promises is necessary for the covenant of grace to be effectual demonstrates the existence of different parties involved in covenanting in the two covenants and justifies Edwards' insistence that they be "distinguished" and "not confounded." Believing man is thus a party to the covenant of grace. Edwards writes that when Scripture speaks of God making a covenant with his people and compares it to a marriage covenant, it refers to the covenant between Christ and His people.[30] According to Edwards, "the new covenant as a mutual agreement, or as a conditional promise, is only with Christ."[31] The crucial covenant, of course, is the cove-

---

28. "Miscellanies," No. 617, Yale MSS. Cf. above pp. 138-139.
29. Gerstner, *Steps to Salvation,* p. 177. "When God gave Christ to die for the elect, he looked on them as they are in themselves; but in actually bestowing eternal life, he does not look on them as they are in themselves, but as they are in Christ."
30. "Miscellanies," No. 617, Yale MSS.
31. "Miscellanies," No. 165, Yale MSS.

nant of "absolute promise," the covenant of grace which is identified with, rather than distinguished from, the covenant of redemption. But the covenant of grace in its temporal and historical expression has the Triune God, especially the Son, and man as its covenanting parties. And man, a created being living in time, gives to the covenant of grace its temporal dimension.

As with Reformed theologians in general Edwards is careful to affirm man's lack of power to autonomously fulfill "conditions" for salvation.[32] This appears in his first note on the covenant in the "Miscellanies" where he speaks of the difficulties arising from calling faith the condition of the covenant. Such talk, according to Edwards, "is doubtless the foundation of Arminianism," and it tends "to make men value themselves for their own righteousness." His conclusion is that "if we should leave off distinguishing the covenant of grace and the covenant of redemption, we should leave all these matters plain and unperplexed."[33] Since in this same entry Edwards speaks of a "wrong distinction" between the two covenants, and since, as we have seen, he does himself distinguish the two, we must conclude that Edwards saw a "right distinction" between the covenant of grace and the covenant of redemption. He passionately wanted to guard against an unwarranted distinction that would result in an autonomous ability on the part of fallen man to fulfill the "conditions" of the covenant. Edwards, as we have seen, does not hesitate to use covenantal language, nor does he eliminate the designation of faith as the condition of the covenant.

While the whole question of faith in relation to the covenant of grace will be dealt with in a separate chapter, the

---

32. A representative Reformed theologian and a favorite author of Edwards is Peter van Mastricht, who, for example identifies the parties of the covenant as the Triune God and elect man and speaks of mutual requirements and promises. He makes it emphatically clear that man is a party without any autonomous ability for covenanting and without the power to fulfill the required conditions. Mastricht, *Theoretico-practica Theologia* (*Lib.* V, *Cap.* I, xv-xix), pp. 396-397.

33. "Miscellanies," No. 2, Yale MSS.

issue needs to be introduced here. The Pauline confession of faith apart from works is fundamental to biblical theology, and theology stemming from the Reformation is a most notable example. The statement of the doctrine does not mean it is adequately fathomed, and a correlation is involved that has frequently in theology become unbalanced.

The Bible clearly teaches that justification, or salvation, is a free gift. Equally clear, however, is that justification is by faith, and faith is an act of the believing subject. If salvation is "by" faith, what does the copula "by" signify? How is "forensic" justification as an absolute, sovereign act of God's free grace related to the "necessity" of faith? How do we have one aspect without losing the other? How is the human subject participating in that which is a free gift?

Looking through the eyes of history, we see it as *the* critical issue for Luther. Calvin compared faith to an empty vessel which is capable only of receiving grace. In this way "we do not take the power of justifying away from Christ."[34] This truth was expressed throughout Reformed theology by referring to the instrumental character of faith. The Westminster Confession states: "Faith, thus receiving and resting on Christ and his righteousness, is the alone instrument of justification."[35]

The instrumental nature of faith demonstrates that it is a nonmeritorious act. Turretin writes, "... what is only the instrument for receiving righteousness cannot be our righteousness itself formally."[36] Edwards was sensitive to this same truth in his use of covenantal terms. The fundamental covenant, the covenant of redemption, "was made with Christ," and in that covenant the condition "is Christ's perfect obedience and sufferings."[37] By contrast, the covenant with man "is a free offer ... of life ... whereby he holds it

---

34. Calvin, *Institutes* (III, xi, 7), I, 733.
35. "Confession of Faith," XIII, ii.
36. Turretin, *Institutio* (*Loc.* XVI, Q. VII, vi), II, 732.
37. "Miscellanies," No. 2, Yale MSS.

out in his hand to sinners and offers it without any condition."[38] Herein is Edwards' unhappiness with calling faith a condition, even though he himself calls faith a condition. In the context of the offer of life Edwards writes: "Faith can't be called the condition of receiving, for it *is* the receiving itself."[39]

The doctrine of the covenant of grace is fundamentally an effort to express the saving activity of God in relation to man in a way that honors the monopleuric and dipleuric elements of Scripture.[40] The covenant of grace, originating out of the wholly undeserved grace of God, when established,

---

38. "Miscellanies," No. 2, Yale MSS.
39. "Miscellanies," No. 2, Yale MSS.
40. It may be instructive to realize that a twentieth century theologian the stature of Karl Barth, while unsympathetic to covenant theology, acknowledges the biblical grounds for the depth of the covenant idea. Karl Barth, *The Doctrine of Reconciliation, Church Dogmatics,* IV, 1, trans. G. W. Bromiley (Edinburgh, 1961), pp. 22-26. The title of Barth's chapter is "The Covenant as the Presupposition of Reconciliation," but with regard to federal theology, which in the second half of the seventeenth century "was the ruling orthodoxy of the Reformed Church," he concludes that they "imported" the concept of covenant as an interpretive key and therefore "we cannot follow this theology even in its first and formal statements" (p. 56). In spite of this, Barth sees in the biblical use of the word a foundation that is not contradictory to the (right or wrong) formulations of Reformed theology via covenant theology. "Covenant . . . is the Old Testament term for the basic relationship between the God of Israel and His people. . . . It denotes an element in a legal ritual in which two partners together accept a mutual obligation. . . . We can hardly agree . . . that the covenant may be dissolved. . . . It is 'unalterable, lasting and inviolable. . . .' The Old Testament covenant is a covenant of grace. It is instituted by God Himself in the fulness of sovereignty. . . . But the concept of mutuality must now be elucidated. . . . The word 'covenant' does not denote a two-sided contract between two equal partners, but a more or less one-sided decree. . . . The New Testament . . . διαθήκη brings out exactly the meaning of the Old Testament *berith*. It is 'in every respect the arrangement of God. . . .' For that reason it was rightly described by the Reformed federal theologians of the 17th century as a *foedus μονόπλευρον*. . . . It is always 'my covenant' " (pp. 22-25). Barth, in dealing with the "new covenant" (Jer. 31:31), argues that the "elements" are the same. "We cannot therefore speak of a 'replacement. . . .'" Yet he sees a difference. ". . . The circle of the covenant which in its earlier form is open on man's side will in its new form be closed: not because men will be better, but because God will deal with the same men in a completely different way, . . . He Himself will turn them to Himself. . . ." *Because* God sovereignly acts, a mutual element comes into the monopleuristic covenant. "The covenant—God Himself will make it so—will then be one which is mutually kept, and to that extent a *foedus δίπλευρον*" (pp. 32-33).

imposes mutual obligations on both God and man. The absolute sovereignty of God and man's responsibility meet in the covenant of grace. Both represent true biblical data and must not be played off against each other, since in Scripture they are interrelated. The covenant of grace in its eternal origin has an organic character. Election of individuals happens "in Christ," with Christ as the Head of the body or the second Adam. Coupled with that, however, is the fact that Scripture teaches the realization of this in history in a way that fully honors the rational and moral nature of man.

In his treatise on "Qualifications for Communion" Edwards stresses the reality of the whole man involved in "owning" the covenant of grace.

> The covenant to be owned or professed, is *God's covenant*, which he has revealed as the method of our spiritual union with him, and our acceptance as the objects of his eternal favour; which is no other than the *covenant of grace*. . . . To own this covenant, is to profess the consent of our *hearts* to it; and that is the sum and substance of true piety. It is not only professing the asset of our understandings . . . but it is to profess the consent of our *wills*, it is to manifest *that we do comply with it*.[41]

According to Edwards there is *no* covenant without the consent of both parties.

> In every covenant there is required the consent of both parties. Consent on man's part to God's covenant is only an acceptance of the covenant proposed by God. . . . The reason is very plain why it is faith that is required, because consent to a covenant is

---

41. "An Humble Inquiry," *Works*, I, 443. Printed as an "Appendix" to this work (pp. 479-484) is a letter to Edwards from Thomas Foxcroft "in answer to" Edwards' "request of information concerning the opinion of Protestant Divines and Churches in general, of the Presbyterians in Scotland and Dissenters in England in particular, respecting Five Questions" relating to the communion controversy. The third question is: "Whether it be not the general opinion, that persons admitted to the Lord's table ought to profess saving faith and repentance; meaning that faith and repentance, which are the terms of the covenant of grace?" (p. 482). The casual way Edwards assumes the covenant of grace terminology in asking this question would assume that Edwards was one with the consensus among the Reformed on this doctrine, Perry Miller notwithstanding. Foxcroft's answer stated that he "could easily produce a *cloud of witnesses* . . . on the *affirmative* side."

necessary to the very [being of] that covenant. A man can't be in any covenant till he consents to it.[42]

As with his theological ancestors Edwards' insistence on the necessity of faith is not in conflict with his proclamation of salvation by grace, but it stands instead in closest harmony with the Gospel of grace. In a sermon on the text "Therefore it is of faith that it might be by grace" (Rom. 4:16), Edwards expounds this doctrine: "That the grace of God in the new covenant eminently appears in that . . . it proposes justification only by faith."[43] In this sermon Edwards teaches that the "great and main design of God in the gospel" is "to magnify the riches and sovereignty of his grace." The means to that end is salvation by faith alone, and persons trusting in their own righteousness "exceedingly derogate from the glory of the gospel or new covenant."[44] If the new covenant, which Edwards calls the covenant of grace in this sermon, were not of pure grace, if faith as the condition of the covenant implied any merit at all, Jonathan Edwards would disown the doctrine of the covenant of grace on the basis of this sermon. That he did not disown the covenant of grace as a theological doctrine illustrates the firm conviction of Edwards that this doctrine in no way conflicts with the biblical theme of *sola fide*.

---

42. "Miscellanies," No. 299, Yale MSS. The added phrase, "being of," is a conjecture of what is missing from a torn corner of the manuscript.
43. Sermon on Romans 4:16, Yale MSS, p. 3.
44. Sermon on Romans 4:16, Yale MSS, pp. 18-19. Cf. Bavinck, *Gereformeerde Dogmatiek,* III, 187-228. It is indicative of the way the covenant of grace functions in Reformed theology when Bavinck handles this doctrine in the chapter "Over Christus." The context is sinful man becoming aware that *if* there is redemption, "de verlossing moet komen van boven" (p. 187). Bavinck especially stresses the "monopleurisch karakter" (p. 194) and God's sovereignty in salvation being of pure grace (pp. 223 ff.).

9

The Covenant of Grace in Relation to the Two Dispensations and the Covenant of Works

Two aspects of the covenant of grace have been dealt with which might appear to be inconsistent with each other. On the one hand we have seen the covenant of grace likened to Christ's last will and testament. Now a will or testament becomes effective in no other way than by the death of the testator. On the other hand, Edwards clearly teaches that the covenant of grace was in effect with Adam long before Christ's incarnation and subsequent death. One might expect the covenant not to be in effect until the actual death of Christ.

Edwards' answer is alluded to in a sermon on John 14:27. "For though the covenant of grace indeed was of force before the death of Christ, yet it was of force no otherwise than by his death; so that his death did virtually intervene; being already undertaken and engaged."[1] The relationship to the eternal covenant of redemption is again apparent. The acceptance by Christ of the work of redemption through his death was absolutely and infallibly certain of fulfillment because the covenant of redemption is part of the eternal counsel of God. Gerstner writes:

> Were the saints before the incarnation and atonement devoid of the benefits of grace? Were they awarded them posthumously?

---

1. Sermon on John 14:27, *Works,* II, 90.

No, the benefits of the covenant of grace were in operation from the moment that man fell; but this was in anticipation of the death of Christ. The benefits were administered in advance on the supposition that Christ in the fullness of time would merit them for his people. They were, however, awarded on no other ground than the death of Christ.[2]

Edwards enunciates the unity of both testaments, and in so doing he reflects what is a central feature in Reformed theology. Given this unity the question emerges as to how the Old and New Testaments are related and how the covenant of grace relates to the covenant of works.

William Ames, a favorite of Edwards, writes: "Although the free, saving covenant of God has been one and the same from the beginning, the matter of the application of Christ or the administration of the new covenant has not always been so."[3] Ames distinguishes between the promise and the appearance of Christ, the general and specific revelations, and the differences "in quality and quantity."[4]

Turretin equates the covenant of grace with the new covenant, which is called new "not only because it succeeded the old covenant of works, and . . . renewed in Christ . . . but also because it is eternal, and immutable, and never to be abrogated."[5] He speaks of different modes but the same substance, and he gives explanations of why God worked through this twofold economy. But he insists the only real difference is in mode.[6]

In a "Miscellanies" entry Edwards compares the dispensations of Moses and Christ. They agree in the "same salvation," the "same mediator," the same application of Christ's redemption by the Holy Spirit, the same method of justification with faith or the condition or qualification for justification, the same external means, the same benefits, the same

---

2. Gerstner, *Steps to Salvation,* p. 178.
3. Ames, *The Marrow of Theology,* p. 202.
4. Ames, *The Marrow of Theology,* pp. 202-206.
5. Turretin,*Institutio* (*Loc.* XII, Q. I, ix), II, 188 (Eng. p. 292).
6. Turretin,*Institutio* (*Loc.* XII, Q. V-VIII), II, 210-262 (Eng. pp. 310-354).

the Two Dispensations and the Covenant of Works   143

revelation of these benefits, and the same promise of future blessings.[7] He then declares them to "differ only in manner and circumstances." In the Old Testament spiritual truth was "under a cover," and where it was direct, it was "imperfect."[8] The implicit results from the two differences also made the difference seem greater.

In his published discourse on "Justification by Faith Alone" Edwards responds to those who interpret Paul's statement "not by works of the law" as a reference to the ceremonial law. This view, which Edwards considers a misunderstanding of Paul, implies that Paul is speaking of a law given long after the Abrahamic covenant. The reference is to the Mosaic administration and not the covenant of works as such.[9] The works of the law referred to by Paul is a contrast of the covenant of works and the covenant of grace and pre-dates Sinai.

> This transaction the Jews in the apostle's time misinterpreted; they looked upon it as God's establishing that law as a rule of justification. Against this conceit of theirs the apostle brings this invincible argument, viz. that God would never go about to disannul the covenant with Abraham, which was plainly a covenant of grace, by a transaction with his posterity, that was so long after it, and was plainly built upon it. He would not overthrow a covenant of grace that he had long before established with Abraham, for him and his seed, (which is often mentioned as the ground of God's making them his people,) by now establishing a covenant of works with them at mount Sinai, as the Jews and judaizing Christians supposed.[10]

The contrast is between the covenant of works, made with Adam originally, and the covenant of grace, first revealed to Adam after the fall and continuing eternally.

One is alerted to the fact that Edwards is using the designation of first and second covenants in a different connection than in the comparison of the covenant of redemption and

---

7. "Miscellanies," No. 1353, Yale MSS.
8. "Miscellanies," No. 1353, Yale MSS.
9. "Justification by Faith Alone," *Works*, I, 630.
10. "Justification by Faith Alone," *Works*, I, 630-631.

the covenant of grace. The covenant of works is another covenant, a third covenant, in the context of what Edwards called a twofold covenant pertaining to our salvation. In the chronology of historical revelation, however, the covenant of works is called the first covenant, and the covenant of grace, though founded in eternity, is called the second covenant or a new covenant.

Such a designation takes the covenant of redemption and the covenant of grace in their unity rather than in their dual aspect and compares it as *one* covenant beside another covenant of works. But Edwards qualifies even this legitimate distinction. Viewed from one perspective the "three" covenants are neither three nor two but one only.

> The covenant of grace or redemption (which we have shewed to be the same) cannot be called a new covenant, or a second covenant, with respect to the covenant of works; for that is not grown old yet, but is an eternal, immutable covenant, of which one jot nor tittle will never fail. There have never been two covenants, in strictness of speech, but only two ways constituted of performing of this covenant: the first constituting Adam the representative and federal head, and the second constituting Christ the federal head; the one a dead way, the other a living way and an everlasting one.[11]

The basis for such a statement will become more apparent when we compare the covenant of works with the covenant of grace. Edwards is careful to show the works aspect within the covenant of grace.

Whether we speak of two ways of performing one covenant or, as Edwards normally did, distinguish them as two covenants, the covenant of works was that covenant which God made with Adam before the fall. Adam was the federal head of the covenant of works analogous to the federal headship of Christ in the "second" covenant, or the covenant of grace. In his notes on Genesis 1:27-30 Edwards clearly states that the blessings referred to in these verses were "given to Adam as the public head of mankind" and "given him in the

---

11. "Miscellanies," No. 35, Yale MSS.

name of the whole race."[12] Adam knew this, and so also "when Adam is threatened with being deprived of all these in case of his disobedience, Adam must understand it in like manner as a calamity to come on the whole race."[13] The covenant was with Adam *and* his posterity.

In one of the "Miscellanies" Edwards says this covenant with Adam is clearly a covenant, agreeable to the Scripture's use of that word. It promises "favor in case of compliance as well as threatening of wrath in case of disobedience."[14] The covenantal aspect is pointed out in the notes on Genesis 1: 27-30 mentioned above. "God's making them in his own image and then blessing them, implies his bestowing those blessings pronounced on the subject blessed, on the condition of its continuing such an excellent subject as he had made it...."[15]

It is the conditional nature of this covenant with its requirement of obedience and, pending Adam's performance, the corresponding blessing or judgment which so emphatically distinguishes this as a works covenant. We err, however, if we fail to see Edwards' insistence that the first covenant was a gracious covenant.

> The goodness of God appeared in the first covenant which proposed justification by works. It was an act of God's goodness and condescension toward man to enter into any covenant at all with him and that he would become engaged to give eternal life to him upon his perfect obedience.[16]

In a sermon on Zechariah 4:7 Edwards says God was not obliged to make man happy even if he persevered in obedience.[17]

The rationale behind the presence of grace in the cove-

---
12. "Notes on the Bible," *Works,* II, 689.
13. "Notes on the Bible," *Works,* II, 689. Cf. "Miscellanies," No. 717, Yale MSS, which deals with "why only Adam's first transgression is imputed to us."
14. "Miscellanies," No. 1215, Yale MSS.
15. "Notes on the Bible," *Works,* II, 689.
16. Sermon on Romans 4:16, Yale MSS, p. 3.
17. Sermon on Zechariah 4:7, Yale MSS, p. 3. Edwards goes on to say how the second covenant is a covenant of grace in a way quite different from the first.

nant of works is indicated in this doctrine from a sermon on Luke 17:9: "That God don't thank men for doing those things which he commands them."[18] Adam's obedience as the condition of the covenant of works would in no way merit eternal life, and Adam would have received such a reward, if he had persevered, in no other way than by God graciously determining to honor such a covenant. Edwards states further in this sermon:

> If he had strictly required obedience not only to the moral law and abstaining from the forbidden fruit, but many other positive precepts, without any promise or hopes of reward, it would have been most reasonable that he should obey, and God could no way be accused of injustice if he had bestowed no reward. Much less can fallen man by obedience to God's law deserve of God that he should forgive his sins and should be brought from the state of misery into eternal life.... God is laid under no obligation by men's obedience to hear their prayers.[19]

Ames makes a similar point in a chapter on God's "Special Government of Intelligent Creatures."[20] The point pertaining to government is that this covenant is not between equals but between lord and servant. Ames writes:

> 9. From this special way of governing rational creatures there arises a covenant between God and them. This covenant is, as it were, a kind of transaction of God with the creature whereby God commands, promises, threatens, fulfills; and the creature binds itself in obedience to God so demanding. Deut. 26:16-19....
>
> 10. This way of entering into covenant is not between those who are equal before the law but between lord and servant. It, therefore, rightly pertains to the government. It is very rightly called the covenant not of man but of God, who is the author and chief executer. Deut. 8:18....
>
> 11. In this covenant the moral deeds of the intelligent creature lead either to happiness as a reward or to unhappiness as a punishment. The latter is deserved, the former not.[21]

---

18. Sermon on Luke 17:9, Yale MSS, p. 2.
19. Sermon on Luke 17:9, Yale MSS, pp. 3-4.
20. Ames, *The Marrow of Theology*, pp. 110-113.
21. Ames, *The Marrow of Theology*, p. 111. Cf. G. C. Berkouwer, *Sin*, trans. Philip C. Holtrop (Grand Rapids, 1971), pp. 207-208: "We err if we interpret this distinction as though God's original covenant had to do with *our*

the Two Dispensations and the Covenant of Works

Deserved punishment and undeserved happiness is a scriptural contrast relevant to either covenant, and it is prevalent in the covenant thought of Edwards even as it is very much present in Ames' view of the covenant.

The gracious character of the covenant of works was prevalent among the Reformed theologians of the century preceding Edwards and was reflected confessionally in the Westminster Confession where the covenant with Adam is described as a "voluntary condescension on God's part."[22] Such a phrase would certainly reflect the mentality of Edwards that God is not obliged to "thank men for doing those things he commands them," and even less is He obliged to offer a way of salvation to sinful man.

The Westminster Confession, with which Edwards was in agreement, is suggestive of the way in which he dealt with the covenant of works. The covenant God made with Adam is summarized in these words: "The first covenant made with man was a covenant of works, wherein life was promised to Adam; and in him to his posterity, upon condition of perfect and personal obedience."[23] In a later chapter, "Of the Law of God," there is this further statement concerning the covenant of works:

> God gave to Adam a law, as a covenant of works, by which He bound him and all his posterity to personal, entire, exact, and perpetual obedience, promised life upon the fulfilling, and threat-

---

work or *our* achievement or *our* fulfillment of his law, while the later covenant of grace has reference to the pure gift of his *mercy* apart from all *our works*. . . . We interpose the notion of an impersonal legalism within the original relation of God and man. . . . Therefore whoever burdens the so-called 'covenant of works' with the notion of achievement and presumes that we gain God's favor in that way, must endorse the idea of a 'nomological' ur-existence of man and must cut asunder the law of God from the fellowship of God."

22. "Confession of Faith," VII, i. "The distance between God and the creature is so great, that although reasonable creatures do owe obedience unto Him as their Creator, yet they could never have any fruition of Him as their blessedness and reward, but by some voluntary condescension on God's part, which He hath been pleased to express by way of covenant."

23. "Confession of Faith," VII, ii.

ened death upon the breach of it, and endued him with power and ability to keep it.[24]

In one of his notes Edwards speaks of this law or "rule of duty" God gave to Adam.

> Concerning the declaration or manifestation which God made of his mind to Adam concerning the rule of his duty to God and what [God] expected of him enforced with threatenings of his displeasure in case of a violation of that rule and promises of his favour in case of a compliance, especially Adam's consent being supposed, I say as to this being called a COVENANT we have this to warrant us in it that it is agreeable to the sense in which the Scripture uses the word covenant every where.[25]

The results of compliance with this covenant was a blessed and never-ending life; the results of disobedience was summarized with the word "death."

Edwards on many occasions made it very clear that the penalty of death, which resulted when the covenant of works was violated, includes far more than mere natural death when the body returns to dust. He deals with this fact in several places in *Original Sin*. For example, one of the answers Edwards makes to the objection that the giving of posterity to Adam is inconsistent with the threatening of death depends on such a definition of death. When Adam violated the covenant of works, "he then died spiritually," "spiritual death was one great thing implied in the threatening," and "in the language of Scripture, he is *dead*, that is in a state of condemnation to death."[26] Later in the book in a section answering John Taylor's observations on Romans 5:12 ff., he cites the biblical contrast of death and eternal life to prove that the death referred to is primarily the second death, or eternal death.[27]

In one of the "Miscellanies" which speaks of the death threatened in the covenant of works Edwards states that it is

---

24. "Confession of Faith," XIX, i.
25. "Miscellanies," No. 1215, Yale MSS. Cf. also "Miscellanies," Nos. 400, 401, and 720, Yale MSS.
26. *Original Sin*, pp. 258-259.
27. *Original Sin*, pp. 306 ff.

the Two Dispensations and the Covenant of Works 149

"not only or principally temporal death," but rather "it was the utter, final and sensible ruin or destruction of . . . [the] whole man."[28] He goes on at considerable length listing eleven reasons which confirm that "eternal death" is intended. There are three entries in "Notes on the Bible" on Genesis 2:17 which likewise stress the eternal aspect of the death. The verse reads, "In the day that thou eatest thereof, dying thou shalt die." Edwards comments:

> This expression denotes not only the certainty of death, but the extremity of it. Thou shalt die, in the superlative and to the utmost degree; and so it properly extends to the second death, the death of the soul. . . .
>
> Because such a repetition or doubling of a word, according to the idiom of the Hebrew tongue, is as much as our speaking a word once with a very extraordinary emphasis.
>
> . . . His not dying that day a natural death, is no more difficult to reconcile with truth, than his never suffering at all that death that was principally intended, *viz.*, eternal damnation. . . .[29]

Edwards comments on this same verse in his "Interleaved Bible." "It don't seem to me necessary that we should understand this that death should be executed upon him in that day when he ate."[30] He suggests that this may be understood in a parallel way with 1 Kings 2:37 where Solomon said to Shimei, "On the day thou goest out, and passest over the brook Kidron, thou shalt know for certain that thou shalt surely die." Edwards makes the point that "death was executed upon Shimei many days after he had done that thing," and what God signifies to Adam in this verse is that when he eats of the fruit, "he shall be bound to die."[31]

As the reality of eternal death is emphasized as the actual result of the covenant of works, it should not be forgotten that there was also "a promise of immortal and more glorious

---

28. "Miscellanies," No. 785, Yale MSS.
29. "Notes on the Bible," *Works,* II, 691.
30. "Miscellaneous Observations on Holy Scriptures," written in an interleaved Bible, hereafter cited as "Interleaved Bible," Yale MSS, p. 9. This is folder number 6 in the Yale Collection and is quoted with their kind permission.
31. "Interleaved Bible," Yale MSS, p. 9.

life for obedience given to Adam in his first estate."[32] This is evident not only in the Genesis history but from elsewhere in Scripture. Romans 2:7, 10 refers to the covenant of works which promises not only wrath upon disobedience but eternal life to those abiding in the covenant.[33] Three Pauline references to the law are cited as clearly showing a promise of life upon obedience to it: Galatians 3:12, Romans 10:5, and Romans 7:10.[34] So also Romans 3:23 in stating that "all have sinned and come short of the glory of God" indicates that sinners "have lost all hope of that glory of God, that glorious state in immortality which God promised and to which man would have been entitled by his obedience."[35] And citing the use of the word "covenant" in Hosea 6:7, Edwards concludes that Adam was "under a covenant of life." The reason for this is that "there must be a promise of life as well as a threatening of death to make a law become a covenant."[36]

When the condition of the covenant of works is stated to be obedience, it must be understood that perfect obedience is intended. This is why one transgression brought the threatened ruin. According to Edwards, perfect obedience as the "condition of the first covenant," the covenant of works, "is implied in the words of the command as God expressed it to Adam."[37] The reference is to Genesis 2:17: "Thou shalt not eat thereof for on the day that thou eatest thereof thou shalt surely die...."

The obedience required of Adam represented a rather limited sphere. The "principle" and "habit" of perfect obedience are the same for all times, but the circumstances, the

---
32. "Miscellanies," No. 1074, Yale MSS. Edwards acknowledges Isaac Watts' *Ruin and Recovery of Mankind* (1740) as the source of his argument in this entry. The source of notes 33 to 36 is from Watts as well, though they are not direct quotations.
33. "Miscellanies," No. 1074, Yale MSS.
34. "Miscellanies," No. 1074, Yale MSS.
35. "Miscellanies," No. 1074, Yale MSS.
36. "Miscellanies," No. 1074, Yale MSS.
37. "Miscellanies," No. 786, Yale MSS.

happiness

relation to God, the way He deals with us, and what he expects of us may be quite diverse. Such is the content of a "Miscellanies" entry on "Adam's Innocency and Gospel Holiness Compared."

> So gospel holiness differs greatly from the holiness of man in innocency. Man had the Holy Ghost then as the Spirit of God but now he must have it as the Spirit of the Son of God, the Spirit of a Redeemer, a Mediatour between God and us and a spiritual Husband &c. . . .
> . . . A man is perfectly holy when his love to God bears a just proportion to the capacities of his nature under such circumstances. . . .
> There were many things were innocent in Adam in his circumstances that would be exceeding sinfull in us. Adam might be earthly minded in a sense wherein it would be corrupt and abominable in Christians to be.[38]

What matters as far as the covenant of works is concerned is that obedience be perfect. Whatever the circumstances, the "principle" or "habit" of total obedience must remain constant. "The covenant agreement bound man to a perfect obedience to the divine decree; even a momentary lapse of obedience was sufficient to cancel the covenant."[39]

The abrogation of the covenant of works is attributed to Adam. Adam failed in his duty to abide by the terms of the covenant. Edwards, in the language of covenant theology, saw Adam as a federal head. All men were involved in the covenant of works through Adam in his capacity as a public

---

38. "Miscellanies," No. 894, Yale MSS. Cf. "Justification by Faith Alone," *Works,* I, 639: "The thing required was perfect obedience. It is no matter whether the positive precepts were the same, if they were equivalent. The positive precepts that Christ was to obey, were much more than equivalent to what was wanting, because infinitely more difficult. . . . As that act of disobedience by which he fell, was disobedience to a positive precept that Christ never was under, *viz.* that of abstaining from the tree of knowledge of good and evil; so that act of obedience by which principally we are redeemed, is obedience to a positive precept that Adam never was under, *viz.* the precept of laying down his life. It was suitable that it should be a positive precept, that should try both Adam's and Christ's obedience."

39. Wilcox, "New England Covenant Theology," p. 75. Wilcox makes this statement in a discussion of the covenant with Adam and is representative of covenant theology in general.

person, and thus all men share in the abrogation of that covenant with the resulting alienation from the God of the covenant.[40]

The result of Adam's breaking the covenant of works is universal and leaves all of mankind under the "dominion of sin." On the basis of the covenant of works alone this leaves man in a hopeless situation. In a manuscript sermon on Romans 6:14, Edwards states what is a primary reason for this hopelessness:

> ... By the law no provision is made for men's deliverance from sin either from the guilt or strength of it. The law indeed strictly forbids sin and not only so but very severely threatens the commission of it, but yet administers no other principle to preserve from it but only a servile fear, the spirit of bondage, which principle can never deliver the heart from the love and so the power of sin or make them sincere and hearty in their obedience, and therefore is called a dead letter.[41]

The covenant of works, once violated and hence abrogated, served only to condemn.

Not only did the covenant of works offer no provision for salvation for fallen man, it positively discouraged them and increased their hostility to God. In his "Notes on the Bible" dealing with the same text of the sermon just referred to (Rom. 6:14), Edwards makes the following comments regarding the "dominion of sin" and the contrast of being "under the law" and "under grace":

> The law, or covenant of works, is not a proper means to bring the fallen creature to the service of God. It was a very proper means to be used with men in a state of innocency, but it has no tendency to answer this end in our present weak and sinful state. . . .
> 1. It would have tended to discourage persons from any attempts to serve God, because under such a constitution it must

---

40. Though Edwards breaks new ground in his treatment of the imputation of Adam's sin in the way he attributes the unity of the race to the "arbitrary constitution" of divine wisdom, it in no way breaks with the essential teaching in Reformed theology regarding Adam as the federal head with the result that all men are taken up in Adam's sin. Cf. *Original Sin,* pp. 389-412, and also Holbrook's comments in the "Editor's Introduction" (pp. 41-60).

41. Sermon on Romans 6:14, Yale MSS, pp. 1-2.

necessarily have been looked upon as impossible to please him and serve him to his acceptance....
2. God must necessarily have been looked on as an enemy.... A fallen creature held under the covenant of works cannot look on God as a father and friend, but must necessarily look on him as an enemy; for the least failure of obedience by that constitution, whether past or future, renders him so.[42]

If there is a positive aspect in the covenant of works for fallen men, it is in the sense that it is now "a schoolmaster to lead to Christ." The giving of the moral law at Sinai is cited by Edwards as an example of such a "schoolmaster." "It is an instrument that the great Redeemer makes use of to convince men of their sin, misery, and helpless state ... in order to make men sensible of the necessity of Christ as a Saviour."[43]

The fundamental reality facing man is the sin of Adam with its universal imputation and the resulting state of condemnation for all mankind. Sin radically altered man's relationship to God. The change is so radical and total that "the second covenant ... may by way of distinction be called the covenant of grace," and "the free and sovereign ... grace of God appears in ... that it proposes justification by faith alone."[44]

Edwards uses a hypothetical situation to illustrate the greatness of this distinction. Even if faith were seen as a good work—Edwards of course calls faith a gift of God—the covenant of grace would still not be a covenant of works.

> In the first covenant after man had consented, he was yet to do that work which was the condition of the covenant and therefore that is a covenant of works. In the second covenant there is nothing to do but only to consent. There is no work to be done afterwards; the work is done by Christ. This therefore is not a covenant of works, for although faith be a good work, yet in such a case tis no more properly called a work than Adam's consenting

---

42. "Notes on the Bible," *Works*, II, 799.
43. "History," *Works*, I, 547.
44. Sermon on Romans 4:16, Yale MSS, p. 3. Cf. Ames, *The Marrow of Theology*, p. 150: "The application by which God fulfills ... what was contained in a covenant formerly made and broken is called in the Scriptures the *New covenant ... a covenant of life, salvation, and grace....*"

> to the first covenant was part of the work of that covenant.... This consent of their's whereby in their souls they accept of the second covenant to be performed by Christ is justifying faith....[45]

The covenant must be consented to before it is a covenant, and then the question of works can come up for discussion.

The contrast between law and grace is central to a sermon Edwards preached on Romans 6:14. "By grace is meant the dispensation of God's grace in Christ or the covenant of grace.... If you seek to be justified by the covenant of works, then you have departed from the gospel or the covenant of grace."[46] After stating the sermon doctrine, "that the gospel or new covenant is eminently a dispensation of grace," he further defines grace.

> By grace is meant God's free love and kindness to his creatures.... That for which principally the kindness and bounty of God is called grace is the freeness of it. The freeness of love and kindness consists in its exercise being unmerited, not what can be demanded, and secondly in its being disinterested... and not from self-interest."[47]

It is in this context that "the new covenant is eminently a dispensation of grace."

Later in this same sermon Edwards considers how the new covenant is "a covenant of grace in distinction from the first." They differ first of all as to their nature:

> ... The grace of the new covenant is distinguished from that of the first, both as to its freeness and as to its greatness.
> 1. It is distinguished as to the freeness of the grace... in its being offered and given to those that had no excellency and in its being offered to offenders without satisfaction made by them. Eternal life was not offered to offenders by the first covenant.... Neither was eternal life offered to a creature that was not excellent....
> 2. The last covenant is distinguished in the greatness of the grace: (1) The gift is greater in itself, communion with Christ; (2) but abundantly greater if compared with the state that we were found in by the first covenant.[48]

---

45. "Miscellanies," No. 299, Yale MSS.
46. Sermon on Romans 6:14, Yale MSS, p. 2.
47. Sermon on Romans 6:14, Yale MSS, pp. 3-4.
48. Sermon on Romans 6:14, Yale MSS, p. 12.

The covenant of grace also differs from the covenant of works "as to what they have procured to mankind":

> The gospel may be called a dispensation of grace to distinguish it from the first covenant as to ... the influence they have upon us in fact. 2 Corinthians 3:7-11: ["But if the ministration of death, written and engraven in stones, was glorious, ... How shall not the ministration of the spirit be rather glorious? ... For if that which is done away was glorious, much more that which remaineth is glorious."][49]

In a manuscript sermon on Zechariah 4:7 Edwards acknowledges the grace of God in covenanting with man at all. It was a gracious act of God to provide a covenant of works, but Edwards sees this important difference:

> ... This grace would not have been such as the grace of the Gospel, for he would have been saved upon the account of what he himself did. ... Salvation of the Gospel is given altogether freely. Romans 11:6. "And if by grace, then it is no more of works: otherwise grace is no more grace. But if it be of works, then it is no more grace: otherwise work is no more work."[50]

Though grace is a factor in both covenants, the grace-works distinction of these two covenants is absolute.

Edwards compares these two covenants in the sixth sermon of a series on Hebrews 12:22-24.[51] He summarizes the newness of the covenant of grace under two headings: because it succeeds the covenant of works in time and replaces it and because of its "superior excellency."[52] The excellency of the covenant of grace is demonstrated by its being a "covenant of promise." According to Edwards that is the meaning of Ephesians 2:12. Not that the covenant of works was without promises, "but the covenant of grace may be especially

---

49. Sermon on Romans 6:14, Yale MSS, p. 12.
50. Sermon on Zechariah 4:7, Yale MSS, p. 3.
51. Sermons on Hebrews 12:22-24 (VI), Yale MSS, pp. 5-11. Comparing the covenant of works with the covenant of grace was commonly done in the systematic works of Edwards' day and earlier. Cf. for example, Ames, *The Marrow of Theology*, pp. 150-152, where he cites nine differences between the two covenants; Turretin, *Institutio* (*Loc.* XII, Q. IV, i-xii), pp. 208-210, where he lists five things wherein they agree and ten things wherein they differ; and Mastricht, *Theoretico-practica Theologia* (*Lib.* V, *Cap.* I, xxv-xxxiii), pp. 399-402.
52. Sermons on Hebrews 12:22-24 (VI), Yale MSS, p. 11.

called a covenant of promises because the promises of it are... full and absolute."[53] The covenant of works depended upon "man's free will and good works" in order to receive the promises. The covenant of grace, however, cannot fail because it depends on God and not man's works.

It would be a complete misrepresentation of Edwards if one concluded from a comparison of the two covenants that the covenant of works ceased to be in effect after Adam's sin. We know that Edwards freely spoke of the covenant of redemption, the covenant of grace, and the covenant of works as three separate covenants. Yet we also know that he viewed the three covenants as two or one, depending on what aspects were under consideration. We cited previously from "Miscellanies," No. 35, where Edwards says the covenant of grace or redemption is not a new covenant in the sense that the covenant of works "is not grown old yet, but is an eternal, immutable covenant." The two covenants are seen by Edwards as "two ways constituted of performing of this covenant."[54] According to Edwards "the covenant God made with man stating the condition of eternal life" is "the covenant of works." This, he says, was *never* abrogated, and "the covenant of grace is not another covenant... but a covenant made with Christ to fulfill it."[55] Christ, as the federal head, takes the place of Adam and fulfills the covenant of works. Those united with Christ via the "marriage covenant," the covenant of grace, thus possess as their own the merited blessings their spouse receives as the promise of the covenant of works. The covenant of works was thus abrogated as far as man's ability to succeed in its desired end. It was not, however, abrogated as being the only means provided by God to grant the blessing of eternal life to man.

It is apparent that this truth is at the very foundation of the whole biblical teaching of the atoning work of Christ.

---

53. Sermon on Ephesians 2:12, Yale MSS, p. 37.
54. "Miscellanies," No. 35, Yale MSS. Cf. above p. 156.
55. "Miscellanies," No. 30, Yale MSS. Cf. above p. 114.

When Scripture says, "Was it not necessary?" when it speaks of Christ's suffering and death, we are reminded of the fact that the covenant of works has indeed "not grown old yet."

Not surprisingly we find the emphasis of Christ fulfilling the work which Adam and the rest of mankind have failed clearly taught in Edwards' great treatise on justification.

> If Adam had finished his course of perfect obedience, he would have been justified: and certainly his justification would have implied something more than what is merely negative; he would have been approved of, as having fulfilled the righteousness of the law, and accordingly would have been adjudged to the reward of it. So Christ, our second surety, (in whose justification all whose surety he is, are virtually justified,) was not justified till he had done the work the Father had appointed him, and kept the Father's commandments through all trials; and then in his resurrection he was justified.[56]

Christ suffered not as a private person but as a representative. But what He did, He did as fulfillment of the conditions of the covenant of works. When Christ agreed to His redeeming work in the covenant of redemption, the fulfilling of the condition of the covenant of works was contained in the condition of the covenant of redemption.

In this same treatise on justification Edwards writes:

> Justification by the righteousness and obedience of Christ, is a doctrine that the Scripture teaches in very full terms; Rom. v. 18, 19. "By the righteousness of one, the free gift came upon all men unto justification of life." ... We have justification by Christ's righteousness. ...[57]

Edwards sees in this both a propitiation, or "bearing a penalty of a broken law in our stead," and a "voluntary submitting" to this suffering as a positive and righteous obedience to the Father.[58]

According to Edwards the covenant of works is very broad precisely in its simplicity.

---

56. "Justification by Faith Alone," *Works*, I, 623.
57. "Justification by Faith Alone," *Works*, I, 638.
58. "Justification by Faith Alone," *Works*, I, 638.

> There is indeed but one great law of God, and that is the same law that says, "If thou sinnest, thou shalt die;" and "cursed is every one that continues not in all things contained in this law to do them." All duties of positive institution are virtually comprehended in this law.... It may moreover be argued, that all sins whatsoever are breaches of the law or covenant of works, because all sins, even breaches of the positive precepts, as well as others, have atonement by the death of Christ: but what Christ died for, was to satisfy the law, or to bear the curse of the law....
>
> So that Christ's laying down his life might be part of that obedience by which we are justified, though it was a positive precept not given to Adam.[59]

In short, "what Christ did was to fulfil the covenant of works."[60]

The covenant of grace promises salvation in a mediated way. The direct promise of the covenant of grace, as can be seen in its first revelation in Genesis 3:15, is Christ Himself. The promise of a person is why Edwards can use the marriage analogy, and what Christ merits becomes the possession of the bride through the marriage union. Christ fulfilled the covenant of works in order that his people might be saved by grace.

The covenant of works had to be fulfilled either by man himself or for him by another acceptable to God. In one of the "Miscellanies" where Edwards contrasts the two covenants he writes:

> The covenant of works and the covenant of grace as to their condition or that which they propose to be complied with by us in order to eternal life are in some respects the same tho in other respects exceeding diverse. They propose the very same duties, tis the same law, the revelation of the same holy God, and in general the same holy acts and exercises that are now proposed to us as the way to our possession of eternal life that was before in the covenant of works....[61]

The very important difference, however, is that the covenant of works is what we give to God, "something acceptable and

---

59. "Justification by Faith Alone," *Works*, I, 639.
60. "Justification by Faith Alone," *Works*, I, 646.
61. "Miscellanies," No. 1030, Yale MSS.

well pleasing to him," but the covenant of grace is "an expression of acceptance of something offered *by God to us* most profitable and good for us."[62]

This difference, which is of the utmost importance for the sinner, must not cause us to miss the unchangeable demands of the covenant of works.

> But yet the dispositions and acts by which both one and the other of these covenants is complied with are fundamentally the same, because it is still the same God that we have to do with in both.... There is implied an agreeableness between us and this God in either case whether we offer to God that which is acceptable, amiable to the will of his infinite majesty and holiness, or whether we on the other hand entirely and sincerely yield to the offers he makes of himself to us as our beneficent friend, Saviour and all sufficient portion. This can't be without an agreeableness between us and him, so that tis the same agreeableness to the same glorious God that is requisite in both cases, but this agreeableness includes all holiness, and all our duty that we are directed to both under the covenant of works and the covenant of grace.[63]

The holiness and justice of God could not be compromised. The covenant of works would be fulfilled, or the just consequences would result. Salvation, or eternal life, depends upon its fulfillment.

The good news of the Gospel is that Christ provided the condition, the fulfillment, of the covenant of works. A manuscript sermon on Psalm 40:6-8 has as its doctrine, "that the sacrifice of Christ is the only sacrifice that is upon its own account acceptable to God."[64] The burden of this sermon is to show how the Old Testament sacrifices were not acceptable on their own account and how and why the sacrifice of Christ is.

The doctrine of the covenant of grace, as it functions in the theology of Edwards, is a doctrine of comfort and assurance. This was seen when the covenant of grace was expressed as "firm and sure" because it is a manifestation of the

---

62. "Miscellanies," No. 1030, Yale MSS.
63. "Miscellanies," No. 1030, Yale MSS.
64. Sermon on Psalm 40:6-8, Yale MSS, p. 5.

covenant of redemption, and the covenant of redemption is between the divine Persons who are eternal and unchanging. Because Christ is the party of the covenant of redemption, we can depend on his covenant faithfulness. So also Christ is a party to the covenant of works, a substitute for the first Adam who represented us, and since it is God Himself representing the sinner, we can be infallibly assured that He fulfilled the condition of the covenant of works *for us* if we are united with Him in the covenant of grace. As long as eternal life depended upon "man's free will and good works," uncertainty prevailed. Once Adam sinned, the perseverance question became a moot point, since all were in a state of condemnation. The covenant of grace, however, promised salvation. Not only did it restore man to a right relationship to God, it removed the uncertainty of the previous covenant of works. The covenant of grace, because it depends on God and not man, cannot fail.

The covenant of grace, therefore, is foundational for the doctrine of perseverance. It is not surprising that we find Edwards comparing the covenant of works and the covenant of grace in his remarks "Concerning the Perseverance of Saints." The deficiency of the first covenant, according to Edwards, was that perseverance was intrusted to man himself.

> ... Therefore, God introduces a better, which should be an everlasting covenant, a new and living way; wherein that which was wanting in the first should be supplied, and a remedy should be provided against that, which under the first covenant proved man's undoing, *viz.* man's own weakness and instability; by a Mediator being given, who is the same yesterday, to-day, and for ever; who cannot fail.... It is not fit that in a covenant of grace, wherein all is of mere, free, and absolute grace, that the reward of life should be suspended on the perseverance of man, as dependent on the strength and stedfastness of his own will. It is a covenant of works, and not a covenant of grace, that suspends eternal life on what is the fruit of a man's own strength.
> ....
> The first covenant failed of bringing man to the glory of God, through man's instability.... But God had made a second covenant in mercy to fallen man.... The first covenant, that God

the Two Dispensations and the Covenant of Works 161

made with Adam, failed, because it was weak.... Therefore God introduces another better covenant, committed not to his strength, but to the strength of one that was mighty and stable, and therefore is a sure and everlasting covenant. God intrusted the affair of man's happiness on a weak foundation at first, to show man that the *foundation* was weak, and not to be trusted to, that he might trust in God alone. The first was only to make way for the second.[65]

In a sermon on "The Final Judgment" (Acts 17:31) the demands of the law or the covenant of works is shown to be still in effect.

The book of Scripture will be opened, and the works of men will be tried by that touchstone. Their works will be compared with the word of God.... That which God hath given us to be our rule in our lives, he will make his own rule in judgment.

The rule of judgment will be twofold. The *primary* rule of judgment will be the law.... The law will so far be made the rule of judgment, that not one person at that day shall by any means be justified or condemned, in a way inconsistent with that which is established by the law.... The righteous will be so far judged by the law, that although their sentence will not be the sentence of the law, yet it will by no means be such a sentence as shall be inconsistent with the law....

It will be inquired concerning every one, both righteous and wicked, whether the law stands against him, or whether he hath a fulfilment of the law to show. As to the *righteous*, they will have fulfilment to show; they will have it to plead, that the judge himself hath fulfilled the law for them.... But as to the wicked, when it shall be found ... that they have broken the law, and have no fulfilment of it to plead, the sentence of the law shall be pronounced upon them.

A *secondary* rule of judgment will be the gospel, or the cove-

---

65. "Miscellaneous Remarks," *Works*, II, 596, 599. As the weakness of the first covenant instructs us of our need to trust God alone, so also Edwards finds a pedagogical value in the remaining death and afflictions which are the curse of the law. Concerning the question of how such affliction can be reconciled to the covenant of grace, he writes: "... It seems part of the curse of the law still remains taken away for none, but is unavoidable by believers as well as others. I answer, the same death that was the curse of the law remains, but the curse of the law remains not.... Those adversities and death, that were so many degrees of that curse, are, according to the new covenant, so many steps that are necessary in order to deliverance from that curse...."

"Such is the state of man already before his redemption, that he can't be completely redeemed without he passes through death in order to it." "Miscellanies," No. 235, Yale MSS.

nant of grace, wherein it is said, "He that believeth shall be saved, and he that believeth not shall be damned. . . ." By the gospel, or covenant of grace, eternal blessedness will be adjudged to believers. When it shall be found that the law hinders not, and that the curse and condemnation of the law stands not against them, the reward of eternal life shall be given them, according to the glorious gospel of Jesus Christ.[66]

In the sermon on Deuteronomy 32:35, where the plight of sinners in the hands of an angry God is vividly set forth, Edwards makes it very clear that God is under no obligation "to keep any natural man out of hell one moment." God made no promises of eternal life *but* "what are contained in the covenant of grace," and they "who are not the children of the covenant" and who "have no interest in the Mediator of the covenant" surely "have no interest in the promises of the covenant of grace."[67] Outside of the covenant of grace whatever a man does in no way obliges God. The universal condition of all persons outside the covenant of grace is that they "are held in the hand of God over the pit of hell"; God is in no way bound to hold them at all; and "all that preserves them every moment is the mere arbitrary will, and uncovenanted, unobliged forbearance, of an incensed God."[68] The application of this sermon is to call those outside the covenant of grace, that is outside of Christ, to "awake and fly from the wrath to come." Outside the covenant of grace and union with Christ natural man is under the covenant of works on his own behalf. As a party to the covenant of grace he is still under the covenant of works, but it is fulfilled on his behalf by Jesus Christ.[69]

---

66. Sermon on Acts 17:31, *Works*, II, 196.
67. Sermon on Deuteronomy 32:35, *Works*, II, 9.
68. Sermon on Deuteronomy 32:35, *Works*, II, 9.
69. The blessings of the covenant of grace have an added blessing beyond that promised in the covenant of works. In a sermon on Ephesians 1:10, Edwards states that "being brought through Christ to dwell forever in the highest heavens . . . is a benefit procured by Christ alone. It is a promise of the covenant of grace established in Christ. It was not a promise of the first covenant." It promised eternal life, but not that it "should be enjoyed in heaven." Edwards speculates that had Adam not sinned God might have later made such a provision,

Since faith is union with Christ and the means whereby we appropriate the blessing merited by Christ in the covenant of works, and since faith is the "condition" of the covenant of grace, Edwards predictably teaches a close relationship between the covenant of grace and justification by faith alone. Concerning the doctrine of justification by faith alone he writes: "It is in this doctrine that the most essential difference lies between the covenant of grace and the first covenant."[70]

> But the great and most distinguishing difference between that covenant and the covenant of grace is, that by the covenant of grace we are not thus justified by our own works, but only by faith in Jesus Christ. It is on this account chiefly that the new covenant deserves the name of a covenant of grace, as is evident by Rom. iv. 16. "Therefore it is of faith, that it might be by grace."[71]

Indeed Edwards argues the importance of the doctrine he is expounding on justification by faith precisely because it is the doctrine that chiefly distinguishes the two covenants.

This comparison between the covenant of works and the covenant of grace comes at the end of a major discourse on absolute solafideism. That Edwards would give such prominence to the covenant of grace in a doctrinal exposition so central to his theology not only confirms his adherence to the covenant of grace, but it demonstrates as well that he saw no conflict whatsoever between the covenant of grace rightly understood and unmitigated Calvinism with its absolute sovereignty. Nor were the Reformation principles of *sola fide* and *sola gratia* in any way jeopardized by his covenant doctrine.

---

but heaven is "peculiarly a blessing of the second covenant." Sermon on Ephesians 1:10, Yale MSS, pp. 26-28.
70. "Justification by Faith Alone," *Works*, I, 652.
71. "Justification by Faith Alone," *Works*, I, 653.

10

The Role of the Covenant Concept in Edwards' Theology

The concept of covenant presents itself as a biblical concept. If for no other reason, that certainly makes it a legitimate topic of theological reflection. The covenant theology of Edwards gives a priority, both logically and chronologically, to the covenant of redemption. This covenant, existing as it does from eternity, precedes the covenant of works and the covenant of grace. It prepares the way for them. In time, however, the covenant of works is God's first covenant with man, and this is followed, after the fall, by the covenant of grace.

The development of covenant theology, however, expanded far beyond the purely theological doctrine of the covenant of grace. The covenant of grace became the foundation for what were known as church and civil covenants. Whether such developments were legitimate is not the issue with which we are concerned. What does matter is that such a diverse use of the covenant concept may cause confusion about the specific doctrine of the covenant of grace. It is for that reason that this danger was brought out at the conclusion of Chapter 1 on "Contemporary Considerations."[1] The problem appears when one concludes that a particular theologian, in this case Edwards, accepts, rejects, or alters the doctrine of the covenant. Frequently it is not clearly dis-

---

1. Cf. Chapter 1 above, pp. 14-16.

tinguished which covenant or what aspect of the covenant is meant.

In his book *The Covenant Idea in New England Theology, 1620-1847,* De Jong at one point mentions seven ways the covenant concept is used within Calvinistic churches.[2] This does not even get into the Anabaptist or Arminian use of the covenant concept. The more common division is threefold: the civil covenant, the church covenant, and the covenant of grace.[3]

It is obviously true that the covenant doctrine had implications for Puritans far beyond the purely theological realm. Aldridge writes that, "like all Puritans, Edwards was obsessed by covenants," and "the covenants between God and man ... filled his sermons."[4] "Obsessed" may be a loaded word, but the fact of the covenant concept pervading Edwards' thought cannot be ignored. Further qualification is needed, however, if Edwards' view is going to be in perspective.

The burden of this thesis is to see Edwards' view of the covenant of grace from a theological perspective. Such an approach would undoubtedly be profitable even within a broad covenantal framework. However, for Edwards such an approach is even more justified since he is far less concerned with the broader, nontheological aspects of the covenant which occupied many of his contemporaries. In an article on Edwards and the covenant Conrad Cherry points out this difference between Edwards and the general Puritan emphasis:

---

2. De Jong, *The Covenant Idea in New England Theology, 1620–1847,* p. 50.

3. Cf. Schneider, *The Puritan Mind,* pp. 19-25; and De Jong, *The Covenant Idea in New England Theology, 1620–1847,* pp. 78 ff. On the relation of the covenant of grace to the civil or national covenant, cf. McKee, "The Idea of Covenant in Early English Puritanism (1580-1643)," pp. 207-208, 234, 236. On the relation of the covenant of grace to the church covenant, cf. Edmund S. Morgan, *Visible Saints: The History of a Puritan Idea* (New York, 1963), p. 55, where the one is that "between God and a saved individual, the other between God and a group of presumably saved individuals."

4. Aldridge, *Jonathan Edwards,* pp. 133-134.

The Role of the Covenant Concept in Edwards' Theology   167

> The scope of the Puritan covenant-idea was narrowed for Jonathan Edwards in this sense: it did not assume for him the same importance for an understanding of the saints' social and political life as it had for his forefathers. This is accounted for in large part, of course, by the fact that Massachusetts had long since lost her charter (1684), New England became inclusive of more church groups than "New Israel" congregationalists, and the covenant of grace and the political-social covenants could no longer be considered strictly commensurate.[5]

In ascertaining the role of the covenant in Edwards' theology such qualification becomes extremely helpful in focusing attention on the soteriological relationship between God and man.

It is necessary to take a brief detour from the strictly theological path to see the state of degeneration of covenantal thinking out of which Edwards emerged. The detour is down the path of the Halfway Covenant, and according to some interpreters, it is a path inherent in covenant theology. C. C. Goen shares the rather prevalent feeling that covenant theology tends to Arminianism. According to Goen "Federal Theology . . . was far from impregnable."

> It contained a built-in equivocacy whereby the Arminian camel could get his nose under the Puritan tent so unobtrusively that few of the insiders noticed when the stakes of orthodoxy began to loosen. . . . Theoretically, God still chooses whom he wills, and only the elect can accept the covenant. But practically all of New England's ecclesiastical, political, and social life was interpreted under rubrics derived from the Federal Theology; and the covenant of grace with individual saints was easily transmuted into an external covenant with the nation. As experiential piety waned, it was natural for leaders of the holy commonwealths to stress men's "natural power" to obey the terms of the external covenant, so that if they did what they could . . . possibly God would enable them . . . to believe unto salvation.[6]

The concern became "what, if anything, a sinner might do to

---

5. Conrad C. Cherry, "The Puritan Notion of the Covenant in Jonathan Edwards' Doctrine of Faith," *Church History*, XXXIV (September, 1965), p. 329.
6. "Editor's Introduction" in *The Great Awakening*, p. 11. It should be noted that on the basis of Edwards' distinction of moral and natural necessity in *Freedom of the Will*, he would be totally in opposition to the statement that "only the elect *can* accept the covenant."

prepare himself for conversion and entrance into the covenant of grace," and the resultant doctrinal effect was the Halfway Covenant.[7]

In Reformed theology election and human responsibility are both maintained as essential elements of revelation about the relationship of God with man. It is a foreboding of difficult times for Christ's church whenever either election or human responsibility is emphasized in a way to exclude or weaken the other. In the seventeenth century there was a movement toward such an overemphasis. "Thus out of the undue and unseasonable emphasis which the Puritan theology laid upon the divine sovereignty and man's inability there had sprung a blighting influence which . . . was beginning to deplete the churches of members."[8]

According to Peter de Jong, "their overemphasis on divine election at the expense of human responsibility led them to condone, if not to excuse, the halfheartedness of many birthright members."[9] As a disjunction between the covenant of grace and the church covenant began to appear within the churches,

> the leaders taught that there was "no certain, but only a probable connexion between federal Holyness and Salvation." Hence it was comparatively easy for them to allow those who were merely federally holy to continue as church members. If God did not choose to grant them a vivid experience of regeneration and conversion, they would acquiesce in their fate. Surely it could not be expected of them to force the will of God, who plainly elected some and rejected others according to His own inscrutable purpose. . . . Because the churches affirmed the sovereignty of God in the way in which they did, many used it as an excuse for being

---

7. "Editor's Introduction" in *The Great Awakening*, p. 12.
8. Foster, *A Genetic History of the New England Theology*, p. 31. That which created the Halfway Covenant was "simply the passive theology of the times, which waited for God in the matter of conversion as for a sovereign whose gifts of grace were in his own inscrutable disposal, and without whom man was absolutely unable to do anything" (pp. 34-35).
9. De Jong, *The Covenant Idea in New England Theology, 1670-1847*, p. 107.

content with half-way membership. Increasingly . . . people no longer sought salvation earnestly. . . .[10]

The Halfway Covenant was the method chosen to remedy a problem within the church. It was a case where the remedy may be as bad as the original problem.

> It is not easy to determine whether the Half-way Covenant was the cause or the result of the decline in religious interest so manifest since 1660. To a certain extent it seems to have been both. From these days on until the time of Jonathan Edwards the ministers uttered their lamentations and prophesied their woes over the spiritually unfortunate but materially prosperous and complacent settlements.[11]

At any rate what was a defect or an abuse within this earthly sphere, namely, a credible profession by an unregenerate, became a legitimate half-way point between the totally depraved and the regenerate.

Stoddard's position on the Lord's Supper, says Peter de Jong, is "the logical and necessary outcome" of the Halfway Covenant.

> He allowed the unregenerate to enlarge their use of church privileges and ordinances. . . . In order that the churches might still maintain their hold on the people of the land, the ministers began to emphasize as never before the use of the means. Although it was recognized that only the Lord could change the sinner's heart, he could place himself in a more or less favorable situation to receive divine favor. These included regular attendance upon public worship, prayer and a decent life. To this list Stoddard would add Communion as still another "converting ordinance. . . ." He refused to demand a "relation of the work of God's Spirit upon their hearts" as requisite to Communion. All that was required was a profession of faith and repentance. . . . Stoddard surrendered the Puritan conception of the sacraments as the privilege of the experiential saints only by claiming that the Lord's Table was a "converting ordinance."[12]

---

10. De Jong, *The Covenant Idea in New England Theology, 1620-1847*, p. 121.
11. De Jong, *The Covenant Idea in New England Theology, 1620-1847*, p. 122.
12. De Jong, *The Covenant Idea in New England Theology, 1620-1847*, pp. 128-129.

Haroutunian summarizes the matter simply when he sees the Halfway Covenant and Stoddardism as "moral sincerity" in contrast to "gracious sincerity."

> It was clear to Stoddard and those whom he left to the charge of Edwards that "moral sincerity" is quite sufficient a "qualification for communion." In "owning the Covenant," the believer bound himself to God and to the other people in the church, promising to "profess" the truths of religion and to live a good life. What more could be expected from him than that he should do this with "moral sincerity"! Edwards hesitated for a long time, but at last he came forth with his convictions.[13]

Though Edwards' convictions led to his dismissal from his long pastorate at Northampton, he was later vindicated, and his position prevailed not only in Northampton but throughout New England.[14]

Edwards was not unaware of the problem that existed. He knew there were those who professed publically their faith in Christ who were without true saving faith. Edwards opposed, however, the legitimatizing of such persons as members of the covenant. De Jong writes:

> Edwards repudiated the distinction between an external and an internal covenant. He claimed, however, that one could be a member of the Covenant of Grace either externally or internally, depending on whether or not one was subjectively in possession of saving grace.... What Edwards sought to do was to make active faith as the fruit of God's saving grace requisite for attending Communion. Thus he vigorously opposed Stoddardeanism. Those whose minds were willing to accept Christ but whose con-

---

13. Haroutunian, *Piety versus Moralism,* p. 98.
14. Walker, *Jonathan Edwards: A Profile,* p. 107: "It is interesting to note that one, at least, of those of Edwards' congregation prominent in procuring his removal, and esteemed by the Northampton pastor his most energetic opponent, Joseph Hawley, Edwards' cousin, and a leading lawyer and politician, afterward not only privately but publicly avowed his regret and repentance for what had been done. And Edwards' contention in the principal subject of this controversy was not without abundant ultimate fruitage. His friends, notably his pupil, Rev. Dr. Joseph Bellamy, carried forward his attack on Stoddardeanism and the Halfway Covenant, with the result that, by the first decade of the nineteenth century, when Edwards had been fifty years in his grave, the system had been generally set aside by the Congregational churches."

duct was not in harmony therewith he claimed "are not truly pious" but have "guile, disguise, and false appearance."[15]

Writing on the qualifications for communion, Edwards does not absolutely reject the use of the distinction between "the internal and external covenant." But he makes it clear that it must not be understood as "really and properly *two* covenants of grace; but only that those who profess the one only covenant of grace, are of two sorts."[16] The distinction, according to Edwards, is between "those who comply with it *internally* and really, and others who do so only *externally*, that is, in profession and visibility."[17] But the important dimension which Edwards insisted upon is that the only legitimate external or visible professing of the covenant of grace is a profession that one is really and internally a member of the covenant of grace.[18] Haroutunian states Edwards' position in these words:

> The covenant with which a member of the church binds himself to God is a "covenant of grace," so that none but those whom the operation of the Holy Spirit in their hearts has regenerated into the spiritual life may or really can "own the Covenant."[19]

The covenant concept has a broad usage in Puritan thought. It would be wrong to conclude that Edwards rejected or ceased to use the concept in its broader implica-

---

15. De Jong, *The Covenant Idea in New England Theology, 1620-1847*, pp. 145-146.
16. "An Humble Inquiry," *Works*, I, 443. Bavinck reflects the same sort of concern in opposing a twofold external and internal covenant. *Gereformeerde Dogmatiek*, III, 227: "Het verbond der genade is één; en de uit- en inwendige zijde ervan, schoon hier op aarde niet samenvallend, kunnen en mogen niet van elkander losgemaakt en naast elkaar gelegd worden." Berkhof, *Reformed Dogmatics*, I, 272, writes that the dualism of an external and internal covenant "is not warranted by Scripture." "The impression is created that there is a covenant in which man can assume an entirely correct position without saving faith; but the Bible knows of no such covenant." Expressing the same concern of Edwards, Berkhof acknowledges the view of those who speak of "an external and internal side to the covenant of grace." He cites Mastricht as an example. Cf. also De Jong, *The Covenant Idea in New England Theology, 1620-1847*, p. 250.
17. "An Humble Inquiry," *Works*, I, 443.
18. "An Humble Inquiry," *Works*, I, 443.
19. Haroutunian, *Piety versus Moralism*, p. 99.

tions. But primarily the covenant for Edwards meant the covenant of grace, a use that was pre-eminently theological. Thus when he uses the covenant concept, it appears most frequently in the context of salvation history and the relationship of saving faith. As already alluded to, and as will become more apparent in our chapter on faith, the covenant was used by Edwards to illustrate the nature of the relationship between God and man which is fundamentally the faith-relationship.

Conrad Cherry indicated the narrowing of the covenant concept by Edwards and emphasizes the primacy of the faith-relation. He writes that "covenant theology was most valuable to Edwards for a description of the nature of the saints' relation to God in faith."[20] Cherry finds "two recurrent motifs" in Edwards' doctrine of the covenant of grace which are fundamental to his doctrine of faith and its relationship to the covenant scheme. The one is "God's 'indebtedness' to man in the covenant of grace," and the other is "man's faith as the 'condition' of the covenant with God."[21] Both of these will be fundamental issues in the doctrinal discussion in Part III.

Some have criticized Edwards for this emphasis. De Jong, specifically referring to "The History of Redemption," criticized Edwards as "individualistic."

> His emphasis was individualistic and thus did not do justice to organic relations. Without a conception of the covenant which takes its rise in the organic relation in which the members of the race stand to their head, and again the relations between that head and God, and finally the relations obtaining between the three persons of the Godhead, the whole idea of the covenant becomes no more than an anthropomorphic representation of God's dealings with men, which must sooner or later lose its hold on religious thought and life.[22]

---

20. Cherry, *The Theology of Jonathan Edwards*, p. 109.
21. Cherry, *The Theology of Jonathan Edwards*, p. 109.
22. De Jong, *The Covenant Idea in New England Theology, 1620-1847*, p. 150. See pp. 198-200 where he indicates the men of the "New Divinity" continued this individualized concern.

Jan Ridderbos sees a dualism in Edwards between the revivalism emphasis on spirituality and the natural realm.[23] Closely connected with this "dualism," he also finds an individualism in Edwards which he feels is unwarranted.[24] These critics believe Edwards emphasized the individual, spiritual relationship between God and man at the expense of the broader organic relationship between God and the whole of creation.

While we do not feel this criticism is justified and while we believe Edwards had an unusually healthy view of the organic relationship between God and the whole of creation, these criticisms of individualism point up the fact of Edwards' awareness that the covenantal relationship between the individual and his Creator is central to biblical Christianity. This can never be an area of either/or, but the reality of both unity and individualism must be maintained. Redemption is the message of biblical Christianity, and while God works within covenantal relationships of communities—His people—each member of that community stands individually before the countenance of God (*coram Deo*).

In man's relationship to God regeneration is the work of the Holy Spirit upon an individual heart; faith is the response of the individual; and the covenant blessings are promised to the individual. One may only conclude that if such "individualism" contradicts the organic relationships revealed in Scripture, then the central message of Scripture contradicts the organic relationships revealed in Scripture. Edwards is unaware of any such contradiction, and he is in good company with such a view.

The covenant of grace, as a way of describing the saints' relation to God, is a doctrinal feature that has been present in differing degrees of elaboration throughout the history of Reformed theology. The distinguishing mark of Calvinism is often identified as an emphasis on the absolute sovereignty of God. Properly understood, that is an accurate designation. Such a

---

23. Ridderbos, *De Theologie van Jonathan Edwards*, p. 314.
24. Ridderbos, *De Theologie van Jonathan Edwards*, p. 315.

description, however, may never be permitted if it is intended to deny the emphasis of Calvinism on human responsibility. Scripture honors the human activity no less than the divine sovereignty. Edwards saw, as his Calvinistic forefathers saw, that the covenant was a biblical idea capable of expressing the correlation between divine sovereignty and human responsibility.

If the covenant of grace is open to abuse, it is in part because the Scriptures are open to abuse. The danger is not only potential but real that a false emphasis on divine sovereignty can result in hypercalvinism or fatalism, and a false emphasis on human ability can and has resulted in Arminianism or historic liberalism.

The striking feature about Jonathan Edwards is his awareness—indeed his struggles against—both of these dangers. His use of the covenant concept as well as his activism militate against any charge of neglecting human responsibility. Yet if ever there was an opponent of Arminianism and defender of divine sovereignty, it is Edwards. The moral inability taught in *Freedom of the Will* in no way precluded Edwards' doctrine of the covenant of grace. Man's role in the covenant is to believe, but Edwards never suggested that occurred outside the divine initiative in which God granted the elect the gift of faith. "It never seems to have occurred to him that anyone would suppose that there was any inconsistency between his predestinarianism and his covenant doctrine."[25] Edwards' use of the covenant of grace without surrendering to Arminianism should suggest the error in trying to conclude that he either lost his Calvinism *or* threw over the covenant. To Edwards, "no reconciliation seemed necessary where no inconsistency existed."[26]

The task for the interpreter becomes one of ascertaining where the boundaries are in utilizing a covenant framework. In terms of this study, what are the relations and implications of crucial theological perspectives for the covenant of grace as set forth in Edwards' writings.

---

25. Gerstner, *Steps to Salvation*, p. 186.
26. Gerstner, *Steps to Salvation*, p. 186.

PART III

DOCTRINES RELATED TO THE COVENANT OF GRACE

In efficacious grace we are not merely passive, nor yet does God do some, and we do the rest. But God does all, and we do all. God produces all, and we act all. For that is what he produces, *viz.* our own acts. God is the only proper author and fountain; we only are the proper actors. We are, in different respects, wholly passive and wholly active.

In the Scriptures the same things are represented as from God and from us. God is said to convert, and men are said to convert and turn. God makes a new heart, and we are commanded to make us a new heart. God circumcises the heart, and we are commanded to circumcise our own hearts; not merely because we must use the means in order to the effect, but the effect itself is our act and our duty. These things are agreeable to that text, "God worketh in you both to will and to do."[1]

---

1. "Miscellaneous Remarks," *Works,* II, 557.

11

Jonathan Edwards
and Divine Sovereignty

It is appropriate that a consideration of doctrines in Edwards' theology explicitly or implicitly related to the covenant of grace begin with the doctrine of the sovereignty of God. This doctrine was subjectively crucial for Edwards' conversion, even as it is objectively essential to any conversion, and it remained a fundamental and determinative factor in his theology. In fact it is this doctrine of absolute sovereignty that in the eyes of some interpreters militates against Edwards being an advocate of the covenant of grace.

Edwards' own description of his conversion emphasizes a recognition of the absolute sovereignty of God in salvation. What "used to appear like a horrible doctrine" to Edwards became a "*delightful* conviction" at his conversion: "Absolute sovereignty is what I love to ascribe to God. But my first conviction was not so."[1] The full awareness of divine sovereignty was for Edwards not a doctrine only, but a "sense." "... There came into my mind so sweet a sense of the glorious *majesty* and *grace* of God, as I know not how to express."[2] This "conviction" remained with Edwards throughout his life and is a necessary factor in how his covenant doctrine is interpreted.

The centrality of the sovereignty doctrine is not missed by the biographers. Edwards' first address at the "public lecture" in Boston in the spring of 1731 is given great promi

---

1. "Memoirs," *Works,* I, liv-lv.
2. "Memoirs," *Works,* I, lv.

nence in many books. It was to be his first published work and was entitled "God Glorified in Man's Dependence." Alexander Allen, a biographer of the last century, saw this sermon as representative and said of Edwards, ". . . Like an ancient prophet he felt called to deliver his burden."[3] The burden was the absolute dependence of man upon God.

Perhaps no one has put any more interpretive value on Edwards' Boston lecture, nor done it in such a brilliant and fascinating way, than Perry Miller. The first chapter of his biographical study, *Jonathan Edwards,* is almost entirely given over to this one lecture and its circumstances.[4] The argument for Miller's influential interpretation of Edwards can be found there. But the importance of this lecture in Miller's opinion, and its historical significance as a contrast to the Puritanism from which he will extricate Edwards, may be seen in the paragraph Miller chooses to place at the very end of the last chapter of his two-volume work on *The New England Mind.* At the end of two massive volumes dealing with New England Puritanism, he closes with a paragraph on Edwards that sounds like the dawning of a new age.

> By the end of 1730 it was evident that everybody had spoken from whom ideas or words were apt to come, had indicated what he might or might not contribute to the solution. Or rather, all except one. The next spring it was known that Jonathan Edwards would come to the Harvard Commencement, and he was pressed to give the Thursday lecture. Solomon Stoddard's successor announced that he would speak on *God Glorified in the Work of Redemption, by the Greatness of Man's Dependence upon him, in the Whole of it.* That man must depend upon God in the work of the covenant was always a basic axiom of New England. That he should depend upon God in reforming the sins he committed in his independence was the premise of all jeremiads. Yet somehow, in a century of American experience, the greatness of man's dependency had unaccountably become a euphemism for the greatness of man. Possibly that was because this greatness had not yet been thoroughly considered in the whole of it.[5]

---

3. Allen, *Jonathan Edwards,* pp. 56-57.
4. Miller, *Jonathan Edwards,* pp. 3-34.
5. Miller, *NEM: Colony to Province,* p. 485.

An understanding—or rather a misunderstanding—of Edwards and his doctrine of sovereignty is the foundation on which Miller's interpretation of Edwards and the covenant is built. The fundamental issue is here brought into focus. Puritans professed to believe the doctrine of sovereignty. Their profession is not at issue. The issue, as Miller saw it, was the co-existence of the covenant doctrine. He saw in the covenant idea, or "Federal Theology" as it was called, "a way for human enterprise in the midst of a system of determinism."[6] However, in the Boston lecture Edwards presented what Miller saw as unmitigated Calvinism, and the inference he drew from that fact became his manifesto. "The Federal Theology is conspicuous in his sermon by its utter absence."[7]

Significant revision of Miller's interpretation has occurred in numerous writings. To a large extent, however, the retreat is only partial. Conrad Cherry, for example, argues repeatedly against Miller's view. However, Cherry's conclusion is that Edwards was a covenant theologian almost against his better judgment.[8] The uneasiness remains that arises from a presumption of a necessary conflict between the doctrines of covenant and sovereignty.

We return to Miller briefly, not because he is alone, but because his interpretation is so influential and places the issue in such bold relief. The redeemed are in everything dependent upon God, and so the choice was clear. As Miller paraphrases John Taylor and claims Edwards' approval, one must either return to "unmitigated Calvinism, wherein the naked will of God decrees and compels every action," or "jettison

---

6. Miller, *Jonathan Edwards*, p. 30.
7. Miller, *Jonathan Edwards*, p. 30.
8. Cherry, *The Theology of Jonathan Edwards*, pp. 122-123. "During Edwards' 'better moments,' . . . he was careful to designate faith as the 'condition' of the covenant only in the sense that in faith the covenant and its blessings are concretely *received*." Did Edwards ever imply more? Evidently Cherry thinks so. ". . . He continued to speak with some abandon of faith as the human condition of the covenant, thereby involving himself in the same problems which had faced his Puritan forefathers."

the theology of election and predestination."⁹ Anyone conversant with historical Reformed theology will readily note the gratuitous nature of the assumption that covenant and sovereignty are mutually exclusive.

Two factors were undoubtedly influential in the failure to properly understand Edwards in relation to these two doctrines. One is an error of historical interpretation concerning the Puritan's alleged "modification" of the doctrine of sovereignty. The other is the error, historically or theologically, in grasping the doctrine of sovereignty.

The first bias affecting our understanding of Edwards is the widely accepted thesis that Puritanism represented a modification of Calvinism, especially in regard to the doctrine of sovereignty. In her biography, Ola Winslow states that New England changed the "unfathomable, unpredictable God of Calvin" into a "reasonable being."

> In fact, Calvin's God had not crossed to the American continent at all, but by 1620 had already suffered comfortable modification at the hands of various Cambridge divines: John Preston, William Perkins, Richard Sibbes, and notably William Ames, whose *Medulla Sacrae Theologiae* became the vade mecum of Harvard and Yale divinity students for another hundred years.¹⁰

Perry Miller is convinced the covenant doctrine was not intentionally a departure from Calvinism or an inculcating of free will, but it was "a marvelous strategem for getting around an immovable obstacle in theology," namely, sovereign election.¹¹ Miller sees an "implicit antagonism" between the "theological conception of God and the God of the covenant." Again their sense of a sovereign God would not permit them to do this intentionally.

> However, even while paying the proper respect to the terror and the fury of God, they could contrive to take many steps in these

---

9. Miller, *Jonathan Edwards*, p. 115.
10. Winslow, *Jonathan Edwards, 1703-1758*, pp. 154-155.
11. Miller, *NEM: 17th Century*, p. 395. Miller's position is based on a separation of election and covenant, something the Puritans generally would not do. Certainly Edwards held them in close relationship.

directions as soon as they had seized upon their brilliant discovery that the absolute monarch had voluntarily engaged Himself to regular procedures and bottled up His prerogative in a covenant. The rest followed surely and easily from this promise....[12]

One marvels at the surprise, as though the covenant was a totally new discovery with the Puritans.

When Miller concludes that Edwards returned to "pure, unmitigated Calvinism" in rejecting the covenant and teaching absolute sovereignty, he is not only short-changing Edwards but Calvin as well. Marsden writes:

> Thus when Miller pictures the reformer turning in his grave as William Ames announces that since Abraham there has been one covenant, "yet the manner ... of administering this new Covenant, hath not always beene one and the same, ..." Miller is failing to recognize that in this very instance, "Ames is merely quoting Calvin, as every Calvinist theologian did."[13]

Marsden refers to Calvin's sermons on Deuteronomy as providing the "fullest exposition of the implications of the covenant of grace for understanding God's sovereignty and man's responsibility" and concludes:

> These sermons leave no doubt that Perry Miller was mistaken in supposing that the Puritan contrived the covenant concept in order to circumscribe the sovereignty of Calvin's God or to transform "the hitherto stern Deity" into a "condescending," "kindly and solicitous being."[14]

While there were no doubt various abuses of the covenant concept in an un-Calvinistic direction, the covenant concept is present in Calvin and Edwards, as well as the Reformed-Puritan tradition in between.

Calvin's strong doctrine of absolute sovereignty did not preclude the covenant; nor did the Puritan covenant doctrine preclude absolute sovereignty. Certainly Edwards did not see a contradiction. Yet his sermon "God Glorified in Man's Dependence" is used to prove otherwise. Goodwin makes an

---

12. Miller, *NEM: 17th Century*, pp. 485-486.
13. Marsden, *Church History*, XXXIX, 102.
14. Marsden, *Church History*, XXXIX, 102.

important point in reminding us that Edwards' contemporaries did not see this sermon as an innovation.

> Edwards' first public lecture and first published work has been treated as a crucial signpost in American intellectual life on the grounds that it marked the first presentation by a New Englander of Calvinism unrelieved by the softening effects of either the covenant or covert Arminianism. Did contemporaries consider Edwards an innovator? Far from it. They thought his sermon a strong and vigorous statement of traditional doctrines. Thomas Prince and William Cooper praised it precisely because the sermon taught New England's established theology.[15]

Edwards' doctrine of the covenant of grace and divine sovereignty is difficult to fully appreciate if his predecessors are falsely seen as modifying the doctrine of sovereignty. The interpretive error is to assume that absolute sovereignty and the covenant of grace are necessarily in conflict. The overwhelming response of how Reformed theologians have dealt with these issues would confirm that an assumption of conflict is gratuitous.

The second factor hindering a proper evaluation of Edwards, closely related to the first, is an incorrect understanding of the Calvinistic doctrine of sovereignty. If one accepts the equation that Calvinist sovereignty equals predestination equals fatalism, and if one accepts the fact that Edwards held to the Calvinist doctrine of sovereignty, the conclusion that he would reject a covenant doctrine which honored human activity seems plausible.

Peter Gay represents just such an errant view of Calvinist sovereignty in his view of Edwards.

> ... Edwards set man's historical situation into a supernatural frame: man is helpless in the hands of God, incapable of resisting the influx of grace or the decree of condemnation. The Calvinist drama—it is worth saying once again—is wholly predestined: its resolution—eternal salvation or eternal damnation—is unaffected

---

15. Goodwin, *New England Quarterly*, XLI, 228. Cf. the "Advertisement to the Reader" for this sermon written by Prince and Cooper, *Works*, II, 2.

by the actions of men, and takes place not in this world but in the next.[16]

To say that salvation or damnation "is unaffected by the actions of men" is so totally contrary to Calvinism that one feels almost apologetic in stating it. The notion that God drags a person screaming and kicking into heaven against that person's will, or that he condemns to eternal damnation those who willingly choose to receive eternal life in Christ, is as contrary to Edwards as it is to Scripture. It is precisely that it does matter what a man does that the covenant concept tries to elucidate.

In "The Marrow of Puritan Divinity" Perry Miller calls Arminianism an attempt to relate God and man, and the basic error he claims is not one of the "five points" but "its exaltation of human reason."[17] In light of Miller's designation of Calvin's hidden, inscrutable God one can see his bias. Miller thus sees Edwards as a return to the "irrational" God of Calvin. However, for the orthodox and clearly for Edwards, the issue was precisely that the Arminian position was irrational. One need only read *Freedom of the Will* to see this. Miller nevertheless sees in the covenant almost a kind of cheating by professing Calvinists to explain what was inexplicable. They professed full sovereignty, "but in practical life the dogmatic rigors of absolute predestination are materially softened."[18]

It is quite clear that Miller's understanding of sovereignty and his evaluation of what Puritans had done to the doctrine is a liability in looking at Edwards accurately. Because Miller is a brilliant scholar, he is not unaware of the Puritan's own insistence to the contrary of his conclusions. But what he gives with one hand he takes away with the other. In answer

---

16. Peter Gay, "Jonathan Edwards: An American Tragedy," *Jonathan Edwards: A Profile*, p. 243.
17. Miller, "The Marrow of Puritan Divinity," *Errand into the Wilderness*, pp. 56-57.
18. Miller, "The Marrow of Puritan Divinity," *Errand into the Wilderness*, p. 73.

to his students' questions as to why Puritans exerted themselves at all since they believed that everything was predestined, Miller writes:

> ... What is hard to get moderns to comprehend about the founders of New England is, first, that for them the doctrine of predestination did not have as a psychological consequence the surrender of all volition but rather that it was a powerful stimulus to activity; second and more important, this tremendous exertion being made in a social context, the incentive was therefore strengthened by an awful realization that without it the whole enterprise might fail.[19]

Having affirmed the fact that predestinarian Puritans vigorously believed in exertion, he yet will deny that Edwards held to the covenant with its implicit exertion on the basis of a sermon Edwards preached on sovereignty!

In general it can be seen that more recent students of Puritanism have retreated from Miller's strained interpretation of Calvin's God as "an arbitrary despot" with Puritanism softening of that doctrine. However, the issue is not settled thereby, and the question of Edwards' sovereignty doctrine and the covenant of grace remains.

In ascertaining the role of sovereignty in Edwards' thought it is instructive to note first that in his theology absolute sovereignty was essential if there was to be salvation at all. The biblical presupposition for this is found in Edwards' manuscript sermon on Romans 3:13-18 in which the doctrine is that "the nature of man in his fallen state is utterly and universally corrupt."[20]

In another manuscript sermon on John 5:43, Edwards declares that "God is the great and first author of the whole affair," and salvation "has its foundation in the eternal counsels and purposes of God," who "appointed the Saviour" and "called the Saviour to His work."[21] This is necessary since

---
19. Perry Miller, "The Resolution of Nonconformity," *Puritanism and the American Experience,* p. 235.
20. Sermon on Romans 3:13-18, Yale MSS, p. 4.
21. Sermon on John 5:43, Yale MSS, p. 5.

Jonathan Edwards and Divine Sovereignty

man is opposed to the Gospel by nature; his heart is against God and Jesus Christ and "is opposite to the benefits of Christ that the Gospel reveals and offers."[22] In regard to the dreadful condition of those in a natural or unsaved condition Edwards says:

> They have nothing on which to depend for conversion. They have nothing in the world, by which to persuade themselves that they shall ever be converted. Left to themselves, they never will repent and turn to God. If they are ever converted, therefore, it is God who must do it.... It is but a peradventure, whether God will ever give them repentance to the acknowledging of the truth. 2 Tim. ii. 25.[23]

In a sermon on Hosea 13:9 Edwards' doctrine is that the sinners who are saved are saved by God.[24] Connected with this is the fact that man is unable to save himself since he offended an infinite God and "an infinite price must be offered to satisfy for the injury . . . which price God alone can be the author of."[25] The doctrine of a sermon on Revelation 17:4 states: "Those that are Christ's and belonging to him 'tis of God that they are so."[26] Left to themselves, says Edwards, "they would be like the rest of the world," separated from Christ and His benefits.[27]

In his sermon "God Glorified in Man's Dependence" Edwards points to the absolute dependence upon God's sovereign grace for salvation as he contrasts the covenant of works with the covenant of grace (the sermon Miller uses to prove Edwards threw over the covenant doctrine).

> But now we are dependent on the grace of God for much more; we stand in need of grace, not only to bestow glory upon us, but

---

22. Sermon on John 5:43, Yale MSS, pp. 5-8.
23. Sermon on Acts 16:29-30, *Works*, II, 823. Cf. Haroutunian, *Piety versus Moralism*, p. 46.
24. Sermon on Hosea 13:9, Yale MSS, p. 1.
25. Sermon on Hosea 13:9, Yale MSS, pp. 1-2.
26. Sermon on Revelation 17:4, Yale MSS, p. 4.
27. Sermon on Revelation 17:4, Yale MSS, p. 4. According to Edwards those in Christ did not distinguish themselves, "but that God distinguished them from the day of eternity . . . He gave Him in His eternal decree and covenant all that should afterwards should be with him . . ." (p. 5).

> to deliver us from hell and eternal wrath. Under the first covenant we depended on God's goodness to give us the reward of righteousness; and so we do now: but we stand in need of God's free and sovereign grace to give us that righteousness; to pardon our sin, and release us from the guilt and infinite demerit of it.
> ... We are dependent on the goodness of God for more now than under the first covenant. ... We are now more dependent on God's arbitrary and sovereign good pleasure. ... Now when fallen man is made holy, it is from mere and arbitrary grace.[28]

In the first covenant by God's grace man contributed something—his obedience which when perfect is righteousness. As sinner, man is without that option, and if he is saved, God must sovereignly provide both the righteousness and the reward of that righteousness.

In a sermon on John 1:47 Edwards argues that conversion is a great thing because God does it. " 'Tis no very great thing to [be] externally an Israelite, ... to be baptized and come to meetings, ... to put on external show of devotion, [or] ... to have religious affections. ..."[29] However, conversion is a great thing because it is "the fruit of the eternal ... love of God," and being "drawn to Christ is the fruit of God's everlasting love" which "is a particular love."[30] So great is the change involved that the person "becomes a new creature."[31]

God's sovereignty is even manifest in ordering events so as to teach us our need and take away our self-confidence. Edwards notes the trial of Peter at the hands of Satan and observes that from God's sovereign perspective the goal was to sift him as wheat "that there might be a separation made between you and your corruptions, your pride and self-confidence, as wheat is separated from chaff by sifting."[32]

In Edwards' own life the doctrine of absolute, divine sovereignty was no abstract doctrine. His personal conversion

---

28. Sermon on 1 Corinthians 1:29-31, *Works*, II, 4.
29. Sermon on John 1:47, Yale MSS, pp. 4-5.
30. Sermon on John 1:47, Yale MSS, pp. 6-8.
31. Sermon on John 1:47, Yale MSS, p. 13.
32. "Notes on the Bible," *Works*, II, 790.

is described in his own words with a tremendous awareness of the role of the sovereign God in the whole affair and his own resistance to the idea prior to conversion.[33] The life of Edwards became dominated with rapturous expressions of his passionate sense of the glory of God and His sovereign activity.[34]

Schneider in his *The Puritan Mind* says Edwards' doctrine was seen as "old-fashioned" by the older clergy, but its power and influence came from the fact that "it was a fruit of his own inner struggles."[35] Allen in his biographical work indicates the change which occurred in his conversion had the result of "putting him in sympathy with the tenets of Calvinistic theology."[36]

Edwards would concur in this implicit equation between genuine conversion, a right knowledge of God's sovereignty, and the tenets of Calvinistic theology. His comments on the conversion of a man he loved deeply, David Brainerd, confirm Edwards' own position on the matter.

> His conversion was no confirming and perfecting of moral principles and habits . . . but entirely a supernatural work. . . .
> A very little while before, his mind was full of the same cavils against the doctrines of God's sovereign grace, which are made by Arminians. . . .
> In his conversion, he was brought to see the glory of that way of salvation by Christ, that is taught in what are called the *doctrines of grace*. . . . And if his conversion was any real conversion . . . then this one grand principle, on which depends the whole difference between Calvinists and Arminians, is undeniable, *viz.* that the grace or virtue of truly good men not only differs from the virtue of others in *degree*, but even in *nature* and *kind*. . . .
> . . . .

---

33. "Memoirs," *Works*, I, liv-lv.
34. Cf. for example, Joseph G. Haroutunian, "Jonathan Edwards: Theologian of the Great Commandment," *Theology Today*, I (October, 1944), pp. 361-377. "God blessed Jonathan Edwards with a unique sense and knowledge of His glory. . . . A love of God's 'infinite perfections' is . . . the clue for understanding both his life and writings" (p. 361).
35. Schneider, *The Puritan Mind*, p. 105.
36. Allen, *Jonathan Edwards*, p. 36.

> So that it is very evident, Mr. Brainerd's religion was wholly correspondent to what is called the *Calvinistical scheme*, and was the effect of those doctrines applied to his heart. . . .[37]

Edwards was of the conviction that until a man acknowledged his own helplessness, and until he willingly accepted the absolute sovereignty of God with joy, the gift of free grace could have no meaning for him.

In a sermon on Romans 9:18 Edwards teaches that "God exercises his sovereignty in the eternal salvation of men" and provides the following definition of sovereignty:

> The sovereignty of God is his absolute, independent right of disposing of all creatures according to his own pleasure. . . .
> 1. In opposition to any constraint. . . .
> 2. In opposition to its being under the will of another. . . .
> 3. In opposition to any proper obligation.[38]

In this same sermon he further states that "God can either bestow salvation on any of the children of men, or refuse it, without any prejudice to the glory of any of his attributes, except where he has been pleased to declare, that he will or will not bestow it."[39]

The close relationship between covenant, sovereignty, and election is not new to Reformed theology. Heppe cites Wyttenbach: " 'Since the covenant of grace is the execution of the testament of grace, and this testament is identical with the decree of election, it is manifest that God's eternal election is the foundation of the covenant of grace.' "[40] Wilcox in his study on "New England Covenant Theology" stresses this:

> Although the foundation of the covenant of grace is laid in the covenant of redemption, the key which unlocks the covenant for man is the doctrine of predestination. . . . Thus it is through the decree of God concerning the final end of man, that the creature

---

37. "Some Reflections and Observations on the Preceding Memoirs, &c of the Rev. David Brainerd," *Works*, II, 453-454.
38. Sermon on Romans 9:18, *Works*, II, 850.
39. Sermon on Romans 9:18, *Works*, II, 850.
40. Heppe, *Reformed Dogmatics*, p. 379.

is engrafted into the covenant of grace. Without predestination and election there is no possibility of man covenanting with God.[41]

Wilcox then relates this to sovereignty:

The importance of the doctrine of predestination is the emphasis that it places upon the sovereignty of God. . . . All is of God. . . . The material cause of the covenant of grace is election. . . . The desired emphasis is that God alone is the initiator of the covenant of grace.[42]

Edwards refers to the ninth chapter of Romans as "a more minute discussion of the sovereignty of God in electing some to eternal life, and rejecting others, than is found in any other part of the Bible."[43] In a sermon on 1 Peter 2:9, Edwards teaches that "Christians are chosen by God from the rest of the world." "No foreseen excellency in the elected is the motive that influences God to choose them," rather "election is only from his good pleasure."[44] In one of his "Miscellanies" Edwards emphasizes that there are no preconditions from the side of man and that one does not know whether he is elect until the promise is performed.[45] Election, therefore, demonstrates the sovereignty of God.

God's thus electing a certain definite number from among fallen men from all eternity, is a manifestation of his glory. It shows the glory of the divine sovereignty. God hereby declares himself the absolute disposer of the creature; he shows us how far his sovereignty and dominion extend, in eternity choosing some and passing by others, and leaving them to perish. God here appears in a majesty that is unparalleled.[46]

One dare not miss the point that for Edwards sovereignty was absolute, not only in terms of quality but also quantitatively. The full title of Edwards' first public lecture in Boston was "God Glorified in the Work of Redemption, by the Greatness of Man's Dependence upon Him in the Whole of

---

41. Wilcox, "New England Covenant Theology," p. 118.
42. Wilcox, "New England Covenant Theology," p. 127.
43. Sermon on Romans 9:18, *Works*, II, 849-850.
44. Sermon on 1 Peter 2:9, *Works*, II, 937.
45. "Miscellanies," No. 163, Yale MSS.
46. Sermon on 1 Peter 2:9, *Works*, II, 938.

It." The burden on Edwards' heart was to destroy the notion that man contributed anything to his salvation. The dependence is "absolute and universal." "... They are dependent on him for all, and are dependent on him every way."[47]

The absolute dependency on God inherent in the doctrine of sovereignty parallels a statement of Edwards in his remarks on "Efficacious Grace."

> ... God has contrived to exclude our glorying; that we should be wholly and every way dependent on God, for the moral and natural good that belongs to salvation; and that we have all from the hand of God, by his power and grace. And certainly this is wholly inconsistent with the idea that our holiness is wholly from ourselves. . . .[48]

Thus in a sermon on 1 Corinthians 10:11, Edwards warns those seeking salvation not to "trust in the works of their own hands as the children of Israel did."[49] He drew the analogy of the Israelites in the wilderness making an idol out of their golden ear-rings and ornaments which they trusted instead of the God of Israel and sinners making "an idol of their own righteousness" and trusting that "to bring them to heaven."[50]

In the application of a sermon on Romans 9:18 Edwards makes this statement on sovereignty as pertains to the comprehensiveness of it:

> Hence we learn how absolutely we are dependent on God in this great matter of the eternal salvation of our souls. We are dependent not only on his wisdom to contrive a way to accomplish it, and on his power to bring it to pass, but we are dependent on his mere will and pleasure in the affair. We depend on the sovereign will of God for every thing belonging to it, from the foundation to the top-stone.[51]

Edwards, as with all proponents of the Reformed doctrine of sovereignty and predestination, affirmed that means as well

---

47. Sermon on 1 Corinthians 1:29-31, *Works*, II, 3.
48. "Miscellaneous Remarks," *Works*, II, 560.
49. Sermon on 1 Corinthians 10:11, Yale MSS, p. 33.
50. Sermon on 1 Corinthians 10:11, Yale MSS, pp. 33-34.
51. Sermon on Romans 9:18, *Works*, II, 853.

as ends, secondary causes as well as primary causes, are predestined. Though this will be dealt with more in a later chapter, it is important to affirm the truth of it now as part of Edwards' understanding of sovereignty.

The implications for the covenant of grace are obvious once it is clear that an elect person's believing is part of God's sovereign predestination. In "Miscellany" No. 63 Edwards states clearly what is foundational throughout his thought.

> If God ever determined in the general, that some of mankind should certainly be saved, and did not leave it altogether undetermined, whether ever so much as one soul of all mankind should believe in Christ; it must be that he determined, that some particular persons should certainly believe in him....[52]

On the principle, articulated in *Freedom of the Will*, that an effect is only as certain as the cause, God's *not* predestinating the belief (faith not given by God) would mean "it was not as yet determined whether he should ever redeem one soul, or have any mediatorial kingdom at all."[53]

Thus it is that faith is the means to salvation; indeed it is a necessary means and thus called a "condition" of the covenant of grace, and yet belief may not be called the "cause" of salvation in the sense it moves God's will. Ames would be representative here in reflecting both Edwards and Calvinism in general:

> Here it is rightly said that God wills one thing to exist in order to produce another. But it cannot be said that that one thing is properly a cause whereby the will of God is moved internally to appoint the other thing.... There is no cause of God's will outside of itself.
> ....
> ... Although he wills many things which will not take place except upon some antecedent act of the creature, God's act of willing does not itself properly depend upon the act of the creature. And it is not right ... to attribute to God that imperfect willing which is called "woulding" [velleitas] in the schools. This

---

52. "Miscellanies," No. 63, Yale MSS.
53. "Miscellanies," No. 63, Yale MSS.

does not agree with an omniscient, omnipotent, and infinitely blessed nature.[54]

The use of such terms as "means," "cause," "instrument," and "condition" of the covenant must be seen in light of this understanding of sovereignty.

When Edwards attributes salvation to God, he means that God is the author of all the circumstances in the application of the redemptive work of Christ.[55] Not only is God "the author of all the ordinances of the Gospel,"[56] but He does what needs to be done upon the heart of man in order to receive salvation.[57]

> 'Tis God that excites and enables men to do all that they do in order to their salvation after a principle of grace is infused.... 'Tis God that makes them rise up and open the door and let him into the hearts and make them willingly yield themselves unto him to be his, 'tis the Father that draws and makes him run as it were into the arms of his grace and love. He does this by shining into the heart and making a discovery of the sufficiency and excellency of Jesus. And 'tis of God that Christians are enabled to live a holy life, which is necessary to eternal life as it is the way of it, tho Godly men can't exert one holy action without God....[58]

God does elect, and part of the decree is changed hearts and holy acts.

What must be said time and time again in light of fre-

---

54. Ames, *The Marrow of Theology*, p. 98. Concerning this and notes 52 and 53 above, it should be noted that Edwards expressed himself differently from Ames inasmuch as he used certainty and necessity interchangeably with regard to predestined means. Ames writes: "The will of God does not imply a necessity in all future things, but only a certainty in regard to the event. Thus the event was certain that Christ's bones should not be broken.... But there was no necessity imposed upon the soldiers...." *The Marrow of Theology*, p. 99. The use of "imposed" suggests that their intent was the same. Edwards would equate "imposed" with his distinction of "natural necessity," while not considering an action resulting from a "moral necessity" as "imposed." Charles Hodge, however, feels that Edwards' distinction does not relieve the conflict and prefers to distinguish between certainty and necessity. *Systematic Theology*, 3 volumes (Grand Rapids, n. d.), II, pp. 284-288. The desire is to express the same truth, though Edwards' use is more consistent.
55. Sermon on Hosea 13:9, Yale MSS, p. 4.
56. Sermon on Hosea 13:9, Yale MSS, p. 5.
57. Sermon on Hosea 13:9, Yale MSS, pp. 6-7.
58. Sermon on Hosea 13:9, Yale MSS, pp. 9-10.

quently propounded "evidence" that Edwards threw over the whole covenant scheme is that he advocated the active responsibility of man even as he advocated absolute sovereignty. God is sovereign in salvation, even "in the whole of it." But part of that whole decreed by God is our "willing," our "believing," our "obeying," and our "covenanting." Paul, Augustine, Calvin, the majority of the Puritans, and Edwards all found a sovereign God and an active man to be not only biblical but consistent. Precisely what Miller calls "consistent Calvinism" is neither Calvinism nor consistent in a theology informed by Scripture. It is also un-Edwardsean.

Allen was mystified at Edwards' preaching sermons of exhortation while holding to a "philosophical necessitarian" view. Allen writes: "That there is here an emphatic contradiction requires no proof."[59] So puzzled is Allen that he takes Edwards' epistemological conclusion that "we must continue to speak in the old way about things" and applies it to his preaching.[60] The implication is that Edwards merely linguistically pretended that we have a kind of freedom even though he knew better. Such a view is without foundation to say the least.

Perry Miller shows the same misunderstanding. In a different context he speaks of New England's concern for reform in the second half of the seventeenth century. His point is that the leaders were torn between the need to call the people to reform and their doctrine of "divine determinism." Miller's assumption is that you "could not merely preach repentance and expect . . . men to obey" unless one can legitimatize the notion that "they could if they would."[61] Contrary to Edwards, Miller sees a contradiction between sovereignty and a call to reform because for him sovereignty means fatalistic determinism. And the message of *Freedom of*

---

59. Allen, *Jonathan Edwards*, p. 109.
60. Allen, *Jonathan Edwards*, pp. 109-110.
61. Perry Miller, "'Preparation for Salvation' in Seventeenth-Century New England," *Journal of the History of Ideas*, IV (June, 1943), pp. 253-254.

the Will, which should have prevented false conclusions from the Boston lecture, is that "they *could* if they would" but they *will not* if they would not.

Claude Newlin makes the incredible comment that because of Edwards' emotional and intellectual devotion to the absolute sovereignty of God, "he therefore minimized the independence of man and his efforts."[62] If by "independence" is meant a kind of autonomy, Edwards did not minimize it, he eliminated it! On the other hand, if "independence" refers to the legitimate activity of man in Edwards' theology, he in no way minimized it but maintained it strongly.

Edwards nowhere says it any clearer than with one phrase in his remarks on "Efficacious Grace": "God does all, and we do all."[63] Haroutunian's statement on that phrase bears repeating:

> Such a statement deserves a whole volume as a commentary. A proper understanding of it would obviate the vicious character of the theological dilemma of "determinism and free-will." The problem is based upon a confused assumption to the effect that divine causation and natural causation are commensurate, so that what is natural cannot also be divine.[64]

"We are," says Edwards, "in different respects, wholly passive and wholly active," and "in Scriptures the same things are represented as from God and from us."[65]

Edwards was very much a pastor, and his doctrines were almost never abstracted from real needs. Sovereignty and the sovereign use of means come across in a sermon on Luke 22:31 where he states "that Christ's intercession is that which will effectually secure believers from ever totally and finally falling away from grace."[66] Perseverence is founded in sovereignty. There is nothing in us that "would keep us

---

62. Newlin, *Philosophy and Religion in Colonial America,* pp. 64-65.
63. "Miscellaneous Remarks," *Works,* II, 557.
64. Joseph Haroutunian, "Jonathan Edwards: a Study in Godliness," *The Journal of Religion,* XI (July, 1931), p. 415.
65. "Miscellaneous Remarks," *Works,* II, 557.
66. Sermon on Luke 22:31, Yale MSS, p. 3.

from . . . falling away"; the power of God keeps believers from falling; and Edwards closes the sermon with the words, "thank Christ he prayed for you."[67]

Assurance is a frequent theme for Edwards. The role of the doctrine of absolute sovereignty is reflected in the last point of a sermon on Romans 9:18 whose main theme was the sovereignty of God. "We may make use of this doctrine to guard those who seek salvation from two opposite extremes—presumption and discouragement."[68] Because God is sovereign, we dare not presume on the mercy of God, says Edwards. But discouragement is also ruled out of order on the basis of the same sovereignty. His reason is the closing sentence of the sermon: "Let you be what sinner you may, God can, if he pleases, greatly glorify himself in your salvation."[69]

---

67. Sermon on Luke 22:31, Yale MSS, pp. 8, 10, 16.
68. Sermon on Romans 9:18, *Works*, II, 854.
69. Sermon on Romans 9:18, *Works*, II, 854. John von Rohr demonstrates a relation between covenant and assurance in early English Puritanism. ". . . The force of the covenant idea in relation to assurance is to thrust men back to a dependence upon God's declaration of his sovereign mercy. It is to turn men, therefore, to the objective fact of God's Word and its promises of a new heart and a new life as sheer acts of grace. In the Covenant, in this final sense, grace does all, and reliance must be upon this promise." *Church History*, XXXIV, 201-202.

12

The Self Binding of a Sovereign God in the Covenant of Grace

Implicit throughout this work is the awareness of a close relationship between the sovereign election of God and the covenant of grace. An aspect of the covenant concept with an important bearing on the doctrine of sovereignty is the "binding" of the parties to the covenant. The critic's question resulting from this relationship is whether a sovereign God who arbitrarily predestinates is not incompatible with the idea of God being a party to a covenant in which He is bound. Puritan theology in general, including Edwards, would offer a resounding "No" to that question.

As indicated before, Perry Miller does not so much dispute what the Puritans claimed or intended, but he disputes the consistency of it and credits the attempt of holding to both sovereignty and covenant for weakening, if not eliminating, the doctrine of absolute sovereignty. He who was unfettered "proposed that He be chained," and "in the Covenant He is ruled by a law."[1] John Gerstner provides an excellent summary of the issues involved:

> Many students seem to assume that the two doctrines are incompatible. It is said by some that according to the doctrine of election God is sovereign and arbitrary while the covenant involves God in a contract and confines and limits him. One has God bound—the other, unbound. Many students of historical theology see the post-Calvin development of the covenant doctrine as a short-circuiting of the absolute predestinarianism of John Calvin. Some even represent Edwards as virtually eliminating the doctrine

---

1. Miller, *NEM· 17th Century*, p. 379.

of the covenant (which we have already shown is clearly not the case), returning to the purer Calvinism of Calvin.

If God elected, he therein bound himself. He was arbitrary in electing, to be sure. That is, he did not need to elect at all. But as soon as he did elect to save some, he bound himself to save by some covenant or no covenant. He would have been bound by nothing but his own veracity; but he would have been bound by that.[2]

The same historical interpretation prejudices are thus present which suggest election and covenant cannot rightly co-exist. This further statement by Gerstner shows the fallacy in such an alleged dilemma:

... The covenant of grace is nothing other than the way by which God decrees to carry out what he has committed himself to do. He is already bound by his decree; this covenant can bind him no tighter. It binds him more specifically. That is, it binds him with respect to a particular plan, which he has imposed upon himself. The covenant in no sense "relieves" the doctrine of the decrees.[3]

If one grasps the fact that the covenant binds God "no tighter" than His decree and that the covenant does not "relieve" the doctrine of unconditional election, he will be at the heart of Edwards' theology.

Looking to Edwards himself we find a consistent expression of "boundness" within the framework of election. According to Edwards God's "faithfulness" or "boundness" was the result, not the cause, of election.

So that perfection of God which we call his faithfulness, or his inclination to fulfil his promises to his creatures, could not properly be what *moved* him to create the world; nor could such a fulfilment of his promises to his creatures be his *last* end in giving the creatures being. But yet *after* the world is created, *after* intelligent creatures are made, and God has bound himself by promise to them, then that disposition, which is called his faithfulness, may move him in his providential disposals towards them; and this may be the end of many of God's works of providence, even the exercise of his faithfulness in fulfilling his promises, and may be in the *lower* sense his *last* end. ... Thus God may have ends of

---

2. Gerstner, *Steps to Salvation*, p. 185.
3. Gerstner, *Steps to Salvation*, p. 185.

particular works of *providence*, which are ultimate ends in a lower sense, which were not ultimate ends of the creature.[4]

What is significant here is the reference of God binding Himself in a work devoted to what God as Sovereign proposed to do in the first instance before the creation.

The sermon on Romans 9:18, cited in the last chapter, is one of the clearest and strongest statements by Edwards on the sovereignty of God. The whole sermon is given over to expounding that one doctrine. Significantly, it is in the application of this sermon that we find one of Edwards' strongest statements on God binding Himself.

> Hence we learn what cause we have to admire the grace of God, that he should condescend to become bound to us by covenant; that he, who is naturally supreme in his dominion over us, who is naturally proprietor, and may do with us as he pleases, and is under no obligation to us; that he should, as it were, relinquish his absolute freedom, and should cease to be merely sovereign in his dispensations towards believers, when once they have believed in Christ, and should for their more abundant consolation, become bound. So that they can challenge salvation of this Sovereign; they can demand it through Christ, as a debt. And it would be prejudicial to the glory of God's attributes, to deny it to them; it would be contrary to his justice and faithfulness. What wonderful condescension is it in such a Being. . . . He hath bound himself by oath.[5]

In Calvinist fashion Edwards emphatically rejects the notion that a believer has any righteousness of his own with which to demand salvation from God as a debt. In those terms Edwards would find the whole notion obnoxious. But a legitimate use of debt or boundness is not thereby excluded. Showing the crucial difference, Cherry writes: "Man does not 'tie up' God, but God ties himself to man in the covenant."[6]

The boundness involved in the covenantal relation is closely tied to the nature of God. In a manuscript sermon on

---

4. "The End for which God Created the World," *Works*, I, 96.
5. Sermon on Romans 9:18, *Works*, II, 854. Cf. Sermon on Psalm 111:5, Yale MSS, p. 2: "God is . . . under no obligation to his creatures, yet pleased to lay himself under obligation, an instance of his wonderful condescension."
6. Cherry, *The Theology of Jonathan Edwards,* p. 112.

Numbers 23:19 Edwards makes the following doctrinal statements: "That God never changes his mind"; "He never repents of anything that he has done"; and "God never changes his mind with respect to the rules which he fixed for himself to act by."[7] Concerning these statements Edwards writes: "What I have principally respect to is the covenants that God has entered into with his reasonable creatures."[8]

The covenants Edwards mentions are the covenant of works and the covenant of grace. The covenant of works is "an eternal rule of righteousness," and God will never depart from it. "God in the covenant fixed perfect obedience as the condition of eternal life, and he will never depart from it."[9] It was on this basis that Edwards could in one sense reduce all covenants to this one with differences only in how they were fulfilled.

Edwards applies this same doctrine of the unchangeableness of God to the covenant of grace which God entered into with respect to men. According to Edwards the "promises and threatenings are rules which God has fixed to himself, and he never will change his mind concerning 'em."[10] Edwards lists three causes which could result in a change in God's mind: "either ignorance or error or change of nature."[11] He quickly shows the hypothetical nature of such a statement. "It cannot be from ignorance or error because God is omniscient; he knows all things that ever have been or are or shall be."[12] So also "God's nature and disposition is never changed."[13] Such a change in God would imply a dependency upon a cause outside of Himself, a situation Edwards would utterly reject.

In a note in his "Interleaved Bible" on 2 Samuel 23:5

---

7. Sermon on Numbers 23:19, Yale MSS, pp. 2, 5.
8. Sermon on Numbers 23:19, Yale MSS, p. 5.
9. Sermon on Numbers 23:19, Yale MSS, p. 5. Cf. Chapter 9 above.
10. Sermon on Numbers 23:19, Yale MSS, p. 6.
11. Sermon on Numbers 23:19, Yale MSS, p. 6.
12. Sermon on Numbers 23:19, Yale MSS, p. 7.
13. Sermon on Numbers 23:19, Yale MSS, p. 9.

concerning the certainty of the "everlasting covenant," Edwards sees "an allusion to a legal ordering of a covenant bond . . . so ordered every way according to law that there is no flaw or defects or room for any evasion."[14] As is often the case, the practical application is not separated from the doctrine but a part of it. On the one hand sinners should be awakened to the fact that God's threatenings are for real and change not; on the other hand there is comfort in the certainty of the promises.[15]

In the covenant of grace the attribute of righteousness brings joy and certainty of salvation, rather than terror and certainty of damnation. The arbitrariness and unsearchableness of the Almighty is, within certain defined areas, limited by God Himself. He binds Himself to a rule that is self-imposed. In "Miscellany" No. 453 Edwards writes:

> The righteousness of a judge consists in his judgment according to law, or to the rule of judgment which has been fixed by rightful legislators. . . . But God, in the blessings He adjudges to His people, judges according to the fixed rule of judgment which is His covenant. God shows His holiness by fulfilling His promises to His people. God's faithfulness is part of His holiness, and this is what is meant by righteousness.[16]

Without infringing His sovereignty God establishes a covenant relationship with the elect. "He was still the absolute monarch, although He had given His subjects a bill of inviolable rights."[17]

In the beginning of "A History of the Work of Redemption" Edwards attributes the happiness of the church to the covenant of grace, but he makes it clear that this is dependent upon God's "righteousness" in fulfilling the covenant. Though he emphasizes that in the first instance it was "free and sovereign grace," a grace "altogether undeserved," that provided the covenant and its blessings, "yet as God has been

---

14. "Interleaved Bible," Yale MSS, p. 258.
15. Sermon on Numbers 23:19, Yale MSS, pp. 14-16.
16. *The Philosophy of Jonathan Edwards,* p. 184.
17. Miller, *NEM: 17th Century,* p. 381.

pleased, by the promises of the covenant of grace, to bind himself to bestow them, they are bestowed in the exercise of God's righteousness or justice."[18]

This in no way denies the fact that Edwards explicitly denies that God is indebted to man. In his discourse on "Justification by Faith Alone" Edwards emphatically teaches "that justification respects a man as ungodly."[19] The sinner is justified as sinner, not as righteous. If the sinner wants to speak to God about debts, the result is disastrous.

In a sermon on Romans 3:19, "The Justice of God in the Damnation of Sinners," Edwards teaches that God is under no obligation to redeem any sinner and that he could justly decide to save none.[20] Thus God was not bound or indebted to save anyone. In a sermon on Psalm 46:10 with the published title, "The Sole Consideration, that God Is God, Sufficient to Still All Objections to His Sovereignty," Edwards says objecting to God saving some and not others is based on a wrong view of sovereignty.

> With this sinners often quarrel; but they who upon this ground quarrel with God, suppose him to be *bound* to bestow his grace on sinners. For if he be bound to none, then he may take his choice, and bestow it on whom he pleases; and his bestowing it on some brings no obligation on him to bestow it on others. Has God no right to his own grace? . . . for a person cannot make a present of that which is not his own, or in his own right. It is impossible to *give a debt*.[21]

Here is Calvinism with its unconditional election.

Yet as we have already seen, such disavowal of God owing salvation to sinners in no way caused Edwards to throw out the covenant concept or the notion of debt and boundness inherent in it. Cherry properly indicates that Edwards considered "the notion of God's indebtedness to man for salvation" "in two distinct ways, or on two different levels":

---

18. "History," *Works,* I, 533.
19. "Justification by Faith Alone," *Works,* I, 622.
20. "The Justice of God in the Damnation of Sinners," *Works,* I, 668-679.
21. Sermon on Psalm 46:10, *Works,* II, 110.

In his condemnation of the idea of debt he is rejecting all Pelagian and Arminian claims to salvation on the basis of what man is or does (including the act of belief). Here "debt" is to be understood in a "non-covenantal" way. In his adoption of the debt idea, Edwards is attempting to take seriously the meaning of the Incarnation as God's condescension to man in history. On this level "debt" takes on a very restricted meaning within the context of Biblical representation of faith as a covenant-relation between God and man and excluded the notion that God is indebted by human performance.[22]

Such a twofold understanding must be kept in mind when Edwards deals with the subject of debt. One meaning is utterly contrary to Scripture in Edwards' view; the other is legitimate precisely because it bears the opposite meaning of an Arminian view. Man may "challenge salvation" from God in faith not because man deserves it but because God promised it. The very faith in which salvation is "challenged" or "demanded" from God is a faith the essence of which is acknowledgment that God was under no obligation to save. In a sermon on Luke 16:16 Edwards teaches that in seeking, or "pressing into the Kingdom," God "may" save, "though God has not bound himself to any thing that a person does while destitute of faith, and out of Christ."[23] Here we see both that God is not bound by what man does, and that He *is* bound by faith, though as Edwards teaches elsewhere, faith is a gift of God. Thus God is not indebted or bound to anything man does (i.e., Arminianism), yet He is bound to the covenant which He has established. God is not bound unless He binds Himself.

The Christological foundation is very evident in Edwards' writing. It was clear in the covenant of redemption which presupposes the covenant of grace, and it was evident in the ongoing validity of the covenant of works which only Christ fulfills. The sinner who by faith demands salvation does so only through Christ. His union with Christ provides the believer with the perfect holiness—an imputed holiness—which

---
22. Cherry, *The Theology of Jonathan Edwards*, p. 111.
23. "Pressing into the Kingdom of God," *Works*, I, 659.

God must reward with salvation since He is just and righteous.

The binding of God in relation to His sovereignty and its Christological foundation is seen in the sermon on Romans 9:18:

> ... God's sovereignty in the salvation of men implies ... that God can either bestow salvation on any of the children of men, or refuse it, without any prejudice to the glory of any of his attributes, except where he had been pleased to declare, that he will or will not bestow it. ... Concerning some, God has been pleased to declare either that he will or that he will not bestow salvation on them; and thus to bind himself by his own promise. ... But God exercised his sovereignty in making these declarations. God was not obliged to promise that he would save all who believe in Christ. ... But it pleased him so to declare.[24]

In a manuscript sermon on John 3:8 Edwards refers to the covenant of redemption in which the elect "are spoken of as given in Christ before they are converted. John 17:2 ... And so God's grace is said to be given to the elect in Christ before the world began. 2 Tim. 1:9."[25] Edwards here indicates the priority of election even with regard to the covenant of redemption.

> But however the persons of the Trinity may be obliged one to another, that obligation is only within God himself. But he lies under no obligation to any creature. ...
> And with respect to those hidden promises of the Father to the Son in the covenant of redemption, God is arbitrary in them. The Father was under no obligation to make such promises to the Son of conversion to such and such persons.[26]

In the sermon on Deuteronomy 32:35 Edwards states that God is under no obligation to sinners *except* in Christ which is through the covenant of grace.

> God has laid himself under *no obligation*, by any promise, to keep any natural man out of hell one moment. God certainly has made no promises either of eternal life ... but what are contained in the covenant of grace, the promises that are given in Christ, in whom all the promises are yea and amen. But surely

---

24. Sermon on Romans 9:18, *Works*, II, 850.
25. Sermon on John 3:8, Yale MSS, p. 2.
26. Sermon on John 3:8, Yale MSS, p. 2.

> they have no interest in the promises of the covenant of grace who are not the children of the covenant, who do not believe in any of the promises, and have no interest in the Mediator of the covenant.
> ... Whatever pains a natural man takes in religion, ... God is under no manner of obligation. ...
> ... Neither is God in the least bound by any promise to hold them up one moment. ... All that preserves them every moment is the mere arbitrary will, and uncovenanted, unobliged forbearance, of an incensed God.[27]

The application begins with the statement that such "is the case of every one of you that are out of Christ."[28]

The ever present assumption in Edwards' covenantal theology is that "in Christ," in the covenant of grace, God has obligated Himself. There is no hope outside of that covenant; there is certain hope within it. Because of the infinite condescension of God in Christ, sinful man can enter into a covenant relationship with the Creator. The Creator was under no obligation, but He willingly bound Himself and became obligated to the covenant of grace.

The self binding of God in the covenant brings the assurance motif to light. Edwards writes in *Religious Affections:*

> And the nature of the covenant of grace, and God's declared ends in the appointment and constitution of things in that covenant, do plainly show it to be God's design to make ample provision for the saints having an assured hope of eternal life, while living here upon earth.[29]

He refers to Hebrews 6:18 which states "it was impossible for God to lie" and speaks of the command to Christians to obtain assurance.[30]

The manuscript sermon on Isaiah 55:3 states that "the excellency of this covenant and the great desireableness of an interest in its blessings is set forth here by 2 things: 1. that it is an everlasting covenant, and 2. that the mercies promised in it are sure."[31] In a manuscript sermon on Psalm 111:5,

---

27. Sermon on Deuteronomy 32:35, *Works*, II, 9.
28. Sermon on Deuteronomy 32:35, *Works*, II, 9.
29. *Religious Affections*, p. 169.   30. *Religious Affections*, p. 169.
31. Sermon on Isaiah 55:3, Yale MSS, p. 2.

having indicated how God is faithful in fulfilling the covenant engagements, he states the primary application is "confidently to trust God."[32]

Without the covenant "binding" God there would be no assurance. But because of that covenant, because it depends solely on Christ, there is certainty. Edwards sees the certainty of salvation via the covenant as illustrative of the "Wisdom of God."

> Yea, it is so ordered now that the glory of these attributes *requires* the salvation of those that believe. The justice of God that required man's damnation, and seemed inconsistent with his salvation, now as much requires the salvation of those that believe in Christ, as ever before it required their damnation. Salvation is an absolute debt to the believer from God, so that he may in justice demand it, on account of what his surety has done. . . . It is a thing that may be challenged. . . . And again, the believer may demand eternal life, because it has been merited by Christ, by a merit of condignity. . . . Justice that seemed to require man's destruction, now requires his salvation.[33]

Strong as Edwards makes this language, it is never a reason for presumption. All is of grace, even the assurance that the covenant provides.

In a sermon on 2 Samuel 23:5 Edwards declares: " 'Tis only through our unbelief and our sinful . . . disposition of heart that we stand in need of . . . confirmation."[34] But faith which is covenant faith is not something we bring in our hands as our contribution to the covenant. True faith "understands the covenant." Faith "does not see the covenant as an empty scheme . . . but it hears the word of grace and knows that the decision does not rest with us."[35]

---

32. Sermon on Psalm 111:5, Yale MSS, pp. 8-10.
33. Sermon on Ephesians 3:10, *Works*, II, 149.
34. Sermon on 2 Samuel 23:5, Yale MSS, p. 18.
35. G. C. Berkouwer, *Faith and Perseverance*, trans. Robert D. Knudsen (Grand Rapids, 1958), p. 215. Cf. Bavinck, *Gereformeerde Dogmatiek*, p. 195. "God kan en mag zijn verbond niet verbreken; Hij heeft er zich vrijwillig, uit zichzelf, met een duren eed toe verbonden; zijn naam, zijn eere, zijn wezen zelf hangt eraan. . . . Het verbond, dat van God uitgaat en ons opneemt, vermaant en verplicht ons tot eene nieuwe gehoorzaamheid. Maar als wij dan somtijds uit zwakheid in zonden vallen, zoo moeten wij toch daarom aan Gods genade niet

As for the interpreters of Edwards, many seem unable to conceive him as both a covenant and a Calvinist theologian. The problem for them lies in the area of sovereignty and boundness. McGiffert, for example, says Edwards clearly distinguishes himself from Calvin.

> Calvin could not talk of God as bound; God does not act in a certain way because it is right; it is right because he acts that way. Like certain ancient Greeks, Edwards conceived of a power superior even to God....[36]

Apart from his conclusion regarding Calvin, he is certainly in error in suggesting Edwards conceives of a "power superior even to God." The fact that the boundness of God is anchored in His sovereignty shows McGiffert's criticism arising from a false dilemma.

McKee in his dissertation on "The Idea of the Covenant" acknowledges that God binds Himself to the covenant.[37] Yet he believes "a denial of the absolute majesty and freedom of God" is implied in this, with the goal of eliminating "arbitrariness" and "capriciousness" in the actions of God.[38] "Covenant theology took its point of departure from man's despair and man's need rather than from God's providence. Its orientation, therefore, was anthropological."[39] Though McKee is dealing with a period prior to Edwards, this thinking on the covenant is prevalent in Miller as well and colors how one deals with Edwards. Miller likewise suggests that anthropological concerns caused the Puritans to "contrive" the boundness of the covenant to make God "less inscrutable," "less mysterious," and "less unpredictable."[40] It is

---

vertwijfelen noch in de zonden blijven liggen, want het verbond der genade ligt vast in het onveranderlijk welbehagen Gods."
36. Arthur Cushman McGiffert, *Jonathan Edwards* (New York, 1932), p. 159.
37. McKee, "The Idea of Covenant in Early English Puritanism," p. 152.
38. McKee, "The Idea of Covenant in Early English Puritanism," p. 153.
39. McKee, "The Idea of Covenant in Early English Puritanism," p. 155.
40. Miller, "The Marrow of Puritan Divinity," *Errand into the Wilderness*, pp. 55-56. Miller somehow conceives God's promise as not providing the kind of certainty that would make Him "less inscrutable." In fact, he puts the commit-

simply not the intention nor the essence of the covenant that it detracts from the absolute majesty and freedom of God. While human needs are met and assurance is given, it is nevertheless misleading to suggest such needs as the source of the covenant doctrine. It is, as Edwards believed it to be, revealed in Scripture as God's provision and not man's.

---

ment of the covenant over against the divine promise. "This arrangement between the two is not simply a promise on God's part, it is a definite commitment. These authors in fact, practically do away with the conception of God as merely promising, and substitute a legal theory of God's delivering to man a signed and sealed bond" (p. 62). It is hard to imagine what Miller means by "simply a promise" or "merely promising." Does a promise from God have no commitment? Clearly the Bible does not give the impression that the promise of God lacks anything to make it absolutely dependable. One wonders at the distinction between promise and commitment. Such a tension was unknown to Edwards. Cf. "The End for which God Created the World," *Works,* I, 96, where he indicates that God is bound "by his promise." This binding is what Miller would set in opposition to promise.

13

Grace and the Holy Spirit in the Covenant of Grace

It is not without good reason that the covenant pertaining to salvation is designated as gracious. Jonathan Edwards reflects the essence of the Scriptures when he attributes salvation to the absolute, sovereign grace of God.[1] The Reformation cry of *sola gratia* and *sola fide* reverberates throughout his writings.

Edwards' strong position on absolute sovereignty would demand the conclusion that if there is salvation, it is completely a matter of grace. Unconditional election by definition places salvation in the area of grace and not debt. That there is a covenant of works, but especially that there is a covenant of redemption which results in salvation, is wholly of grace. That the Holy Spirit should do His spiritual surgery upon the heart of sinful man can be accounted for only by divine grace.

It should be emphasized that the doctrine of grace is extremely important in Edwards' theology. As with any biblical theologian, grace is a fundamental doctrine. But Edwards went beyond many writers in dealing with the nature of grace, what it is, and how it functions. The epistemological relevance of the Holy Spirit's gracious activity (no new knowledge but a new "taste" or "relish") is a major study of

---

1. "The gospel dispensation is finished wholly and entirely in free and glorious grace...." Sermon on Zechariah 4:7, Yale MSS, p. 3. "That the gospel or new covenant is eminently a dispensation of grace." Sermon on Romans 6:14, Yale MSS, p. 3.

Edwards in itself. Our intent, therefore, is not to give an exposition of Edwards' doctrine of grace and the Holy Spirit but to elucidate those areas with a direct bearing on the covenant of grace.

Basic to Edwards' view is an absolute distinction between "common grace" and "saving grace." In his "Treatise on Grace" Edwards lists eight ways "that common and saving grace differ, not only in degree, but in nature and kind."[2] There is a difference between a natural and spiritual birth, between the flesh and the spirit, and partaking or not partaking of "the divine nature." Those without saving grace "have no degree of that relish and sense of spiritual things"; they are without "charity," and "they have no communion or fellowship with Christ." The existence of a truly "gracious principle in the heart" is "inconsistent with a man's being a sinner," and the presence of the grace of conversion is thus represented in Scripture "as a work of creation" or "a resurrection."

The freeness of grace is essential to saving grace. Edwards in one of his notes defines free grace as what is "given without retribution by way of condition, or without the receiver's profiting or pleasuring the giver."[3] The Romans 4:16 sermon lists "these three things that contribute to the freedom of a gift":

> 1. When a gift is given to an offender without satisfaction made by him. . . .
> 2. When it is given without the giver's receiving or expecting profit by it. . . . It is not given in recompense for any kindness we have done God. . . .
> 3. When it is given without worthiness or without any excellency in our persons or actions to move the giver to love and beneficence. . . .[4]

---

2. *Treatise on Grace and Other Posthumously Published Writings,* ed. Paul Helm (Cambridge, England, 1971), hereafter cited as *Treatise on Grace,* pp. 25-33.
3. "Miscellanies," No. 191, Yale MSS.
4. Sermon on Romans 4:16, Yale MSS, pp. 16-17.

This is paralleled in a sermon where the freeness is said to consist "in its exercise being unmerited . . . and . . . in its being disinterested, that which is done only from a mere inclination to beneficence and kindness and from mere goodwill and not from self-interest."[5]

In a "Miscellanies" entry on "Free grace" Edwards lists three ways a gift may be bestowed freely:

> 1. if it [be] bestowed without any prerequisite qualification or condition whatsoever. 2. if it be bestowed only for such a suitableness in the nature. . . . 3. if it be given only for the actual exercise of such an agreeableness and suitableness of nature and inclination in accepting and closing with the offer.[6]

In the first category Edwards places "election" and the giving of "Christ's sufferings and obedience"; in the last two he places the "effectual calling" with its consequent faith and justification *by* that faith.[7] Thus while Edwards sees a "natural fitness" in faith, yet faith does not require justification in its own right.

The nature of grace as manifest in the Spirit's work is highlighted by the natural condition of man. A distinctive feature of Edwards' thought is his emphasis on the absolute necessity of grace, but which grace is to be understood not as an improvement of man's natural faculties or new knowledge. In an important discourse on Psalm 94:8-11 entitled "Man's Natural Blindness in the Things of Religion," Edwards sets forth the following doctrinal observation basic to his theology:

> THAT THERE IS AN EXTREME AND BRUTISH BLINDNESS IN THINGS OF RELIGION, WHICH NATURALLY POSSESSES THE HEARTS OF MANKIND.—This doctrine is not to be understood as any reflection on the *capacity* of the human nature; for God hath made man with a noble and excellent capacity. The blindness I speak of, is not a merely *negative* ignorance; such as in trees and stones, that know nothing. . . . There is no fault to be found with man's *natural* faculties. God has given men faculties

---

5. Sermon on Romans 6:14, Yale MSS, p. 4.
6. "Miscellanies," No. 417, Yale MSS.
7. "Miscellanies," No. 417, Yale MSS.

truly noble and excellent; well capable of true wisdom and divine knowledge. Nor is the blindness... from want of necessary opportunity....

The blindness that is in the heart of man, which is spoken of in the text and doctrine, is neither for want of *faculties,* nor *opportunity* to know, but from some positive cause. There is a principle in his heart, of such a blinding and besotting nature, that it hinders the exercises of his *faculties* about the things of religion; exercises for which God has made him well capable, and for which he gives him abundant opportunity.[8]

Not new knowledge but a new heart is required.

The only solution to man's natural blindness is for the Holy Spirit to totally change man's nature, a change indicated in Scripture by names such as "born from above," "regeneration," "a new heart," and "a new creation." An extremely important sermon, published under the title "A Divine and Supernatural Light," deals with this work of the Holy Spirit. The doctrine of the sermon states: "That there is such a thing as a spiritual and divine light, immediately imparted to the soul of God, of a different nature from any that is obtained by natural means."[9] "This spiritual light is not the suggesting of any new truths or propositions not contained in the word of God," but "the prejudices of the heart, against the truth of divine things, are hereby removed."[10] Edwards draws a clear distinction between "having an *opinion,* that God is holy and gracious, and having a *sense* of the loveliness and beauty of that holiness and grace."[11]

---

8. "Man's Natural Blindness in the Things of Religion," *Works,* II, 247. The relevance of this understanding for Edwards' position on natural theology is obvious. He writes: "There is no one thing whatsoever more plain and manifest, and more demonstrable, than the being of a God. It is manifest in ourselves, in our own bodies and souls, and in every thing about us wherever we turn our eye.... And yet how prone is the heart of man to call this into question! So inclined is the heart of man to blindness and delusion, that it is prone to even atheism itself" (p. 252). Not the weakness of the demonstration but the inclination of the will against God is the trouble spot.

9. Sermon on Matthew 16:17, *Works,* II, 13.

10. Sermon on Matthew 16:17, *Works,* II, 13-14.

11. Sermon on Matthew 16:17, *Works,* II, 14. For further discussions on this aspect of Edwards' teaching on the Spirit's work see especially, Cherry, *The Theology of Jonathan Edwards,* pp. 25-43; Elwood, *The Philosophical Theology*

At the close of the sermon on "A Divine and Supernatural Light," Edwards speaks of the "effectual" influence it has upon the soul.

> This light, and this only, will bring the soul to a saving close with Christ. It conforms the heart to the gospel, mortifies its enmity and opposition against the scheme of salvation. . . . It causes the whole soul to accord and symphonize with it . . . and it effectually disposes the soul to give up itself entirely to Christ.[12]

This "closing" with Christ, which is faith or union with Christ, is the marriage of the believers to Christ in the covenant of grace. The soul "closes," "conforms," and gives itself up to the Gospel, but clearly it is totally dependent upon the Spirit's "bringing." Thus the covenant relation is affirmed in the very place where the sinner's part in the covenant is shown to be the work of the Spirit. The doctrine of a sermon on John 6:45 is that those who come to Christ do so because they are "infallibly drawn to him."[13] This is essentially another way of saying God Himself provides the condition of the covenant, which is the precise teaching of Reformed theology on the covenant of grace.

In our consideration of the doctrine of sovereignty we saw Edwards' insistence upon the sinner's "absolute and universal dependence" on God for their salvation,[14] which depends solely on His "sovereign grace" to save "if he pleases."[15] In encouraging sinners to seek salvation Edwards says, "If ever God bestows mercy upon you, he will use his sovereign pleasure about the time when," and "when you have done all, God will not hold himself obliged to show you mercy at last."[16]

For there to be salvation "grace is the one thing need-

---

of *Jonathan Edwards,* pp. 113-149; Gerstner, *Steps to Salvation,* pp. 117-137; and Miller, *Jonathan Edwards,* pp. 44-45, 64-68, 187-188, 241-242, and 325.
  12. Sermon on Matthew 16:17, *Works,* II, 17.
  13. Sermon on John 6:45, Yale MSS, p. 4.
  14. Sermon on 1 Corinthians 1:29-31, *Works,* II, 3-4.
  15. Sermon on Romans 9:18, *Works,* II, 854.
  16. "Pressing Into the Kingdom of God," *Works,* I, 658-659.

ful."[17] That is the doctrine of Edwards' sermon on Luke 10:42 where he teaches grace is needful for "our happiness," our obtaining heaven, and our "escaping eternal death."[18] He calls grace the "good part." " 'Tis called the good part by way of eminency as being incomparably the best part," and the many benefits are distinguished especially in that it shall never be taken away from those who possess it.[19] This is confirmed in a sermon on the same text preached some years later which has as its doctrine: "That which God gives to the saints for their part is the best good that ever any of the children of men obtain."[20]

Not only is grace the one thing needful, it is needed in all the parts. The manuscript sermon on Zechariah 4:7 teaches that as its doctrine and emphasizes that "every part of the great work of redemption" is begun and finished "in glorious grace."[21] Edwards writes that "God ... has provided a Saviour for us and Christ has come and died," but "the application of the redemption of the Gospel by the Holy Spirit is of mere grace."[22] "If we will but accept ... Christ" (here Edwards states the condition of the covenant of grace), redemption is ours, but with reference to Ephesians 2:8-9, Edwards states, "We are not able to do that of ourselves, but it is the free gift of God" (the condition is provided by God).[23]

Because salvation is totally of God, Edwards says we "dishonor God and the Gospel" if we depend on anything but God's grace.[24] A manuscript sermon on Deuteronomy 9:4-6 stresses our acceptance to be in no way dependent upon our righteousness. He says such would be "inconsistent with the

---

17. Sermon on Luke 10:42 (1), Yale MSS, p. 2.
18. Sermon on Luke 10:42 (1), Yale MSS, pp. 5-7.
19. Sermon on Luke 10:42 (1), Yale MSS, pp. 9-13.
20. Sermon on Luke 10:42 (2), Yale MSS, p. 3.
21. Sermon on Zechariah 4:7, Yale MSS, p. 3.
22. Sermon on Zechariah 4:7, Yale MSS, p. 9.
23. Sermon on Zechariah 4:7, Yale MSS, p. 9.
24. Sermon on Zechariah 4:7, Yale MSS, p. 13.

nature of grace and mercy," "inconsistent with the state of man," "inconsistent with the law of God," and "inconsistent with the whole method of redemption by Jesus Christ."[25] As a second doctrine in this same sermon Edwards teaches the "vast consequence" of properly understanding this since Scripture teaches God's "indignation manifested toward self-righteous professors," and reason teaches self-righteousness to be "hateful" and "opposite to the glory of God."[26]

The same emphasis is found in another manuscript sermon on Titus 3:5 which contrasts our righteousness and God's mercy. The doctrine states "that there are none saved by their own righteousness," or, as he further expresses it, "there are none saved upon the account of their own moral excellency."[27] "Those that God is pleased to convert and call unto Jesus Christ, them he justifies. Rom. 8:30 . . . They have a righteousness given them. . . . This is the way paid of Christ's obedience and death. . . ."[28] Edwards mentions several reasons "why we can't be saved by our own righteousness," the last of which is that it is "contrary to God's design of glorifying his free grace by Jesus Christ."[29]

Edwards uses the doctrine of justification by faith alone as evidence that the new covenant is of free grace.

> We are taught that we are justified freely through grace (Rom. 3:24), and it appears in this that we are justified only by faith, Ephes. 2:7, 8: "That in the ages to come he might shew the exceeding riches of his grace in his kindness toward us through Jesus Christ for by grace are ye saved through faith."[30]

Accordingly, "those who are in a state of salvation are to attribute it to sovereign grace alone, and to give all the praise

---

25. Sermon on Deuteronomy 9:4-6, Yale MSS, pp. 5-7.
26. Sermon on Deuteronomy 9:4-6, Yale MSS, pp. 21, 24. Cf. "Miscellaneous Remarks," *Works,* II, 544: "The doctrine of men's being the determining causes of their own virtue, teaches them, not to do so much, as even the proud Pharisee did, who thanked God for making him to differ from other men in virtue, Luke xviii."
27. Sermon on Titus 3:5, Yale MSS, p. 3.
28. Sermon on Titus 3:5, Yale MSS, p. 5.
29. Sermon on Titus 3:5, Yale MSS, p. 5.
30. Sermon on Romans 4:16, Yale MSS, pp. 16-17.

to him, who maketh them to differ from others."[31] Contrariwise, "those doctrines that detract from free grace are contrary to the gospel."[32]

In a sermon on Ruth 1:16 Edwards lets us see that a complete dependence upon grace in no way negates man's actively using ordained means to obtain salvation. Concerning the proper use of the means "appointed in order to our becoming some of the true Israel," he writes: "A choosing of their God, and their people, with a full determination, and with the whole soul, is the condition of an union with them."[33] This is equivalent to entering into the covenant of grace. But to leave no doubt of the role of sovereign grace in so choosing, Edwards adds: "No man doth ever heartily choose God and Christ, and the spiritual benefits that Christ has purchased, and the happiness of God's people, till he is converted."[34] The natural man is wholly lacking of both an awareness of the excellency of God's provision and a desire for it.

If no one chooses Christ until he is converted, it becomes important to define conversion. Edwards writes: "Conversion is a great and glorious work of God's power, at once changing the heart and infusing life into the dead soul; though that grace that is then implanted does more gradually display itself in some than in others."[35] In his "Treatise on Grace," after contrasting the qualitative differences between common and saving grace, Edwards draws the inference *"that it must needs be that conversion is wrought at once"*:

---

31. Sermon on Romans 9:18, *Works,* II, 854.
32. Sermon on Romans 6:14, Yale MSS, p. 13.
33. "Ruth's Resolution," *Works,* I, 666.
34. "Ruth's Resolution," *Works,* I, 666.
35. *The Great Awakening,* p. 177. Edwards' qualification regards the subjective realization of an objective event. "But as to fixing on the precise time when they put forth the very first act of grace, there is a great deal of difference in different persons; in some it seems to be very discernible when the very time of this was; but others are more at a loss. In this respect there are very many that don't know the time (as has been already observed), that when they have the first exercises of grace, don't know that it is the grace of conversion, and sometimes don't think it to be so till a long time after. . . ."

Grace and the Holy Spirit in the Covenant of Grace 217

That knowledge, that reformation and conviction that is preparatory to conversion may be gradual, and the work of grace after conversion may be gradually carried on, yet that work of grace upon the soul whereby a person is brought out of a state of total corruption and depravity into a state of grace, to an interest in Christ, and to be actually a child of God, is in a moment.[36]

It must be so, argues Edwards, since a person is brought into a state "entirely different in nature and kind from all that went before."[37] In an instant one is translated from a state of utter lack of any saving grace to a state of grace and acceptance as a child of God.

That grace is absolutely necessary is demonstrated by the need of man in a natural state. Two sermons Edwards preached on the third chapter of Romans have as their respective doctrines: "All that natural men do is wrong,"[38] and "the nature of man in his fallen state is utterly . . . corrupt."[39] Edwards acknowledges "degrees of sinfulness" and "external fulfilment," but the main thing, utterly absent in natural man, is "a spiritual service to God."[40]

In a manuscript sermon on John 5:43 Edwards gets to the essence of the matter. "Man's H[eart] is naturally wholly opposite to the gospel."[41] He speaks of the contrast between our "sinful nature," our "misery" and "condemnation to hell" and the "glad tidings of peace and reconciliation with God and salvation from hell and eternal life."[42] The reaction we should expect, says Edwards, is that men would rejoice in this deliverance. "But man is a creature of such perverseness that 'tis quite otherwise with him. When the gospel is preached to him, he don't rejoice at it; he hears it with coldness. . . ."[43]

As Edwards indicates in *Freedom of the Will*, the measure

---

36. *Treatise on Grace,* pp. 33-34.
37. *Treatise on Grace,* p. 34.
38. Sermon on Romans 3:11-12, Yale MSS, p. 4.
39. Sermon on Romans 3:13, Yale MSS, p. 4.
40. Sermon on Romans 3:11-12, Yale MSS, pp. 4, 7, 11, 13.
41. Sermon on John 5:43, Yale MSS, p. 3.
42. Sermon on John 5:43, Yale MSS, p. 3.
43. Sermon on John 5:43, Yale MSS, p. 4.

of virtue is not in the act as such but rather the "disposition" of the doer.[44] His contention is that natural man has a sinful disposition and thus "all that a natural man doth is sin." He compares a possible external conformity from a wrong disposition with an unloving wife. "Let a woman seek to give all the content to her husband that may be, not out of any love to him but only out of love to another man; he abhors all that she doth."[45] In a sermon expounding the total depravity of man, Edwards admits a man may do the right thing for a wrong or selfish reason. The rightness that is crucial concerns the "subject" and his "spiritual service to God," and "this is altogether wrong in all that natural men do."[46]

It is precisely the sinner's sinful disposition that causes the "blindness" in things of religion. The problem and the solution are clearly set forth in two sermons, "Man's Natural Blindness in the Things of Religion" and "A Divine and Supernatural Light." It is also a recurring theme in the "Miscellanies."

Edwards, for example, draws our attention to the fact that our "natural temper oftentimes very much blinds us in similar affairs."[47] He has in mind such occasions as when a man is "melancholy, or jealous, cowardly, and the like." Conversion concerns the removal of such blindness. Conversion thus "is the alteration of the temper and disposition and spirit of the mind," giving a new "principle of life and action" and giving the mind a "sense" of the "excellency, glory, and delightfulness" of "divine things."[48] "Ratiocination, without this spiritual light, never will give one such an advantage to see things in their true relations and respects to other things, and to things in general."[49]

Edwards defines faith in one of the "Miscellanies" as a "divine or a spiritual conviction of the truth of things of

---

44. *Freedom of the Will,* pp. 320-342.
45. *The Philosophy of Jonathan Edwards,* p. 244. ("Miscellany" No. 676).
46. Sermon on Romans 3:11-12, Yale MSS, pp. 7-13.
47. *The Philosophy of Jonathan Edwards,* p. 248. ("Miscellany" No. 248).
48. *The Philosophy of Jonathan Edwards,* p. 249. ("Miscellany" No. 397).
49. *The Philosophy of Jonathan Edwards,* p. 249. ("Miscellany" No. 408).

religion."[50] The Holy Spirit graciously provides such a "spiritual conviction" or "knowledge."

> That spiritual light that is let into the soul by the Spirit of God discovering the excellency and glory of divine things. It not only directly evidences the truth of religion to the mind—as this divine glory is an evident stamp of divinity and truth—but it sanctifies the reasoning faculty and assists it to see the clear evidence there is of the truth of religion in rational arguments, and that two ways, viz., as it removes prejudices and . . . as it positively enlightens and assists. . . .[51]

The truth of the Gospel of God's provision for salvation is accessible to all men. Natural man, however, is so sinfully disposed that he finds it distasteful, and thus it is only in the gracious work of the Spirit changing the sinner's disposition that he is "drawn" to and "delights" in the Gospel.

The situation is one of an infinite chasm between man in a natural estate and man in a state of salvation, and that chasm can be bridged only by grace from God's side. The second of two inferences Edwards drew from a comparison of common and saving grace is that *"it is impossible for men to convert themselves* by their own strength and industry."[52] The doctrine of a sermon on Romans 5:6 states: "We are all in our selves utterly without any strength or power to help our selves."[53]

That a large number from mankind, helpless in themselves, do choose Christ and his salvation via the covenant of grace must be attributed solely to the sovereign, gracious, irresistible operation of the Holy Spirit. Concerning efficacious grace Edwards writes:

> It is manifest that the Scripture supposes, that if ever men are turned from sin, God must undertake it, and he must be the doer of it; that it is his doing that must determine the matter; that all that others can do, will avail nothing, without his agency. . . . According to Dr. Whitby's notion of the assistance of the Spirit,

---

50. *The Philosophy of Jonathan Edwards*, p. 251. ("Miscellany" No. 1090).
51. *The Philosophy of Jonathan Edwards*, p. 251. ("Miscellany" No. 628).
52. *Treatise on Grace*, pp. 37-38.
53. Sermon on Romans 5:6, Yale MSS, p. 3.

> the Spirit of God does nothing in the hearts or minds of men beyond the power of the devil.... For he supposes that all the Spirit of God does, is to bring moral motives and inducements to mind, and set them before the understanding, &c.[54]

Edwards would say that no amount of inducements or persuasion will avail if God does not change the sinner's disposition.

By disposition Edwards meant the inclination of the will. In the spiritual realm the will is inclined either favorably or unfavorably to divine truth. Edwards would say natural man is inclined unfavorably. In this light, Edwards declares the dispute over whether grace is resistible or irresistible to be "perfect nonsense":

> For the effect of grace is upon the will; so that it is nonsense, except it be proper to say, that a man with his will can resist his own will, or except it be possible for him to desire to resist his own will; that is, except it be possible for a man to will a thing and not will it at the same time, and so far as he does will it.[55]

Elsewhere Edwards writes: "The very first effect of saving grace that touches the will is to abolish its resistence and to incline the will.... Opposition of the will is overcome by divine grace or rather abolished."[56]

The inconsistency of the notion of "resistible" grace is paralleled by the inconsistency of thinking a man can convert himself:

> As to man's inability to convert himself—In them that are totally corrupt there can be no tendency towards their making their hearts better, till they begin to repent of the badness of their hearts.... But they cannot begin sincerely to repent of the badness of their hearts till their hearts begin to be better, for repentance consists in a change of the mind and heart. So that it is not men's repentance that first gives rise to their having a better heart; and therefore it cannot be any tendency in them to make their hearts better, that gives rise to it. The heart can have no tendency to make itself better, till it begins to have a better

---

54. "Miscellaneous Remarks," *Works*, II, 543.
55. "Miscellaneous Remarks," *Works*, II, 551. This same statement is found in the "Miscellany" lettered "O" in the Yale MSS.
56. "Miscellanies," No. 665, Yale MSS.

tendency; for therein consists its badness, *viz.* its having no good tendency or inclination. And to begin to have a good tendency, or, which is the same thing, a tendency and inclination to be better, is the same thing as to begin already to be better. And therefore the heart's inclination to be good, cannot be the thing that first gives rise to its being made good. For its inclination to be better, is the same thing with its becoming better.[57]

In a series of sermons on John 16:8, Edwards says "the work of the Holy Ghost" is "to make men understand the way of sinners' reconciliation and acceptance with God through Christ."[58] This is called the "exalted operation of the Spirit," the giving of "divine light" "into the heart of converts," and the "primary operation of the Spirit of God when he first enters into the soul."[59] Later in this series, Edwards states it in these words:

1. The Holy Ghost convinces of the reality of this way of reconciliation and acceptance by the righteousness of Christ. Though natural men they do believe, that Christ is a Saviour, and they hear a great deal about it, and they don't contradict it; . . . yet for all that it don's seem real to them. . . . The Holy Spirit, when he enters, he lets in that divine light, which discovers truth and makes it appear as truth, and shows the way of salvation. . . .
2. The Holy Ghost convinces of the suitableness and sufficiency of this way of salvation. The believing soul, when thus enlightened sees a suitableness. . . .
3 and lastly. The Holy Ghost causes to see a glorious excellency in this way. It all appears with a lust[re] of glory upon it. . . . Natural men see no glory in this dying love of Christ.[60]

Edwards insists that "there is the greatest liberty in this his government" since men are not "forced and compelled" but are freely drawn by "the sweet and gracious influences of Christ upon the will."[61]

---

57. "Miscellaneous Remarks," *Works,* II, 553.
58. Sermons on John 16:8, Yale MSS, p. 33.
59. Sermons on John 16:8, Yale MSS, p. 33.
60. Sermons on John 16:8, Yale MSS, pp. 53-56.
61. Sermons on John 16:8, Yale MSS, pp. 98-99. Edwards compares this free dominion of Christ with the "tyranny of that monster that the rest of the world are under" (p. 99). In the first sermon Edwards related the work of Christ to the work of the Holy Spirit. "The Holy Ghost don't only immediately apply Christ's redemption, but 'tis he that does what is necessary to be done upon men's

The relevance for the covenant of grace is clear. Before there will be faith, which is the condition of the covenant of grace, the heart must be changed.

> There must be the principle before there can be the action, in all cases; there must be an alteration made in the heart of the sinner, before there can be action consequent upon this alteration; yea, there must be a principle of holiness before holiness is in exercise. Yea, this alteration must not only be before the effect, but also in time; if this embracing of Christ as a Saviour be a successive action, that is, an action where one thought and act of the mind in any wise follows another, as it certainly is.[62]

It is in this sense of a holy principle preceding the act of faith that Edwards will sometime speak of sanctification preceding faith (and hence justification) in distinction from the usual treatment in Reformed theology.

In defining terms in *Freedom of the Will* Edwards lays down the following principle: "The will is always determined by the strongest motive," and "the will always is as the greatest apparent good is."[63] Many do not come to Christ, says Edwards, because they "don't know him" and "what manner of person he is."[64] Christ is not their greatest good. Those who do come, however, do so because they are "infallibly

---

hearts in order to it. What Christ does immediately is not upon men's souls but for them, which yet their souls would never be the better for were not something done immediately upon their soul. Whatever in the work of redemption is done immediately in or upon men's souls is the work of the Spirit, whether it be actually making them partakers of this redemption by converting them and uniting them with Christ ... and making of them perfect in holiness in heaven and filling them with happiness, but also convincing men of sin, making of them sensible" (p. 4).

62. "Miscellanies," No. 77, Yale MSS. William Ames speaks similarly of the grace of God exerting its influence on the will. Cf. Ames, *The Marrow of Theology*, p. 159: "The passive receiving of Christ is the process by which a spiritual principle of grace is generated in the will of man"; "this grace is the basis of that relation in which man is united with Christ"; "the will is the ... subject of this grace; the conversion of the will is the effectual principle in the conversion of the whole man"; and "the enlightening of the mind is not sufficient to produce this effect because it does not take away the corruption of the will."

63. *Freedom of the Will*, p. 142. Cf. Elwood, *The Philosophical Theology of Jonathan Edwards*, pp. 190-191, where he shows a parallel with Peter van Mastricht, "whose psychology of the will Edwards essentially adopts."

64. Sermon on John 6:45, Yale MSS, p. 5.

drawn to him."⁶⁵ They come to Him because the Holy Spirit illuminated them to see Christ's true loveliness and excellency, which is now their greatest good, and they are "infallibly drawn" because of the principle stated above concerning the will. When one realizes that because of the sinner's perverted will, his greatest apparent good is an abomination to the Lord, then it becomes clear why the grace by which men are saved is both grace and irresistible.

That Edwards held the doctrine of the covenant of grace has been demonstrated, and that he used conditional language will be clearly shown in a later chapter. In his doctrine of grace and the Holy Spirit one can see the way Edwards would go. Misunderstanding is not thereby relieved. Elwood writes: "Edwards opposed the synergism implied in the Federalist notion of a conditional covenant."⁶⁶ He certainly opposed synergism, but his doctrine of grace clearly shows that he did not exclude the conditional but rather attributed it solely to sovereign grace. Elwood appeals to Edwards' warnings about conditional language and his emphasis on the unity of the twofold covenant, but he errs in excluding the concept of condition, contrary to Edwards, and in failing to clearly distinguish between the covenants of redemption and grace, as Edwards had said we must.

In the covenant of grace the Holy Spirit becomes the connecting link between God's part and man's part. This is in accord with Edwards' statement that "God does all, and we do all"⁶⁷ and honors the absolute sovereignty of grace in salvation. God grants the new motivation for the will so that men work, yet it is God working in them.

It is only in this framework that one can rightly understand Edwards' doctrine of the covenant of grace. Our entrance into the covenant is totally a matter of free grace. In

---

65. Sermon on John 6:45, Yale MSS, p. 4.
66. Elwood, *The Philosophical Theology of Jonathan Edwards*, p. 194, note 93.
67. "Miscellaneous Remarks," *Works*, II, 557.

his sermon on Romans 6:14 Edwards defines grace, in distinction from the law, as "the dispensation of God's grace in Christ or the covenant of grace or the gospel."[68] God was without obligation to bestow it, without "expectation of any recompense for it," and without there being any "excellency to merit or attract it."[69]

That Edwards maintained the covenant doctrine without any compromise to Arminian synergism is manifest in his teaching that the Holy Spirit, without whom one would never enter the covenant, is precisely "the sum of the blessings" Christ purchased.

> The sum of the blessings Christ sought, by what he did and suffered in the work of redemption, was the *Holy Spirit*.... The Holy Spirit is the subject matter for the promise, both of the eternal covenant of redemption, and also of the covenant of grace. This is the grand subject of the *promises* of the Old Testament, so often recorded in the *prophecies* of Messiah's kingdom; and the chief subject of the promises of the New Testament; and particularly of the covenant of grace delivered by Jesus Christ to his disciples, as his last will and testament, in the 14th, 15th, and 16th chapters of John; the grand legacy that he bequeathed to them, is so often called the *Spirit of promise*, and emphatically, *the promise, the promise of the Father*, &c.[70]

This is the teaching of a manuscript sermon on Galatians 3:13-14. The Holy Spirit "is the sum of the blessings that Christ purchased for us in the work of our redemption," "the great promise of the covenant of grace made by Christ to believers," and the "legacy that Christ left ... at his death."[71]

In "God Glorified in Man's Dependence," Edwards emphasizes the sovereignty of each person of the Trinity in

---

68. Sermon on Romans 6:14, Yale MSS, p. 2. Berkhof writes: "This covenant may be called a gracious covenant (1) because in it God allows a surety to meet our obligations; (2) because He himself offers the surety in the person of His Son, who meets the demands of justice; and (3) because, by his grace, revealed in the operation of the Holy Spirit, He enables man to live up to his covenant responsibilities.... It is grace from the beginning to the end for the sinner." *Reformed Dogmatics*, I, 262.
69. Sermon on Romans 6:14, Yale MSS, pp. 4-11.
70. "An Humble Attempt," *Works*, II, 288.
71. Sermon on Galatians 3:13-14, Andover MSS, pp. 2-4.

accomplishing man's salvation. The Holy Spirit has the unique task of placing man in the covenant. "We are dependent on the Holy Ghost, for it is *of him that we are in Christ Jesus;* it is the Spirit of God that gives faith in him whereby we receive him, and close with him."[72] In his sermons on John 16:8 Edwards writes:

> 'Tis the Holy Ghost that makes application of Christ's redemption. That is to say, that altho Jesus Christ prepares the way for men's salvation by his righteousness and sufferings, yet 'tis the immediate work of the Holy Ghost actually to make men partakers of that salvation. 'Tis he that doth the finishing stroke. Whatsoever Christ has done, yet if men were not brought to repentance, faith, union with God and Christ, all would be to no purpose. And it is the work of the Holy Ghost to bring this to pass.[73]

The covenant of grace is consummated by the Holy Spirit by effectually uniting the elect to Christ through faith. It is an everlasting covenant relation because the perseverance depends completely on God.

It would be totally contrary to Edwards' thought to fail to honor the human activity in the covenant relationship of faith. Grace does not preclude men receiving the salvation offered in the covenant. In the application of the sermon on Zechariah 4:7 which emphatically proclaims salvation by grace, Edwards exhorts all "to accept the grace of the gospel."[74] Salvation by grace in no way exempts anyone from the responsibility to accept God's goodness which is offered to them. The doctrine of a sermon on Revelation 22:17 states: "Nothing is required in order to having all the blessings of the gospel but willingly receiving."[75] Likewise, the Gospel of grace does not rule out good works but requires

---

72. Sermon on 1 Corinthians 1:29-31, *Works,* II, 3.
73. Sermon on John 16:8, Yale MSS, p. 3. Cf. Ames, *The Marrow of Theology,* p. 149: "Application is the making effectual, in certain men, of all those things which Christ has done and does as mediator." It "is attributed to the Holy Spirit.... But it depends, first, upon the Father's decree and donation by which he has given Christ certain men to be redeemed and saved, John 6:39."
74. Sermon on Zechariah 4:7, Yale MSS, p. 15.
75. Sermon on Revelation 22:17, Yale MSS, p. 1.

them. In this same sermon which states nothing is required but receiving, Edwards states: "Indeed we can't have gospel blessings without good works, not because works are a prerequisite condition, but because they are a part of the gospel blessing."[76] Everything is of grace, but there is no antinomianism. Man's activity is fully honored, but there is no synergism.

It is Edwards' conviction that any self-righteousness whatsoever "reflects upon the Holy Ghost, as tho he came into the world to convince men of lies":

> If it be so that your righteousness is the cause of your acceptance, then the Holy Ghost in coming to convince men of righteousness, comes to convince men of that that is not true. He comes to convince men that the righteousness of Christ is that alone by which we can have acceptance. But this is a lie if man's own righteousness be sufficient.[77]

There is no doubt in Edwards' mind that Scripture teaches salvation to be wholly of grace and grace alone. Anything that derogates from this in the least is equivalent to making God a liar. When Edwards teaches the covenant of grace, therefore, we dare not judge his intention as anything less than relating how the sovereign God freely and graciously applies the gift of salvation.

"Everyone that believes," says Edwards, "is beloved of God."[78] That love of God for the saints not only exists from eternity but is exercised from eternity.[79] The only "cause" of this in the fullest sense of the word is divine grace. But the means chosen by God to realize it in time is the covenant of grace, a covenant which, as we have seen, has its foundation in the eternal counsel of God.

---

76. Sermon on Revelation 22:17, Yale MSS, p. 13.
77. Sermons on John 16:8, Yale MSS, p. 63.
78. Sermon on Romans 8:29-30, Yale MSS, p. 4.
79. Sermon on Romans 8:29-30, Yale MSS, p. 5.

14

Justification by Faith in the Covenant of Grace

If the covenant of grace cannot exist in harmony with the clear proclamation of Scripture that justification is by faith alone, the covenant of grace must be discarded. Jonathan Edwards would be first in line of those who would go on record as accepting such a consequence. For Edwards, however, the issue retained its hypothetical status.

To take away the covenant of grace from Edwards requires both a misunderstanding of the covenant and an ignoring of what he wrote on the subject. Perry Miller is surely guilty of both when he declares that "the scandal of Edwards' discourses on justification . . . was his rejection of the covenant."[1] In this very discourse, "Justification by Faith Alone," Edwards ummistakably unites justification by faith alone with the covenant of grace.

> . . . By the covenant of grace we are not thus justified by our own works, but only by faith in Jesus Christ. It is on this account chiefly that the new covenant deserves the name of a covenant of grace, as is evident by Rom. iv. 16. "Therefore it is of faith, that it might be by grace."[2]

A consideration of the nature of faith, especially its designation as "union with Christ," will further clarify this faith-covenant relation.

---

1. Miller, *Jonathan Edwards*, pp. 115-116.
2. "Justification by Faith Alone," *Works*, I, 653.

The Nature of Covenant Faith

A fundamental aspect of justification by faith is that it is contrasted to justification by works or self-righteousness. The difference is fatal. The doctrine of a sermon on Romans 9:31-32 states, "That it's of fatal consequence to men's souls for 'em to trust in their own righteousness."[3] Edwards hammers away at this theme throughout the sermon. The error he sees in self-righteousness is "too high a notion of . . . our own supposed goodness" and "too light an apprehension" of God's displeasure with us.[4] Similarly, in another place Edwards writes:

> For a man to trust in his own righteousness, is to conceive hopes of some favour of God, or some freedom from his displeasure, from a false notion of his own goodness or excellency, and the proportion it bears to that favour; and of his own badness, and the relation it bears to his displeasure. . . . For men to trust in their own righteousness, is to entertain hope of escaping any displeasure, or obtaining any positive favour from God, from too high a notion of our own moral excellency, or too light a notion of our badness, as compared with or related to that favour or displeasure.[5]

The trouble with trusting our own righteousness is that it is justification by works, which is impossible.[6] It is also "contrary to the method revealed in the Gospel"; it is "contrary to God's eternal design to glorify his free grace"; and it is "a way not consonant to the honor of God's attributes."[7]

Because it is "faith alone by which men are united to Christ," "trusting their own righteousness will effectually prevent being saved in any other way."[8] The error of a man trusting his own righteousness is its supposition

> that he is justified already, at least in part. It supposes, that God's anger for sin is at least partly appeased, and that God is more

---

3. Sermon on Romans 9:31-32, Yale MSS, p. 2.
4. Sermon on Romans 9:31-32, Yale MSS, pp. 2-3.
5. "Miscellaneous Remarks," *Works,* II, 582.
6. Sermon on Romans 9:31-32, Yale MSS, p. 12.
7. Sermon on Romans 9:31-32, Yale MSS, p. 12.
8. Sermon on Romans 9:31-32, Yale MSS, p. 13.

favourably inclined to him for his excellency's sake, in that he is disposed to give him converting grace, or do something else towards his conversion upon that account.[9]

In his sermon on Titus 3:5 Edwards again emphasizes the fatal nature of trusting one's own righteousness.

> You must be emptied of yourself and be brought to trust in Christ's sufficiency and come to God only in his name if ever you are accepted. If your own righteousness is what you build upon, you build your house upon the sand, and when the wind blows and the rain descends and the floods of death come upon you, you'll fall and great is likely to be your fall.[10]

The contrast is between self-sufficiency or Christ's sufficiency.

It is not surprising then to see Edwards define faith as "the acquiesence of the soul in the divine sufficiency."[11] His doctrine of faith goes hand in hand with his important sermon "God Glorified in Man's Dependence." In that sermon on divine sovereignty Edwards gives this important statement on the nature of faith:

> Hence we may learn a reason why faith is that by which we come to have an interest in this redemption; for there is included in the nature of faith, a sensible acknowledgment of *absolute dependence* on God in this affair. It is very fit that it should be required of all in order to their having the benefit of redemption, that they should be sensible of, and acknowledge, their dependence on God for it. It is by this means that God hath contrived to glorify himself in redemption. . . . Faith is a sensibleness of what is real in the work of redemption; and the soul that believes doth entirely depend on God for all salvation, in its own sense and act. Faith abases men, and exalts God. . . .[12]

This is why faith is not a matter of degree. One either has an "absolute dependence" on God for salvation, or he does not.

---

9. "Miscellaneous Remarks," *Works*, II, 582.
10. Sermon on Titus 3:5, Yale MSS, p. 44.
11. Sermon on Habakkuk 2:4, Yale MSS, p. 4. Edwards acknowledges the broader definition of faith which includes trusting God for "all concerns," but the more restricted definition "respects . . . Christ in the particular concern of the salvation of souls" (pp. 4-5).
12. Sermon on 1 Corinthians 1:29-31, *Works*, II, 7.

Those in a state of damnation are "wholly destitute of it" and not merely with too little of it.[13]

True faith in its very nature looks outside itself; it is God directed. "It is necessary in order to saving faith, that man should be emptied of himself. ..."[14] In the second of two manuscript sermons on John 3:36 Edwards says "a sense of our own utter unworthiness of any mercy" must accompany true and saving faith.[15] It is an awareness of our inability and God's sovereignty in bestowing faith that undergirds the believer's assurance of persevering in faith.

> It is one act of faith to commit the soul to Christ's keeping in this sense, *viz.* to keep it from falling. The believing soul is convinced of its own weakness and helplessness, its inability to resist its enemies, its insufficiency to keep itself, and so commits itself to Christ, that he would be its keeper.... Faith (on our part) is the great condition of salvation; it is that *by* which we are justified and saved. But in this faith, the perseverance that belongs to it is a fundamental ground of the congruity that faith gives to salvation.... And it is looked upon as if it were a property of that faith by which the sinner is then justified. God has respect to continuance in faith; and the sinner is justified by that, as though it already were; because by divine establishment it shall follow.... Without this ... it would be needful that the act of justification should be suspended till the sinner had persevered in faith.[16]

From beginning to end we are dependent upon God "in the whole of it."

Faith has value not in itself but because it lives off grace.

---

13. Cf. "Miscellaneous Remarks," *Works*, II, 593-594, where Edwards shows how the difference between common and saving faith is not a matter of degree but of nature and kind.

14. Sermon on 1 Corinthians 1:29-31, *Works*, II, 7. Cf. G. C. Berkouwer, *Faith and Justification*, trans. Lewis B. Smedes (Grand Rapids, 1963), where he shows this emphasis to be characteristic of Reformed theology. "... Faith ... recognizes and accepts the exclusiveness of God's salvation" (p. 18). "... Faith has significance only in its orientation to its object—the grace of God. Thus, *sola fide*, instead of directing our attention to the believer, points us away from him to grace and God" (p. 29). "... Faith does nothing but accept, or come to rest in the sovereignty of His benefits" (p. 43). "Faith is not a human act that compliments God's act of grace.... Faith holds us in fellowship with Him who is our justification" (p. 45). "Our contribution amounts to precisely zero" (p. 89).

15. Sermon on John 3:36 (2), Yale MSS, p. 3.

16. "Miscellaneous Remarks," *Works*, II, 598.

Edwards suggests that "believing," rather than "choosing or loving," is the key designation in order to prevent the misunderstanding that there is some "moral goodness" in it.[17] Faith by definition is without merit.

> But in the act of that faith which God requires in order to a sinner's justification, he looks on himself wholly as a sinner or ungodly. He has no consideration of any goodness or holiness of his own in that affair but merely and only the righteousness of Christ, and thus he seeks justification of himself as in himself ungodly and unrighteous by the righteousness of another. And so it is that God looks on him in justifying him. God has no . . . consideration of any goodness in him when he justifies by faith. . . .[18]

Faith then is not a good work which replaces all other good works.

> When it is said we are not justified by works nothing else is implied than that nothing that we do procures justification of God for us by virtue of the goodness or loveliness of it. . . . In the first covenant respect was had to the goodness or loveliness of works in fixing them as the condition of life. But 'tis not so under the second covenant.[19]

This is at the heart of his disagreement with the Arminians and their notion of a "self-determining" will. The Arminian view involves a neonomian understanding of faith, and in a letter to John Erskine, Edwards makes the following important observations:

> The doctrine of a self-determining will . . . teaches a kind of absolute independence on all those things, that are of chief importance in this affair; our righteousness depending originally on our own acts, as self-determined. Thus our own holiness is from ourselves, as its determining cause, and its original and highest source. And as for imputed righteousness, that should have any merit at all in it, to be sure, there can be no such thing. For self-determination is necessary to praise and merit. But what is imputed from another is not from our self-determination or action. And truly, in this scheme, man is not dependent on God; but God is rather dependent on man. . . .
> The nature of true faith implies a disposition, to give all the

---

17. "Miscellanies," No. 329, Yale MSS.
18. "Miscellanies," No. 1161, Yale MSS.
19. Sermon on Romans 4:26, Yale MSS, p. 15.

glory of our salvation to God and Christ. But this notion is inconsistent with it, for it in effect gives the glory wholly to man. For that is the very doctrine that is taught, that the merit and praise is his, whose is the original and effectual determination of the praiseworthy deed.[20]

According to Edwards "that which makes our obedience the matter of our justification" is "contrary to the gospel doctrine of justification by faith."[21]

In his notes on Romans 4:3-4 Edwards emphasizes the significance of the apostle's stress on the words "counted" or "imputed."

> If he had had a righteousness, that is, of his own, upon the account of which the reward was of proper debt, it would not have been expressed in this manner, as he evidently argues in the following verses. Abraham's believing God was not righteousness, but was only *imputed* for it. It was of God's mere grace looked upon as supplying the room of righteousness.[22]

The situation is again seen to be either one's own righteousness or righteousness given by God.

In the application of a sermon on Romans 2:10 Edwards poses the inquiry, "What must I be brought to in order to get to heaven?" He lists seven requirements, but the first two are of the essence in illuminating his doctrine of faith. First, "You must be brought entirely to renounce all hope of obtaining heaven by any thing that you can do by your own strength," and "you must be brought off from all confiding in your own strength" and "renounce your own righteousness as the price of heaven."[23] Secondly, "Your heart must be brought to close with him who has purchased heaven"; and being drawn to Him, "it must be pleasing and sweet to you to have heaven as a free gift."[24]

Essential to Edwards' understanding of faith is his emphasis on one's coming to Christ being done willingly, indeed,

---

20. *Freedom of the Will*, pp. 468-469.
21. "Miscellanies," No. 474, Yale MSS.
22. "Notes on the Bible," *Works*, II, 798.
23. Sermon on Romans 2:10, *Works*, II, 903.
24. Sermon on Romans 2:10, *Works*, II, 904.

being drawn to Christ by a desire for His "excellency." Justifying faith is defined as

> a sense and conviction of the reality and excellency of Christ as a Saviour that entirely inclines and unites the heart to him. There is the act of the whole soul in it, of every faculty entirely embracing and acquiescing in the gospel that reveals Jesus Christ as our Saviour. . . . There is an entire yielding of the mind and heart to it and a closing with it with the belief, with the inclination and affection, it being the complex act of the whole soul and of each faculty together.[25]

Faith involves correct knowledge, the truth of Christ and the Gospel, but it is infinitely far from saving faith unless there is a "taste" or "relish" or "new sense of divine things." It is the "divine and supernatural light" that removes the "natural blindness in things of religion." This is the point of Edwards' teaching that the Holy Spirit's work is upon the heart or the will. Not new knowledge but a new taste is necessary. Such a "taste" is a "divine and supernatural light" and the gift of God's grace.

The gratuitous nature of faith with its emphasis on believing rather than doing does not negate the fact that it is man who believes. The doctrines of sovereignty and grace, as well as the doctrine of faith, in no way jeopardize the biblical emphasis on man's being active and responsible. It is precisely the fact that man is active in faith which makes the covenant concept a legitimate form for expressing the relationship between God and the elect.

In "Justification by Faith Alone" Edwards deals with the question of how it is "by faith *alone.*" Faith is the sole "qualification," he says, "because it is that in him which, *on his part,* makes up this union between him and Christ."[26]

---

25. Sermon on Romans 4:16, Yale MSS, pp. 7-8. Cf. Miller, *NEM: 17th Century*, p. 30: The Holy Spirit may [sic] use argumentation, but it goes much farther and enables the soul to see intuitively as well as through the point-by-point demonstrations of logical discourse. . . ." The "much farther" is the work of the Spirit according to Edwards, but the natural knowledge is not by-passed in a mystical or antinomian fashion. Cf. Carse, *Jonathan Edwards and the Visibility of God*, pp. 114-129.

26. "Justification by Faith Alone," *Works*, I, 625.

Edwards' concern is primarily to show that faith unites us to Christ, and in that union is the basis of the sinners' justification. But man is active in entering that union.

> ... I suppose there is nobody but what will allow, that there may be something that the true Christian does *on his part*, whereby he is *active* in coming into this relation or union; some *uniting* act, or that which is done towards this union or relation (or whatever any please to call it) *on the Christian's part*. Now faith I suppose to be this act.[27]

Edwards stresses that this union or interest in Christ is not a *"reward* for faith," but they are united because faith *is* the "soul's *active* uniting with Christ... *on their part."*[28] "God... treats men as reasonable creatures, capable of act and choice...."[29]

The essence of man's being is not by-passed, but sanctified, in saving faith. Man as a unified, whole being believes.

> Upon the whole, the best, and clearest, and most perfect definition of justifying faith, and most according to the Scripture, that I can think of, is this, faith is the soul's entirely embracing the revelation of Jesus Christ as our Saviour.... It is the whole soul according and assenting to the truth, and embracing of it. There is an entire yielding of the mind and heart to the revelation, and a closing with it, and adhering to it, with the belief, and with the inclination and affection.[30]

James Carse points out that Edwards' identification of "faith as the action of the soul" was much bolder than, though not contrary to, the Reformers.[31] Calvin and the Reformers were struggling against the "works righteousness" prevalent within the Roman Church. They were not opposed to the idea of the soul's activity in faith. "The Reformers did not want to

---

27. "Justification by Faith Alone," *Works*, I, 625.
28. "Justification by Faith Alone," *Works*, I, 626.
29. "Justification by Faith Alone," *Works*, I, 626. Cf. G. C. Berkouwer's discussion on "concurrence" in *The Providence of God*, trans. Lewis B. Smedes (Grand Rapids, 1961), pp. 125-160. The fundamental truth from which the discussions arise is seen in the statement: "... Scripture nowhere suggests that God's work is limited by human activity or that God's activity negates human enterprise" (p. 127).
30. "Miscellaneous Remarks," *Works*, II, 580.
31. Carse, *Jonathan Edwards and the Visibility of God*, p. 115.

say that man could be saved by his own actions, but they did want to say that his salvation necessitated action."[32]

If Edwards saw the whole man involved in faith, yet it was a unified and single act. In plain language faith is receiving. The doctrine of a sermon on Revelation 22:17 states: "Nothing is required in order to have all the blessings of the gospel but willingly receiving."[33] He does emphasize that knowledge is essential to this receiving. One must know what it is he is receiving.[34] In a sermon on Luke 14:16 Edwards compares guests being freely invited to a feast to sinners being freely invited to receive the Gospel blessings. God "requires nothing of us for it," and if we were to buy it, we are without the price.[35] This receiving is reminiscent of Calvin's comparison of faith to an empty vessel.

The receiving "is the hearty receiving of Christ and his gospel" and involves the heart as compared to a mere outward receiving.

> A person may receive a thing and yet his heart not receive it. A woman that is sought in marriage may . . . receive her lover when her heart don't receive him. . . . The door that Christ stands at and knocks and calls for entrance is the door of the heart.[36]

Such an attitude of the heart involves an understanding of the Gospel of Jesus Christ which realizes the gratuitous character of salvation "through the worthiness and righteousness of Christ."[37] In this sermon Edwards explicitly teaches that "God opens the understanding of a believer to see this," and "the soul is drawn to Christ Jesus" with the consent of the mind and heart.[38]

Man is thus active in faith, but his faith is a gift of God. Edwards attributed faith to the efficacious grace of God which is an "immediate power" above "second causes."

---

32. Carse, *Jonathan Edwards and the Visibility of God*, p. 117.
33. Sermon on Revelation 22:17, Yale MSS, p. 1.
34. Sermon on Revelation 22:17, Yale MSS, pp. 2-3.
35. Sermon on Luke 14:16, Andover MSS, p. 7.
36. Sermon on Galatians 5:6 (1), Yale MSS, pp. 5-6.
37. Sermon on Galatians 5:6 (1), Yale MSS, p. 7.
38. Sermon on Galatians 5:6 (1), Yale MSS, pp. 9-11.

> In that text in Ephesians the apostle speaks of faith, "the power that works in us that believe." So in this text in Colossians, "ye are risen through faith." Again, 2dly, in Ephesians, together with what there follows, chap. ii. he compareth believing to a rising from the dead.... It is called faith of the operation or effectual working of God, and as there God is said to be the author, the same that raised up Christ, and to work faith in them, as here it is the faith of the operation of God who raised Christ from the dead, so that, every way, one place is parallel with the other.... But that the apostle means the operation of God in giving faith, appears by verse 11. which introduces these words, where the apostle says, "In whom ye are circumcised with the circumcision made without hands, in putting off the body of the sins of the flesh by the circumcision of Christ." The phrase, *made without hands*, in Scripture, always denote God's immediate power above the course of nature, and above second causes.[39]

The danger is real in stressing the human activity of faith that it will be interpreted in a synergistic manner. One must be very careful in the use of language to avoid such a pitfall. Edwards would state that man's activity is neither contrary to or apart from, but a part of, God's sovereign election. In a sermon on 1 Peter 2:9 in which election is set forth as the decisive factor for Christians, he teaches that the doctrine of election shows us "that faith itself is the gift of God, and that the saints persevering in a way of holiness unto glory, is also the fruit of electing love."[40]

As a Calvinist Edwards taught moral inability, but he saw in this no exclusion of the covenant idea. Consistently Edwards emphasized the responsibility of man to embrace the covenant of grace by faith (receiving), while insisting that God alone gave the disposition in the elect to believe. Man's part in the covenant has its origin in the eternal counsel of God.

When Edwards, in describing efficacious grace, said, "God does all, and we do all," when he writes, "God is said to

---

39. "Miscellaneous Remarks," *Works*, II, 545.
40. Sermon on 1 Peter 2:9, *Works*, II, 938. Cf. "Miscellanies," No. 705, Yale MSS: "Tho giving an interest in Christ is evermore an act of meer sovereignty, yet denying an interest in Christ may be a judicial act."

convert, and men are said to convert,"[41] he is affirming not only what he believes to be the teaching of Scripture but a long tradition before him. Ames for example stresses that receiving, which is necessary, depends upon God:

> 26. Active receiving is an elicited act of faith in which he who is called now wholly leans upon Christ as his savior and through Christ upon God. John 3:15, 16, *Whoever believes in him;* I Peter 1:21, *Through him believing in God.*
> 27. This act of faith depends partly upon an inborn principle or attitude toward grace and partly upon the action of God moving before and stirring up. John 6:44, *None can come to me, unless the Father . . . draws him.*
> 28. It is indeed called forth and exercised by man freely but also surely, unavoidably, and unchangeably. John 6:37, *Whomever my Father gives me will come to me.*
> 29. With this faith in which the will is turned to possessing the true good, there is always joined repentance, in which the same will is turned to doing the true good and comes to turn away from and hate the contrary evil or sin. Acts 19:4; Mark 1:15, *Repent, and believe in the gospel.*[42]

Similarly, Turretin expresses the same idea when he writes of faith and repentance:

> Although these two duties are commanded by God, as works due from man, still they are also promised by him, as his gifts; so that they are here to be considered at the same time, both as the duties of man, and as the blessings of God, Ezek. xxxvi. 27, *I will put my spirit within you, and cause you to walk in my statutes,* etc.[43]

So Edwards likewise stresses the gift of the Holy Spirit as the "cause" of faith and good works. In his series of sermons on John 16:8, Edwards attributes to the Spirit the believer's "embracing," "consenting," and "closing" in regard to Christ. "All prevailing opposition ceases"; "the soul quits all other endeavors for reconciliation"; and trusting in Christ alone, "there follows a quiet rest and calm of the mind."[44] Later when he stresses that "men are justified freely by faith

---

41. "Miscellaneous Remarks," *Works*, II, 557.
42. Ames, *The Marrow of Theology*, p. 159.
43. Turretin, *Institutio* (Loc. XII, Q. II, xxx), II, 202 (Eng. pp. 302-303).
44. Sermons on John 16:8, Yale MSS, pp. 57-58.

in Jesus" and are "sure of heaven" once they "believe in Christ," he speaks to those who imply one need not trouble with good works.[45]

> ... The gospel secures good works, tho men are justified only by faith, and not by the works of the law. For the work of the Holy Ghost in conversion don't only consist in convincing men of righteousness, but also of judgment. He don't only show them the sufficiency of Christ's righteousness to justify 'em, and to make 'em receive him as a Saviour from punishment, but also shows the glory of Jesus Christ as Lord and King, and makes them receive him heartily and entirely as their Lord and King. . . . That is, he makes them to submit to his rule and government. . . . Conviction of righteousness and of judgment always go together. The Holy Ghost does not give one without the other. The preceding conviction of sin is in order to both these, and these are always given together in conversion.[46]

The Spirit works upon the will, providing a new disposition and spiritual "taste," and because the will follows the strongest motive or apparent good, the regenerated person freely *and* necessarily will follow that which is God's command since that is now what he loves and desires above all else.[47] As a sound apple tree will necessarily produce good apples, so the sinner whose evil disposition has been converted to a good disposition will necessarily be inclined to good works and do them. It would be a contradiction for the Holy Spirit to give one without the other.

Edwards sees the covenant of grace and justification by faith alone as descriptions of the same phenomena.[48] The

---

45. Sermons on John 16:8, Yale MSS, pp. 91-92.
46. Sermons on John 16:8, Yale MSS, p. 92. Cf. "Miscellanies," No. 1354, Yale MSS, where Edwards says "obedience is . . . insisted on as a thing consequentially necessary."
47. The principle here is precisely the burden of Edwards' *Freedom of the Will,* a work so foundational to his thought that much of his theology is inexplicable without it. Cf. especially Part I of *Freedom of the Will* where "will," "determination of the will," "necessity," "moral and natural necessity," and "freedom" are defined.
48. Cf. "Justification by Faith Alone," *Works,* I, 653. ". . . By the covenant of grace we are not justified by our own works, but only by faith in Jesus Christ."
Bavinck, *Our Reasonable Faith,* pp. 277-278, deals with the covenant as honoring man's activity. ". . . The covenant of grace . . . realizes itself in a way

Justification by Faith in the Covenant of Grace

covenant concept honors both the sovereignty of God and the moral nature of man. Immediately after defining faith as a "being drawn to Christ," he writes:

> The freeness of the covenant of grace is represented thus, that the condition of finding is only seeking; and the condition of receiving, asking; and the condition of having the door opened, is knocking. From whence I infer, that faith is a hearty applying unto God by Christ for salvation, or the heart's seeking it of God through him.[49]

"Hearty applying" and "being drawn" are correlates in Edwards' theology.

Faith as man's part in the covenant of grace is implied in "An Humble Inquiry" where "profession" is equated with "owning" the covenant. "... It is a duty ... *to make an explicit open profession of true religion, by owning God's covenant; or, in other words, professedly and verbally to unite themselves to God in his covenant by their own public act.*"[50]

Faith as Union with Christ

One cannot read Edwards in any depth without being sensitive to the importance to him of designating faith as union with Christ. It was not a new doctrine but an increased emphasis. "... Calvinistic theologians did not usually stress faith as a uniting with Christ in the penetrating way in which

---

which fully honors man's rational and moral nature.... Behind the covenant of grace lies the sovereign and omnipotent will of God, which is penetrated by Divine energy, and which therefore guarantees the triumph....

"But that will is not a necessity, a destiny, which imposes itself on man from without, but is, rather, the will of the Creator of heaven and earth, One who cannot repudiate His own work in creation or providence, and who cannot treat the human being He has created as though it were a stock or stone....

"This accounts for the fact that the covenant of grace, which really makes no demands and lays down no conditions, nevertheless comes to us in the form of a commandment, admonishing us to faith and repentance (Mark 1:15).... But in order that as promise and gift it may be realized in us, it takes on the character of moral admonishment in accordance with our nature.... The will of God realizes itself in no other way than through our reason and our will."

49. "Miscellaneous Remarks," *Works*, II, 579.
50. "An Humble Inquiry," *Works*, I, 441.

Edwards did."[51] For Edwards union with Christ is both a doctrine and an experience; it is truth and beauty. The value of faith is not in itself but in its object. Faith unites the believer with Him who *is* our righteousness.

In his discourse on justification Edwards discusses what is meant when it is said that we are justified *by* faith. He refers to the common designation of faith as an "instrument," and while he does not feel there was anything wrong in the intention of those who called faith an instrument, he finds it to be a less than ideal expression for faith.

> ... It was not intended that faith was the instrument wherewith God justifies, but the instrument wherewith we receive justification; not the instrument wherewith the justifier acts in justifying, but wherewith the receiver of justification acts in accepting justification. But yet, it must be owned, this is an obscure way of speaking, and there must certainly be some impropriety in calling it an instrument wherewith we receive or accept justification; for the very persons who thus explain the matter, speak of faith as being the reception or acceptance itself; and if so, how can it be the instrument of reception or acceptance?... If faith be an instrument, it is more properly the instrument by which we receive Christ, than the instrument by which we receive justification.[52]

It is in the framework of Edwards' uneasiness with the

---

51. Gerstner, *Steps to Salvation*, p. 141. Cf. Schafer, *Church History*, XX, 58, 65, notes 33, 34, for references to Ames, Turretin, and Mastricht. John Cotton was a covenant theologian, and this summary of his position on the doctrine of union with Christ is found in Foster, *A Genetic History of the New England Theology*, p. 26: "Mr. Cotton seems, at first sight, to have been farther from the truth than his colleagues, and was brought with some difficulty to a partial agreement with them. He held that our 'union with Christ' is complete before and without the work or act of faith though not before or without the 'habit' or gift of faith. It is evident from his own subsequent expressions that he was after all in substantial agreement with the rest, for he says, 'I looked at union with Christ as equivalent to regeneration.' This as the divine part in conversion does at least logically precede the act of faith. But, however they might be divided upon this point, Mr. Cotton and all the rest were united in viewing man as passive in faith. For the sake of securing the honor of God as the author of regeneration, they held views of divine sovereignty, inability, and regeneration which in effect rendered man totally passive till the indispensable condition was fulfilled, upon which faith followed, as a spontaneous act, it is true, but still as necessary."

52. "Justification by Faith Alone," *Works*, I, 624.

instrumental designation of faith that one can appreciate his preference for the union concept.

> It is certain that there is some union or relation that the people of Christ stand in to him, that is expressed in Scripture, from time to time, by being *in Christ*, and is represented frequently by those metaphors of being members of Christ, or being united to him as members to the head, and branches to the stock, and is compared to a marriage union between husband and wife.[53]

Especially the marriage union is important in relation to the covenant doctrine, but it also illustrates the unmeritorious nature of faith.

> Indeed, neither salvation itself, nor Christ the Saviour, are given as a reward of any thing in man: they are not given as a reward of faith, nor any thing else of ours: we are not united to Christ as a reward of our faith, but have union with him by faith, only as faith is the very act of uniting or closing *on our part*. As when a man offers himself to a woman in marriage, he does not give himself to her as a *reward* of her receiving him in marriage. Her receiving him is not considered as a worthy deed in her for which he rewards her by giving himself to her; but it is by her receiving him that the union is made, by which she hath him for her husband. It is *on her part* the unition itself. . . . It appears how contrary to the gospel of Christ their scheme is, who say that faith justifies as a principle of obedience. . . .[54]

Faith then is our nonmeritorious uniting with Christ.

This emphasis is found throughout Edwards' preaching. In the sermon on Habakkuk 2:4 he defines faith as "that by which the soul is united to Christ."[55] "Faith is the . . . uniting act of the soul towards Jesus Christ whereby it receives and closes with him, and being thereby united to Christ, believers become his members and he is their head to communicate vital influences."[56] In the second of two sermons on John 3:36 he defines faith as the "soul's entirely uniting and closing with Christ for his Saviour."[57] In a sermon on Romans 4:16 one of Edwards' designations for faith is a

---

53. "Justification by Faith Alone," *Works*, I, 624.
54. "Justification by Faith Alone," *Works*, I, 640.
55. Sermon on Habakkuk 2:4, Yale MSS, p. 10.
56. Sermon on Habakkuk 2:4, Yale MSS, p. 10.
57. Sermon on John 3:36 (2), Yale MSS, p. 3.

"sense and conviction" which "entirely inclines and unites the heart to Christ as Saviour."[58]

The "Miscellanies" also abound in similar references. Concerning justifying faith, Edwards says faith justifies "not for the goodness or loveliness of the grace of faith . . . but only because 'tis that act on their part which makes 'em one."[59] In "Miscellany" No. 617 Edwards contrasts the covenants of redemption and grace, comparing the latter to a marriage covenant, which is the "marriage" union between Christ and believers.[60] In the first half of chapter 9, we saw Edwards' use of the marriage analogy to describe the covenant of grace. In speaking of faith as union with Christ, we are merely expanding the implications of that same concept.

In another "Miscellany" Edwards calls faith "an active uniting of the person to Christ."[61] The importance of this for the covenant of grace is obvious. "God the Father makes no covenant and enters into no treaty with fallen man distinctly by themselves; he will transact with them in such a friendly way no other way than by and in Christ Jesus as members and as it were parts of him."[62] Justification is *by* faith because faith unites us to Christ. "That it is by uniting us to Christ so that we should properly be looked upon as IN HIM by the following places as the words are in the Greek. Gal. 2:17, justified in Christ; Eph. 4:32, in Christ hath forgiven you—Gal. 3:11-14."[63]

Edwards, as would be expected from all that has gone before, attributes the act of uniting to the grace of God.

---

58. Sermon on Romans 4:16, Yale MSS, p. 12. This hearty assent, according to Edwards, "implies a yielding of the whole soul. . . . A true conviction of the reality and excellency [of Christ as Saviour] causes an adherence of the soul to him. . . . To believe is to have the heart drawn to Christ."
59. "Miscellanies," No. 568, Yale MSS. He adds: "God sees it fit that they only that are one with Christ by their own act should be looked upon as one in law."
    60. "Miscellanies," No. 617, Yale MSS.
    61. "Miscellanies," No. 632, Yale MSS.
    62. "Miscellanies," No. 1091, Yale MSS.
    63. "Miscellanies," No. 1250, Yale MSS.

Justification by Faith in the Covenant of Grace

Union with Christ is a fruit, and not the root, of God's grace.[64] Those united with Christ are one and the same as the elect. Edwards writes: "Jesus Christ is the great medium and head of union in whom all elect creatures in heaven and earth are united to God and to one another."[65] In a sermon on Galatians 3:16 the importance of the covenant and Christ as the covenant head is indicated. "All the rewards God promised to Christ were promised to Christ's mystical [body]," and the members of that body were "chosen in Christ before the world began."[66] "Christ and his elect church are respected as one mystical person in the purchase that Christ made."[67] Christ acted not only for Himself but "for them as one," and "all that Christ purchased was for Christ's mystical [body]."[68] And the wisdom of God is displayed in salvation in that Christ also purchased for the elect the faith which is given them, "whereby they shall be [actively] united to Christ, and so have a [pleadable] title to his benefits."[69]

The covenant implications have already been mentioned. Edwards explicitly equates saving faith with both union with Christ and "joining the covenant."

> But the union, cleaving, or joining of that covenant, is saving faith, the grand condition or the covenant of Christ, by which we are in Christ. This is what [on our part] brings us *into the Lord*. For a person explicitly or professedly to enter into the union or relation of the covenant of grace with Christ, is the same as professedly to do that which on our part is the uniting act, and that is the act of faith. To profess the covenant of grace, is to profess it, not as a spectator, but as one immediately concerned in the affair, as a party in the covenant professed; and this is to profess *that* in the covenant which belongs to us *as a party*, or to profess *our part* in the covenant; and that is the soul's believing acceptance of the Saviour. Christ's part is salvation, our part is a

---

64. Sermon on Zechariah 4:7, Yale MSS, p. 12.
65. Sermon on Ephesians 1:10, Yale MSS, p. 5.
66. Sermon on Galatians 3:16, Yale MSS, p. 12.
67. Sermon on Galatians 3:16, Yale MSS, p. 13.
68. Sermon on Galatians 3:16, Yale MSS, p. 13.
69. "The Wisdom of God, Displayed in the Way of Salvation," *Works*, II, 146-147.

saving faith in him; not a feigned, but unfeigned faith; not a common, but special and saving faith; no other faith is the condition of the covenant of grace.[70]

Though the covenant of grace in its eternal origin is one-sided, yet in the historical application of it there is a mutuality, a profession on the part of both Christ and man, a consent of the heart as in marriage.

> The transaction of that covenant is that of espousals to Christ; on our part, it is giving our souls to Christ as his spouse. There is no one thing that the covenant of grace is so often compared to in Scripture, as the marriage-covenant; and the visible transaction, or mutual profession, there is between Christ and the visible church, is abundantly compared to the mutual profession there is in marriage. In marriage the bride professes to yield to the bridegroom's suit, and to take him for her husband, renouncing all others, and to give up herself to him to be entirely and for ever possessed by him as his wife. But he that professes this towards Christ, professes saving faith. They that openly covenanted with God according to the tenor of the institution, Deut. x. 20. visibly united themselves to God in the union of that covenant. They professed on their parts the union of the covenant of God, which was the covenant of grace.[71]

In one of the "Miscellanies" Edwards compares union with Christ to marriage and calls faith the "bride's reception of Christ as a bridegroom."[72] This involves an acceptance of Christ as a "shelter from the wrath of God," and "Christ will not receive those as the objects of his salvation who trust to themselves, their own strength or worthiness, but those alone who entirely rely on him."[73]

In an outlinish manuscript sermon on Hosea 3:1-3 Edwards says, "The covenant . . . between God and a professing people is like a marriage covenant" where they "profess and oblige themselves to renounce all others" and to belong to each other forever.[74] The text refers to Hosea's marriage to

---

70. "An Humble Inquiry," *Works*, I, 443.
71. "An Humble Inquiry," *Works*, I, 443.
72. "Miscellanies," No. 37, Yale MSS.
73. "Miscellanies," No. 37, Yale MSS.
74. Sermon on Hosea 3:1-3, Yale MSS, pp. 1-3.

Justification by Faith in the Covenant of Grace

her who would "play the harlot," and Edwards cites 1 Corinthians 6:16-17 which states, "He which is joined to an harlot is one body.... But he that is joined unto the Lord is one spirit."[75] It is the unity with the Lord through which salvation comes.

In the "Miscellanies" Edwards writes: "The new covenant itself evidences that it is made with Christ, and not with believers considered as distant from him."[76] In the first entry on the "covenant" in the "Miscellanies" Edwards emphasizes that "Christ is a common head and representative of believers." Thus he writes, "It is very improper to say that a covenant is made with men any otherwise than in Christ."[77] The covenant union with Christ is the key to "our" success in the covenant. "By Christ's performing the condition of the covenant, the condition is as if it were performed by them."[78] One recognizes in this critical "as if" a parallel with the "as if" involved in the doctrine of imputation of Christ's righteousness to the believer "as if" it were his own.

In the sermon on Galatians 3:16 Edwards' theme is that in God's work of salvation "Christ and believers are considered as ... one mystical person" and are so considered "in that covenant that God has entered into in order to their salvation."[79] In his notes on this text, he quotes Locke approvingly that "seed" refers to "Christ, and his mystical body."[80]

The union as a gift of God and an act of man is paralleled by the covenant of redemption and the covenant of grace. According to Edwards there is a primary and a secondary ground for this union. The "primary ground" is "the act of the Father and Son"; the "secondary ground" is "the act of

---
75. Sermon on Hosea 3:1-3, Yale MSS, p. 4.
76. "Miscellanies," No. 163, Yale MSS.
77. "Miscellanies," No. 2, Yale MSS.
78. "Miscellanies," No. 2, Yale MSS.
79. Sermon on Galatians 3:16, Yale MSS, pp. 2, 5. Cf. p. 11 with references to Titus 1:2, 2 Tim. 1:9, and Eph. 1:4.
80. "Notes on the Bible," *Works,* II, 802.

believers."[81] The primary ground is the "eternal donation of them to Christ" from God the Father and Christ's love to them.[82] Though they are "given to Christ from eternity," yet they are "not actually in Christ till they have believed in him," and thus the designation of man's belief as a secondary ground.[83] Included in the application is the question whether the hearer has "consented to the covenant of grace" and the admonition to seek that union with Christ.[84]

Faith then is the unique qualification that results in the believer's justification. As Edwards never tires of saying, our justification is not by works. Nothing we *do* procures reconciliation. "God don't justify us in this manner upon the account of any act of ours, whether it be the act of faith or any other act whatsoever, but only upon the account of what the Saviour did."[85]

Yet it is by *faith alone* and not without faith that a sinner is justified. Edwards speaks of a suitableness or agreeableness in faith, however, which does not conflict with justification apart from works.

> But tis something that we do that renders it in God's account as the case now stands (there being a Saviour) a meet thing that God should let go his anger and admit us into his favour, as it may render it a meet thing in the sight of God that we and [sic] particular should be looked upon as united to the Saviour, and having the merit of what he did and sufferd ... by reason of its being the primary and most simple and direct exercise of uniting, harmony and agreement in the soul with that Saviour and his salvation, and the way of it, and the proper act of reception of him or closing and uniting with him.... This is quite a different thing from the former.[86]

Justification by faith alone does not refer to our own merit

---

81. Sermon on Galatians 3:16, Yale MSS, p. 16.
82. Sermon on Galatians 3:16, Yale MSS, p. 17. Edwards cites scriptural references where Christ speaks of the Father giving them to Him.
83. Sermon on Galatians 3:16, Yale MSS, p. 18.
84. Sermon on Galatians 3:16, Yale MSS, pp. 21, 25.
85. "Miscellanies," No. 416, Yale MSS.
86. "Miscellanies," No. 416, Yale MSS.

or excellency but to the uniqueness of faith as that which unites us to Christ, by which we possess what He possesses. Edwards speaks of a "fitness" of faith in justification without violating the doctrine of absolute grace in salvation by using a distinction between a moral fitness and a natural fitness. "Miscellany" No. 647 contains this distinction which also shows up in Edwards' discourse on "Justification" where he spells out this important distinction:

> A person has a moral fitness for a state, when his moral excellency commends him to it. . . . A person has a natural fitness for a state, when it appears meet and condecent that he should be in such a state or circumstances, only from the natural concord or agreeableness there is between such qualifications and such circumstances; not because the qualifications are lovely or unlovely, but only because the qualifications and the circumstances are like one another, or do in their nature suit and agree or unite one to another. And it is on this latter account only that God looks on it fit by a natural fitness, that he whose heart sincerely unites itself to Christ as his Saviour, should be looked upon as united to that Saviour, and so having an interest in him; and not from any moral fitness there is between the excellency of such a qualification as faith. . . . God's bestowing Christ and his benefits on a soul in consequence of faith, out of regard only to the natural concord there is between such a qualification of a soul, and such an union with Christ. . . . God will neither look on Christ's merits as ours, nor adjudge his benefits to us, till we be in Christ: nor will he look upon us as being in him, without an active unition of our hearts and souls to him. . . . A moral suitableness or fitness to a state includes a natural: . . . but such a natural suitableness as I have described, by no means necessarily includes a moral.
>
> This is plainly what our divines intend when they say, that faith does not justify as a *work*, or a righteousness, *viz*. that it does not justify as a part of our moral goodness or excellency. . . .[87]

In one of the "Miscellanies" Edwards gives a sevenfold answer repudiating the objection that such a "natural fitness" puts the foundation of a believer's justification "in nature and not in God's pleasure."[88] For Edwards that is a false

---

[87]. "Justification by Faith Alone," *Works*, I, 627. Cf. "Miscellanies," No. 647, Yale MSS.
[88]. "Miscellanies," No. 831, Yale MSS.

dilemma since God stands prior to and above any such arrangement.

From the distinction between moral and natural fitness Edwards states the following corollary: "They therefore that hold that sincere obedience is the condition of being in Christ, as such a moral fitness as is above described, they maintain what is contrary to the Scripture doctrine of justification by faith alone."[89] "When it is said forgive and ye shall be forgiven, ... there is no necessity of supposing that 'tis out of respect to the moral fitness ... for there is a natural fitness and suitableness between these things."[90] In another "Miscellany" which Edwards intends as a continuation of the one just mentioned, he refers to such "conditional" promises as "not conditions of salvation the same way as faith is."[91] He explained this in the prior entry thus: "Men are saved only by faith but yet they are saved by evangelical obedience so far as it is an expression of faith."[92]

Evangelical obedience is thus in the same category as the works to which James attributes justification. They are necessary as an effect and not as a cause. The doctrine of a sermon on Galatians 5:6 states: "Only that sort of faith that works by love avails anything before God."[93] Edwards means a working faith, a faith that is not alone, and one which "brings forth the proper fruits of it in the life."[94] Good works arise from true faith and flow from love. Thus "evangelical obedience flows from love and not principally from fear."[95]

As we bring to a conclusion our consideration of faith in general and union with Christ in particular, it would be well to note the blessed fruit of this faith for those who believe.

---

89. "Miscellanies," No. 647, Yale MSS.
90. "Miscellanies," No. 670, Yale MSS.
91. "Miscellanies," No. 714, Yale MSS.
92. "Miscellanies," No. 670, Yale MSS.
93. Sermon on Galatians 5:6 (1), Yale MSS, p. 4.
94. Sermon on Galatians 5:6 (1), Yale MSS, pp. 13-14.
95. Sermon on Galatians 5:6 (1), Yale MSS, p. 15.

Justification by Faith in the Covenant of Grace 249

Such a concern brings us squarely to the necessity of faith in uniting us with Christ and the covenant of grace.

Justification is by faith alone precisely because justification is by works. Though this may at first seem contradictory, it will become clarified as soon as one realizes that our Puritan defender of solifidianism believed the only ground for justification is actual righteousness, without which none will inherit eternal life. This was seen in the chapter dealing with the covenant of works, which covenant Edwards says has "not grown old yet." What Edwards, and what Reformed theology, means by justification by faith is really justification by the works Christ did for us. Gerstner writes:

> The justification of the sinner is by his union with Christ, who is justified not by faith but by works. So in the ultimate sense of the word the sinner too is justified by works—not his own, originally and actually, but none the less his own by faith.[96]

God as judge justifies only those who possess perfect righteousness, either their own or righteousness imputed to them.

Apart from union with Christ in the covenant of grace by which the sinner and Christ are looked upon as one person, there would be no righteousness in any creature, and none would ever be justified. To be "in Christ" is the only way the eternal life purchased by Christ will ever be applied to man.

The reason justification is by faith alone is because faith unites the sinner with Christ. And the reason justification is by union with Christ alone is clearly stated in Edwards' discourse on justification: "What is *real* in the union between Christ and his people, is the foundation of what is legal."[97] Edwards explains:

> ...It is something really in them, and between them, uniting them, that is the ground of the suitableness of their being accounted as one by the Judge.... No wonder that... he should accept the satisfaction and merits of the one for the other....
> And there is a wide difference between its being suitable that

---

96. Gerstner, *Steps to Salvation*, pp. 148-149.
97. "Justification by Faith Alone," *Works*, I, 626. Cf. "Miscellanies," No. 568, Yale MSS.

> Christ's satisfaction and merits should be theirs who believe, because an interest in that satisfaction and merit is a fit *reward* of faith ... and its being suitable that Christ's satisfaction and merits should be theirs, because Christ and they are so united that in the eyes of the Judge they may be looked upon ... as one.[98]

Later Edwards states: "Believers are represented in Scripture as being so in Christ, as that they are legally one, or accepted as one, by the Supreme Judge...."[99]

When Jesus Christ was about to leave His disciples, He said, "Peace I leave with you, my peace I give unto you" (John 14:27). Jonathan Edwards preached on this text and saw in it a reference to the believer's union with Christ. The peace which Christ left, says Edwards, is the same peace Christ Himself enjoys.

> It is as being united to Christ, and living by a participation of his life, as a branch lives by the life of the vine. It is as partaking of the same love of God; John xvii. 26. "That the love wherewith thou hast loved me may be in them."—It is having a part with him in his victory over the same enemies: and also as having an interest in the same kind of eternal rest and peace.[100]

The blessing of the covenant of grace, analogous to the marriage covenant, is that all our sin and unrighteousness is Christ's, and all His blessings and righteousness are ours.

Those who have fulfilled the condition of the covenant of grace, who by faith are united with Jesus Christ, may know with the certainty of God's Word, which cannot lie, that they shall inherit eternal life. Conrad Cherry writes:

> The demanding of salvation from God as an "absolute debt" is a palatable act for Edwards, therefore, when it is an act of faith.... The relation of faith is a non-moral or non-meritorious dependence-relation. In terms of the covenant idea, this means that in faith man demands from God, sues God for, the salvation promised in Christ. But the demand is simply the prayer of faith enabled by first being united with Christ, a union given man by God through the conjoined operation of Word and Spirit.[101]

---

98. "Justification by Faith Alone," *Works*, I, 626.
99. "Justification by Faith Alone," *Works*, I, 637.
100. Sermon on John 14:27, *Works*, II, 91.
101. Cherry, *Church History*, XXXIV, 335. Cf. Cherry, *The Theology of Jonathan Edwards*, p. 116.

The faith relationship is pre-eminent in Edwards' thought. The "mechanical," "commercial," arrogant "striking of a bargain" with God and "incipient Arminianism" charges so frequently leveled at covenant theology are, if anything, conspicuous by their absence in Edwards' writings.

15

Faith as the Condition of the Covenant of Grace

Jonathan Edwards clearly refers to "saving faith" as "the grand condition of an interest in Christ"[1] and "the great condition of the covenant of grace."[2] The first of these descriptions is from his remarks "on faith" and the second from his remarks "on efficacious grace." In a "Miscellanies" entry on the covenant Edwards writes, "Salvation is not offered to us upon any condition, but freely and for nothing."[3] In the understanding of these two seemingly contrary statements lies the key to Edwards' view of the covenant and the conditionality of faith.

Edwards' position did not emerge in a vacuum. It should be observed that his emphasis on both a conditionality and nonconditionality regarding the covenant has an impressive historical precedent in Puritan and Reformed theologians.

In early English Puritan theology the covenant of grace was said to have a twofold nature. It was seen to be both conditional and absolute. John von Rohr, writing on the covenant in early English Puritanism, summarizes the twofold nature thus: "Faith is required as a condition within it antecedent to salvation, but that very faith is already granted by it as a gift consequent of election."[4] John Murray, in refer-

---

1. "Miscellaneous Remarks," *Works,* II, 595.
2. "Miscellaneous Remarks," *Works,* II, 546.
3. "Miscellanies," No. 2, Yale MSS.
4. Von Rohr, *Church History,* XXXIV, 201. Von Rohr writes: "The conditional character of the Covenant is, of course, expressed in the idea of compact and mutual obligation. The Covenant is of grace because God's gifts within it are

ence to the British Isles in the seventeenth century, states that "no theologian within the Reformed camp took the position that ... the thought of condition is to be completely eliminated." However, "There was no thought of the covenant as contingent upon human autonomy."[5]

Turretin and van Mastricht are both favorites of Edwards and representative of continental Reformed theology. Turretin with his usual precision deals with the question by stating it clearly and showing that the covenant of grace is conditional, but only if condition is understood in the appropriate way.[6]

> If the condition is taken antecedently and *a priori* for the meritorious and impulsive cause, and for a natural condition, the covenant of grace is rightly denied to be conditioned; because it is wholly gratuitous.... But if it is taken consequently and *a posteriori* for the instrumental cause, receptive of the promises of the covenant, and for the disposition of the subject, admitted into the fellowship of the covenant, which flows from grace itself, it cannot be denied that the covenant is conditionate.[7]

Turretin gives the scriptural evidence that it *is* thus conditional and shows how faith is the condition of the covenant.[8]

---

those of mercy to the undeserving, but it is conditional because the promises are to those who present faith, a sincerity, a 'pitching on Christ.' Grace is given if conditions are fulfilled. But to leave the covenant idea at that point was to commit grievous error and to be guilty of serious absurdity in Puritan understanding. One absurdity, as Robert Jenison put it, was that then the benefit men have by Christ would be as uncertain as that which men once had in Adam and which was 'lost when it was left to his owne keeping.' Here is the recognition of man's impotence and his inability to turn himself from sin to faith. Another absurdity, said Jenison, would be that the difference 'between the Children of God and of this World, as suppose betweene Peter and Judas, should be wholly made from nature, not from grace.' Here is the recognition of the divine sovereignty in election and the affirmation that in the last analysis the chosen are God's chosen and not simply those who choose themselves. So the conditional covenant, as final word, foundered on the shoals of man's depravity and God's sovereignty and could be rescued only by being subordinated to the New Covenant which was absolute" (pp. 199-200).

5. Murray, *The Encyclopedia of Christianity*, III, 208-209. For full quote, cf. p. 66 above.
6. Turretin, *Institutio* (*Loc.* XII, Q. III, ii), II, 202 (Eng. p. 303).
7. Turretin, *Institutio* (*Loc.* XII, Q. III, iii), II, 202-203 (Eng. p. 303).
8. Turretin, *Institutio* (*Loc.* XII, Q. III, iii-xvii), II, 203-207 (Eng. pp. 303-307).

"The construction exemplified in Turretine, whereby the covenant is conceived of as conditioned upon faith and repentance, is in accord with the classic formulation in terms of *stipulation, promise, astipulation,* and *restipulation.* ..."[9]

Peter van Mastricht treats the subject in a similar fashion. He first lists five ways in which the covenant of grace is not conditional, but he then declares the covenant to be conditional with respect to its mutual obligations and promises.[10] In specifying what the condition is, he speaks of all obedience relating to the covenant in a broad sense, but in the narrower sense as to what puts the covenant into effect, van Mastricht says, "*Faith alone* is the condition of the covenant of grace."[11] Later on he stresses the importance of avoiding the danger of a meritorious understanding of condition. On that level the covenant is "absolute," since man is dead in sin, and justification depends solely on the free and gracious will of God.[12] This does not, however, take away what he said earlier of a legitimate use of faith as a condition of the covenant of grace.

Speaking not only of the limited representatives we have mentioned, but referring to Reformed theologians in general, Murray concludes a discussion of the conditionality question with these words which speak to the heart of the issue:

> It should be understood that the insistence upon this conditional feature of the Covenant of Grace, within the frame of thought espoused by these theologians, impinged in no way upon the sovereignty of God's grace nor upon the covenant as a disposition of grace, and they are unanimous in maintaining that the fulfilment of the conditions proceeded from operations of grace which were not themselves conditional.[13]

The question of the conditionality of faith is not merely an

---

9. Murray, *The Encyclopedia of Christianity,* III, 211.
10. Mastricht, *Theoretico-practica Theologia* (*Lib.* V, *Cap.* I, xx-xxi), pp. 397-398.
11. Mastricht, *Theoretico-practica Theologia* (*Lib.* V, *Cap.* I, xxii), p. 398.
12. Mastricht, *Theoretico-practica Theologia* (*Lib.* V, *Cap.* I, xxxvii), pp. 400-401.
13. Murray, *The Encyclopedia of Christianity,* III, 211-212.

historical issue but is ever present when one tries to do justice to the biblical data regarding the role of faith.

Charles Hodge made the distinction between a meritorious condition and a condition which is meant in the sense of a *sine qua non* with no merit involved. In the covenant of redemption Christ provides the condition by His work and merits our salvation; in the covenant of grace faith is the condition on the part of man in the sense of a *sine qua non* without merit. "In either case the necessity is equally absolute" since "without the work of Christ there would be no salvation; and without faith there is no salvation."[14] Berkhof stresses the gratuitous nature of salvation when he says, "Faith itself is a fruit of the covenant."[15] Yet he also distinguishes clearly the way in which the covenant of grace is both conditional and unconditional.[16]

What human language describes as conditional in one of two different meanings is required in order to be a recipient of the covenant blessings. Murray writes:

> The necessity of keeping the covenant on the part of men does not interfere with the divine monergism of dispensation....
>
> ...The conditions in view are not really conditions of bestowal.... In a word, keeping the covenant presupposes the covenant relation as established rather than the condition upon which its establishment is contingent.
>
> It should be noted also that the necessity of keeping the covenant is bound up with the particularism of this covenant.... This particularization is correlative with the spirituality of the grace bestowed and the relation constituted and it is also consonant with the exactitude of its demands.[17]

Berkouwer writes: "Justification through faith alone was the confession pre-eminent, the confession *sine qua non*."[18]

---

14. Hodge, *Systematic Theology*, II, 364-365.
15. Berkhof, *Reformed Dogmatics*, I, 261. Cf. Bavinck, *Our Reasonable Faith*, pp. 267, 274.
16. Berkhof, *Reformed Dogmatics*, I, 266-267.
17. Murray, *The Covenant of Grace*, pp. 18-20.
18. Berkouwer, *Faith and Justification*, p. 47.

Faith as the Condition of the Covenant of Grace

The intent is the same as the nonmeritorious use of condition, though it is said in the context of an approving look at the Canons of Dort in their rejection of "faith" as a "condition of salvation." Having designated faith as the *sine qua non* of salvation, Berkouwer also refers to the Scripture's teaching of the "*necessity* of faith" as the "central point" of his study.[19] Because faith by definition is not autonomous and honors the "exclusiveness of divine grace," because faith is a gift, Berkouwer says it "excludes faith as a condition."[20] With his stress on the necessity of faith as the confession *sine qua non,* however, his quarrel is surely with the use of the word "condition" in the meritorious sense. The intention of honoring Scripture's emphasis on the gratuitous nature of faith *and* its necessity is one with Reformed theology.

As we turn to Edwards himself, it should be clear that one may not make prejudgments about his view of the conditionality of faith. Edwards saw no conflict between his covenant doctrine and absolute predestination. We may not assume one excludes the other. Nor may one determine in advance that speaking of a condition of the covenant implies merit or autonomy or incipient Arminianism.

Edwards' initial "Miscellanies" entry on the covenant begins with his objections to calling faith "the condition upon which God has promised salvation." It is instructive to note that he does not begin with an assertion that such language is wrong, but begins: "Many difficulties used to arise in my mind...."[21] "Difficulties" are not evidence against its validity, and his phrase "used to arise" might well suggest the difficulties, while real, have been adequately dealt with to his own satisfaction.

The difficulties are real. Edwards cites, for example, that "work" in divinity normally means "something to be done as a condition," as in the covenant of works with Adam. In this

---

19. Berkouwer, *Faith and Justification,* p. 185.
20. Berkouwer, *Faith and Justification,* pp. 188-191.
21. "Miscellanies," No. 2, Yale MSS.

context Edwards said: "Talking thus, whether it be truly or falsely, is doubtless the foundation of Arminianism and neonomianism and tends very much to make men value themselves for their own righteousness."[22] Edwards' concern is the parallel between Adam in the covenant of works and Christ in the covenant of redemption. In the latter covenant Christ performed the condition. "Salvation is not offered to us upon any condition, but freely and for nothing. We are to do nothing for it; we are only to take it."[23]

Edwards suggests that had Adam finished his obedience in the Garden, God would have invited him to eat of the tree of life "that he might live forever."[24] Christ is now the "tree of life," says Edwards, and we stand where man would have been *if* he had "finished his righteousness." "We are . . . invited . . . to come to him to take and eat without any other terms because the condition of righteousness is fulfilled already by our surety."[25]

Receiving is contrasted to condition as a "work." "Faith can't be called the condition of receiving, for it *is* the receiving itself."[26] Edwards does not hesitate to say "those that don't believe are not saved," but he questions calling "receiving salvation" the "condition of receiving it."

> But I must confess after all, that if men will call this free offer and exhibition a covenant, they may; and if they will call the receiving of life the "condition" of receiving life, they are at their liberty. But I believe it is much the more hard to think right, for speaking so wrong. Christ and his church are one in law; that is, they are one in respect of the covenant. By Christ's performing the condition of the covenant, the condition is as it were performed by them.[27]

It should be understood that "Miscellany" No. 2, which provides the main evidence of Edwards' opposition to calling

---

22. "Miscellanies," No. 2, Yale MSS.
23. "Miscellanies," No. 2, Yale MSS.
24. "Miscellanies," No. 498, Yale MSS.
25. "Miscellanies," No. 498, Yale MSS.
26. "Miscellanies," No. 2, Yale MSS.
27. "Miscellanies," No. 2, Yale MSS.

Faith as the Condition of the Covenant of Grace

faith a condition, is aimed at rejecting a wrong separation of the covenants of redemption and grace. If the covenant of grace is given an autonomy, then the conditional aspect indeed takes on a meritorious tendency. Edwards' concern is that the covenant of grace is a manifestation of the covenant of redemption, and Christ performed the condition of the covenant of redemption. The covenant of grace pertains to our uniting or closing with Christ (the marriage analogy), the condition of which is faith (still nonmeritorious), and the result of which is an interest in Christ's merited reward.

This concern of Edwards over the use of conditional language regarding faith does show up in his discourse on "Justification by Faith Alone."

> ... Though faith be indeed the condition of justification so as nothing else is, yet this matter is not clearly and sufficiently explained by saying that faith is the condition of justification; and that because the word seems ambiguous, both in common use, and also as used in divinity. In one sense, Christ alone performs the condition of our justification and salvation; in another sense, faith is the condition of justification; in another sense, other qualifications and acts are conditions of salvation and justification too.[28]

His concern here is with a proper understanding of how the word is used in relation to salvation and the covenant. The uses "are understood in very different senses by different persons," yet significantly Edwards says "we are forced to use" such language.[29]

Unfortunately, Edwards' concern with and criticism of the difficulties in calling faith the condition of the covenant result in misinterpretation. William Morris in his dissertation quotes from "Miscellany" No. 2 and then boldly declares:

---

28. "Justification by Faith Alone," *Works,* I, 623.
29. "Justification by Faith Alone," *Works,* I, 623. William Ames was himself very cautious with the use of conditional faith. Ames representatively taught that predestination rested on no prior condition in man, and in comparing the two covenants he says the "present covenant requires no ... prior condition." Yet he is in need of a designation to show the role of faith and chooses the expression "a following or intermediate condition." *The Marrow of Theology,* pp. 151, 153.

260   *Faith as the Condition of the Covenant of Grace*

> Edwards regards the view that faith is a necessary condition of the Covenant of Grace as sheer Arminianism.... There is no condition of acceptance; no work that we must or can do, to be one of the elect.[30]

This is totally misleading and not what Edwards says. It ignores his explicit references to faith as the condition of the covenant of grace; it equates "condition" with "work" which Edwards clearly states he does not mean when he does use it in the covenantal framework; and it equates conditional covenant (which Edwards does teach) with "conditional election" (which Edwards would utterly reject).[31]

Edwards' uneasiness with the conditional language, his warnings against Arminianism, neonomianism, and self-righteousness, point out one very striking conclusion. In light of his explicit and frequent designations of faith as the condition of the covenant of grace, his caution can only be interpreted to mean that he saw as clearly as, if not more clearly than, his critics the dangers and boundaries of covenant terminology. It demonstrates again not only his acceptance of the doctrine of the covenant of grace, but how far he was from any incipient Arminianism.

Despite the linguistic limitations, Edwards felt obliged to use the designation of faith as the condition of the covenant of grace. How he understood "condition" is closely related to his covenant doctrine. It was indicated above how "Miscellany" No. 2, which was most critical of using "condition" in regard to the covenant, was concerned about a proper relationship between the covenants of redemption and grace. This concern is clarified in later entries in his "Miscellanies" notebook.

In a major entry on the covenant Edwards says both covenants are conditional. The condition of the covenant of redemption between God the Father and Christ is the work

---

30. Morris, "The Young Jonathan Edwards," pp. 773-774.
31. Edwards calls conditional election "absurd" and "nonsense." "Miscellaneous Remarks," *Works*, II, 537.

Christ did to "procure redemption." "The condition of Christ's covenant with his people or of the marriage covenant between him and men is that they should close with him and adhere to him."[32] In comparing the covenants further he writes: "Thus regeneration and closing with Christ is one of the promises of the covenant of the Father with Christ but is the condition in the covenant of Christ with his people."[33]

In yet another "Miscellany" Edwards again spells out the distinction.

> The covenant of grace, if thereby we understand the covenant between God the Father and believers in Christ, the covenant that he ordains in the hand of [a] Mediatour and the promises given us in him, is indeed without any proper conditions to be performed by us. Faith is not properly the condition of this covenant but the righteousness of Christ.... But the covenant of grace, if thereby we understand the covenant between Christ himself and his church or his members, is conditional as to us. The proper condition of it, which is a yielding to Christ's wooings and accepting his offers and closing with him as a Redeemer and spiritual husband is to be performed by us.[34]

The importance of the marriage analogy for understanding the covenant of grace is again apparent.

This teaching appears in his preaching also. In a sermon on Hebrews 9:15-16, having dealt with the twofold covenant, he writes:

> ... Not only are the parties covenanting different, but the conditions are entirely different. The condition of the Covenant that God the Father makes with Christ and his church ... is all that Christ has done and suffered.... The condition is wholly performed by Christ. But the condition of the covenant between Christ and his people ... is to be performed by believers, and is faith in Jesus Christ....[35]

---

32. "Miscellanies," No. 617, Yale MSS.
33. "Miscellanies," No. 617, Yale MSS. E. C. Smyth edited some of Edwards' unpublished works, including portions of some of the "Miscellanies." In a connecting note between No. 2, where Edwards was critical of the conditional language, and No. 617, which is cited above, he writes: "Much later, in another essay, he treats of the two covenants of grace and redemption, as follows,—not so much changing his ground, as finding room for the former by precise definition." This can be found in a recently published work, *Treatise on Grace*, p. 96.
34. "Miscellanies," No. 1091, Yale MSS.
35. Sermon on Hebrews 9:15-16, Yale MSS, p. 7.

The requirement of faith as the means of being in the covenant of grace cannot be by-passed. Edwards had used the illustration of a man courting a woman, and he said this was not a covenant without her acceptance. He then states: "Neither do I think that the gospel is called a covenant in Scripture, but only when the engagements are mutual."[36] In *Religious Affections* the all or nothing of faith is noted:

> There is no promise of the covenant of grace belongs to any man, till he has first believed in Christ; for 'tis by faith alone that we become interested in Christ, and the promises of the new covenant made in him: and therefore whatever spirit applies the promises of that covenant to a person who has not first believed, as being already his, must be a lying spirit. . . .[37]

As Edwards writes in a sermon on Matthew 19:22, "There are some persons that wish they had salvation and yet won't comply with the necessary means of it."[38]

Edwards is but stating what is the clear message of Scripture. "Faith is the qualification whereby they become entitled unto life according to the terms of the covenant of grace; John 3:36. He that believeth in the Son hath everlasting life. . . ."[39] Faith is called the "qualification that God has respect to in us in his looking upon us as being in Christ and so imputing to us his righteousness."[40] Two sermons on John 3:36 have as their respective doctrines: "he that don't believe on the Lord Jesus Christ, the wrath of God abideth on him," and "unless persons believe on Jesus Christ they shall never see eternal life."[41]

In a sermon on Revelation 22:17 Edwards relates "receiving" to "terms" or conditions. "They that do indeed willingly receive and accept of the blessings of the gospel, they

---

36. "Miscellanies," No. 617, Yale MSS.
37. *Religious Affections,* p. 222.
38. Sermon on Matthew 19:22, Andover MSS, p. 5.
39. Sermon on Habakkuk 2:4, Yale MSS, p. 9.
40. Sermon on Habakkuk 2:4, Yale MSS, p. 10.
41. Sermon on John 3:36 (1), Yale MSS, p. 1, and sermon on John 3:36 (2), Yale MSS, p. 3. Cf. also "Miscellanies," No. 855, Yale MSS, where this believing is seen to involve accepting Christ in His kingly *and* priestly office, and it is called "the proper condition of salvation."

Faith as the Condition of the Covenant of Grace

accept them as they are offered"; "they accept them upon the terms upon which they are offered"; and "they that receive salvation receive it upon God's terms."[42] These terms include accepting it "of God and as his gift," as a "free gift," and as given in Christ to whom they are to come.[43]

The essence of the matter is this: "Christ don't promise ... redemption but upon condition, and we haven't performed that condition till we have believed."[44] Faith in no way merits salvation in the covenant, but it is the condition of the covenant in that without this qualification on man's part he will not receive the blessings of the covenant. It is, in the language of the second of two meanings of condition, the condition *sine qua non*.

When it is said we are justified by faith alone or faith only, it is clear that faith is not *a* condition but *the* condition. In stating that "faith justifies as the condition" Edwards is concerned with the "ambiguity" in the expression and clarifies it in a sermon on Romans 4:16 in these words:

> In one sense of the word Christ alone performs the condition of our justification....
>
> And in another sense of the word there are other graces besides faith that are the condition of justification. If we mean ... that with which we shall be justified and without which we shall not, so is love to God and so is repentance and so is a spirit of obedience....
>
> Faith is that in them which God has respect to upon the account of which God judges it meet that they should be looked upon as having Christ's righteousness belonging to 'em. God sees it meet that some men rather than others should have Christ's righteousness imputed to 'em.... And this is the qualification that God has respect to in 'em, even faith, upon the account of which God in his wisdom sees it proper that they should have an actual communion with Christ in his righteousness. And that because faith is that grace that is most directly and immediately uniting of the soul to Christ as a Saviour. It is the proper act of reception of him or closing with him as a Saviour.[45]

---

42. Sermon on Revelation 22:17, Yale MSS, p. 8.
43. Sermon on Revelation 22:17, Yale MSS, pp. 8-9.
44. "Miscellanies," No. 329, Yale MSS.
45. Sermon on Romans 4:16, Yale MSS, pp. 13-14. This parallels the

We are not justified without "other graces," but faith is uniquely that "grace" which God provided and through which He looks upon us as "in Christ" and thus acceptable to Him. In the closing part of the application of this sermon Edwards pleads: "Let us earnestly seek faith in Jesus Christ which is the qualification that God has a primary respect to in imputing Christ's righteousness unto men. . . ."[46]

Edwards frequently refers to the qualification of faith as the condition of salvation or the covenant of grace. "Faith in Christ is the condition of salvation."[47] "Saving faith . . . is abundantly insisted on in the Bible, as in a peculiar manner the condition of salvation. . . . Saving faith . . . is the grand condition of an interest in Christ, and his great salvation."[48] In his remarks "Concerning Efficacious Grace" Edwards calls saving faith "the great condition of the covenant of grace."[49]

Edwards sees a fuller revelation of the covenant of grace in the call of Abraham, including a clearer revelation of faith as "the great condition of the covenant of grace."[50] In "An Humble Inquiry" we read it as well. "Christ's part is salvation, our part is a saving faith in him," and he adds that "no other faith is the condition of the covenant of grace."[51] And later he states: "Their professing faith in Christ was visibly owning the covenant of grace, because faith in Christ was the grand condition of that covenant."[52]

Such a designation of faith as the condition shows up in his preaching also. In the sixth of seven sermons on Hebrews 12:22-24 Edwards states, "The great condition of the covenant is faith in Jesus whereby the believer does with all his

---

threefold look at condition in "Justification by Faith Alone," *Works*, I, 623, where in different senses he says "Christ performs the condition," "faith is the condition," and "other qualifications and acts are conditions."
46. Sermon on Romans 4:16, Yale MSS, p. 22.
47. "Miscellaneous Remarks," *Works*, II, 591.
48. "Miscellaneous Remarks," *Works*, II, 595.
49. "Miscellaneous Remarks," *Works*, II, 546.
50. "History," *Works*, I, 543.
51. "An Humble Inquiry," *Works*, I, 443.
52. "An Humble Inquiry," *Works*, I, 444.

heart close with Christ as the Saviour, renouncing all other saviours...."[53] In his sermon on Ruth 1:16 Edwards speaks of the use of means and then goes on to say, "A choosing of their God ... with a full determination, and with the whole soul, is the condition of an union with them."[54]

For Edwards faith is the one, unique condition. In one of the "Miscellanies" he writes:

> The condition of justification ... is but one and that is faith. There is nothing else that has a like concern in the affair of justification as that hath. Repentance and faith are not two distinct things.... Faith comprehends the whole of that by which we are justified or by which we come to have an interest in Christ, and there is nothing else that has a parallel concern with it in the affair of our salvation.[55]

In this "Miscellany" Edwards spends a great deal of space elaborating that point. A similar statement is found in "Justification by Faith Alone."

> From these things we may learn in what manner faith is the only condition of justification and salvation. For though it be not the only condition, so as alone truly to have the place of a condition in an hypothetical proposition, in which justification and salvation are the consequent, yet it is the condition of justification in a manner peculiar to it, and so that nothing else has a parallel influence with it; because faith includes the whole act of union to Christ as a Saviour. The entire active uniting of the soul, or the whole of what is called coming to Christ, and receiving of him, is called faith in Scripture; and however other things may be no less excellent than faith, yet it is not the nature of any other graces or virtues directly to close with Christ as a mediator, any further than they enter into the constitution of justifying faith, and do belong to its nature.[56]

The doctrine of *sola fide* is thus anchored in the concept of union with Christ and the covenant relation.

Edwards sees a "natural fitness" in all this, but he sees in it no distraction from the sovereign will of God.[57] "Faith is

---

53. Sermon on Hebrews 12:22-24 (6), Yale MSS, pp. 4-5.
54. "Ruth's Resolution," *Works*, I, 666.
55. "Miscellanies," No. 669, Yale MSS.
56. "Justification by Faith Alone," *Works*, I, 628.
57. "Miscellanies," No. 1260, Yale MSS.

appointed the condition of an interest in Christ because there is a PROPRIETY in it . . . that such only should be looked upon as in him or one with him whose hearts are united to him as their Saviour."[58] Edwards sees the wisdom of God in using means with a propriety in proportion to reality. God saw fit to unite us to God through a Mediator, that the Mediator die, and that

> God will not bestow the benefits of the Mediatour on them that are not united to him because there is no propriety in it. . . . And God's insisting on this propriety is not the least inconsistent with the highest possible freedom of his grace. . . . There can be no propriety in looking on intelligent beings capable of act and choice as united to Christ that don't consent to it and while their hearts are disunited; therefore active voluntary union is insisted on. But neither does this in the least infringe on any possible freedom of grace in the method of salvation.[59]

There is thus a natural fitness between faith and justification, but there is no moral fitness in that our faith merits justification.

The covenant of grace, beginning as it does with Adam after the fall, has the same essential condition in both Testaments. "The prophecies of the Old Testament concerning the glorious times of the gospel shew plainly, that the way of acceptance with God and the CONDITIONS OF SALVATION are the same under the gospel, as they were under the Old Testament."[60] Comparing the sameness of the Mosaic and Christian dispensations, Edwards writes: "The grand qualification for justification was faith, the active unition of the heart to Christ, attended with repentance, conviction of sin &c. . . . differed only . . . by different degrees of revelation."[61]

As the condition is necessary, so will the resulting blessing necessarily follow. In the application of a sermon on Hebrews 13:8, having dealt with the unchangeableness of the

---

58. "Miscellanies," No. 1331, Yale MSS.
59. "Miscellanies," No. 1346, Yale MSS.
60. "Miscellanies," No. 874, Yale MSS.
61. "Miscellanies," No. 1353, Yale MSS.

eternal covenant, Edwards speaks of encouragement for sinners.[62] He pleads with them "to come to Christ, and put their trust in him for salvation." Christ invites them and promises to accept those who come. Edwards further calls attention to "how Christ has treated those that have come to him heretofore," concluding, "we read of none that ever were rejected by him." God is eternally the same and faithful to the covenant, and if we "come" we will be saved and not rejected. In a sermon on Psalm 25:11 concerning the infinite mercy of God Edwards says, "Christ *will not refuse* to save the greatest sinners, who in a right manner come to God for mercy."[63] He says further, "Pardon is as much *offered and promised* to the greatest sinners as any, if they will come aright to God for mercy."[64] To "come aright" and "in a right manner" is faith alone, the essential qualification for the bestowal of the covenant promises. It is the *sine qua non,* the condition of the covenant of grace.

It is important to consider in more detail the crucial qualification which has been a part of our discussion on the conditionality of faith. According to Edwards, God provides the condition. Here too we must be careful to distinguish. On the one hand Edwards teaches that the condition of our righteousness is fulfilled by our surety, that Christ is our righteousness, and that justification is by His righteous obedience.[65] Christ fulfills the condition. Yet when the covenants of redemption and grace are distinguished, there is a condition in the latter filled by man which is not to be confused with the condition Christ fulfills. Our condition is the act of union with Christ (faith) in order to receive the benefits of the condition He has already fulfilled. This condition of the covenant of grace, however, is no less a gift of God than the gift of Christ as our righteousness.

    62. Sermon on Hebrews 13:8, *Works,* II, 953.
    63. Sermon on Psalm 25:11, *Works,* II, 112.
    64. Sermon on Psalm 25:11, *Works,* II, 112.
    65. Cf. for example, "Miscellanies," No. 498, Yale MSS; "The Final Judgment," *Works,* II, 196; "Justification by Faith Alone," *Works,* I, 638.

Faith as the Condition of the Covenant of Grace

That faith, the condition of the covenant of grace, is a gift of God is evident from the sinful state of natural man from whom the condition is required. One of the clear teachings of Edwards' work on *Original Sin* is "that all mankind are under the influence of a prevailing effectual tendency in their nature . . . which implies their utter and eternal ruin."[66] In writing on "qualifications for communion" Edwards says a natural man is not really willing to fulfill the condition of the covenant of grace because natural man is without true faith which is the required condition.[67] The issue between Edwards and Stoddard on qualifications for communion (and the halfway covenant) settles around a clear distinction between faith (a saving grace) and something the unregenerate can do. If Edwards refuses moral sincerity as sufficient, and that is all the unregenerate can do, then it is obvious that the condition of the covenant of grace depends not on man but God.[68]

The absolute necssity for divine intervention accords with Edwards' express belief that the gracious work of the Holy Spirit is upon the will of man. Man's inability is a "moral inability." That unregenerate man will not perform the required condition is absolutely certain.

> Free will. 'Tis very true that God requires nothing of us as condition of eternal life but what is in our own power, and yet 'tis very true at the same time that it's an utter impossible thing that ever man should do what is necessary in order to salvation, nor do the least towards it, without the almighty operation of the Holy Spirit of God—yea, except everything be entirely wrought by the Spirit of God. True and saving faith in Christ is not a thing out of the power of man, but infinitely easy. 'Tis entirely in a man's power to submit to Jesus Christ as a savior if he will. But the thing is, is [it] man's will that he should will it, except God

---

66. *Original Sin,* pp. 120 ff.
67. "An Humble Inquiry," *Works,* I, 446.
68. In "Truth Vindicated," *Works,* I, 503, Edwards writes: "There is no such thing as moral sincerity, in the *covenant of grace,* distinct from gracious sincerity. . . . *Unsanctified* men, while such, cannot with any sincerity at all testify a *present* cordial compliance with the covenant of grace . . . neither can they with any sincerity promise a *future* compliance with that covenant."

Faith as the Condition of the Covenant of Grace 269

works it in him? To will it, as to do it, depends on a man's will and not on his power, 'tis an impossibility that he should ever do it except he wills it, because submission to Christ is a willing.[69]

Translated into homiletical terms: "A natural man may choose deliverance from hell; but no man doth ever heartily choose God and Christ ... till he is converted. On the contrary, he is averse to them; he has no relish of them...."[70]

When Edwards preached the Boston lecture, "God Glorified in Man's Dependence," he did not reject the use of "means" but said, "It is of God that we have these means of grace, and it is he that makes them effectual."[71] The Arminians admit to a partial dependence, but according to Edwards, "whatever scheme is inconsistent with our *entire* dependence on God ... is repugnant to the design and tenor of the gospel."[72] In discussing election Edwards clearly rejects the notion that "faith and good works" are the first things in the order of God's decree. First is God's will to "communicate his happiness, and glorify his grace." Faith as the condition is not of the "very nature of grace"; it "is only a certain way of the appointment of God's wisdom."[73]

According to Edwards "all the decrees of God are harmonious," but it is improper to say "one decree" is "a condition of another."[74] "God in the decree of election is justly to be considered as decreeing the creature's eternal happiness antecedently to any foresight of good works.... But faith and good works is not supposed in the first things in order to the decree of election."[75]

---

69. *The Philosophy of Jonathan Edwards*, p. 155. ("Miscellany" No. 71).
70. "Ruth's Resolution," *Works*, I, 666.
71. Sermon on 1 Corinthians 1:29-31, *Works*, II, 4.
72. Sermon on 1 Corinthians 1:29-31, *Works*, II, 7. Perry Miller was correct in seeing the emphasis of Edwards on God's absolute sovereignty but erred in seeing an Arminianizing tendency in a conditional faith via a "self-determining power" within the will of men. This was certainly not true of Edwards' use of conditional language. Cf. Miller, *Jonathan Edwards*, pp. 112-113.
73. "Miscellaneous Remarks," *Works*, II, 540.
74. "Miscellaneous Remarks," *Works*, II, 527.
75. "Miscellanies," No. 700, Yale MSS.

> It is very nonsense, to call such a conditional election as they talk of, by the name of election, seeing there is a necessary connection between faith in Jesus Christ and eternal life.... What nonsense is it therefore, to talk of choosing such to life from all eternity.... A predestination of such to life is altogether useless and needless.... And what do they mean by an election of men, to that which it is in its own nature impossible that it should not be, whether they are elected to it or no? and so to say, that God chose them that had a right to eternal life, that they should have eternal life.[76]

The "nonsense" of the Arminian notion of conditional election is also spoken of in a sermon on Numbers 23:19 where Edwards concludes that their doctrine implies "God must be liable to change with respect to his will."[77]

According to Edwards one may indeed speak of decrees "depending" on one another if care is taken to properly distinguish what it means.

> What divines intend by *prior* and *posterior* in the affair of God's decrees, is not that one is before another in the order of time, for all are from eternity; but that we must conceive the view or consideration of one decree to be before another, inasmuch as God decrees one thing out of respect to another decree that he has made; so that one decree must be conceived of as in some sort to be the ground of another, or that God decrees one because of another; or that he would not have decreed one, had he decreed that other.[78]

He further clarifies how decrees are conditional and unconditional:

> There are no conditional decrees in this sense, *viz.* that decrees should depend on conditions of them, which in this decree, that depends on them as conditions, must be considered, like themselves, as yet undecreed. But yet decrees may, in some sort, be conditions of decrees; so that it may be said, that God would not have decreed some things, had he not decreed others.[79]

There is a connection but not a mechanical one.

A discussion of Edwards and the conditionality of the

---

76. "Miscellanies," No. 63, Yale MSS.
77. Sermon on Numbers 23:19, Yale MSS, p. 13.
78. "Miscellaneous Remarks," *Works*, II, 540.
79. "Miscellaneous Remarks," *Works*, II, 542.

Faith as the Condition of the Covenant of Grace 271

covenant leads inevitably into the "harmonious," "natural fitness" concepts and on to his understanding of cause and effect. Edwards' position is "that God decrees all things harmoniously and in excellent order." He writes, for example: "When God decrees to give the blessing of rain, He decrees the prayers of His people; and when He decrees the prayers of His people, He may very comparatively decree rain; and thereby there is a harmony between these two decrees. ..."[80]

In a sermon-lecture on Romans 8:29-30, a predestination passage, Edwards specifically brings together the doctrine of decrees and the harmonious, sequential events through which those decrees are actualized. The sermon doctrine states: "The things which God doth for the salvation and blessedness of the saints are like an inviolable chain reaching from a duration without beginning to a duration without end."[81] Cause and effect function within predestination, not in the sense that causes are autonomous conditions, but in the sense that they are part of the decree. In his sermon on Revelation 22:17 Edwards writes: "Indeed we can't have gospel blessings without good works, not because works are a prerequisite condition but because they are a part of the gospel blessings."[82]

Henry Rogers calls the premise "every effect must have a cause" the "one postulate" of *Freedom of the Will.* He further adds: "... Of the thousands who have denied the conclusiveness of Edwards' reasoning, perhaps scarcely one was

---

80. *The Philosophy of Jonathan Edwards,* p. 154. ("Miscellany" No. 29). Cf. Miller, *NEM: 17th Century,* p. 239: "... If God enacts events in sequences within the realm of nature, must He not also ordain sequences within the realm of grace? If He establishes a succession of 'means' for combustion, surely He must create one for conversion." Miller says Locke changed all this (p. 245), and as we have seen, he would have Edwards return to the "arbitrary determinism" of Calvin. Edwards, however, in no way discards the "sequence" aspect, but merely the mechanical understanding of sequence.
81. Sermon on Romans 8:29-30, Yale MSS, p. 3.
82. Sermon on Revelation 22:17, Yale MSS, p. 13. Cf. Miller, *NEM: 17th Century,* p. 392, re: conditions as secondary causes.

ever absurd enough to deny his premises."[83] There is a close relation of this with the conditionality of faith.

In his notes on "The Mind" Edwards defined cause as "that, after or upon the existence of which (or the existence of it after such a manner), the existence of another thing follows."[84] In *Freedom of the Will* Edwards is careful to qualify and define the use of the word "cause."

> ...I sometimes use the word "cause," in this inquiry, to signify any antecedent, either natural or moral, positive or negative, on which an event, either a thing, or the manner and circumstance of a thing, so depends, that it is the ground and reason, either in whole, or in part, why it is, rather than not; or why it is as it is, rather than otherwise; or, in other words, any antecedent with which a consequent event is so connected, that it truly belongs to the reason why the proposition which affirms that event, is true; whether it has any positive influence, or not.[85]

The last phrase, "whether it has any positive influence, or not," is crucial to Edwards' position. A cause can be the *sine qua non* via the decree of God without a mechanical or autonomous "positive influence."

Edwards' use of the word "effect" is similarly qualified. "...I sometimes use the word 'effect' for the consequence of another thing, which is perhaps rather an occasion than a cause, most properly speaking."[86] The stress on "occasion" instead of "cause" is again indicative of Edwards' opposition to a purely mechanical understanding. In fact in his early writing Edwards sets forth this corollary in his notes "Of Being": "... There is no such thing as mechanism if that

---

83. "An Essay on the Genius and Writings of Jonathan Edwards," *Works*, I, iv.
84. "The Mind," *The Philosophy of Jonathan Edwards*, p. 36.
85. *Freedom of the Will*, pp. 180-181.
86. *Freedom of the Will*, p. 181. Cf. Miller, *Jonathan Edwards*, p. 81, where he states that faith "is not an instrument which works an effect, but is part of a sequence within a system of coherence." Later Miller writes that Edwards "did not take 'cause' in the positivistic sense of that which determines the effect, but rather as that which is necessarily and aesthetically antecedent" (p. 257). See further pp. 82, 96, 121, and 122. Carse, *Jonathan Edwards and the Visibility of God*, pp. 117-123, deals with the way faith can be active without works righteousness if the causal relation is not seen in a mechanistic way.

Faith as the Condition of the Covenant of Grace

word is taken to be that whereby bodies act each upon other purely and properly by themselves."[87]

Having made these clarifications Edwards' premise can be stated without equivocation. "I assert," says Edwards, "that nothing ever comes to pass without a cause."[88] In this framework faith may be called the cause and salvation the effect without jeopardizing the absolute sovereignty of electing grace in the affair of salvation. Faith is the condition in that it is the *sine qua non* of justification. In the very place where Edwards rejects faith as a condition in a meritorious sense he affirms that faith is the *sine qua non* and in such a qualified sense a condition. "'Tis true, those that don't believe are not saved, and all that do believe are saved: that is, all that do receive Christ and salvation, they receive it; and all that will not receive salvation, never do receive it and never have it."[89] Elsewhere in his "Miscellanies" notebook Edwards defines condition in this more restricted sense. "But for any thing to be the condition of justification is to be that with which justification shall be, and without which it shall not be."[90]

Faith is that condition, the *sine qua non* of justification. Concerning the benefits Christ purchased, Edwards says that "God sees it to be a more meet and suitable thing that it

---

87. "Of Being," *The Philosophy of Jonathan Edwards*, p. 19. This statement is an expression of Edwards' belief in the absolute and utter dependence of everything in creation upon the sovereign Creator. This viewpoint is especially prevalent in his criticism of the deists.
88. *Freedom of the Will*, p. 181. Cf. Elwood, *The Philosophical Theology of Jonathan Edwards*, pp. 52 ff.; Miller, *NEM: 17th Century*, pp. 234-235; Miller, *Jonathan Edwards*, pp. 78-79; and Cherry, *The Theology of Jonathan Edwards*, pp. 98 ff.
89. "Miscellanies," No. 2, Yale MSS.
90. "Miscellanies," No. 659, Yale MSS. Cf. Ames, *The Marrow of Theology*, p. 98: "... God wills one thing to exist in order to produce another. But it cannot be said that the one thing is properly a cause whereby the will of God is moved internally to appoint the other thing." Charles Hodge, *Systematic Theology*, II, 365, distinguished a twofold definition of condition: "But in other cases, by condition we merely mean a *sine qua non*. . . . It remains a gratuitous favor; but it is, nevertheless, suspended upon the act of asking. It is in this last sense only that faith is the condition of the covenant of grace. . . . In either case the necessity is equally absolute."

should be assigned to some rather than others, because he was then differently qualified; that qualification ... is that in us by which we are justified."[91] Without Christ fulfilling the condition of salvation in the meritorious sense, nothing in us would matter. However, because Christ fulfilled the condition of the covenant of redemption, the covenant of grace is effectual. God established a connection (real) between faith (union with Christ), the condition which God gives, and salvation.[92] There is a "natural fitness" or "suitability" in this relation, but the boundness and necessary connection is a sovereign decision by God. Cause and effect is applicable, but only in the nonmechanistic sense where faith is a cause in that it is antecedent to the effect consequent upon the cause, namely salvation.

There is yet another facet of Edwards' use of the word "condition" that must be emphasized. We mentioned earlier[93] the different ways Edwards understood "condition." Within this framework Christ performs the condition, faith is the condition, or other qualifications are conditions. In the latter sense faith is not the *only* condition, though this in no way contradicts the truth that justification is by faith *alone* in a unique sense.

It is in his discourse on "Justification by Faith Alone" that Edwards explicitly speaks of other conditions. It is even spoken of in the *sine qua non* context.

> If it be that with which, or which being supposed, a thing shall be, and without which, or it being denied, a thing shall not be, we in such a case call it a condition of that thing. But in this sense faith is not the only condition of salvation or justification; for there are many things that accompany and flow from faith, with which justification shall be, and without which it will not be; ... such are love to God, and love to our brethren, forgiving men their trespasses, and many other good qualifications and acts.

---

91. "Justification by Faith Alone," *Works*, I, 624.
92. "Justification by Faith Alone," *Works*, I, 626.
93. Cf. above p. 259.

And there are many other things besides faith . . . to be pursued or performed by us, in order to eternal life.⁹⁴

Edwards makes it very clear that if faith is "the only condition of justification in this sense," it does not adequately express the scriptural expression of "being justified by faith."⁹⁵ The "by" has a deeper meaning than just an inseparable connection.

Obedience is one of these "conditions" of salvation. Obedience is necessary to salvation.⁹⁶ Another requirement or condition is perseverance in faith. "The perseverance of faith is necessary to a congruity to salvation . . . several places in Scriptures."⁹⁷ It is a means of continuing in a state of justification.⁹⁸ Concerning perseverance Edwards writes: "The promise of acceptance is made only to a persevering sort of faith."⁹⁹

In one of the "Miscellanies" Edwards compares the condition of faith as the "first closing with Christ" to the other conditions of perseverance and holiness. He is using the marriage analogy here and says: "There is the like difference between them as there is between a woman's consenting to be the wife and accepting for her husband him that offers himself to her and . . . her covenant promises . . . *viz.* . . . being faithful to him. . . ."¹⁰⁰ Edwards says they are both conditions "but not in the same respects."

> For the former is so much the condition along that as soon as she has performed it, she is at once entitled to him as an husband and so to his love. . . . But yet her being actually faithfull to him till death may also be so much the condition. . . .¹⁰¹

---

94. "Justification by Faith Alone," *Works*, I, 623.
95. "Justification by Faith Alone," *Works*, I, 623.
96. "Miscellanies," No. 488, Yale MSS. Cf. "Miscellanies," No. 876, Yale MSS.
97. "Miscellanies," No. 808, Yale MSS.
98. "Miscellanies," No. 1186, Yale MSS.
99. "Miscellaneous Remarks," *Works*, II, 596. Cf. "Miscellanies," No. 729, Yale MSS.
100. "Miscellanies," No. 617, Yale MSS.
101. "Miscellanies," No. 617, Yale MSS.

276   Faith as the Condition of the Covenant of Grace

In another "Miscellany" Edwards mentions both sorts of conditions, but he further states that no amount of "good works" without faith would render it a "fit and proper thing in God's esteem that he should be saved."[102] Faith does render it so.

In dealing with the fact that "repentance is often spoken of as the special condition of remission of sins," Edwards emphasizes the scriptural teaching that "remission of sins is by faith in Jesus Christ," and he concludes "that faith and repentance are not to be looked upon as properly two distinct things ... but that evangelical repentance is a certain exercise of faith in Jesus Christ."[103] This is consistent with Edwards' teaching of the biblical truth that a good tree (antecedent) will necessarily (consequence) bear good fruit. Thus there is no salvation without "good works," but there is no salvation because of them. In a sermon on "The Manner of Seeking Salvation" Edwards, having stated works do not merit salvation, sums up the matter in these words: "Men are not saved on the account of any work of theirs, and yet they are not saved without works."[104]

It is not necessary, therefore, for one to be left up in the air with various interpretations about Edwards' acceptance or rejection of the covenant, the conditionality of faith, and related issues if we will only hear him when he distinguishes how he uses the word "condition." The sense in which Christ alone performs the condition of justification confirms his Calvinism. The sense where faith is the condition of justification (the *sine qua non*) makes it clear that his Calvinism was consistent with his doctrine of the covenant of grace. The third sense, where other things are conditions of justification, places him opposite the antinomians and their neglect of the necessity of good works as fruits of justification.

Edwards' doctrine of the covenant of grace and its condi-

---

102. "Miscellanies," No. 315, Yale MSS.
103. "Miscellanies," No. 943, Yale MSS.
104. Sermon on Genesis 6:27, *Works*, II, 53.

tion in comparison to the covenant of works is handled in the same manner as the mainstream Reformed covenant theologians and in the tradition of the Reformation theology with its contrast between law and gospel.

> The condition both of the first and second covenant, is a receiving, compliance with, or yielding to, a signification or declaration from God, or to a revelation made from God. . . . There is indeed obedience in the condition of both covenants, and there is faith or believing God in both. But the different name arises from the remarkable different nature of the revelation or manifestations made. The one is a law; the other a testimony and offer. The one is a signification of what God expects that we should do towards him, and what he expects to receive from us; the other a revelation of what he has done for us, and an offer of what we may receive from him.[105]

In one of the "Miscellanies" we find the following among a list of some benefits of the covenant of grace: "The grand means, Jesus Christ and his mediation, with the qualifications or condition[s] of an interest in the Saviour. . . ."[106] The condition of the covenant is thus a benefit of the covenant; it is not a synergistic cooperation on the part of the sinner.

Writing about efficacious grace Edwards says "that neither the salvation, nor the condition of it, shall be of our works, but . . . we are God's workmanship and his creation antecedently to our works; and his grace and power . . . are all prior to our works and the cause of them."[107] Concerning divine decrees Edwards writes that "God has regard to condi-

---

105. "Miscellaneous Remarks," *Works*, II, 584.
106. "Miscellanies," No. 1353, Yale MSS. Turretin writes that the covenant of grace is so named because "all things in this covenant are gratuitous, and thus even the conditions." Turretin says God wanted the whole covenant to depend upon his promise, "not only with regard to the reward promised by him, but also with the duty demanded from us; so that God performs here not only his own part, but also ours." *Institutio* (*Loc.* XII, Q. I, ix, xi), II, 188-189 (Eng. pp. 291-292). So also van Mastricht writes that the Reformed did not mean that the covenant of grace demands faith through man's own strength, but it results rather from the strength of the promise of the covenant. He shows this by a contrast to the covenant of works, by the promise of the covenant of grace to give a new heart through which the condition is performed, and by the express teaching of Scripture that faith is a gift of God. *Theoretico-practica Theologia* (*Lib.* V, *Cap.* I, xxxix), p. 405.
107. "Miscellaneous Remarks," *Works*, II, 560.

tions in his decrees," and He in His wisdom decreed an order and connection so that "one part of the wise system of events would not have been decreed, unless the other parts had been decreed."[108] According to Edwards conditions are commanded, and rightly so in the order of things, even though (and because) they are decreed by God from all eternity.[109]

It is as much an error to deny that Edwards taught the covenant and conditionality of faith as it would be to conclude that his acceptance of them jeopardized his Calvinism. Edwards' understanding of the conditionality of faith and the covenant is clearly implied in this portion of a sermon on Luke 17:9:

> It is the gift of God to us that we are enabled . . . to do anything, and therefore we can't deserve any thanks of God for what we do. Obedience to God's commands is God's gift. 1 Corinthians 4:7. What hast thou that thou didst not receive. . . . If some men live sober and orderly lives that is God's gift to them; 'tis because God makes him to differ that he is not vicious; . . . 'tis owing to the restraining grace of God. Or if a man seeks and strives for salvation and takes a great deal of pains, . . . this is God's gift. 'Tis because God awakens and convinces him otherwise; he would be as stupid and senseless as any body. . . . And how unreasonable is it to suppose that God is obliged to men for being what he makes them, or for having what he gives them.[110]

---

108. "Miscellaneous Remarks," *Works*, II, 540.
109. "Miscellanies," No. 415, Yale MSS. "As persons are commanded and counselled to repent and be converted, tho it is already determined whether they shall be converted or no; after the same manner and with like propriety, persons are commanded and counselled to persevere, altho by their being already converted 'tis certain, they shall persevere."
110. Sermon on Luke 17:9, Yale MSS, pp. 7-8.

16

Seeking Salvation in the Framework of Calvinist Covenant Theology

The Puritan doctrine of "seeking" is integral to Edwards' theology. The way in which this doctrine functioned in his thought would provide a major study in itself. It is also one of the most difficult aspects of his thought to correctly grasp. The difficulty arises when he vigorously asserts an area of "ability" in natural man—an ability closely but not infallibly connected with God's sovereign bestowing of saving grace— within the context of a Calvinism which affirms man's inability in the affair of salvation.

While we believe Edwards' doctrine of seeking is not inconsistent with his Calvinism, it is obvious that many see this as "one more" example of Edwards' departure from the Calvinism of Calvin. We choose the phrase "one more" advisedly, since there is a likelihood that those who see an un-Calvinistic ability in man's participation in the covenant of grace will also see an un-Calvinistic ability in man's seeking salvation. Because it is a gross error to see these as parallel paths leading away from Calvinism to Arminianism, it is important to take at least a brief look into Edwards' position and its implications for his doctrine of the covenant. We will preface Edwards' position on "seeking" with his comments on God's use of "means" and with something of the historical context for the doctrine of seeking or "preparation."

Perry Miller, expressing New England thought in the seventeenth century as he saw it, stresses their use of means. "God chooses whom He will, and he rejects regardless [sic] of merit, but His ministers must proceed upon the assumption that if they can drive images of doctrine deep enough into the mind . . . they can then . . . become the means of election. . . ."¹ The "spoken word" was an important "means." Elsewhere Miller wrote:

> Normally the instruments by which He engenders faith in an individual are the sermons of ministers and the sacraments of the church. These ordinances, it should be noted, are not in themselves the causes of faith, they are simply the 'means.' Though God is at perfect liberty to summon a man by a direct call, in the vast majority of cases He will work upon him through these secondary causes.²

That God "rejects regardless of merit" is contrary to Scriptures and an unfair representation of Puritanism. One also suspects that anyone in the Calvinist-Puritan family would be puzzled at what Miller intends by God summoning a man "by a direct call."

Miller's emphasis on "means" in New England theology is accurate, though Edwards would accept the inclusion of sacraments as means to engender faith only with extreme qualification. The idea of God using means to accomplish His purposes is common to Edwards. In "God Glorified in Man's Dependence" Edwards gives a good summary of his understanding of the use of means: "And though means are made use of in conferring grace on men's souls, yet it is of God that we have these means of grace, and it is he that makes them effectual."³ This description of how means function parallels the way faith as man's part in the covenant of grace functions for Edwards. Interestingly, it is this sermon from which Miller concluded that Edwards had thrown over the covenant of grace and "returned" to the "absolute" and "arbitrary" God of Calvin!

---

1. Miller, *NEM: 17th Century*, p. 295. Cf. pp. 285-286 where he speaks of reason and its use as a "means."
2. Miller, "The Marrow of Puritan Divinity," *Errand Into the Wilderness*, p. 68.
3. Sermon on 1 Corinthians 1:29-31, *Works*, II, 4.

It is precisely within the predestinarian framework that Edwards frequently speaks of "means." In his remarks "Concerning Divine Decrees" he deals with the fatalistic objection.

> They say, to what purpose are praying, and striving, and attending on means, if all was irreversibly determined by God before? But, to say that all was determined before these prayers and strivings, is a very wrong way of speaking, and begets those ideas in the mind, which correspond with no realities with respect to God. The decrees of our everlasting state were not before our prayers and strivings; for these are as much present with God from all eternity, as they are the moment they are present with us. They are present as part of his decrees, or rather as the same; and they did as really exist in eternity, with respect to God, as they exist in time, and as much at one time as another. Therefore, we can no more fairly argue, that these will be in vain, because God has foredetermined all things, than we can, that they would be in vain if they existed as soon as the decree, for so they do, inasmuch as they are a part of it.[4]

Edwards finds the command to persevere and the threatenings for defection perfectly in order "notwithstanding its being certain that all that have true grace shall persevere" and "notwithstanding all that are elected shall undoubtedly be saved."[5] The point he stresses is that "decree or no decree, every one that believes shall be saved, and he that believes not shall be damned."[6] It is a condition *sine qua non* whether it is decreed or not, and according to Edwards, it is a means or a condition which is a part of the decree itself.

In a sermon on Matthew 19:22 Edwards speaks of those who desire salvation but "won't comply with the necessary means of it." "They wish they might go to heaven"; they know the law and understand justice; they are afraid of

---

4. "Miscellaneous Remarks," *Works*, II, 527. Cf. "Miscellanies," No. 82, Yale MSS.
5. "Miscellaneous Remarks," *Works*, II, 596. This is paralleled by Edwards' remarks on means and decrees in areas other than saving faith. Cf. "Miscellaneous Remarks," *Works*, II, 527: "God decrees rain in drought, because he decrees the earnest prayers ... or ... he decrees the prayers ... because he decrees rain.... *God decrees a thing because,* is an improper way of speaking; but not more ... than all our other ways...." Cf. also, *The Philosophy of Jonathan Edwards*, pp. 153-154. ("Miscellany" No. 29).
6. "Miscellaneous Remarks," *Works*, II, 596.

death; "they do many things in order to their salvation"; "yet they will not comply with the necessary means of it."[7] In the application of the sermon he calls it folly to prefer "sin and the world before eternal life and deliverance from eternal death."[8]

These "necessary means" and their use are given by God. The manuscript sermon on Hosea 13:9 abounds with Edwards' teaching that God provides the application as well as the ground of salvation.[9] "God ... is the author of all the ordinances of the gospel by means of which he communicates grace," and these include prayer, preaching, the Sabbath, and church discipline.[10] But God also does what needs to be done upon the heart of man in order for salvation to occur.[11] "'Tis God that excites and enables men to do all that they do in order to their salvation, . . . to lay hold on Jesus Christ and to embrace him," and to "let him into their hearts and make them willingly yield themselves unto him."[12] By enlightening the heart to the sufficiency and excellency of Christ "the Father . . . draws and makes him run as it were into the arms of his grace and love."[13]

The Word of God is one of the most important "means" used by God in salvation. In his series of sermons on John

---

7. Sermon on Matthew 19:22, Andover MSS, pp. 5-8.
8. Sermon on Matthew 19:22, Andover MSS, p. 16.
9. Sermon on Hosea 13:9, Yale MSS, p. 4.
10. Sermon on Hosea 13:9, Yale MSS, p. 5.
11. Sermon on Hosea 13:9, Yale MSS, pp. 6-7.
12. Sermon on Hosea 13:9, Yale MSS, p. 9.
13. Sermon on Hosea 13:9, Yale MSS, pp. 9-10. Cf. Haroutunian, *Piety versus Moralism*, pp. 45-46. "It is now easy to understand why Edwards could take this religious affection to be nothing less than 'super-natural.' The natural affections, being qualitatively different from the sense of divine glory, do not and cannot produce it. . . . Edwards does not deny that the natural man may be good. But he will not permit himself to lose sight of the fact that to be religious and to be moral are two different things. Morality is natural, religion is supernatural. The latter is based upon a 'new principle,' derived, not from nature, but from God. The sense of the divine is produced by the Divine, through the operation of the indwelling Spirit of holiness, introducing a 'new principle' and a new object of affection."

16:8 Edwards leaves no doubt as to the dependence on the Spirit of God to make the Word effectual.

> Thus we learn where ministers should have their dependence in their endeavors, even upon the Holy Ghost. The word of God indeed is sharp as a two-edged sword and is quick and powerful; but it is so only through the cooperation of that Spirit that gave the word. The word alone, however managed, explained, confirmed and applied, is nothing but a dead letter without the Spirit....[14]

Edwards says our eyes "should be to God to reform men that are vicious in their lives...."[15]

Edwards' insistence on the necessity of means is part and parcel of his doctrine of absolute sovereignty. In a sermon on John 3:8 he cautions against the abuse of the doctrine that God is sovereign in the work of conversion. To those who interpret the sovereignty of God to imply that "it is not worth the while for any person to take any care about the matter," Edwards replies that "God don't accept persons without means," and a neglect of these means will result in their being no hope of obtaining salvation.[16] "God carries on his work by means, and therefore those that don't use the means can't expect to obtain the end.... He appoints the means and the end together."[17]

The beginning and the end of the matter is God's good pleasure. "... It is his [God's] will to give converting grace in the use of means, among which this is one, *viz.*, to lead a moral and religious life, and agreeable to our light, and the convictions of our conscience."[18] The significance of the use of means in seeking salvation or preparation for salvation is the acknowledgment of a nonmeritorious ability on the part of natural man, an ability which he is obliged to exercise but which in *no way* obligates God. This seeking is, however, the

---

14. Sermons on John 16:8, Yale MSS, p. 101.
15. Sermons on John 16:8, Yale MSS, p. 102.
16. Sermon on John 3:8, Yale MSS, pp. 20-21.
17. Sermon on John 3:8, Yale MSS, pp. 21-22.
18. Sermon on Psalm 25:11, *Works*, II, 113.

normal means God has sovereignly chosen to decree as the way His election is applied.

While an historical survey cannot be attempted here,[19] we must at least indicate the issue as it relates to Calvin and Calvinism. This is needed both because of the indebtedness of Puritans to Calvin and because Perry Miller's judgments about Puritan theology are often contrasted to Calvin.

In his article "Calvin and Covenant Theology" Emerson provides a good summary of Calvin and criticizes Miller's overly narrow view of Calvin.

> Another difference exists between covenant theology and the older Reformed theology, according to Miller. Since the covenant cannot be accepted unless sinners first learn what is proposed, the covenant idea had the effect of suggesting that there must be a time between depravity and conversion when the transaction of the covenant is proposed. This learning period, it is argued, wrought a fundamental change in Reformed theology. Since conversion does not come like a flash of lightening, it can be prepared for. Men can perform some parts of conversion. . . .
>
> But Calvin, at least in passing, also refers to a kind of preparation for salvation. ". . . The commencement of faith is knowledge: the completion of it is a firm and steady conviction. . . ." T. H. L. Parker has summarized Calvin's teachings on this point: "There is . . . according to Calvin, a certain knowledge which precedes and begets faith; which is, indeed a *praeparatio fidei."* Because of this concept, Calvin was able to declare in a sermon that ". . . we cannot profit from Him [Christ] except by knowledge of Him . . . Jesus Christ justifies only through the knowledge one has of Him."[20]

Concerning Calvin Pettit writes: "While he held that man is totally depraved, and can do nothing of his own to prepare for grace, he did not deny preparation as such. Nor did he dismiss the biblical exhortations to preparation as 'useless.' "[21] Calvin saw no autonomy or merit for man in this.

---

19. An historical survey with a wide selection of representative figures is Norman Pettit's, *The Heart Prepared.* This survey covers the period from the beginnings of Continental Reformed theology to the time of Edwards. For the seventeenth century specifically, cf. Miller, *Journal of the History of Ideas,* IV, pp. 253-286.
20. Emerson, *Church History,* XXV, 140.
21. Pettit, *The Heart Prepared,* p. 40.

"Being 'previously prepared,' said Calvin, does not mean that man has his 'own share' in the work. There can be no 'flexibility of the human heart' other than that 'supplied by the grace of God.'..."[22]

From the time of Calvin to Edwards' day the issue of preparation within a Calvinist context was an ongoing discussion. To what extent heterodoxy resulted is not our present concern. There was clearly an effort made on the part of most participants in the Reformed camp to remain true to the Calvinistic doctrines of grace, sovereignty, and inability.

Williston Walker applies his analysis of how Calvinism declines in four stages, from its pure state through Arminianism and ending in religion as morality, to the time period with which we are concerned. Historically, Walker sees Edwards' arrival on the scene at the beginning of the fourth stage where Arminianism degenerates to moralism, and he sees Edwards' significance in his turning back this current for almost a century.[23] Apparently without fully appreciating Edwards' distinction between moral and natural ability, Walker sees Edwards as less than an absolute Calvinist because of his teaching on man's "natural ability."[24]

J. Ridderbos agrees with the conclusion that the beginning of the eighteenth century represented a decline in Reformed theology.[25] The third of three areas of decline he cites concerns preaching and theology. There was a "slackening of zeal for the purity of doctrine." Though they concurred with the confession of their fathers, "nevertheless the preaching soon began to bear a weaker Arminianizing character."[26] Ridderbos sees this weakening as a compromise between a concern for morality and the doctrine of inability, a

---

22. Pettit, *The Heart Prepared,* pp. 42-43.
23. Walker, "Jonathan Edwards," *Jonathan Edwards: A Profile,* pp. 95-97.
24. Walker, "Jonathan Edwards," *Jonathan Edwards: A Profile,* p. 97.
25. Ridderbos, *De Theologie van Jonathan Edwards,* p. 5.
26. Ridderbos, *De Theologie van Jonathan Edwards,* p. 8. (Translation mine.)

middle way. According to Edwards, however, this is a false dilemma in a true Calvinistic framework.

Nevertheless, the more common interpretation of Edwards has been to see his revival preaching, his covenant doctrine, and his doctrine of seeking as inconsistent with pure Calvinism. Foster, for example, believes Edwards theoretically held to a doctrine of inability but practically he rejected it. He believes Edwards did not see the "fact" that the doctrine of inability was the source of deadness in religion. So Edwards theoretically preached "inability." In practice, however, Foster sees Edwards contradicting this.

> ... Yet there is an appeal to "press" and "do" and "hold out," which has a ring anticipatory of later and better preaching; and this tone of exhortation to action which sounded through all Edwards' preaching—the thrilling, intense activity of his ardent soul—this it was which moved men to repentance and conversion, and this first actually broke down the doctrine of inability. That doctrine has never played any actual part in the thinking of men in times of real revival.[27]

Foster's view of Edwards is paralleled by Miller's view of Puritans in general (if not Edwards). The issue is similar. The Puritan doctrine, according to Miller, was incipient Arminianism, and the true Puritan is seen in the application (practical) and not in the doctrine. Miller writes:

> The real tendency of a Puritan discourse is seldom to be found in its "doctrine," nor even in its considered "reasons," but entirely in its "applications." Hooker and Shepard shamelessly improve the concept of preparation to mean that every man can perform the requisite actions.... Let predestination be what it may, the world calls him mad who argues, "I can do nothing for my self, therefore I will take a course that no man shall do any thing for me." The conclusion is inescapable: "Therefore I must attend upon God in those means which he useth to do for all those he useth to do good unto." ... In short, then, New England, following the lead of Hooker and not of Cotton, having weathered the storm of Antinomianism, could insist, "doe what you are able to doe, put all your strength, and diligence unto it."[28]

---

27. Foster, *A Genetic History of New England Theology*, pp. 55-56.
28. Miller, *NEM: Colony to Province*, pp. 64-65. This dichotomy between theory (election) and practice (human exertion) is a view Miller set forth in his

As with the doctrine of the covenant, so here, Miller is unable to grasp the possibility of a both/and theology.

In a chapter entitled "The Expanding Limits of Natural Ability" Miller traces what he believes to be a growth of an idea within covenant theology. The covenant idea began with no intention of weakening absolute predestination, but through the stages of urging rededication, contractual terms, and negotiating with the Almighty the door was opened, according to Miller, for human ability.[29] In his article on "Preparation" Miller writes: "By the beginning of the eighteenth century, preparation had come to mean for all practical purposes, that every man was able to predispose himself for grace, that his fate was in his own hands, even though grace was given by God."[30]

As has been suggested more than once in this study, Miller is representative of those who seem unable to grasp the concept of biblical predestination as other than fatalistic determinism. There is a blindness to the doctrine that man is active and responsible in history without detracting from the truth that his activity is a "secondary cause" within a predestinarian framework. If one begins with such a predisposition against a correlation between predestination and responsible moral agency, it will preclude in advance the possibility that a Calvinist can consistently maintain a doctrine of the covenant or a doctrine of seeking. This is not to say there is a precise parallel between the covenant and seeking. Seeking, or preparation, is something man does in the sense that he is

---

earlier volume, *NEM: 17th Century,* p. 59: "Puritan orators did not usually thump the rostrum or gesticulate like their successors in the camp-meeting and the revival. Their tone was restrained and their manner surgical, but among the first generation the sermons glowed therefore with all the whiter heat. The ministers grappled with the metaphysical problems of free will and foreordination, but in their pulpits, when they thought the occasion demanded, they put aside all such abstruseness and, regardless of logic, demanded of their followers wholehearted, continuous, and heroic exertions."

29. Miller, *NEM: Colony to Province,* p. 55.
30. Miller, *Journal of the History of Ideas,* IV, 283. Cf. Goen in *The Great Awakening,* p. 12.

active, but there is not cause-effect or condition-promise relation to such seeking and salvation. In the covenant of grace faith, as the condition, is something man does in the sense that he is active, but here the resulting salvation will infallibly occur. The point of contact is that in either case the absolute and arbitrary sovereignty of God is honored, and all results pertaining to salvation rest in the sovereign grace of God.

One need only read the massive literature, debates, and divisions that preceded Edwards in regard to the controversy over "preparation" to realize how much an effort was made to be judicious and precise in giving due reverence for Scripture's teaching. These differences, though painful and with important practical consequences, were *not* major theological or doctrinal differences. They were rather shades of meaning and application within a Reformed, Calvinistic framework. As we look at Edwards' doctrine of seeking, it is not surprising to see the same intention of remaining true to the Reformed, Calvinistic tradition, while dealing honestly with scriptural admonitions to seek, press, and prepare.

Though more recent scholarship has tended to deny both the covenant and seeking in Edwards in order to preserve his Calvinism, an honest evaluation sees the presence of these doctrines and must conclude either that they are in harmony with Calvinism or that Edwards departed from Calvinism.

Allen makes an incredible interpretation of Edwards at this point, one which we have alluded to before. He sees Edwards as a "philosophical necessitarian"; yet he is amazed that Edwards' "sermons abound in appeal and in pathetic exhortations, as if the will had the power of choosing."[31] He mentions specifically the sermon "Pressing into the Kingdom of God" and concludes "that there is here an emphatic contradiction." Allen refers to his epistemological conclusion that "we must continue to speak in the old way ... because of ... the defects of human language," and he concludes,

---

31. Allen, *Jonathan Edwards*, p. 109.

Calvinist Covenant Theology

"we may infer, then, that though he does not believe in the freedom of the will he sees no impropriety in using the customary language."[32] That is the way of "Scripture and of the common usuage of life." Allen mentions as a secondary reason for "Edwards' inconsistency" a point made by Dwight about the distinctions in *Freedom of the Will,* but his primary explanation shows his prejudice against the co-existence of seeking and predestination.[33]

Some writers are prone to skirt the issue and acknowledge the presence of "seeking" in Edwards but only as an exceptional digression and not the "true Edwards." Sidney Rooy, for example, speaking of the series of sermons published as "A History of Redemption" writes:

> These sermons undergirded the great new wave of revival.... They were not "threatening, imprecatory" sermons, but, like most of his preaching, they were Biblical and ethical in character. [Surely Edwards would not want to imply that "threatening, imprecatory" sermons are "unbiblical."] His simple, unrelenting logic persuaded men of their need.... Edwards' most famous imprecatory sermon, *Sinners in the Hands of an Angry God,* vividly pictured God's judgment upon human sin.... We may view it more as typical of contemporary sermonization than as Edwards' main method to secure revival.[34]

In fairness to Rooy, it must be stressed that he goes on to say that Edwards' Enfield sermon

> is typical of this theological pattern in demonstrating that man's moral judgments and his seeking of God through repentance can-

---

32. Allen, *Jonathan Edwards,* pp. 109-110.
33. Allen, *Jonathan Edwards,* pp. 110-111. Cf. Dwight's comment in "Memoirs," *Works,* I, xcii: "There are individuals, who, having received their theological views from the straitest sect of a given class of theologians, regard the sermon on 'Pressing into the kingdom of God,' as inconsistent with those principles of moral agency, which are established in the treatise on the 'Freedom of the Will;' and charitably impute the error to the imperfect views of the author at this period. While a member of college, however, Mr. Edwards, in investigating the subject of *Power,* as he was reading the Essay of Locke, came to the settled conclusion, that men have, *in the physical sense,* the power of repenting and turning to God." Natural ability, in contrast to moral ability, is implied in the phrase, "in the physical sense."
34. Sidney H. Rooy, *The Theology of Missions in the Puritan Tradition* (Delft, 1965), pp. 286-287.

not earn God's favor. Man's seeking lies in the universal realm of common grace and natural ability. Nothing but saving grace born of God's transcendent will can rescue a sinner from judgment.[35]

Yet one cannot but detect an uneasiness on Rooy's part with Edwards preaching this way at all.

John Gerstner in his book on Edwards' evangelistic preaching elucidates both Edwards' anti-Arminian method of preaching as well as his encouraging sinners to seek God. One example of this is in his chapter dealing with Edwards' preaching of hell.

> Unlike most modern evangelists, who would either let the matter rest once they had advised men to be born again or would assure them, in Arminian fashion, that they would be born again if they would believe, Edwards tells his hearers to repair to God if, peradventure, he may give them the gift of the new birth. This evangelist does not believe that faith is a potentiality of corrupt natures. Until God gives the disposition to believe men remain unbelieving. There is, therefore, nothing that they can do to produce regeneration. But they can seek God (and Edwards always encourages them) in order that God may, if it is his sovereign pleasure, bestow the gift upon them.[36]

Edwards frequently preached that God has appointed certain days or seasons in which He will exercise mercy and judgment. Seeking is in order at such times as Edwards writes in a sermon on Luke 19:42.

> Every one that lives under the Gospel has a day of Grace a certain limited time wherein God is (waiting?) upon him to be gracious and his spirit striving with him. . . . If men work while this day lasts, they may be able to accomplish this great work, but when the night comes, then no man can work. . . . While this day lasts, . . . those that seek him may find him and those that call upon him may be (comforted?).[37]

It is important to note that those seeking "may find him."

The only connection between seeking and finding is the arbitrary grace of God. What Edwards finds in God's revela-

---

35. Rooy, *The Theology of Missions in the Puritan Tradition*, p. 287.
36. Gerstner, *Steps to Salvation*, p. 29. Cf. pp. 71-109 for an extensive discussion of Edwards' doctrine of seeking.
37. Sermon on Luke 19:42, Yale MSS, p. 4.

tion is that God's arbitrary grace is usually bestowed upon those who are seeking. This twofold aspect is seen in a "Miscellany" on preparation. Edwards writes:

> ... Grace and the exercise of grace is given entirely by the Spirit of God by His free and most arbitrary motions; but that His ordinary method, notwithstanding, is to give grace to those that are much concerned about it, and earnestly and for a considerable time seek it or continue to do things in order to it. That is, 'tis the Spirit's ordinary method first to make them concerned about it so as to convince them that 'tis best to seek it, so far as to make them seek it much, and then to bestow it.[38]

Seeking is thus clearly within the predestinarian framework, at least for Edwards. The decrees of God are harmonious, and according to Edwards, when God "decrees striving, then he often decrees the obtaining the kingdom of heaven; when he decrees preaching of the gospel, then he decrees the bringing home of souls to Christ."[39]

In a sermon on "The Manner of Seeking Salvation" Edwards places seeking within the realm of duty and necessity.

> If we would be saved, we must seek salvation. For although men do not obtain heaven of themselves, yet they do not go thither accidentally, or without any intention or endeavours of their own. God, in his word, hath directed men to seek their salvation as they would hope to obtain it.[40]

In answer to the question why seeking is necessary, Edwards emphatically denies it is because there is any merit in it. "Men are not saved on the *account* of any work of theirs, and yet they are not saved *without* works."[41] After emphasizing that there is no merit in our seeking Edwards states further:

> Though it be not needful that we do any thing to merit salvation, which Christ hath fully merited for all who believe in him; yet God, for wise and holy ends, hath appointed, that we should

---
38. *The Philosophy of Jonathan Edwards*, pp. 109-110. ("Miscellany" No. 116).
39. "Miscellaneous Remarks," *Works*, II, 527.
40. Sermon on Genesis 6:22, *Works*, II, 52.
41. Sermon on Genesis 6:22, *Works*, II, 53.

come to final salvation in no other way, but that of good works done by us.[42]

The intention of Edwards is clearly to assert both the necessity of seeking *and* salvation by grace alone.

Though there is no certain connection between seeking and salvation, there is certainty of perishing without seeking. The doctrine of a sermon on 2 Kings 7:3-4 states "that a possibility of being saved is much to be preferred to a certainty of perishing."[43] On the one hand there is certain destruction via (1) neglect of concern for the soul, (2) "continuing in any way of known sin," (3) seeking salvation but becoming discouraged and giving up, (4) continuing to trust in our own righteousness, and (5) "quarelling with God" and "finding fault with his justice."[44] On the other hand "there is a possibility of salvation for all those that thoroughly reform their lives and set themselves to seek their salvation. . . . So for all sorts of persons that reform and seek salvation there is a possibility of being saved."[45] Accordingly, Edwards says a preference of a possibility of "eternal life" over a certainty of "final destruction and ruin" is self-evident.[46]

The same contrast between a certainty of damnation and a possibility of salvation is seen in Edwards' published sermon, "Pressing into the Kingdom of God."

> . . . If you sit still, you die; if you go backward, behold you shall surely die; if you go forward, you may live. And though God has not bound himself to any thing that a person does while destitute of faith, and out of Christ, yet there is a great probability, that in a way of hearkening to his counsel you will live; and that by pressing onward, and persevering, you will at last, as it were by violence, take the kingdom of heaven.[47]

Seeking in no way binds God (in contrast to faith binding God within the covenant), but without seeking the possibility

---

42. Sermon on Genesis 6:22, *Works*, II, 53.
43. Sermon on 2 Kings 7:3-4, Yale MSS, p. 3.
44. Sermon on 2 Kings 7:3-4, Yale MSS, pp. 3-9.
45. Sermon on 2 Kings 7:3-4, Yale MSS, p. 10.
46. Sermon on 2 Kings 7:3-4, Yale MSS, pp. 14-15.
47. "Pressing into the Kingdom of God," *Works*, I, 659.

of salvation is minute if not nonexistent. It is that way because God so decreed.

Ridderbos finds the seeds of Arminianism in Edwards' doctrine of seeking. The "impression" given from his writings, according to Ridderbos, is that "human inability is relative."[48] Citing Edwards' appeals to the unconverted to seek salvation he writes: "This explains how the theological development to which Edwards gave the impetus relatively quickly passed off into the same Arminianism that he so energetically opposed."[49]

Those who feel Edwards unconsciously aided and abetted the enemy (Arminianism) need to hear his answer to the objection that earnest seeking leads to a trusting of one's own righteousness. Edwards' answer is that those who seek less trust themselves more. "A more awakened conscience will not rest so quietly in moral and religious duties, as one that is less awakened."[50] Edwards thus rejects the objection that seeking leads to a self-righteousness. In fact the reverse is the case. ". . . The more they do, or the more thorough they are in seeking, the less will they be likely to rest in their doings, and the sooner will they see the vanity of all that they do."[51]

The historical fact that New England theology became Arminian a century later does not necessarily imply that Edwards' theology gave the impetus for it. On the contrary, as was indicated in Part I, Edwards was responsible for hold-

---

48. Ridderbos, *De Theologie van Jonathan Edwards,* p. 138. Later Ridderbos states that Edwards failed to escape the common practice of many preachers to call sinners not so much to conversion as to preparation for conversion (p. 284).
49. Ridderbos, *De Theologie van Jonathan Edwards,* p. 139. (Translation mine.)
50. "Pressing into the Kingdom of God," *Works,* I, 657.
51. "Pressing into the Kingdom of God," *Works,* I, 657. Cf. Gerstner, *Steps to Salvation,* pp. 72-74: ". . . Inability is one reason that men must seek. . . . Because sinners are able to seek, it does not mean that, of themselves, they may be able to find. . . . It was because men were unable to believe that they were to seek, not because they were able. They were able to seek, of course, but they were not able to believe. . . . Some strive to believe, and some strive to receive the gift of belief. There is a great difference between these two types of striving. One of them is presumptuous. . . . The other is acceptable to God. . . ."

ing back the flood of Arminianism. That such was the case is further substantiated by the witness of Edwards' contemporaries. Gerstner writes the following against the conclusion of Ridderbos that Edwards helped Arminianism along the way: "While we grant that Edwards' manner of speaking could have been misunderstood, there is no evidence that it was misunderstood."[52] If the Arminian threat was so great that Edwards spent a major portion of his time opposing it, his Arminian opponents (if not his Calvinist colleagues) would surely have utilized any incipiency in opposing Edwards. That Edwards did not have to defend himself against his opponents in this regard is substantial evidence that he was not misunderstood and that he did not let Arminianism in through the back door.

The relativizing of human inability, with which Ridderbos criticized Edwards, is emphasized by his statement that "anyone who is sincere and earnest, who uses all opportunities, etc., shall not fail."[53] One is immediately struck by the contrast of Ridderbos' interpretation that seeking "shall not fail" and Edwards' statement that seeking "may" result in salvation "if God so wills." In a manuscript sermon on Titus 3:5 Edwards poses the objection that if God gives encouragement that He will do something, "why is it not equivalent to a promise," and "why is he not in faithfulness obliged to do it."[54] Edwards' answer is that God's word cannot be understood as encouraging "that every particular person that strives shall be converted."[55] What *is* promised and what encourages us is "that when God does convert any he will ordinarily convert those that he finds in this way, still reserving to himself his sovereign liberty of showing mercy to whom he will show mercy," and "the command to strive

---

52. Gerstner, *Steps to Savlation*, p. 76.
53. Ridderbos, *De Theologie van Jonathan Edwards*, p. 138.
54. Sermon on Titus 3:5, Yale MSS, p. 27.
55. Sermon on Titus 3:5, Yale MSS, p. 27.

infers no more than this."[56] Edwards is thus quite explicit that seeking in no way puts God under obligation.

In his volume on Edwards, Alfred Aldridge makes some straightforward charges of inconsistency in Edwards which in reality reflects a failure to carefully distinguish where Edwards distinguished. The inconsistency, according to Aldridge, resides mainly between Edwards the theologian and Edwards the preacher. In reference to Edwards' sermons he writes:

> ... Some of them are, nevertheless, incompatible with the doctrine of necessity. In his role as an evangelist, inspiring and vitalizing the Great Awakening, Edwards spread the message, "Seek and you will find." As a theologian, however, Edwards privately believed, "Seek but you shall not find."
>
> In his preaching Edwards actually taught that salvation is a "free choice." ... As a theologian he believed that salvation comes entirely through God's grace.... In his sermons, Edwards leaves one with the impression that all men have the power to seek....
>
> But the confusion vanished when Edwards made his evangelistic appeal.[57]

As Aldridge sees it, Edwards was an Arminian in the pulpit and a Calvinist in his theology, a dichotomy that hardly sounds characteristic of Edwards the man.

Two observations are in order concerning Aldridge's comments. From the quote above he moves immediately to cite as evidence a sermon of Edwards which argues against him: "When persons do what they can God usually does for them that which is not in their own power."[58] That statement is in no way inconsistent with Edwards' Calvinistic theology. The second observation is that Edwards does speak of a "seeking" that necessarily "finds," but this is clearly distinguished from the more general doctrine of seeking.

Edwards' doctrine of seeking with its acknowledgment of

---

56. Sermon on Titus 3:5, Yale MSS, p. 27.
57. Aldridge, *Jonathan Edwards,* pp. 96-97.
58. Aldridge, *Jonathan Edwards,* p. 97. The quote is from a sermon on Ecclesiastes 4:5 in the Andover MSS.

certain natural abilities (nonmeritorious) is not to be confused with the activity of man within the covenant of grace, an activity which is the "condition" of the covenant and which is not within our natural ability. Edwards does apparently equate a certain kind of seeking with faith as the condition of salvation. In this use, however, it is seeking with a promise and presupposes regeneration already present. Edwards writes:

> As to that, Matthew vii. 7. "Seek and ye shall find;" it is explained by such places as that, Deut. iv. 29. "But if from thence thou shalt seek the Lord thy God, thou shalt find him, if thou seek him with all thy heart and with all thy soul." And by Deut. xxx. 2-6. "If thou shalt return unto the Lord thy God, and shalt obey his voice with all thy heart and with all thy soul; the Lord thy God will circumcise thine heart, and the heart of thy seed, to love the Lord thy God with all thy heart, and with all thy soul;" which is very parallel with that, "to him that hath shall be given."[59]

In another place Edwards writes: "Seeking God is from time to time spoken of as the condition of God's favour and salvation, in like manner as trusting him."[60] There is, therefore, a seeking which certainly succeeds, but it is itself God-given and not to be confused with the seeking Edwards stresses as within man's ability.

The heart of Jonathan Edwards here as elsewhere is his total commitment to the sovereign and absolute grace of God in the affair of salvation.

> The Scripture teacheth that holiness, both in principle and fruit, is from God. "It is God who worketh in you, both to will and to do of his good pleasure." and Prov. xvi. 1. "The preparation of the heart in man, and the answer of the tongue, is from the Lord." ... Reason shows that the first existence of a principle of virtue cannot be from man himself, nor in any created being whatsoever; but must be immediately given from God....[61]

Edwards leaves no doubt that there is nothing virtuous before faith.

---

59. "Miscellaneous Remarks," *Works*, II, 553.
60. "Miscellaneous Remarks," *Works*, II, 586.
61. "Miscellaneous Remarks," *Works*, II, 553.

When Christ speaks of men being drawn to him, he does not mean any preparation of disposition antecedent to their having the gospel, but a being converted to Christ by faith in the gospel, revealing Christ crucified, as appears by John xii. 32. "And I, if I be lifted up from the earth, will draw all men unto me." Acts xv. 9. "Purifying their hearts by faith." Therefore we are not to suppose God first purifies the heart with the most excellent virtues, to fit it for faith.

The apostle says, "without faith it is impossible to please God." Therefore, it is not possible that persons should have, before faith, those virtues that are peculiarly amiable to God....[62]

According to Edwards "saving grace differs, not only in degree, but in nature and kind, from common grace."[63] It is "done at once"; it is "a work of creation"; and it is "compared to a resurrection."[64]

In each of the previous doctrines considered which had a direct bearing on the covenant of grace, as well as in Edwards' doctrine of seeking, whose relation to the covenant is more indirect, we find Edwards to be both a Calvinist and a covenant theologian. The alleged inconsistencies are seen to be unfounded, and such criticism frequently came from a built-in bias against the possibility of a "pure" Calvinistic doctrine of the covenant of grace. Specifically in regard to seeking, which is admittedly a difficult doctrine to properly maintain and which in some respect distinguishes[65] Edwards,

---

62. "Miscellaneous Remarks," *Works*, II, 558.
63. "Miscellaneous Remarks," *Works*, II, 562.
64. "Miscellaneous Remarks," *Works*, II, 562-563.
65. Gerstner, *Steps to Salvation*, pp. 191-192, provides a good summary of Edwards' uniqueness on this point within the Calvinistic framework: "Probably the most distinctive thing about Jonathan Edwards' evangelistic message is his theory of seeking. A natural man could do certain things (use the means of grace, obey the commandments outwardly, etc.) that would probably issue in his salvation. This theory falls between the Arminian, on the one hand, and the extreme Calvinistic, on the other. According to the Arminian theory of salvation, the sinner was able of himself alone to repent, believe, and be saved: all without the working of regeneration having previously taken place. According to Calvinism, regeneration must precede such gracious acts as believing and repenting.... But if God does not work faith, there is nothing, according to some Calvinists, that the sinner can do. At this point perhaps the Calvinist Edwards is distinctive (though certainly not among Puritans). He insists that there is something that the sinner can do; in that, he agrees with the Arminians. Still, he denies with vigor

we heard his clear affirmation that there is nothing of true or saving virtue in the seeking of an unconverted person. He encouraged the sinner, but the ability he urged them to use was neither a virtuous ability nor an efficacious ability.

Seeking is a natural ability without merit and obnoxious to God when performed by the unregenerate. This is in direct contrast to saving faith which is not a natural ability of sinful man. Faith, in contrast to seeking, is a supernatural gift of God. Natural man cannot produce saving faith, but the sinner to whom faith is given is therein given the condition of the covenant of grace as well and thus is certainly justified. Seeking or preparation is normally prior to faith, but has no necessary connection with faith being given. The encouragement to sinners is only in the fact that God "usually" exercises his sovereign election from among those who are in fact seeking. Edwards does, as we have cited above, speak of a "true seeking" in distinction from the more general doctrine of seeking. This "true seeking" is equivalent to the heart being willing to come to Christ and trust in Him. That "seeking" in distinction from his doctrine of seeking presupposes regeneration already present and is thus equivalent with saving faith and the condition of the covenant of grace.

---

that the sinner can do what the Arminian thinks he can do. But at the same time he disagrees with those Calvinists who say that there is nothing that the sinner can do. According to Edwards, he can do something nonsaving but promising and hopeful: namely, seek."

PART IV

CONCLUSION

... God's righteousness ... is ... his faithfulness in fulfilling his covenant promises to his church, or his faithfulness towards his church and people, in bestowing the benefits of the covenant of grace upon them.
... Salvation is the sum of all those works of God by which the benefits that are by the covenant of grace are procured and bestowed.

* * * * *

... We may see the stability of God's *mercy* and *faithfulness* to his people; how he never forsakes his inheritance, and remembers his covenant to them through all generations. Now we may see what reason there was for the words of the text, "The moth shall eat them up like a garment, and the worm shall eat them like wool; but my righteousness shall endure for ever and ever, and my salvation from generation to generation."[1]

---

1. "History of Redemption," *Works,* I, 533, 618.

18

Conclusion

Jonathan Edwards is one of those unique personalities of history who provides a seemingly endless reservoir for those who would drink from the creative thoughts of the mind of an individual human being. Edwards was keenly aware of his creatureliness and placed himself accordingly under the discipline of the Creator as revealed in the Scriptures and the person of Jesus Christ. It is that combination of individual genius and submission to the Author of truth that provides a reservoir rather than a wasteland.

The priority which Edwards gave to theology placed him within a framework of the Christian Church. More specifically, by his own writing, his preferred authors, and the testimony of his disciples, he is clearly within the theological traditions of the Reformation and Puritanism. The teachings of this tradition on the covenant of grace are thus a relevant factor. But the stature of Edwards was such that he called no man master. His intention was to be a slave to Scripture, not tradition. The primary concern is thus what Edwards himself wrote; the secondary but relevant concern is his background.

In determining where Edwards stood in regard to the covenant of grace, two dominant motifs must be dealt with. These motifs were common to the Reformed and Puritan background from which Edwards came, and they recur frequently in the course of this study.

The first dominant motif is the obvious fact that Edwards was a Calvinist. He was a predestinarian evangelist, the advocate of the absolute sovereignty of God, and the leader of the anti-Arminian forces. The Calvinistic framework has been present explicitly or implicitly throughout this study. It has been the standard against which covenantal thinking was measured. It is dominant in the doctrines dealt with in Part III. And as was seen, it is used as "evidence" against the covenant in the minds of some interpreters.

The second dominant motif is the explicit writing of Edwards on the covenant. In Part II, we have seen the numerous references to the covenant of grace in the notes, sermons, and major treatises of Edwards. In typical Edwardsean fashion he carefully distinguished between the covenants of works, redemption, and grace, showing wherein there was a sameness and wherein we must clearly distinguish them. While Edwards expresses concern with the covenant terminology and the inherent dangers of the conditional language, he nevertheless accepts the concept into his own writing as a way (apparently less dangerous than other possibilities) of expressing the biblical data of man as an active, responsible, moral creature within the context of a sovereign, electing God.

A survey of the literature on Edwards reveals three basic alternatives in understanding these two motifs. One approach is to see them as contradictory and conclude Edwards lived with a major theological contradiction. Such a solution is so contrary to the tenor of Edwards' mentality that it is not a viable option.

A second option can go either of two ways and represents perhaps the prevalent attitude of recent decades. In essence one accepts the two motifs as irreconcilable and concludes that Edwards did not teach or did not really mean one or the other. On the one hand some acknowledge the covenant doctrine in Edwards, conclude insipient Arminianism, and further conclude Edwards did not really mean his Calvinism to which he gave lip service. On the other hand some will find the real Edwards in his Calvinism and conclude that he did not teach the covenant of grace even when he mentions it.

This view became well-known and accepted through the influence of Perry Miller. According to Miller Calvin espoused the doctrine of "naked divine sovereignty," but such "rarefied theological atmosphere" was too thin for his common and practical-minded English followers to live in and was brought "down to earth" by means of a compromise, the covenant.[1] Miller's thesis is that Edwards rejected the pragmatic compromise of the covenant, which was inconsistent with Calvinism, and returned to the unmitigated sovereignty doctrine of Calvin.

The third option, which we believe to be both true to Edwards and to Calvinism rightly understood, is that Calvinism and the covenant of grace are clearly consistent and do not exclude one another. That such a view has frequently fallen on hard times since Edwards' day is in part indicative of a misunderstanding of both Calvinism and the doctrine of the covenant. One may superficially conclude that Calvinism equals fatalistic determinism and the covenant of grace is necessarily Arminian, and Edwards thus becomes the victim of inaccurate and nonhistorical interpretation. The sheer weight of testimony to Edwards' ability of ratiocination and the frequency with which he explicitly teaches Calvinism and the covenant should warn against any such superficial interpretation.

The covenant of grace is not a device of man acting autonomously; it is a provision of the eternal, sovereign, electing God. Thus we see the impossibility of isolating the covenant of grace from the covenant of redemption, which is totally a divine affair within the eternal counsel of the triune God. When Edwards calls the covenant of grace "an expression of" the covenant of redemption,[2] he firmly set his doctrine upon a Calvinistic (and biblical) foundation.

From the sinner's perspective the covenant of redemption

---

1. The language and analogy of Miller's position is that of Professor Gerstner, which he utilized in a classroom situation.
2. Sermon on Hebrews 13:8, *Works*, II, 950.

is the basis for the covenant of grace. For Christ, however, it is a covenant of works and not of grace. Here the "three" covenants begin to be seen in their interrelatedness in the way of redemption. Election, the justice of God, atonement, and faith are all present. Elect sinners are promised to Christ in the covenant of redemption. For Christ, however, it is a covenant of works in the sense that His perfect obedience in fulfilling the law is the condition of that covenant. Therein the justice of God is satisfied and atonement is procured by way of the cross. What Christ did as the "condition" of the covenant of redemption (or works) is then seen as what is promised to man in the covenant of grace. The "condition" for obtaining what is promised is receiving, and receiving is of the essence of saving faith. Faith, or the receiving, is itself a gift of God, and the covenantal frame of reference is right back where it began in the eternal counsel of God.

The covenant of grace is thus concerned with the application of the gift of salvation, and this application is manifested in history. Imputation of Christ's righteousness (His success in fulfilling the covenant of works) occurs when the sinner is really "in Christ," and he is "in Christ" when he by faith is united with Christ. The necessity of this union is why the "conditional" language is used, for without such a union of faith there would be no salvation. The richness of implication from such a union with Christ surely accounts for the prominence of the doctrine of faith as union with Christ in Edwards' thought and the frequent allusions to the marriage analogy in his explication of faith as the condition of the covenant of grace. In the historical manifestation of the covenant of grace, man's part is to believe. The covenant of grace is not in effect till he believes. But Edwards never suggested, implicitly or explicitly, that such believing occurred outside the divine initiative in regenerating the sinner and causing faith to come forth.

The obvious burden of Part III was to ascertain whether major doctrinal teachings of Edwards, primarily doctrines distinguishing him as a Calvinist, were consistent with the doctrine of the covenant of grace. In each case there was no real conflict. Another aspect emerged from this portion of the study which, while not expected, is not surprising when one realizes the role of the covenant in Edwards' writing. In the very doctrines which some interpreters see as precluding the doctrine of the covenant of grace, we find Edwards explicitly affirming it. Especially in his treatment of the sovereignty, the gracious work of the Spirit, and the doctrine of faith, we see the covenant doctrine not as an appendage that needs to be extricated from his "pure Calvinism" but an integral part of it. And the doctrines of "indebtedness" or "boundness" of God, the conditionality of faith, and the doctrine of seeking, areas assumed by some to be inconsistent with the doctrines of Calvinism, are shown to be handled by Edwards in a way which does not jeopardize his Calvinism.

The covenant of grace, as set forth by Edwards, is simply the way the sovereign God has committed Himself to carry out what He has decreed from all eternity as pertains to the redemption of sinners. The atoning work of Christ, and consequently the covenant of grace, is for the elect. In his doctrine Edwards is clearly without Arminianism—insipient or otherwise. The covenant of redemption with its historical manifestation through the covenant of grace is an expression of a sovereign, electing God. Edwards, because of his aversion to Arminianism in any form, pointed out the dangers and the boundaries of the covenant concept more clearly than his critics were able to do. That he would teach the doctrine after acknowledging the dangers should serve to confirm that Edwards saw no conflict between his covenant doctrine properly understood and his Calvinism.

This study began with a reference to the renaissance of Edwardsean studies. The renewed interest in Edwards appropriately resulted in a revival of interest in the vast collection of as yet unpublished works of Edwards. Numerous citations, especially from sermons and the "Miscellanies," are utilized in this study and are important to Edwards' view of the covenant. Some have tended to excuse what we believe to be an error in Perry Miller's interpretation on the basis of his unfamiliarity with the bulk of the unpublished material. There may be a truth element in such an evaluation. He may indeed have been unacquainted with certain items that clearly teach the covenant. But his error, or anyone else with a similar error, is not thereby excused.

Without touching the unpublished material, it is clear that the covenant of grace is a doctrine maintained by Edwards. While not a subject of a specific writing, it is both assumed and explicitly taught in published treatises, sermons, and other writings. The unpublished material is extremely valuable to fill in the gaps and spell out his doctrine more clearly. But a denial of the covenant doctrine in Edwards must be based more on the interpreter's presuppositions than the texts.

Were it not for the fact that it is by no means an accepted view of current scholarship, it would be difficult not to be apologetic about the purpose of this study and its conclusion. For when the relevant material is considered and Edwards' general frame of reference is known, and when all the crucial distinctions are set forth as Edwards intended, and when questionable assumptions by the numerous authors on Edwards are put in perspective, it seems a work of supererogation to show that Edwards taught the doctrine of the covenant of grace.

He not only taught the covenant of grace, but he did so consistently with his Calvinism and his understanding of Scripture. It certainly was not an irrelevant doctrine. Rather it was a comforting doctrine of assurance. The covenant of grace, Edwards preached, "is only that covenant of redemption partly revealed to mankind for their encouragement, faith, and comfort." He then adds that Christ "will never depart from the covenant of grace; for all that was promised to men in the covenant of grace, was agreed on between the Father and the Son in the covenant of redemption."[3]

---
3. Sermon on Hebrews 13:8, *Works*, II, 950.

Bibliography

Primary Sources

Collected Works

The Workss of President Edwards. Edited by S. Austin. 8 vols. Worcester, Mass., 1808-9.
The Works of President Edwards. Edited by Sereno E. Dwight. 10 vols. New York, 1829-30.
The Works of Jonathan Edwards. Edited by Edward Hickman. 2 vols. London, 1879
The Work of President Edwards. Edited and published by Robert Carter and Brothers. 4 vols. New York, 1881.
Works of Jonathan Edwards. General editor: Perry Miller and John E. Smith. New Haven: Yale University Press, 1957–.
   Freedom of the Will. Edited by Paul Ramsey. Vol. I, 1962.
   Religious Affections. Edited by John E. Smith. Vol. II, 1959.
   Original Sin. Edited by Clyde A. Holbrook. Vol. III, 1970.
   The Great Awakening. Edited by C. C. Goen. Vol. IV, 1972.

Selections and Individual Works

"Jonathan Edwards on the Sense of the Heart," edited by Perry Miller, *Harvard Theological Review*, XLI (April 1948), 123-245.
Jonathan Edwards: Representative Selections, with Introduction, Bibliography, and Notes. Edited by Clarence H. Faust and Thomas H. Johnson. New York: Hill & Wang, 1962.
"The Mind" of Jonathan Edwards: A Reconstructed Text. Edited by Leon Howard. Berkeley: University of California Press, 1963.
Observations Concerning the Scripture Oeconomy of the Trinity and Covenant of Redemption. Edited by Egbert C. Smyth. New York: C. Scribner's Sons, 1880.
The Philosophy of Jonathan Edwards from His Private Notebooks. Edited by Harvey G. Townsend. Eugene, Ore.: University of Oregon Press, 1955.
"Six Letters of Jonathan Edwards to Joseph Bellamy," edited by S. T. Williams, *New England Quarterly*, I (April, 1928), 226-242.
Treatise on Grace and Other Posthumously Published Writings. Edited by Paul Helm. Cambridge: James Clarke, 1971.
An Unpublished Essay of Edwards on the Trinity: With Remarks on Edwards and his Theology. Edited by George P. Fisher. New York: C. Scribner's Sons, 1903.

Manuscripts

"Miscellanies" Journal. Sometimes called "Miscellaneous Observations on Theological Subjects," these notes of Edwards represent an ongoing compilation of thoughts from which he frequently drew information for published works and sermons. There are eight volumes and an index volume which are found in Folders XIII-XXI of the Yale Collection, Beinecke Rare Book and Manuscript Library, Yale University. Entries range from brief notes to several pages and are itemized "a" to "z," "aa" to "zz," and 1 to 1360.

"Miscellaneous Observations on Holy Scripture," written in an "Interleaved Bible." Folder VI of the Yale Collection, Beinecke Rare Book and Manuscript Library, Yale University. This is a King James Bible interleaved with blank pages for annotations, paginated by Edwards 1-904. Entries are cross-indexed with entries in his earlier separate manuscript volumes which he calls "Notes on the Scriptures."

"Notes on the Scriptures." Listed by Edwards as books 1-4 and located in Folders III-V of the Yale Collection, Beinecke Rare Book and Manuscript Library, Yale University.

Sermons. Approximately 1,200 autographs are extant, 1,150 of which are in the Yale Collection, Beinecke Rare Book and Manuscript Library, Yale University, and 55 of which are in the Andover Collection, Andover Newton Theological School Library. Of the many manuscript sermons examined 44 from the Yale Collection and 3 from the Andover Collection are cited in this work.

(A considerable amount of this unpublished manuscript material is scheduled for future publication in the Yale University Press edition of Edwards' collected works.)

Secondary Works

With a very few exceptions, only works which have been cited are included in the following list.

Aldridge, Alfred Owen. *Jonathan Edwards.* New York: Washington Square Press, 1964.

Allen, Alexander V. G. *Jonathan Edwards.* Boston: Houghton, Mifflin & Co., 1889.

Ames, William. *The Marrow of Theology.* Translated from the third Latin edition, 1629, and edited by John D. Eusden. Boston: Pilgrim Press, 1968.

Barth, Karl. *The Doctrine of God. Church Dogmatics,* II, 2. Translated by G. W. Bromiley. Edinburgh: T. & T. Clark, 1957.

——————. *The Doctrine of Reconciliation. Church Dogmatics,* IV, 1. Translated by G. W. Bromiley. Edinburgh: T. & T. Clark, 1961.

Bavinck, Herman. *Gereformeerde Dogmatiek.* 4 vols. Kampen: J. H. Bos, 1895-1901.

——————. *Our Reasonable Faith.* Translated by Henry Zylstra. Grand Rapids: Wm. B. Eerdmans, 1956.

Berkhof, Louis. *Reformed Dogmatics.* 2 vols. Grand Rapids: Wm. B. Eerdmans, 1932.

Berkouwer, G. D. *Divine Election.* Translated by Hugo Bekker. Grand Rapids: Wm. B. Eerdmans, 1960.

——————. *Faith and Justification.* Translated by Lewis B. Smedes. Grand Rapids: Wm. B. Eerdmans, 1963.

_____. *Faith and Perseverance.* Translated by Robert D. Knudsen. Grand Rapids: Wm. B. Eerdmans, 1958.
_____. *Man: The Image of God.* Translated by Dirk W. Jellema. Grand Rapids: Wm. B. Eerdmans, 1962.
_____. *The Providence of God.* Translated by Lewis B. Smedes. Grand Rapids: Wm. B. Eerdmans, 1961.
_____. *The Sacraments.* Translated by Hugo Bekker. Grand Rapids: Wm. B. Eerdmans, 1969.
_____. *Sin.* Translated by Philip C. Holtrop. Grand Rapids: Wm. B. Eerdmans, 1971.
Boardman, George Nye. *A History of New England Theology.* New York: A. D. F. Randolph Co., 1899.
Boston, Thomas. *A View of the Covenant of Grace.* Philadelphia: Tower & Hogan, 1827.
Brauer, Jerald C. (ed.). *Reinterpretation in American Church History.* Chicago: The University of Chicago Press, 1968.
Brown, W. Adams. "Covenant Theology," *Encyclopedia of Religion and Ethics,* edited by James Hastings. 12 vols. Edinburgh: T. & T. Clark, 1908-1922. Vol. IV, pp. 216-224.
Buis, H. "Covenants, Biblical," *The Encyclopedia of Christianity,* edited by Philip E. Hughes. 4 vols. Marshallton, Delaware: The National Foundation for Christian Education, 1964- . Vol. III, pp. 219-229.
Calvin, John. *Commentary on the Book of Psalms.* Vol. III. Translated by James Anderson. Grand Rapids: Wm. B. Eerdmans, 1963.
_____. *Commentaries on the First Book of Moses Called Genesis.* Vol. I. Translated by John King. Grand Rapids: Wm. B. Eerdmans, 1963.
_____. *Institutes of the Christian Religion.* 2 vols. Vols. XX and XXI of *Library of Christian Classics.* Edited by J. T. McNeill. Translated by F. L. Battles. Philadelphia: Westminster Press, 1960.
_____. *The Sermons of Master John Calvin upon the fifth booke of Moses called Deuteronomie.* Translated by Arthur Golding. London: Henry Middleton for John Harison, 1583.
Carse, James. *Jonathan Edwards and The Visibility of God.* New York: C. Scribner's Sons, 1967.
Cherry, Conrad C. "The Puritan Notion of the Covenant in Jonathan Edwards' Doctrine of Faith," *Church History,* XXXIV (September, 1965), 328-341.
_____.*The Theology of Jonathan Edwards: A Reappraisal.* Garden City, New York: Doubleday & Co., 1966.
Cragg, C. R. *From Puritanism to the Age of Reason: a Study of Changes in Religious Thought within the Church of England, 1660-1700.* London: Cambridge University Press, 1950.
Christy, Wayne Herron. "John Cotton: Covenant Theologian." Unpublished Th.M. thesis, Pittsburgh-Xenia Theological Seminary, 1942.
Davidson, Edward H. *Jonathan Edwards: The Narrative of a Puritan Mind.* Boston: Houghton Mifflin Co., 1966.
De Jong, Peter Ymen. *The Covenant Idea in New England Theology, 1620-1847.* Grand Rapids: Wm. B. Eerdmans, 1945.
De Jong, Ymen Pieter. *De Leer der Verzoening in de Amerikaansche Theologie.* Grand Rapids: Eerdmans-Sevensma Co., 1913.
Delattre, Roland André. *Beauty and Sensibility in the Thought of Jonathan Edwards: An Essay in Aesthetics and Theological Ethics.* New Haven: Yale University Press, 1968.

De Witt, John. "Jonathan Edwards: A Study," *Princeton Theological Review*, II (January 1904), 88-109.
Elwood, Douglas J. *The Philosophical Theology of Jonathan Edwards.* New York: Columbia University Press, 1960.
Emerson, Everett H. "Calvin and Covenant Theology," *Church History*, XXV (June, 1956), 136-144.
Fisher, George P. *Discussions in History and Theology.* New York: C. Scribner's Sons, 1880.
—————. *History of Christian Doctrine.* New York: C. Scribner's Sons, 1896.
Foster, Frank Hugh. *A Genetic History of the New England Theology.* Chicago: University of Chicago Press, 1907.
—————. "New England Theology," *The New Schaff-Herzog Encyclopedia of Religious Knowledge*, edited by Samuel M. Jackson. 23 vols. Grand Rapids: Baker Book House, 1953. Vol. VII, pp. 130-140.
Gaustad, Edwin S. *The Great Awakening in New England.* New York: Harper & Brothers, 1957.
Gerstner, John H. *Steps to Salvation: The Evangelistic Message of Jonathan Edwards.* Philadelphia: The Westminster Press, 1960.
Goen, C. C. *Revivalism and Separatism in New England, 1740-1800: Strict Congregationalists and Separate Baptists in the Great Awakening.* New Haven: Yale University Press, 1962.
Goodwin, Gerald J. "The Myth of 'Arminian-Calvinism' in Eighteenth-Century New England," *The New England Quarterly*, XLI (June, 1968), 213-237.
Haller, William. *The Rise of Puritanism.* New York: Harper and Row, 1957.
Haroutunian, Joseph G. "Jonathan Edwards: A Study in Godliness," *The Journal of Religion*, XI (July, 1931), 400-419.
—————. "Jonathan Edwards: Theologian of the Great Commandment," *Theology Today*, I (October, 1944), 361-377.
—————. *Piety versus Moralism; the Passing of the New England Theology.* New York: Henry Holt and Co., 1932.
Helm, Paul. "John Locke and Jonathan Edwards: A Reconsideration," *Journal of the History of Philosophy*, VII (January, 1969), 51-61.
Heppe, Heinrich. *Reformed Dogmatics.* Edited by Ernst Bizer. Translated by G. T. Thomson, London: Allen & Unwin, 1950.
Hodge, Charles. "Jonathan Edwards and the Successive Forms of the New Divinity," *Biblical Repertory and Princeton Review*, XXX (October, 1858), 585-620.
—————. *Systematic Theology.* 3 vols. Grand Rapids: Wm. B. Eerdmans, n.d.
Hoekema, Anthony. "The Covenant of Grace in Calvin's Teaching," *Calvin Theological Journal*, II (November, 1967), 130-139.
Holbrook, Clyde A. "Jonathan Edwards and His Detractors," *Theology Today*, X (October, 1953), 384-396.
Hoogstra, Jacob T. (ed.). *American Calvinism: A Survey.* Grand Rapids: Baker Book House, 1957.
Hopkins, Samuel. *The Life and Character of the Late Reverend, Learned, and Pious Mr. Jonathan Edwards, President of the College of New Jersey, Together with Extracts from his Private Writings and Diary, and also Seventeen Select Sermons on Various Important Subjects.* Northhampton, 1804.
James, Sydney V. (ed.). *The New England Puritans.* New York: Harper & Row, 1968.

Kevan, Ernest F. *The Grace of Law: A Study of Puritan Theology.* Grand Rapids: Baker Book House, 1965.
Larson, Robert F. "Jonathan Edwards' Arguments for Divine Sovereignty." Unpublished Th.M. thesis, Pittsburgh Theological Seminary, 1960.
Lawrence, Frank A. "The Decline of Calvinism in New England before Jonathan Edwards." Unpublished Th.M. thesis, Pittsburgh-Xenia Theological Seminary, 1951.
Levin, David (ed.). *Jonathan Edwards: A Profile.* New York: Hill & Wang, 1969.
Marsden, George M. "Perry Miller's Rehabilitation of the Puritans: A Critique," *Church History,* XXXIX (March, 1970), 91-105.
Mastricht, Peter von. *Theoretico-practica Theologia.* Utrecht: Thomas Appels, 1699.
McGiffert, Arthur Cushman. *Jonathan Edwards.* New York: Harper, 1932.
McGiffert, Michael (ed.). *Puritanism and the American Experience.* Reading, Mass.: Addison-Wesley Publishing Company, 1969.
McKee, William Wakefield. "The Idea of Covenant in Early English Puritanism (1580-1643)." Unpublished Ph.D. dissertation, Yale University, 1948.
McNeill, John T. *The History and Character of Calvinism.* New York: Oxford University Press, 1954.
Mendenhall, G. E. "Covenant," *The Interpreter's Dictionary of the Bible,* edited by George Arthur Buttrick. 4 vols. New York: Abingdon Press, 1962. Vol. I, pp. 714-723.
Miller, Edward Waite. "The Great Awakening," *Princeton Theological Review,* II (October, 1904), 545-562.
Miller, Perry. *Errand into the Wilderness.* New York: Harper & Row, 1964.
_____. "The Half-Way Covenant," *New England Quarterly,* VI (December, 1933), 676-715.
_____. *Jonathan Edwards.* Cleveland: The World Publishing Company, 1964.
_____. *The New England Mind: From Colony to Province.* Cambridge, Mass.: Harvard University Press, 1967.
_____. *The New England Mind: From Colony to Province.* Cambridge, Mass.: Harvard University Press, 1971.
_____. *Orthodoxy in Massachusetts, 1630-1650; A Genetic Study.* Cambridge, Mass.: Harvard University Press, 1933.
_____. " 'Preparation for Salvation' in Seventeenth-Century New England," *Journal of the History of Ideas,* IV (June, 1943), 253-286.
Møller, Jens G. "The Beginnings of Puritan Covenant Theology," *Journal of Ecclesiastical History,* XIV (April, 1963), 46-67.
Morgan, Edmund S. *Visible Saints: The History of a Puritan Idea.* New York: New York University Press, 1963.
Morison, Samuel Eliot. *The Intellectual Life of Colonial New England.* New York: New York University Press, 1956.
Morris, William Sparkes. "The Young Jonathan Edwards: A Reconstruction." Unpublished Ph.D. dissertation, University of Chicago, 1955.
Murray, John. *The Covenant of Grace.* London: The Tyndale Press, 1956.
_____. "Covenant Theology," *The Encyclopedia of Christianity,* edited by Philip E. Hughes. 4 vols. Marshallton, Delaware: The National Foundation for Christian Education. 1964- . Vol. III, pp. 199-216.
Newlin, Claude M. *Philosophy and Religion in Colonial America.* New York: Philosophical Library, 1962.
Nichols, James Hastings. *History of Christianity 1650-1950.* New York: The Ronald Press Company, 1956.
_____. Review of *Jonathan Edwards* by Perry Miller, *Church History,* XX (December, 1951), 75-82.

Olmstead, Clifton E. *History of Religion in the United States.* Englewood Cliffs, N. J.: Prentice-Hall, 1962.
Opie, John (ed.). *Jonathan Edwards and the Enlightenment.* Lexington, Mass.: Heath and Company, 1969.
Pettit, Norman. *The Heart Prepared: Grace and Conversion in Puritan Spiritual Life.* New Haven: Yale University Press, 1966.
Porter, Noah. "The Princeton Review on Dr. Taylor and the Edwardsean Theology," *New Englander,* XVIII (August, 1860), 726-773.
Ridderbos, Jan. *De Theologie van Jonathan Edwards.* The Hague: Johan A. Nederbragt, 1907
Rohr, John von. "Covenant and Assurance in Early English Puritanism," *Church History,* XXXIV (June, 1965), 195-203.
Rooy, Sidney H. *The Theology of Missions in the Puritan Tradition.* Delft: W. D. Meinema N. V., 1965.
Schafer, Thomas A. "Jonathan Edwards and Justification by Faith," *Church History,* XX (December, 1951), 55-67.
Schenck, Lewis Bevens. *The Presbyterian Doctrine of Children in the Covenant: An An Historical Study of the Significance of Infant Baptism in the Presbyterian Church in America.* New Haven: Yale University Press, 1940.
Schneider, Herbert Wallace. *The Puritan Mind.* London: Constable and Company Ltd., 1931.
Schrenk, Gottlob. *Gottesreich und Bund in älteren Protestantismus vornehmlich bei Johannes Cocceius.* Darmstadt: Wissenschaftliche Buchgesellschaft, 1967.
Smith, Chard Powers. *Yankees and God.* New York: Hermitage House, 1954.
Smyth, Egbert C. "Jonathan Edwards' Idealism," *American Journal of Theology,* I (October, 1897), 950-964.
Toon, Peter. *Puritans and Calvinism.* Swengel, Pa.: Reiner Publications, 1973.
Townsend, H. G. "The Will and the Understanding in the Philosophy of Jonathan Edwards," *Church History,* XVI (December 1947), 210-220.
Trinterud, Leonard J. "The Origins of Puritanism," *Church History,* XX (March, 1951), 37-57.
Turretin, Francis. *Institutio Theologiae Elencticae.* 3 vols. Utrecht: Jacobum à Poolsum, 1734. All English quotations from Turretin in thi- study are taken from a mimeographed reproduction of portions of a translation by George Musgrave Giger, Professor of Latin at Princeton University (1854-1865). This reproduction was made by the Pittsburgh Theological Seminary in 1965.
Ursinus, Zacharias. *Commentary on the Heidelberg Catechism.* Translated by G. W. Williard. Grand Rapids: Wm. B. Eerdmans, 1956.
Walker, Williston. *A History of the Congregational Churches in the United States.* New York: The Christian Literature Co., 1897.
_____. *Ten New England Leaders.* New York: Silver, Burdette, Co., 1901.
Warfield, B. B. "Edwards and the New England Theology," *Studies in Theology.* New York: Oxford University Press, 1932.
Wilcox, William G. "New England Covenant Theology: Its English Precursors and Early American Exponents." Unpublished Ph.D. dissertation, Duke University, 1959.
Winslow, Ola Elizabeth. *Jonathan Edwards, 1703-1758.* New York: Macmillan, 1941.
Woodbridge, Frederick J. E. "Jonathan Edwards," *Philosophical Review,* XIII (July, 1904), 393-408.

The Jonathan Edwards Center at Yale University

http://edwards.yale.edu

The mission of the Jonathan Edwards Center and The Works of Jonathan Edwards Online is to produce a comprehensive online archive of Edwards's writings and publications that will serve the needs of researchers and readers of Edwards, to support inquiry into his life, writings, and legacy by providing resources and assistance, and to encourage critical appraisal of the historical importance and contemporary relevance of America's premier theologian.

Contact us at:

http://edwards.yale.edu

Jonathan Edwards Center at Yale University
409 Prospect Street
New Haven, CT 06511

Tel: 203.432.5340
Email: edwards@yale.edu

www.ingramcontent.com/pod-product-compliance
Lightning Source LLC
Chambersburg PA
CBHW050616300426
44112CB00012B/1527